# The Complete Book of Cooking Equipment

Second Edition

## Jule Wilkinson

A CBI Book
Published by Van Nostrand Reinhold Company

A CBI Book
(CBI is an imprint of Van Nostrand Reinhold Company Inc.)

Library of Congress Catalog Card Number 81-6104

ISBN 0-8436-2186-9

Printed in the United States of America

*Production Editor:* Becky Handler
*Text Designer:* Katrine Stevens
*Compositor:* TKM Productions
*Cover Designer:* Bruce Kennett

Van Nostrand Reinhold Company Inc.
135 West 50th Street
New York, New York 10020

Van Nostrand Reinhold Company Limited
Molly Millars Lane
Wokingham, Berkshire RG11 2PY, England

Van Nostrand Reinhold
480 La Trobe Street
Melbourne, Victoria 3000, Australia

Macmillan of Canada
Division of Canada Publishing Corporation
164 Commander Boulevard
Agincourt, Ontario M1S 3C7, Canada

16 15 14 13 12 11 10 9 8 7 6 5 4 3 2

**Library of Congress Cataloging in Publication Data**

Wilkinson, Jule.
    The complete book of cooking equipment.

    Includes index.
        1.   Food service—Equipment and supplies.
2.   Kitchen utensils.    I.   Title.
TX912.W54   1981        642'.5'028        81-6104
ISBN 0-8436-2186-9                                AACR2

# Contents

# About this Book

Information on the selection, purchasing, operation, and care of foodservice equipment is of primary importance both to the experienced operator who wants to get the most from his investment and to the student planning to enter the foodservice field. Not only the technical data from manufacturers and designers of foodservice facilities, but also reports from the field telling of uses for items of equipment that have worked well in various establishments, are essential to a well-rounded picture.

Energy saving is a factor that has gained new importance. Throughout this edition energy is a key consideration. Continual emphasis is placed on the need to select, operate, and care for equipment to save energy.

This thoroughly revised second edition offers basic information on major categories of foodservice equipment as well as a selection of specialty equipment items now available. It also includes information on maintenance and cleaning procedures that will extend the life of this equipment.

This is a book about cooking equipment. Cooking is a relationship of temperature and time. Equipment provides the means for achieving the relationship. Relationships, plural, would be a better word because similar cooking results can be achieved by higher temperatures and less time or by lower temperatures and more time. In this book, we will be examining such alternate relationships or combinations.

Every type of cooking equipment on the market has at least one advantage over every other: it cooks fastest; offers least shrinkage; maintains nutritional qualities best; has lowest owning cost; has lowest operating cost; saves the most labor; uses least floor space; requires least operator skill.

No one "advantage" is most important at all times and in all places. Advantages become disadvantages under certain circumstances. For example, "cooks fastest" can be a disadvantage if short cooking time doesn't fit a given schedule. But when we know the characteristics of equipment, then we can use it to *our* "advantage."

But the selection of equipment starts with a menu which, in turn, derives from a marketing concept or conclusion. The marketing conclusion is that a predicted number of persons with recognizable traits need and will purchase prepared food at a specific location. If the establishment, service, and menu meet the desires of those persons, the owner and/or operator will prosper.

In planning a foodservice unit, the designer has to consider such matters as how much the clientele will pay for food and service; how much floor space is needed or available; whether patrons will spend much or little time in the place; the hours of peak service; the availability of labor, its cost and skill; how broad the menu should be.

The tentative answers to these questions enable the operator to create an overall plan for the production of food. We are then ready to consider types and individual pieces of equipment. Each must fit into the overall plan, *unless.* . . .

The *unless* is that once in a while a new item of equipment comes along which does not fit our way of doing things but points to new opportunities and modifies our plan. It may suggest labor saving, quality improvement, a food specialty that will attract business, a take-out department, limited service at a satellite location, a wider menu, addition of breakfast or snack time service—among the infinity of possibilities.

When you think along those lines, the values of this book begin to become apparent. For example: You may already have a foodservice estab-

lishment, and you want to improve efficiency by a broader knowledge of the cooking equipment available. Or, second, you have a plan in mind, and you need to select the equipment that will fit into the plan. Or, third, you want to create a better plan based on knowledge you do not have now. This book can serve any and all of these purposes.

The book does not advocate one type of equipment over another. It attempts to impart a broad understanding of significant characteristics of product types and typical models; it shows what the equipment can produce.

When you understand what today's equipment can do, you can figure out such things as: how many patrons you will be able to serve; how many employees you will need; what time the employees should arrive and when they may leave; what menu items you can offer to attract patronage; how much freezer and refrigerator space you will need; the planned quality level; your food purchasing program—to name a few.

Many foodservice equipment manufacturers, foodservice consultants, designers, and operators have contributed practical answers to common questions: What equipment shall I buy? What will it cook? How much will it cook? How much energy will it require? Will it fit into my plan? Will it *improve* my plan?

# Acknowledgments

Many members of *Restaurants & Institutions* magazine's staff—especially Audrey Garvey, Jane Wallace, and Julie Woodman—provided valuable assistance with the first edition of this book. The late C. L. Staples prepared much of its subsequent revision.

Thanks to those people whose cooperation has made this second edition possible. Russ Carpenter, Editor of *Foodservice Equipment Specialist*, has helped throughout the review and recasting process. Karen Hallberg and Liz Adams of *Restaurants & Institutions'* Food Facilities Awards Program were most helpful in providing access to, and illustrations from, the entries of recent years. Don Garvey of Southern California Gas Company also made available valuable data and photographs from several entries. Many illustrations were also supplied by the *Vulcan Magazine*.

Invaluable assistance for this new edition has also come from many foodservice equipment manufacturers who read the previous version, suggested changes, and provided the latest information about equipment development as well as photographs and valuable information about current use. To all who have helped, I am most grateful.

Jule Wilkinson

# History of Restaurants & Institutions' Award Programs

The kitchen is the nucleus of all foodservice activity. Without a design that meets the challenges of time, space, and energy, the chances of an operation's succeeding diminish greatly.

*Restaurants & Institutions'* Food Facilities Awards Program was initiated in 1946 to provide the first forum for collecting, evaluating, and publicizing the best of the new concepts in kitchen design annually.

Entries are solicited from foodservice consultants, designers, architects, operators, dealers, fabricators—anyone connected with facility design and installation. Entry solicitation is not limited to the United States; North and South America, Europe, and Asia are all included.

To enter this awards program, a kitchen must have been completed or remodeled within the preceding two years, i.e., the 1982 program will accept jobs installed after January 1, 1980. Any type of operation within the industry is eligible to enter: restaurants, hotels/motels, clubs/resorts, hospitals/nursing homes, schools (elementary or secondary), colleges/universities, recreation facilities (stadiums, amusement parks, etc.), or employee foodservice.

Upon receipt of a registration fee to cover the cost of materials, the entrant receives a binder for: 1) a set of forms to insure uniform data for each operation; 2) one or more plans including a schematic flow diagram, if desired; 3) photographs with captions to show design details or overall areas; and 4) a menu or other listing of items served.

Three expert judges are brought into Chicago for two or more days of judging. All entries are evaluated and scored individually by each judge. There are six major criteria: 1) economic soundness; 2) use of labor-saving devices, techniques, and products; 3) ingenuity in meeting routine and/or special problems; 4) working plans and use of space; 5) equipment selection, including sanitation and fabrication; and 6) psychological aspects for employees and patrons.

After each judge has scored each entry individually, the three select the winners as a group. Together they discuss the high scores, re-check data, plans, and photographs speaking for their top choices and, finally, reach a consensus of that year's winners.

To insure objectivity, all designer, consultant, dealer, and fabricator names are removed from the entries and plans.

In 1954, the Interior Design Awards Program was inaugurated to honor establishments that integrated food and service with exceptional surroundings. Both award programs are run simultaneously. An entry may win in both programs and receive a Total Design Concept Award.

The awards programs entries have been a valuable source of excellent ideas and data for operators and designers.

*Restaurants & Institutions*, *Foodservice Equipment Specialist*, and *Service World International* magazines and books such as *The Anatomy of Foodservice Design*, Vols. 1 and 2, publish many of the competitors' ideas. This book describes and pictures many of the recent entries.

Operators who submit entries to the award programs receive well-deserved publicity and also contribute to improvement of the foodservice industry. Anyone interested in entering either awards program can obtain full details from Karen Hallberg, Awards Program Director, *Restaurants & Institutions*, 5 S. Wabash Avenue, Chicago, Illinois 60603. Phone: (312) 372–6880.

# Introduction to Equipment Buying
## Jack Haber

*Mr. Haber's experience in the foodservice equipment field includes work in both the public and private sectors. He was a regional Foodservice Systems Specialist for the U.S. Department of Agriculture's Food and Nutrition Service. Before that he was a representative for a foodservice equipment manufacturer.*

*Mr. Haber has also served as consultant and guest lecturer on foodservice equipment and systems at several universities that offer courses in restaurant and hotel management. Currently he is associated with an executive search company in Palo Alto, California.*

Because the term *equipment* is so all-encompassing, it would be well to define the type with which we will be concerned.

We are, first of all, concerned with Foodservice Equipment. This is also called Kitchen Equipment, but we would like to avoid this term because too often this has been related to domestic or household kitchens and the type of equipment selected has reflected this.

Domestic and Commercial Equipment have the same relationship as a family car and a deliv-

ery truck. Any program serving a minimum of 100 meals should definitely have the commercial equipment to satisfy the required usage and capacity.

The difference is more than just the size of the units. The diversification extends to the research and design of the two types, the kind of manufacturers, and, more directly of interest, the outlets by which these are marketed.

Domestic equipment is a highly promotional, highly competitive line sold at a low markup or profit that leaves little margin for the services and assistance a foodservice operator would need. It is sold by discount stores, department stores and by your friendly neighborhood appliance dealer. Even if the latter has access to the commercial field, it is usually on a single-item basis, and not always for the better graded brands. His experience with the over-all requirements of a good commercial foodservice operation would be comparatively limited, and not conducive to efficiency nor even economy.

Commercial equipment is a more specialized line, usually handled by restaurant equipment and supply companies, and most effective when it is part of a balanced, planned layout, geared to the requirements of the institution involved.

For a number of reasons, including the heavier construction and larger capacity, this equipment is expensive, but it could be money well spent if the purchaser has a basic understanding of the factors involved and how to control these to his or her advantage.

Some of this understanding we hope will be achieved from the material that follows. We have attempted to describe the various kinds of equipment and how they function, and what their relationship is to the over-all kitchen plan.

How to exercise control is a more relative and subjective matter, but the following guidelines may help:

Equipment buying must be treated as a business transaction, and all of the rules and safeguards should be observed.

''Blank checks'' are never desirable nor practical. The purchaser must be specific about his requirements, and who and what it will take to meet them. If he is not specific, then he relinquishes control to the supplier, who will act in his best interests. The most reliable, friendly, honest supplier is still a businessman, and his concern, and rightly so, is to make money for himself and his company.

The purchaser should ask questions—of the dealer salesmen or factory representatives; of other users; of governmental agencies involved. He should learn to listen not only to what is said, but to what is *not* said. No question that bothers him is unimportant, and a purchaser should be wary of anyone who fails to supply a satisfactory answer.

Finally, the purchaser should evaluate the answers. Any piece of equipment and any supplier will have some good features, but it is the total of many good qualities that should govern the selection. As in sport, it is the final score that wins the ball game.

Now, to examine this subject in more detail. Foodservice Equipment can be divided into five categories:

1. Storage
2. Preparation
3. Cooking
4. Serving
5. Clean Up.

Each of these categories will be discussed in the following sections.

## CATEGORIES OF EQUIPMENT STORAGE

Storage, which includes both refrigerated and nonrefrigerated, is by far the most important element in a foodservice operation, and yet very often the most neglected in planning and purchasing.

The purpose of a food program is to serve food. Food, therefore, becomes the stock—the inventory—without which this operation could not do business.

The monetary value of food is high. Food costs account for 50 to 70 percent of every dollar spent, and the protection of this stock is essential to the success of the operation. To put it another way, so many dollars are paid for a given amount of food product at a certain weight and in a certain condition. From this is determined the number of meals that will be served and the price to be charged. Now, if something happens to the food after it is received, such as spoilage, dehydration or contamination, then the full yield is not realized, and the "profit" is diminished to the extent of the food that has to be replaced.

Proper storage is therefore vital to keep food as close as possible to the condition in which it is received.

### Dry Storage

For the storage of nonperishables, comparatively little equipment is needed. Usually an area is allocated that can be reasonably protected. Precautions to observe, however, are:

1.   That the area is well-ventilated and that a temperature of about 70°F. to 75°F. (21° to 24°C) can be maintained. A good wall thermometer should be placed there and checked regularly for both high as well as low temperatures, because in some locations and in some seasons temperatures can go below freezing.

2. That adequate shelving is provided. This should start about 4 to 6 in. (10 to 15 cm) from the floor and sufficient levels should be provided to permit "first-in, first-out" dispensing, adequate aisle space, maximum air circulation, and to avoid too dense a stacking of products such as flour, cereal and sugar.

## Refrigerated Storage

For the storage of perishable food, either at 38°F. to 40°F. (30° to 40°C) or at 0°F., (−18°C) refrigerated cabinets are required. Here understanding, selection and utilization of equipment are most vital to the preservation of food and of the investment it represents.

There are five requirements for refrigerated storage; these are directly concerned with the interior of the cabinets, where the food is kept. Any evaluation of a unit should consider first how well it fulfills these requirements, and only after this is determined should consideration be given to any other features.

These requirements are basic, whether the equipment is a reach-in, roll-in, or walk-in, and at either normal or zero temperature:

1. Air Circulation
2. Humidity (in refrigerators)
3. Temperature
4. Ease of Sanitation
5. Adaptability.

**1. Air Circulation.** By far the most important factor in refrigeration is air circulation. Despite all of the machinery, there is nothing in a refrigerator that makes cold. Instead, the entire principle is based on the removal of heat, from both the product and the interior of the cabinet. Heat is present in any product, whether it is at room temperature or even in the frozen state. The removal of heat is accomplished by transferring the heat to another medium; in this case, the air that circulates inside the area. The air, in turn, gives up its heat by being passed over a coil or evaporator, located in the interior, through which a refrigerant gas is circulated, and to which the heat is transferred.

To put this more simply, consider the example of a hot cup of coffee. When first poured from the pot, it would be difficult to drink without getting burned. If permitted to stand, it will eventually cool enough (give up heat) so that it is comfortable to drink. However, if we want to hurry the process, we blow across the surface and sip the top layer, or pour a small amount at a time into the saucer.

We can, therefore, speed up the cooling rate by either a faster movement of air or by increasing the surface area that is exposed to the air.

It is necessary to undertand this concept to properly evaluate a piece of equipment. All commercial units have forced air circulation, and, if nothing is stored in them, all will work equally well. But as soon as products are put inside, the effectiveness of the air system will be felt. Some systems discharge air from one or two outlets, either at the top of the cabinet or at the bottom. The placement of food or pans solidly across a shelf in a refrigerator can block off the air and prevent it from circulating uniformly, thus causing both freezing of products and spoilage, all within the same unit. A study made on the effects of air circulation showed that it took 8½ hours to lower the temperature of two test containers from 155°F. to 40°F. (68° to 4°C) placed on two 18 × 26 in. (46 × 66 cm) bun pans located at the same level in a refrigerator, as compared to 3½ hours on open shelves.

The most desirable system, therefore, would be one that has multiple cold air outlets, so that it will cool quickly and uniformly even under maximum loading. This cannot be emphasized enough, because the safety factor in a normal temperature unit is only 5° to 7°F. (−15° to −13°C). Poultry, seafoods and hams should not be kept at temperatures above 45°F. (7°C), and this temperature may be exceeded in areas of a unit where the air does not reach.

It is also essential to have good air movement in a frozen food storage cabinet. The tendency is to overload these cabinets, which only compounds a bad situation.

The purpose of a frozen food cabinet is not to freeze food, but to hold product that is already frozen, and the air system is designed to remove any heat that is introduced by the opening of the doors. If the air passage is blocked, then this warm air can be trapped and will affect the food, although no difference in its appearance is apparent. For every degree rise in temperature, the shelf life is decreased, and the result can be a partially or totally spoiled product when it is defrosted.

Good storage requires that the products be stored with adequate spacing—either by the use of shelves or small pieces of wood, to permit air to reach as many surfaces as possible.

**2. Humidity.** In the 38°F. to 40°F. (3° to 4°C) cabinets, humidity is the most important factor. We are, of course, talking about relative humidity, (the amount of moisture that the air can hold at a given temperature); it should be about 80 percent to 85 percent. It is the absence of high humidity that makes peaches look like prunes, puts celery at halfmast, and shrinks high-priced meat from its original weight.

Humidity is, however, controllable by the manufacturer; in his specifications, he should state what relative humidity the equipment will maintain. If humidity is inadequate, the alternative is to wrap or cover all food. But if wrapping can be avoided, it is certainly a great timesaver.

**3. Operation.** As indicated, the mechanical components of a refrigeration system do not make "cold," but are designed to circulate the refrigerant gas into and out of the product zone. The refrigerator manufacturer does not make these components, but does select them and assembles them into the design he has devised.

We have already indicated that his design for discharging air into the interior can influence the preservation of the food. Equally, his selection of components and the incorporation of these into a system will affect the efficiency and economy of its operation.

The components are:

a. Compressors. These are actually pumps that keep the refrigerant circulating through the circuit, at a determined pressure. Run by electricity, they are controlled by temperature or pressure sensing devices, so that they are stopped or started according to the temperature needs of the interior. All have an overload protection device, which cuts off the compressor if it receives a demand or surge of power it cannot handle.

There are standard as well as high-torque compressors, and the difference may be compared to the ability of an automobile motor to start an auto parked on a hill. If the motor cannot overcome the inertia of the vehicle, it will stall. Similarly, a high-torque compressor will be able to start even against high pressure, whereas a standard one may "cut out." To realize fully the capacity of the equipment to operate under difficult conditions, it would be preferable to have high-torque compressors.

b. Condensers. These are the counterpart to the evaporators we mentioned, except that they are on the outside, and in a more recognizable form. They also effect a heat exchange, but in this instance they permit the refrigerant to give off heat. This component is essentially a series of metal fins, about six to the inch, through which a continuous tube, containing the refrigerant, is laced. To effect the heat exchange, it is necessary that the refrigerant be cooled; to do this either a fan is attached, which is an air-cooled condenser, or a water tube, which is a water-cooled condenser. The simplest is the air-cooled, provided that its location permits the easy access of air. This depends a good deal on the design of the cabinet and the location of the condenser.

If it is placed in a small compartment, and near the floor, it can be blocked off readily by objects placed in front of it, or by the fact that the other components will not leave much room for air.

A unit placed on top of the cabinet will have more air to draw on, unless the cabinet is placed under too low a ceiling.

The location of the condenser should also provide easy accessibility for cleaning. Dust and lint in the air drawn across the fins tends to mat up and block the narrow openings. If enough dust builds up, air cannot be pulled through readily and the compressor will overload or the system may not function.

When air circulation or noise of the fan is a problem, then either remove the refrigeration system, or use a water-cooled condenser.

In a remote system, the exterior mechanical components are not part of the cabinet but in a separate location. Actually, the main effect is that the tubing between the exterior and the interior is extended to whatever length is necessary.

However, this extension has an inherent draw-back—i.e., the cost is increased by the additional tubing plus whatever is necessary to physically install it. For example, if the distance is excessive a larger sized compressor may have to be used.

Water-cooled condensers, which can be used on remote or self-contained units, solve some problems, but impose others. Before resorting to this alternative, careful consideration should be given to whether a different brand or additional ventilation could provide better air circulation. Water-cooled condensers are to be used as a last resort, since they are both more costly and more difficult to operate.

In addition to the extra cost of the condenser, a water line has to be brought to it, and a drain line away from it. The water is not reused, which is an added expense, plus the fact that in some areas, hard water will cause liming of the lines that has to be removed periodically. If the amount of water used is excessive, local regulations may require that a water tower be erected; this is quite costly.

c. Insulation. Just as glass fiber replaced cork as an insulating material, so has polyurethane foam replaced glass fiber and been fairly well adopted by refrigerator manufacturers.

In making the change, a number of the users have implied all sorts of properties, but like other elements, these claims should be evaluated in respect to the total result.

It is true that polyurethane foam has twice as much insulative capacity as glass fiber, but this does not necessarily mean that the result will be twice as good. Both have measurable resistances to the introduction of heat, and proper engineering will insure that this factor is taken into account.

The important difference is that glass fiber is made by an insulation manufacturer, whereas foam is made from raw materials by the refrigeration manufacturer, who can vary the formula according to the results he wants to achieve. In other words, it will have no properties that he does not create. Both types require good construction and engineering, as the effect of the insulation can be diminished by poor closing of the doors, leakage through the seams, and inadequate refrigeration. In addition, with foam, errors

cannot be corrected and a manufacturer has to be able to afford to throw away mistakes.

If done properly, though, foam results in a much stronger construction than glass fiber, using the same thickness of metal. The foam bonds to the inner and outer shells and forms a "sandwich", which is stronger and thinner than is the case with glass fiber.

d. Thermometers. Although most of the commercial units have a thermometer, either inside or outside, its function has been generally misunderstood. The thermometer reading is that of the air within the cabinet and not that of the product. Certainly, if the refrigerator has not been opened for a number of hours and the thermometer shows a high reading, then there is something wrong. But in actual use, the instrument's reading will vary as the refrigerator doors are opened and warm air enters.

Furthermore, the reading depends on the location of the sensing bulb, and is not indicative of all areas of the interior.

Other faults are that the thermometer cannot show if the current has been off, and, of course, its effectiveness is limited to visual inspection.

To actually check the efficiency of a unit in respect to product temperature, it is necessary to use one or more good refrigeration thermometers inserted into a glass of water, glycerin, or even into a vegetable or fruit and to take readings from different locations in the cabinet. By averaging the results, one can obtain the effective temperature.

For further protection, it may also be desirable to add an alarm system and/or a recording thermometer, especially when large quantities of food stuff are involved.

The alarm system is battery-operated, with either an audible or visual signalling device located where it can be observed and responded to. It is available for either high- or low-temperature warning or for both.

The recording thermometer uses a spring-driven mechanism, with a chart on which are recorded temperature readings for a 24-hour period. In the case of power failure, the chart will show whether the temperature rose to an unsafe or thawing level and will indicate whether any action need be taken in regard to the food.

**4. Sanitation.** Obviously, no manufacturer will say he puts out a "dirty" piece of equipment, but, again, his design will determine how easily it can be cleaned. In the case of reach-ins, the cabinets should have a minimum of, or, preferably no seams in the interior. Present standards only require that the inside have a cove, which is a rounded, upturned edge, all around, of about a half inch to which are joined the sides and back pieces. Most manufacturers use this method, but some are providing seamless construction. The latter would certainly be more desirable, because spillage and food debris can get into the seams and are difficult to remove by ordinary cleaning methods. This can lead to bacterial growth and mold in the areas where cold air does not reach.

Interior fittings are also important to sanitation. A minimum of corners, extrusions, and crossings is preferable in the shelves, shelf standards, shelf clips, tray or pan slides furnished, as these can all collect spillage and they should be as simple as possible. All of these accessories should also be easily removable, according to the standards of the purchaser, for periodic cleaning.

For walk-ins that are assembled on the site, seams and joinings are an inherent part of the construction, so the consideration here would be how well and close the panels fit into each other and whether they will stay that way.

Most sections are made with a tongue and groove mating, but if this is just foam to foam, the edges can be mashed so that spaces will be left or will result after usage. A stable breaker strip of seasoned wood or wood products, with a soft rubber gasketing, makes for a tighter and more durable juncture. This is particularly important in the floor panels to avoid the possibility of liquids, especially those of an organic nature, getting under the panels.

**5. Adaptability.** In addition to evaluating its capability to preserve food, refrigeration equipment should be selected that will fit the overall plan of operation and add to its efficiency. Toward this end, the use of interior accessories for reach-ins, such as pan or tray slides should be considered in conjunction with, or to replace shelves, for specialized storage.

Tray slides are designed to hold either 18- × 26-in. (46 × 66 cm) baking pans or 14- × 18-in. (36 × 46 cm) cafeteria trays, on as many levels as is consistent with the height of the interior and the items to be stored on them. In use, salads, desserts or other preportioned items are prepared in advance of serving, in so-called "slowtime," put on a pan or tray and inserted into the refrigerator. They are more accessible on the slides, and besides, the capacity of the cabinet can be utilized more fully.

Similarly, 12- × 20-in. (30 × 51 cm) steam table pans can be stored on pan slides and taken directly from the refrigerator to the serving line or cooking equipment. This cuts down on the handling, and avoids the spillage and waste space that occur when they are stored on shelves.

Where larger quantities are involved, pans or trays are put on mobile carts, which can be wheeled directly into a roll-in cabinet, and from there taken to the serving area when needed.

However, when this practice is followed, some precautions will have to be exercised. The carts should not be so tall that they will be difficult to push by the kitchen workers. Also, if the preparation area is excessively warm, the first items put onto the cart may be wilted by the time the cart is fully loaded. The food should also be covered for sanitary reasons and to prevent dehydration.

Finally, two general points should be discussed. One is the question of walk-ins versus reach-ins. A walk-in, by its design and usage, is not as sanitary as a reach-in. Also, because of its size, it must be located first, and then the rest of the equipment is placed in whatever space remains. On the other hand, a reach-in has flexibility, in that it can be placed in a more efficient location, but it is limited in its capacity. It would seem then, that a walk-in should be used if a large amount of bulk, unprepared food is to be stored, whereas the reach-ins should be used in the preparation areas and for storage of prepared food. It is a misguided economy to use a walk-in as a multi-purpose unit or to order a size smaller than 7 ft. deep (223 cm) × 7 ft. wide. (223 cm). And, in accordance with the current trend in foodservice, more walk-in space should be allocated for storage of frozen food than for unfrozen.

The second point is to correct a popular misconception about "freezers." The tendency is prevalent throughout the foodservice industry to speak of 0°F. (–18°C) holding cabinets as freezers; this has led a lot of users to take this term literally. Actually, the more correct term is "frozen food storage cabinet." True, a product put into it will eventually freeze, but the requirement of proper freezing is to reduce the temperature to below 0°F. (−18°C) as quickly as possible, and this can only be done by equipment specifically designed for this purpose, with methods and ingredients that are suitable for the process.

Small amounts of food will freeze and not be affected, but anyone planning to prepare frozen meals in quantity for future use will find using a 0°F cabinet for the purpose not only unsatisfactory, but possibly dangerous.

## Scales

Although not exactly a piece of storage equipment, a scale should be included in the receiving and storage area if any commodities are purchased by weight.

Good practice requires making certain that the weight received corresponds to that shown on the invoice; often deliverymen list their accounts according to whether a scale is used.

Since the scale is a means of protecting the investment in food, get a reliable make, in a size consistent with the type of commodities received. There are small counter models which weigh amounts up to 10 (45 kg) pounds, larger counter scales with a capacity of up to 500 (226.8 kg) pounds, and platform scales that handle amounts up to 1000 pounds (457 kg).

## PREPARATION EQUIPMENT

This category includes a large and varied group of items such as cutters, slicers, and mixers, designed to prepare the food for final consumption or for further processing.

All have one thing in common. They are an extension of one person with one knife or spoon; in other words, we have substituted horsepower to extend human power, i.e., the potential of our workers.

The serving of food at a specified time to a given number of people involves a formula or equation that uses factors such as the number and type of meals to be served, the number of people working, and the time required to prepare and cook this food. If any of these factors are constant, then we can only vary the formula by increasing or decreasing one of the other factors; this is the function of the preparation equipment.

For example, for one person to prepare a certain number of sandwiches, the preparation time could be reduced by using an automatic slicer instead of cutting by hand.

In the same way, other items should be evaluated in order to get the type and size of equipment that will help get the job done. Also consider future needs, and comparisons of cost between the one needed and the next larger size. Frequently, there is a comparatively small difference that may be worth paying in view of the increased capacity.

Once the type and size are determined, then the various makes should be judged on the reliability of the manufacturers; the availability of service and service parts; the design, in regard to ease of sanitation, operation and safety; flexibility in performing a number of operations; and durability.

## COOKING EQUIPMENT

Just as refrigeration is the removal of heat, so cooking is the addition of heat. This can be done in a number of ways. In addition to direct exposure to a heat source, as in broiling; heated air, water, steam, fat or oil, and irradiation are all means of imparting heat to food.

Again, the menu will determine the medium selected, and the quanity of food and the experience of the operator will determine the type.

## Ranges

The basic unit in most kitchens is the electric or gas range with four to six burners on top, and an oven below. It will handle satisfactorily the requirements of up to 100 meals, but for larger capacity, it would be well to consider other types of equipment. For example, there are deck ovens in various sizes and with one, two, or three openings, so that it is not necessary to add another range just to get more oven space.

## Convection Ovens

Where a larger number of meals have to be heated in a short period of time, the convection oven has proved very successful. Basically, the principle is forced air convection, that is, blowing heated air over the food. It provides larger capacity and baking time is figured in minutes rather than hours. Therefore, it is a basic component at the receiving school in a satellite feeding operation.

The various manufacturers have incorporated different features that add to the convenience of operation. But in evaluating their products, the important feature to consider is again the basic one; that is, how well does the oven add heat to the food in all areas of the interior. The design of the air flow will determine whether the full capacity can be used or whether space must be left for circulation. It will also determine if there will be uneven results in baking or heating, especially important for the safety of the food.

Convection ovens can be stacked one on top of the other, but the dimensions should be checked to see if stacking puts either the top or bottom shelves at an inconvenient level.

## Microwave Ovens

Although microwave ovens do not fit the definition of commercial equipment given in the opening paragraphs, their omission here would be rather conspicuous because of their extensive use and popularity in commercial operations.

The microwave oven is one of the by-products of the invention and development of radar. In fact, one of the first brand names used was *Radarange.*

Like its big brother, the microwave oven operates by sending out electronic signals or impulses that excite the water molecules in food rapidly enough to cause them to heat up and cook the food quickly and thoroughly. Metal ware of any kind reflects the impulses, but paper or ceramic, and, of course, organic matter, permit the waves to pass through.

When microwave ovens were introduced in the United States, no standards of acceptable radiation emissions existed so there were many scare headlines and much misinformation. Now, microwave ovens are safe to operate. These ovens conform to standards set by the organizations concerned with sanitation and electrical safety, and by federal agencies such as the FCC (Federal Communications Commission) and the Department of Health and Human Services. (One note of caution: anyone using a pacemaker should stay well away from microwaves because their impulses can disrupt the pacemaker's functioning.)

Although safety is not a problem with microwave ovens, utility and value certainly are. Generally the same kind of unit serves for home or commercial use. The ovens available today are very small, but relatively expensive. Some larger conveyor units have been developed in Europe, but they have not been perfected for the American foodservice industry. Although microwave cooking time for one serving takes mere seconds, cooking time increases proportionately as the operator cooks more servings simultaneously, and the size of the cooking area available limits the number of servings.

If a foodservice manager has to prepare and serve large quantities of food in a short period of time, a microwave oven is neither expedient nor efficient. A serving line delayed by people waiting for the food to come out of the oven, even with a cooking time measured in seconds, is like a stalled car on a highway at rush hour.

Then, why are foodservice operators buying so many microwave ovens? The answer is obvious for sandwich shops and similar operations. On a single-serving basis, the ovens are faster and cheaper than anything else now available. But, they are also valuable to other operations. A restaurant owner can expand his menu, and reduce his risk, by keeping slower-selling specialty items frozen and reconstituting them when they are ordered. The large-volume operator can extend his serving period, without increasing his overhead, by using the microwaves to take care of stragglers and "after-hours" diners. Used in these ways, microwave ovens are a good investment. But, each operator must make his own analysis and resist the temptation to see benefits in microwaves that do not exist for him.

## Steam Cooking Equipment

For cooking large quantities, the steamer and the steam-jacketed kettle are most valuable. Each provides a great deal of versatility plus savings in operating costs, labor and food value.

The steam cooker can be likened to the domestic pressure cooker, while the kettle is like a double boiler. In the first, the steam is introduced directly into the food, and it must be "clean" steam, that is, generated specifically for use in the food.

For the kettle, "house" steam may be used, since it is introduced between the inner and outer shells of the kettle and does not contact the food.

Steam cookers are available in one, two or three compartment sizes and take 12- × 20-in. (30 × 51 cm) cafeteria pans side by side on each level.

Kettles come in various sizes from 5 (18.9 l) up to 150 (566.2 l) gallons with the sizes up to 40 (151 l) gallons available in either tilting or stationary construction.

In determining the proper size, consideration should be given to the menu and the number of choices to be offered each day, the number of portions to be prepared, the time available for preparation, and, also, anticipated future needs.

If only one choice of food is to be offered, obviously, it would be better to get one 60-gal. (226.5 l) kettle, for example, than three 20-gal. (75.5 l) units, because it would be cheaper and take up less space. On the other hand, two kettles would enable two items to be prepared in the same amount of time.

In regard to the steam cooker, each compartment can only take a specified amount of pans and it becomes a matter of arithmetic to see how many compartments would be needed. Or, another way to figure this would be to compute the number of portions each batch would yield, divide that into the total number of portions needed, and multiply the result by the cooking time.

For example, if 400 portions are needed and the steam cooker yields 100 portions, 400 divided by 100 equals 4. If the cooking time is 20 minutes, then a total of 80 minutes would be needed. If the cooking can be scheduled to fit into the serving requirements, that is, the number of portions per minute required, then the equipment may be adequate. If not, then a larger unit may be needed.

There are other variations of steam cooking equipment, such as trunnion kettles and pressure cookers for small batch cooking.

Many accessories are available for steam cooking equipment. Adding some of these and combining two or more provide much flexibility and the ability to handle almost any foodservice operation.

Tilting Braising/Fry Pans are gaining popularity among large-volume foodservice operators. The pan combines the characteristics of the griddle, oven, and steam cooker in one unit without being larger than any one of the three. It can cook "dry" foods such as meat entrees or, with optional equipment, it can operate as a steam cooker. The braising pan can also fry or grill chops, steaks, fish; make large quantities of scrambled eggs; boil oatmeal; cook stew; and grill enough frankfurters to satisfy a Boy Scout troop.

Adding casters gives the tilting braising/fry pan portability for use in point-of-service locations and for events such as meetings or buffets.

The tilting feature and pan-holding arms, similar to those on tilting kettles, permit this equipment to be emptied quickly and safely.

## SERVING EQUIPMENT

It would be difficult to be definitive about this category, because there are so many types and variations available, but there are basic considerations here, too, which will help in the selection.

The first determinant is again the menu. Obviously, the serving of a hot and/or cold plate will call for one type, with the makeup determined by the proportion of hot foods to that of cold.

Then, consider the number to be fed in a given number of periods. The relevant time will be the product of the number of people serving, multiplied by the time it takes to serve each portion. If the line does not move quickly enough, then either a longer serving counter has to be used or more lines added.

The question of mobile as against stationary equipment should also be resolved. By their very nature, stationary lines will take up a specified amount of space, which cannot be used for other purposes. If this is not feasible, then mobile pieces should be used, as in a multi-purpose room, so that they can be cleared and stored after the foodservice period is over.

Custombuilt versus production items is another factor. Custombuilt, obviously, can be made for a specific operation, but is more costly.

With the multiplicity of production-line pieces, these should be checked first because of the cost savings.

Serving equipment also includes insulated carriers for use in transporting food, racks for roll-in storage, and anything else designed to help bring the prepared food to the consumer.

Any of these items should be checked for durability, especially mobile equipment. How well will it stand up under the daily movement? How about sanitation? Does the design promote easy cleanability, or are there built-in dirt catchers? How about safety? Are there sharp corners or edges, which are potential dangers?

If it is insulated equipment, what is the heat loss per hour? Are electrical, gas or steam units adequately safeguarded? Does the equipment have the proper certifications from Underwriters Laboratories and/or National Sanitation Foundation or similar organizations? Is the equipment designed well enough so that additional pieces may be added for future expansion if that should become necessary?

And, no final determination of both equipment and its location should be made without a consideration of its effect on the traffic in and out of the serving area, both in front of the line, as well as from the kitchen.

## CLEAN UP

Clean up should include all of the acts required to sanitize the utensils, equipment, and area involved in foodservice preparation, but here we will consider the sanitizing of utensils such as pots, pans, trays, or plates. Included in this function is the scrapping and disposal of waste food, depositing and stacking of soiled ware, washing and sanitizing of the utensils, and their storage.

All of these tasks can be performed by either people or machines, and the question of which to use will be determined by many factors. There are no magical properties in machines that enable them to perform a function that is not programmed into the machine. A dishwashing machine does not wash dishes by itself; dishes have to be brought to it just the same as dishes are brought to a human being. The same with waste grinders; waste has to be deposited into it the same as into a garbage can.

Thus, the selection of a piece of equipment should be based on its ability to increase the productivity of the people concerned with the food-service operation. One human being, paid a given number of dollars per hour, will take a certain amount of time to wash the utensils concerned. If a machine is used that costs a specified amount to purchase and to operate, how much time will be saved? Will this represent an improvement?

Will the investment in a compactor or waste disposer be realized as a saving over the expense of having a person handle garbage and trash cans?

If workers are difficult to hire, train, and keep, will the presence of machines help, in that it will take fewer people to operate with the machines than without them?

After these questions are answered, then the question arises, which type, size and manufacturer to use? And, the answer to this will be the same as has already been indicated for other categories. How does the equipment chosen meet the requirements of function, sanitation, safety, durability, and service?

In regard to function, it would be helpful again to understand the principles of some of the machines we have mentioned.

## Dishwashers

The actual washing of the dishes is only one phase of the complete operation, which includes scrapping of waste, presoaking, washing, sanitizing, drying, and storage. There are simple machines, which perform just the washing, as well as more complicated ones that perform most of these functions, with the corollary that for every task the machine does, additional cost will be incurred, both in the purchase and in the operation.

Size, alone, does not determine the quantity of dishes that can be washed by a machine. Any rated capacity is optimum; the actual production will be affected by the human factor, the effectiveness of the arrangement of both the soiled and clean dish tables, and the number and kind of functions done by the machines.

Another basic fact is that water has to reach the dishes if they are to be washed. This water is dispensed by the spray arms, and if these get clogged the results will be very poor. Therefore, consider the width of the openings in the spray arms, accessibility for removal and cleaning, and the effectiveness of preventing debris from getting into the arms.

The engineering of any dishwashing machine is governed by the factors of time, and the temperature and amount of water. In order to wash, rinse, and sanitize the dishes properly these factors cannot be disturbed, nor can they be ignored in the design of the equipment. However, the user controls the temperature and availability of water. Therefore, before selecting any system, review the facilities to ascertain that there will be adequate water at the proper temperature not only for the dishwashing operation but also for the other needs of the kitchen.

Many users misunderstand the function of the heater elements in a dishwasher. They are not intended to heat the incoming water, but are to keep the tank water hot and to make up for the heat loss caused by absorption by the dishes and by aeration. This means that 140°F. (60°C) has to be supplied to the machine for washing if it is to do its job. Similarly, the proper temperature has to be supplied for final rinse for the purpose of sanitation. In most machines this is 180°F. (82°C) but some use 160°F. (71°C) with a sanitizing agent, where permitted by local regulations. For sanitation, both will be equally effective, but the hotter water will also permit air drying in a shorter time than will the lower temperature.

To obtain the higher-temperature water needed for the rinsing phase, most installations use a hot-water booster. In effect, a booster is a small water heater located close to the washing machine. By branching the booster directly off from the regular hot-water supply and then connecting the booster to the machine, the regular water supply goes into the "wash" inlet of the machine, while the higher-temperature water from the booster goes into the "rinse" inlet.

The booster can only raise the water temperature a maximum of 40°F. (4°C). If 110°F. (43°C) water is brought to the booster, it will come out at 150°F. (66°C)—not 180°F. (82°C).

Boosters are available with either gas or electric heating, but the buyer should ask the local utility company for a projection of costs and the future availability of fuel before making a selection. Also remember that a gas unit will require venting and is larger than its electric equivalent.

To permit air drying of the dishes, the clean dish table should be long enough to accommodate at least two, and preferably three, racks. Also remember that plastic ware will take longer to dry than will china, due to its lesser absorption of heat.

Any conventional system that results in wet dishes indicates a defect in the layout, inadequate rinse temperatures, or the operators are not allowing sufficient time for air drying. (This presumes the use of conventional machines that have the capacity of rinse at 160°F. (71°C) –180°F. (82°C).

The emphasis on energy saving has focused attention on a new "breed" of washers, popularly called "cold-water" machines. But this euphemism should not be taken literally. These machines do operate at 120° (49°C)–140°F.(60°C) instead of the conventional 160°F. (71°C)–180°F. (82°C). But they require the use of more detergent, sanitizing agents, and other chemical additives. Using water colder than 120°F. (49°C) would make the degreasing exceedingly difficult. Water over 140°F. (60°C) would vaporize the sanitizing agent and destroy its effectiveness.

Although the energy savings of the cooler water is very dramatic and salesworthy, studies have shown that these savings are offset by the increased quantities and cost of the chemicals required, as well as by the energy needed to produce them. So, the energy savings and cost of operation for the two types of systems are about the same.

The "cold-water" machines have drawbacks, however. The sanitizing agent (a chlorine compound—actually laundry bleach) must be dispensed in a specified amount and at a particular time to do an effective job. If the sanitizer runs out and is not replaced, the dishes will not be sanitized and will have to be redone. Some operators, deliberately dilute the sanitizer to save costs—obviously a questionable saving.

Sanitarians and new sanitation codes now require the addition of some audible alarm to signal when the sanitizer has run out or is weak. Manufacturers now have electronic sensing devices available, but they add an extra cost of about $200.

Another significant point that highlights the inherent requirements of a good system is that manufacturers generally have limited their production of the new variety to undercounter and one-rack uprights. As the size and complexity of the machines increases, the problems of the colder-temperature units proliferate. There is no longer parity in operational costs, but, instead, these machines begin to cost more and to present more difficulties than the conventional ones.

As a final factor, remember that dishes rinsed at 140°F. (60°C) will not air dry as quickly as those rinsed at 180°F.(82°C). If the operators become impatient and start to dry the dishes with towels, then the whole sanitizing effort has been negated.

## Waste Disposers

Usually a garbage disposer is included somewhere in the dishwashing layout and can be a valuable time and labor saver.

Depending on the complexity of the dishwashing system, the disposer can be inserted under the prerinse sink or in a special trough with running water.

Before investing in one, though, consider the following:

Is water a problem or a cost factor or will there be an adequate and inexpensive supply?

Is it really needed? If adequate scrapping is done before the dishes come to the dishroom, will a disposer be needed?

Is the design rugged enough to take all scraps, or will it have to be hand fed with selected waste?

Is there a local code which prohibits the use of disposers?

Will the electrical supply be adequate or will the fuses go as soon as it and the dishwasher are turned on?

Does it have a reversing switch? This is very handy when the disposer gets jammed or clogged.

Since it will be used with and around water, are the electrical controls properly safeguarded, so that there is no danger to the operator?

And, by no means, least, who is responsible for the service and warranty on the unit?

Disposers can be useful too in the preparation area, where all of the above questions will apply. However, in regard to "need," the determination will be the form of the food products to be used, that is, fresh or processed. If the former, then obviously there will be a lot of peelings and other waste, which can be conveniently thrown into the disposer.

## Compactors

Although compactors are comparatively new, already a number of companies are producing them. If the compactor is not to be just an expensive toy, then some study should be made to see if it can justify its installation.

How much waste will the kitchen actually produce and what is the cost of disposing of it? This should be determined whether the removal is done by the operation's own personnel or by outside contracted help.

Does the present system represent an undesirable method, from the standpoint of sanitation, pollution, or other determinants?

What happens to the waste after it is compacted or is the problem of disposal entirely solved?

Then, does the machine need special materials such as bags, cartons, or strapping? If so, are these custom designed for the machine, which can represent an added expense, or can any kind be used?

Will the machine take both wet and dry waste or does it require separation, which defeats the labor-saving factor?

Are different sizes available, which will more closely approximate the needs, or is there only a choice of too big or too little?

Does the design have adequate safeguards?

Is there built-in "trouble" or is the mechanism simple enough to operate efficiently with the least amount of service problems?

And, again as with any other piece of equipment, who is responsible for the service and how quickly can it be restored to working condition if service is needed?

## Storage of Dishes and Utensils

Whatever means are used to store the dishes and utensils should not negate the cleaning and sanitizing performed in the washing operation. Generally, the most desirable system is one that requires the least amount of handling between the time the utensils are washed and the next serving of meals, and provides maximum protection of the cleanliness.

For this reason, storage of uncovered utensils in a cupboard is not the best way. If possible, portable carts should be used in the dishwashing area, so that the sanitized and dried items can be stored quickly. These can be protected by a suitable sanitary cover until the next serving period, when the cart can be wheeled over to the serving line and uncovered.

Portable carts are available in various sizes and types that can meet any requirement, from the standpoint of either cost or of application. However, selection should be based on the ease of keeping both the utensils and the cart sanitary; durability of material used; size in relation to portability; type of casters and whether they have locking devices; and design. There are many types of carts; they vary from the simple or general utility to those designed for a particular size dish or tray, with a corresponding increase in cost.

The value of this specialized design should be justified by the requirements of the operation. Do not buy carts that are more sophisticated than needed.

## MATERIALS AND FINISHES

Today's equipment is fabricated from one or more of the following materials. Consider their advantages and disadvantages before selecting a particular item. It should be stressed, though, that this is only one of the many factors involved; do not equate the value or function of an item with its material. In other words, the material used is only a measure of durability not of performance.

The basic materials most commonly used are either ferrous, such as iron or steel, or nonferrous, such as aluminum or fiberglass.

These are not listed in any particular order of desirability. Each does have its own merits and defects, which should be included in the "scorecard" for a particular piece of equipment.

**Steel.**  An iron alloy that has a high degree of strength in relation to its thickness, steel can be alloyed with other metals for special properties, or it can be welded, bent, or drawn to special shapes or design. Impact strength is good and normal damage can dent but probably not penetrate.

**Aluminum.**  This is a softer metal that has gotten the connotation of being rust-free but actually is highly subject to corrosion, especially near high-acid foods. It is usually not alloyed, but can

be treated to have more resistance to corrosion. This is called anodizing, but it is a surface treatment and once the finish is scratched or removed, the base is "raw" aluminum. It can be fabricated like steel, but the nature of the metal requires different handling. Impact strength, though, is much less and normal damage cannot only dent but may penetrate the metal.

**Fiberglass.**  Fiberglass is a new material to the equipment field although it has been successfully used in other fields such as the manufacture of cars and boats. It is made by spraying fiberglass on to a matte and the amount put on will determine the strength of the final hardened material. It can be provided in colors, milled to a particular design, which provides for seamless construction, and can be repaired in the field. Tests indicate a high degree of impact strength.

**Stainless Steel.**  This is a generic term used to designate a group of alloys that have the property of being corrosion-resistant.

As used in the equipment industry, none of these are truly corrosion free and all are subject to rusting under certain conditions. However, some are more resistant than others, and this will depend on the amount of nickel and chromium used. One way to determine whether there is a high resistance is to use a magnet on the metal. Since nickel and chromium decrease the magnetic property, a magnet will not adhere to high corrosion-resistant steel whereas it will to low-content stainless.

A manufacturer should specify, therefore, which stainless steel is being used and on what surfaces. For example, certain "stainless-steel" refrigerators, have "high-content" steel on the faces of the doors only, while the other exterior visible surfaces can be "low-content," the back can be galvanized steel and the interior, aluminum.

The advantages of stainless steel are the degree of corrosion resistance, and the structural strength.

Disadvantages are the added expense without a corresponding increase in function; reliance on the "stainless-steel" to exclude some necessary "housekeeping" practices; the extensive time required to clean this material properly; susceptibility to scratching, and the difficulty of repair in the field.

**Plastic-Coated Steel.** A comparative newcomer to the equipment field is the group of vinyl covered metals. Although aluminum can be processed this way, generally steel is used as a base because of its strength and lower cost.

The process, basically, includes the use of galvanized steel, which can be formed and fabricated by less expensive methods than is the case with stainless. A coating of liquid vinyl is sprayed on to the fabricated parts, which are then baked so the vinyl bonds itself to the metal. If the process is done properly, the vinyl will not peel or flake off. It is possible to cut the surface, but the damage will be restricted to the area of contact, and there will be no rust marks, because of the galvanized steel underneath. It is also possible to repair these scratches in the field.

**Painted Steel.** More commonly known as baked enamel, this finish is less desirable than vinyl, because of its tendency to discolor or "yellow." The process consists of spraying paint on to steel and baking the part to set and harden the paint. However, the steel used is generally not corrosion resistant and scratches in the paint will tend to show rust marks.

Like vinyl, the scratches can be repaired in the field, but in both cases the results are not entirely satisfactory because difference in color will be apparent. This difference is caused by the discoloration of the surrounding area as well as by the fact that the repair material is air dried rather than heat dried.

**Steel with Laminated Finish.** This entails bonding a sheet of material such as formica or vinyl to the metal to achieve a particular color or special effect. It is relatively expensive, equalling the cost of good stainless steel.

**Galvanized Steel.** Galvanizing is the process of coating steel with zinc to provide corrosion resistant properties. It is not as effective for this purpose as is stainless steel, nor is it as attractive. But it is generally adequate and can be used on surfaces not normally visible, such as the backs and tops of refrigerators, canopies, or nonworking surfaces of tables.

**Porcelain.** Porcelainizing is the fusing of glass to steel at extremely high temperatures. Like glass, the result is easily cleaned, hard surfaced, and colorful, but also brittle. It can be damaged easily and cannot be repaired satisfactorily in the field even with so-called touch-up paint.

At one time, this material was quite widely used in the equipment field, but new developments and materials and rising costs have generally excluded the use of porcelain on commercial equipment.

## QUOTATIONS AND CONTRACTS

The stress we have placed on businesslike proceedings and evaluation also encompasses the subject of quotations and contracts.

All of the careful preparations, study, and planning can be negated if specifications and contracts are not stated in a way that will prevent misunderstandings, mistakes, and needless expense. This is not said to imply any shady practices. But it is only fair to both parties—the purchaser and the supplier—to clearly spell out what is needed; what will be supplied; areas of responsibility; and the usually important factor, what will it cost. The purchaser should, therefore, prepare a list of specifications for the equipment to be purchased. This list should include the manufacturer and model number of the equipment—for purposes of standards, not restriction—what optional features are to be included, what services are to be performed, and a starting and completion date. If it is not desirable to show the manufacturer and model number, then at least the specifications should be specific enough to show the grade or standard desired.

The use of the words "or equal" is too vague and should be avoided because it encourages substitution. Equipment design will vary, and the burden falls on the purchaser, sometimes, to prove that a substitute is not equal. Instead, the bids should be based solely on the items specified. Provision can be made for substitution, if the supplier obtains prior approval and indicates on his quotation how the alternate equipment deviates from the original, and how much more or less it will cost.

As to the services to be performed, the purchaser should indicate to what extent the supplier is to be responsible for obtaining the equipment, setting it in place, connecting it to electrical or water lines, cleaning up, and especially, providing service. As to the latter, a clause should be included in the bid request asking for one-year's free service on any operating equipment, plus the name, location, and telephone number of the individual or company that will provide this service.

The request for one-year's free service should be included regardless of whether the equipment has a manufacturer's warranty. Generally, this warranty covers only an exchange of the defective part, and freight and installation charges would be extra.

In any case, it should be the responsibility of the supplier to keep these items operative. He is more knowledgeable and better equipped to deal with these matters.

In responding to this quotation request, the supplier should provide an equally detailed list to show what equipment and services will be provided. The cost for each piece of equipment, especially in reference to an application for governmental assistance, should be a total figure and include freight, setting in place, hook-up and service.

If the project is big enough, the practice is sometimes followed of requiring a performance bond from the successful bidder to guarantee the proper and satisfactory completion of the job or a means of compensation if it is not. This is not usual on smaller installations, but careful selection of the supplier will be almost as good as a guarantee, because he is concerned with his reputation and the good will and recommendation of the purchaser.

## PREVENTIVE MAINTENANCE

If the buyer of foodservice equipment has followed all of the procedures outlined above, he or she does not want all of these efforts negated after the equipment is put into use. To be pragmatic, the buyer has an investment to be protected. Furthermore, inoperative equipment cannot help provide the meals that have to be served.

A few simple rules will insure longer and more efficient operation of these items. The rules are basically good housekeeping or, to give it a fancier title—Preventive Maintenance—but they should be instituted in every kitchen on a regular, scheduled basis.

These are not involved service procedures, but simply tasks that can be performed by the kitchen personnel as part of their regular duties. And they should understand that taking care of these tasks will help them to provide better meals.

The first and foremost rule is to wipe up and remove any spills as quickly as possible. No surface is impervious to the effect of food, especially that with a high-acid content, which is left too long and permitted to harden. If nothing else, cleaning up a fresh spill is less time-consuming and will certainly help preserve the finish.

The next important rule is to clean equipment as soon as its use is over for the day. Equipment should be disassembled and cleaned according to instructions in the manual. This procedure preserves the life of the item, and is equally essential to the maintenance of sanitary and food safety requirements.

Each manufacturer's manual will suggest other preventive maintenance procedures. It is a good practice to make a chart of these procedures and post it prominently near the equipment. In addition, some kitchens post the cost of each piece of equipment to emphasize the importance of proper maintenance.

This preventive maintenance includes proper oiling, small repairs and special cleaning. The latter is especially important in regard to refrigeration systems. As explained in the chapter on refrigeration, the condenser accumulates much dust and lint from the air. If this dirt gets too thick, the system cannot function and will eventually overload and burn out. This is the cause of about 85 percent of refrigeration service calls.

A periodic cleaning of the condenser with a brush or a vacuum cleaner will remove dust and keep the unit running, and also permit a more efficient heat exchange.

For long periods of shutdown, such as those in school lunch operations during school holidays and vacations, consult the manufacturer or the dealer for the best procedure for protecting the equipment.

## SERVICE RECORDS

And, finally, an important step in regard to equipment is the institution of a service record file, which should consist of an index card for each piece showing the item, the manufacturer and model number, the serial number, date and cost

*Suggested form for Service Record—Can be reproduced for loose leaf binder or on 5 × 8 file card.*

## KITCHEN EQUIPMENT SERVICE RECORD

| (Category, e.g., refrigerator stove, mixer, etc.) | (Manufacturer) | (Model No.) |

| (Serial No.) | (Date Purchased) | (Purchase Order No.) |

| (Purchased From) | (Location) | (Invoice No.) |

\_\_NFA Assistance
\_\_Non-NFA Assisted

(Date Installed)
Warranty \_\_Yes
      \_\_No

(Cost)
Specified in Bid Request
  and/or Quotation

\_\_Yes
\_\_No

Period of Warranty

Warranty Covers:

\_\_Replacement of All Parts
\_\_Specified Parts
\_\_Parts and Labor (Free Service)

| | 90 Days | 1 Year | Other |

Warranty Issued by–_____

For Service Call (if different than above)–_____

Bill to–_____

(over)

SERVICE RECORD

| Date | Reason | In Warranty | Out of Warranty (Cost) | Result |
|------|--------|-------------|------------------------|--------|
|      |        |             |                        |        |

of the purchase, the supplier, the warranty and its effective time, the person or company responsible for service, and records of repairs—both costs and dates.

This may seem like a lot of work until the time comes when a piece of equipment breaks down and the search begins for a way to fix it. Depending on someone's memory may be easier but not as effective. Having the file in a safe, available place will remove many complications. This file also proves to be of assistance when an item wears out and has to be replaced. Often the same make or model is then purchased even though the original failed to give adequate value or performance. A service record would have indicated this problem.

**FIGURE   1.1**

The 2-unit hot top range on the cooking battery at Doylestown (Pa.) Hospital is equipped with casters and a flexible electrical cord so it can be wheeled out for easy cleaning. The tilting braising/fry pan and ovens that flank it are also on casters.

# Chapter One

# Ranges

The range qualifies as an energy saver, one of the first requirements for today's cooking equipment. The amount and kind of range space needed varies, but ranges are now designed to fit into all types of operations and to produce at many different rates. They no longer appear only in production kitchens. For example, saute stations combining open burners and even-heat top ranges are frequently set up in semi-exhibition cooking areas.

Like the majority of kitchens in award-winning foodservice establishments, the preparation kitchen at George's Plantation Smorgasbord, San Bernadino, CA was designed for flexible operation. The range was recognized as an essential element since dishes of many kinds can be produced in volume in advance of serving, then held at safe temperatures while workers continue with preparation of other items. All equipment was chosen for repeated and varied use over a longer-than-usual period of time, since primary service at George's is via the smorgasbord.

## HOW RANGES ARE USED

Another California operation, The French Laundry, in Yountsville, uses only a 10-burner range with ovens underneath to produce the best food in Napa Valley or so some residents maintain. The restaurant features a set dinner menu of soup, entree, and salad. A small selection of appetizers and desserts is also available. Range-top cooking is credited with the success of such novel soups as zucchini, green pepper, and sorrel. Slow fusing of flavors on the range creates sauces that are the key to the popularity of such menu specialties as Rabbit in Mustard Cream or Chicken Breasts in Lemon, Mushroom, and Mint Cream Sauce.

Because most of the menu at Cricket's, a Chicago restaurant, is saute-and-sauce-oriented, four rangetop stations were required. Two of the ranges have salamanders for finishing menu items that need quick browning. All four ranges have ovens. A steamer is used to stretch rangetop production for the 3,500 patrons served weekly. It can provide fresh vegetables, seafood items, and eggs.

Combination open-burner/even-heat top ranges provide a saute station in the semi-exhibition entree cooking line at the Foxfire Restaurant in Anaheim, CA. The many varieties of omelets and the showmanship exhibited in their preparation are equally popular with patrons.

"Make it easy on the chef!" Planners of the kitchen on the *U.S.S. Madsen* did so at the range section in three ways. They provided: (1) excellent lighting under the hooded area so it is easy to watch the progress of food cooking on the range; (2) a work table for carving directly across from the range; (3) a dual shelf above the cooking battery that expands the space available for the chef's use. A port opening is located conveniently for passing soiled pots and pans to the potwashing area. Stainless steel diffusers on the face of the exhaust hood furnish tempered air for balancing the air conditioning system. The hood also contains a fire protection system.

At Bob Burns Restaurant, Woodland Hills, CA, an extra aid for the range cook is the nearby trash chute with a removable receptacle underneath (see picture, Chapter 3, *Ovens*).

For all operations, emphasis on quality equipment, fabrication, and installation, as well as on energy conservation, is essential to plan a kitchen that makes the best and most productive use of space, equipment, energy, and personnel.

Referred to as "the command post," the range area of the main cooking battery produces most of the basic menu elements.

Chefs and cooks stationed at the ranges function best when:

- types of range tops match production needs
- ranges do the jobs required: flat-top ranges for cooking and holding; open-top ranges for fast cooking
- pots, pans and other cooking equipment are conveniently at hand
- work space and holding space are within easy reach
- controls for range heat avoid unnecessary overheating of the room
- backsplash area above ranges is protected by single deck, double deck, or flue riser

- ranges are modular, on legs, or with ovens underneath, as requirements dictate

## WHERE GREAT TRADITIONS STARTED

Soups, sauces, stews; newburgs, gravies, ragout; all are at home on the range top. In pots that simmer or bubble, depending on their position and the recipe requirements, such traditional dishes are still guided to perfection on hot top ranges. The great traditions in cuisine all started on the range. Today, despite the variety of cooking equipment available, the range remains the kitchen's jack-of-all-trades.

Open-top cooking is the order of the day at Pope's Cafeteria, Central City Shopping Center, Ferguson, MO. Pope's prefers open-top cooking because it is cool, fast, flexible, low cost, and familiar to the women whom Pope's trains as cooks. This energy-conscious operation has found that it is easier to train operators to turn off open-top burners when nothing is cooking because it is obvious when this type of burner is operating.

Today the range top is often supplemented with other equipment that carries part of its previous production load. However, the range remains essential for vegetables in a hurry for the last in line; a speedy saute for a special order; quantities of soup; varieties of sauces. These items can still be supplied on a demand basis from the range on open-top or high-speed top.

In the kitchen of The Abbey, an Atlanta, GA, restaurant, one cooking battery is composed of hot-top ranges for saute cooking. A three-tiered shelf suspended from the hood holds ready-to-use saute pans that are replenished by the nearby potwasher. The Abbey's menu offers 97 items, including 56 hot entrees, all prepared in the traditional European manner: scratch preparation from fresh ingredients.

Range capacity is also essential in the bake shop. Open-burner and hot-top sections are combined on the range at York, PA, Hospital's bake shop (see picture in Chapter 3, *Ovens*).

Because of the variation in the use of supplementary equipment from one food service to another, it is hard to set hard and fast rules for the amount of range top needed in various types of kitchens.

One rule of thumb for estimating required range-top area has been offered by a food-service designer; he suggests as a tentative basis:

For inplant and school foodservice—
For 300 meals a day—2 ranges
For 500 meals a day—3 ranges
For 1000 meals a day—4 ranges
For hospital foodservice—
One-half the above range space
For restaurants relying primarily on range-top cookery, with griddles and fryers but without steam-cooking provisions—
Add 50 percent to the above range space.

## RANGE-TOP REQUIREMENTS

In determining range-top requirements, the kitchen designer must take into consideration:

* The menu to be offered
* The amount of to-order work required
* Use made of steam kettles and cookers
* Use made of griddles, broilers, and fryers
* Space needed to hold the number and size of pots and pans to meet peak menu loads.

### How to Choose a Range

*Production capacity*
*Reliable temperature controls*
*Warp-free tops*
*Ease of dismantling and assembling*
*Coved corners*
*Flat top easily kept clean*
*Accessibility of moving parts for minor repairs without disturbing line-up or battery of ranges*
*Environmental comfort*

Ranges come in two basic styles: "heavy duty" and "restaurant" or "cafe."

Heavy-duty ranges, designed to meet heavy production requirements, may have solid hot top, a set of open-top burners, a solid griddle, or a combination of these units. Underneath this top there is usually an oven although there may be only a skeleton or modular range with shelves or a storage cabinet.

Restaurant or cafe ranges are suggested for smaller establishments with short order menus or for intermittent use in diet kitchens, churches, etc. A good rule of thumb for selecting a restaurant range is that the range should be used to cook for not more than 50 people. A 36-in. (91.4 cm) range designed to cook smaller-than-steam kettle portions of soup stocks, sauces, and chili can be flush mounted. Top arrangements can be ordered as menu production requirements dictate. Front burners and rear hot tops permit preparation of

## RANGE TOP SPACE IN USE IN 7 ACTUAL OPERATIONS

| Range Sq. Ft. | Area Sq. Meters | Meals Per Week | Type of Institution | Steam Kettles or Cookers | Would Like More Space |
|---|---|---|---|---|---|
| 12 | 1.1 | 1000 | Restaurant | No | 12 sq. ft. (1.1 m²) |
| 10 | 0.93 | 2000 | Cafeteria | Yes | No |
| 23½ | 2.2 | 2100 | Hospital | Cooker only | No |
| 10 | 0.93 | 4000 | Employee Cafeteria | Yes | No |
| 14 | 1.3 | 8500–10,000 | Employee Cafeteria | Yes Yes | No No |
| 24½ | 2.3 | 14,000 | Dept. Store Tearoom | Yes | No |
| 36 | 3.3 | 14,000 | Student Union | Yes | No |

different items at the same time. But restaurant ranges are not built to stand up to continued heavy production requirements.

## NEW RANGE DESIGNS

A radial-fin, hot-top range has been developed recently to combine fast, efficient, cooking, easy maintenance, and low environmental temperatures with production capacity to meet the stiffest demands for food production.

Heavy-duty range sections vary from 32 to 36 in. (81.3 to 91.4 cm) in width and from 36 to 42½ in. (91.4 to 108 cm) in depth. Extensions, commonly half as wide as a range section, may be installed either between two sections or at either side of the range section for extra hot-top, open-top, or fry-top space. The restaurant range may be from 3 to 6 ft. (91.4 to 183 cm) in width and 30 to 32 in. (76.2 to 81.3 cm) in depth.

The first range-top unit specified for a food-service operation usually contains four open burners and is designed primarily for short-order work or items that require fast cooking. Since the whole area on these models can reach uniform temperatures, further additions are usually flat tops for heavy-duty continuous cooking to permit greater flexibility in arranging pots and pans.

## OPERATING PROCEDURES, GAS-FIRED RANGE TOPS

The following operating procedures are said to increase speed and economy of gas-fired range tops.

**Closed Top Ranges.** Usually these have three separate round burners, individually controlled by valves. Turn on all burners to heat top quickly. When operating temperature is reached, turn some of the rings down or off to save as much as 80 percent in fuel. To keep all rings turned on full wastes gas and increases wear on equipment.

During idling period, pilot burner in the center will keep top warm. As heat is well distributed over entire top, you can cover it with utensils and use fewer rings.

**Open Top Ranges.** As these are quickly lighted, only light as many as needed. Be sure operators are trained to turn them off when nothing is being cooked. This is an excellent way to save energy; kitchen will be cooler, too.

**Fry Top and Even-Heat Top Ranges.** Heat top thoroughly before using. It can be kept hot with burners turned partly down; during off period turn burners down or keep only half of top heated.

## CLEANING ROUTINES

To keep range tops clean: Immediately wipe up all spilled foods and boil overs. If, during cooking periods, spills are left to bake and harden on hot surfaces, the cleaning becomes much more difficult.

Make an inspection after each cooking cycle when the equipment has been turned off and is cooling. Clean off obvious grease and other matter immediately.

**Smooth or Closed-Top Ranges.** Allow the range top to cool. Rub all top surfaces, while still slightly warm, with burlap containing a small amount of grease, or use steel wool.

Remove all foreign matter from the top, including any encrustments under flanges, under lids, rings, and top plates. Replace, making sure that all parts are level. Do not slop water over range tops at any time. Sudden immersion in water may crack castings, and water on range linings will cause them to deteriorate rapidly.

Do not allow grease and cooking spillovers to fill up cracks or other openings. When spills do occur, clean off promptly.

AGA (The American Gas Association) suggests that gas service representatives check burner adjustments and connections as needed.

**Open Type and Counter Hot Plates.** When grids are entirely cooled, they may be cleaned in hot water containing a grease solvent, but all encrusted matter should first be removed by scraping. AGA recommends boiling grates and burners in a solution of sal soda or other grease solvent. Clean clogged burner parts with a stiff wire or an ice pick.

## OPERATING PROCEDURES, ELECTRIC RANGES

Many operations also do surface cooking on heavy-duty electric ranges or electric restaurant ranges. Food products can be equally satisfactory whether ranges are gas or electric, but cooking methods with the two fuels differ, so cooks must be trained to use the techniques appropriate to the fuel. Electric fry tops offer three to four thermostats so separate temperature areas can be established to accommodate a variety of items being cooked at the same time. Taking maximum advantage of heat zones makes the most of the available energy whether it comes from electricity or gas.

Using the cooking surface of an electric range to maximum advantage is easy when these directions are followed:

When ready to use the hot plate, wipe the surface clean of all grease and food particles. Place the utensils on the section, arranging them so that as much area as possible is completely covered; set the control at the desired reference number and allow contents to cook.

**Round 10-in. (25.4 cm) French Hot Plates.** These units are used for small-batch cooking of sauces and stocks. The units require only 6½ minutes to boil 2 qt. (1.9 l) of water. Take advantage of the stored heat in the hot plates by continuing cooking 15 to 30 minutes after current is turned completely off.

Stock pots of over 5 gal. (19 l) capacity are not recommended for continuous use on round hot plate sections.

Hot plate surfaces should be scraped with a wire brush (or flexible spatula) after each use.

French hot plates can be kept clean by allowing to cool and then scouring with a damp cloth and mild abrasive. If spillage has carbonized on the surface, remove with fine steel wool. Rinse and wipe dry.

## TOP OF THE RANGE COOKING

The types of cooking usually done on the range include:

*Sauteing:* Frying in small amount of fat. Heat fat in a frying pan on high heat. When fat is hot, switch to low heat and add food. Brown one side, turn, and brown on second side.

*Pan Broiling:* Cooking meats in hot frying pan. Heat frying pan on high heat. Rub hot pan lightly with fat or suet to prevent meat from sticking. Switch to low heat, add meat and brown on one side. Turn and brown on second side. Pour off fat as it accumulates.

*Stewing:* Browning meat in small amount of hot fat, then cooking with liquid in covered utensil. Season meats and dredge in flour, if desired. Brown in hot fat and add liquid. Leave on high heat till food reaches cooking temperature, then switch to low heat for the slow cooking that produces tender foods.

*Stock Kettle Work:* Use high temperature setting to start food boiling. Use high heat only until steam flows freely from edge of utensil cover; then switch to a low heat to continue cooking. If you are following a recipe, start timing when food reaches the boiling point.

## VOTED BY OPERATORS
**"Most Popular from the Range"**

| | |
|---|---|
| Swiss Steak | Pot Roast |
| Spanish Sauce | Soup |
| Lobster Newburg | Gravy |
| Beef a la Deutsch | Sauces |
| Stews | Vegetables |
| Chili | |

Pot and pan cookery requires quick changes from high to low heats. Earmarking different sections of the range for temperatures from low to high makes it easy to shift utensils for a speedy change in cooking temperatures.

Surface cooking utensils should have flat bottoms, straight sides, and tight fitting lids. Utensils should be as light as possible but heavy enough to hold their shape under constant use.

Arrange utensils on surface unit so as much space as possible is covered. This prevents heat loss around sides of utensil, keeps food from sticking, scorching.

**BRAIN TEASER—RANGES**

Have you learned all you should about ranges? Give yourself the following test and if you do not know the answers go over the material a second time.

1. Which of the following foods are cooked on hot-top ranges? (Check right answers)

   SOUPS _____ NEWBURGS _____ PIES _____

   SAUCES _____ FRENCH FRIES _____ BAKED SANDWICHES _____

2. A heavy duty range has one of three different kinds of tops (Fill in):

   (1) _____ (2) _____

   (3) _____

3. You will find a heavy duty range in kitchens where food is cooked in: (Check one answer)

   LARGE QUANTITIES _____ SMALL QUANTITIES _____

4. To start gas-fired ranges, turn on all burners to heat top (Fill in) _____

5. When gas range top is hot, to save fuel turn burners (Check one answer):

   UP _____ DOWN _____ OFF _____

6. To keep gas fired range tops clean, be sure *never* to: (Fill in) _____

   _____

7. Remove food, grease and other wastes from range top by: (Check one answer)

   Washing _____ Scraping _____.

8. First step in using electric range is: (Fill in) _____

   _____

9. To save energy pans of food to be cooked should be placed on electric range top (before) (after) heat controls are turned on.

   (Cross out wrong answer)

10. Hot-top range cooking includes which of the following: (Check right answers)

    SAUTEING _____ BAKING _____

    PAN BROILING _____ STOCK KETTLE WORK _____ STEWING _____

FRENCH FRYING _____   PAN BOILING _____

STEAMING _____

*(For correct answers, see page 249)*

**FIGURE   1.2**
These hot top ranges are used to prepare the delicious soups, sauces, and gravies that help to keep the five dining areas filled to capacity at Foxfire Restaurant in Anaheim, Ca. A conveniently located swivel faucet can be used to fill stockpots in this support cooking line. The open burners which provide fine simmering control hold vegetables for transfer to the cook's dish-up station. The shelf above the range, installed at comfortable height, also serves as a holding area for transfer pans. For added comfort while working, a canopy-type hood with smooth, clean interior lining of highly polished stainless steel and flush-mounted, vapor-proof lights was installed.

Flush-mounted removable filters in the hood are coated and their unique configuration has made them a most efficient filter. They are cleaned weekly, assuring maximum efficiency of the exhaust-ventilating system. Grease collecting receptacles are removable for easy cleaning. Nozzles on either side of swivel faucet are part of the dry chemical fire control system. For added control the wall behind the range is protected with stainless steel.

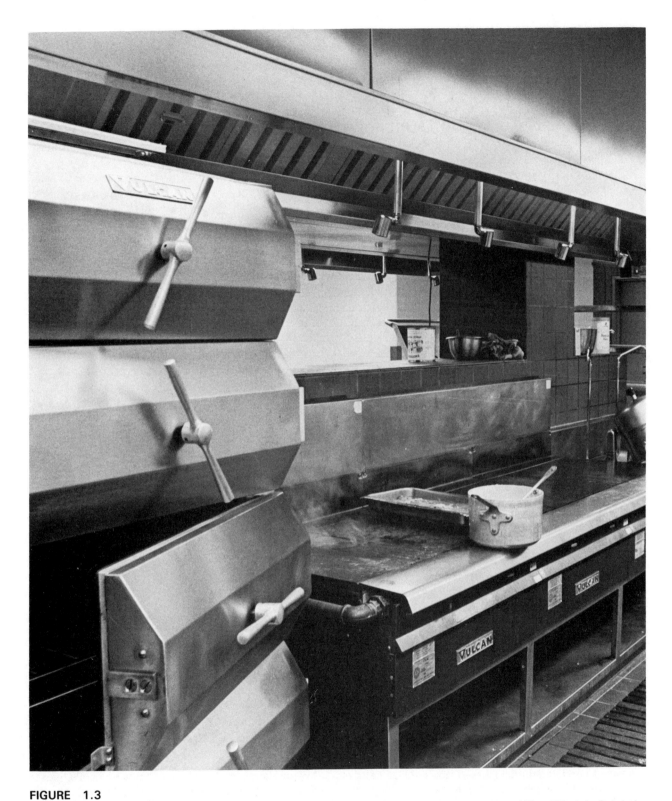

**FIGURE   1.3**
Three modular, heavy duty ranges are located in the main kitchen of the expanded/renovated Hotel Utah in Salt Lake City. Although 30 percent smaller than the old kitchen, the new kitchen has a greater production capacity due to the flow-and-function approach taken by its designers, and the installation of the most productive items of current food-service equipment.

**FIGURE   1.4**

It's easy to understand the pleased look on this chef's face. Careful matching of equipment to menu needs, plus a comfortable working environment, is demonstrated by the heavy duty range in the background equipped with hot top and open burners. This kitchen in the Hyatt Regency Hotel, Lexington, Ky. provides food for two restaurants, one seating 230 and the other 110 patrons, plus private banquets and parties held in the ballroom or meeting rooms. The hotel is part of Lexington Center which also includes a shopping mall, sports and entertainment arena, and a convention center.

**FIGURE   1.5**
At the Sheraton St. Louis Hotel, 8500 meals per week are turned out in two preparation areas. Placement of work table across from ranges speeds work flow. Hoods are automatically washed on a 24-hour cycle.

**FIGURE 2.1**

Ground meat and sauces are prepared in volume in this self-contained steam-jacketed kettle and are then transferred to the stock pots to be held at correct temperature on adjacent 6 open burner unit. A stainless steel extension is attached to the tangent drain valve with one end projecting through the grate of the floor sink. This is done to speed the cleaning and flushing of the kettle and provides safe working conditions. Both the extension and the floor sink grate are removable. A hot and cold water valve with a special swivel fixture is mounted on the stainless steel utility wall. This provides the necessary hot and cold water for the stockpots and the kettle.

# *Chapter Two*

# Steam Cooking Equipment

Quality food items from soup to dessert are turned out in steam-powered kettles and compartment steamers in today's energy-conscious kitchens. Steam is considered by many to be the best source of energy available for cooking; under pressure, it becomes even more efficient. Steam also radiates less heat into the kitchen, reducing cooling costs.

The unique qualities of steam account for the advantages of steam cooking. Steam is an unusual storer, carrier, and deliverer of heat. Although steam is produced by continuously boiling water, there is six times as much heat in the steam as in the boiling water, and this steam heat is delivered constantly without temperature variation.

## WHERE TO GET STEAM

Steam can be supplied from a distant source, from a central system, from a nearby boiler, or from a generator that is part of a compartment steamer or concealed in the base cabinet of a kettle. Steam should be made available in the amounts and pressures listed in manufacturer specifications for the equipment to be installed.

One manufacturer recommends 15 to 35 PSI (1 kg/cm² to 15.9 kg/cm²) steam for kettles, and states the incoming steam line should provide ¼ boiler horsepower (bhp) for each 5-gal. (18.9 l) capacity of kettles. One boiler horsepower produces a bit less than 35 lb. (15.9 kg) of steam per hour. Water connections and floor drains are required for kettles. With certain changes that can be made either at the factory, or after installation in the kitchen, a steam-jacketed kettle can also be used to cool food quickly.

Kettles can be selected from a broad variety of sizes. At the minimum end are 1-qt. oyster kettles, 10- to 20-qt (9.4 to 18.9 l) table models and 5-gal. (18.9 l) stationary, trunnion, and fast-chill models. At the large end, kettles go to 60 gal. (226.5 l) in one manufacturer's line and to 200 gal. (754.9 l) in another's. The ultimate in production is a grouping of a half dozen 150-gal. kettles, with mixers, on both sides of an elevated catwalk. Steam coffee urns are available in a variety of sizes up to 150 gal. (566.2 l).

## STEAM-JACKETED KETTLES

In a steam-jacketed kettle, the steam does not come into contact with the food. The steam clothes the inner bowl of the kettle with higher heat and less temperature variation from point-to-point than a flat cooking surface can. Since the steam-jacketed kettle is composed of two hemispheres or bowls—one inside the other—it is similar to a domestic double boiler.

Steam is made up of tiny molecules of very hot water vapor. When the steam comes into the jacket (in the 2-in. space between the bowls), the molecules touch the inside bowl and condense, or turn back into water. When this happens, the high heat of the molecule goes through the metal into what is being cooked. The water drips down inside the jacket and runs off through the outlet valve, sometimes called the condensate line.

To get a specific temperature, the steam inlet valve is opened either all the way to bring quantities of water to a boil quickly, or only part way for simmering.

Various models of steam-jacketed kettles differ in depth of kettle; steam-jacketed (either full, 2/3 or 1/3 jacketed); mounting—pedestal, legs, or wall; whether tilting or stationary, and method of steam supply, whether direct connected or self generating. Models with their own steam generators conserve energy through fast preliminary heat up and rapid temperature recovery after the product is added. Steam for some models can be generated at temperatures below 212°F. (100°C), though they can also be set at 290°F. (143°C) if necessary.

Full-jacketed and 1/3-jacketed kettles tend to be fixed rather than tilting; their contents are removed through draw-off tubes and valves. Two-thirds-jacketed kettles usually have a trunnion or pivot mechanism so food can be poured or scraped out.

There are also fully-jacketed cylindrical kettles whose inner jackets have bottoms that slope to the draw-off valves. These come in shallow, low, and tall models and trunnion models for 10- to 80-gal. (37.7 to 302 l) units.

Compartment steamers, in contrast to kettles, operate on the principle of the domestic pressure cooker. Since the steam comes into contact with the food, it follows that the steam to be used must be protected against impurities and un-wanted flavors. If the existing supply is contaminated, it can be run to a heat exchanger which will create uncontaminated steam.

A combination of such factors as the shape and size of the cooker; the kinds (perforated or solid) and sizes of the pans used; the pressure and amount of steam used, the position and number of jets or orifices admitting the steam, and the circulation or motion of the steam, determine the cooking time required. On some models thermostats prevent overcooking.

## MAKING YOUR OWN STEAM

What about a steam supply if there is no central source or no large, nearby boiler? Some steam kettles and cookers provide steam-generating equipment, sometimes with enough capacity to power additional steam-using equipment.

Alternatively, a boiler or steam generator (the conventional, heavy "boiler" is usually called a boiler; the "steam generator" is normally a smaller, lighter, steel boiler) may be installed to supply steam for cooking, sanitizing, or cleaning. A number of precautions such as purity of water supply and protection against rupture and explosion must be observed.

If there is a steam supply, but the steam is not pure enough for contact with food in a cooker, a steam-heat exchanger may be installed. The exchanger takes the heat from impure steam and transfers it to potable water, which then becomes pure steam.

### Steam Kettles

The steam-jacketed kettle with its one-stop, no-step operation takes a leading place on any list of essential kitchen equipment. Large quantities of on-premise baked items, popular with patients as well as patrons in the 475-seat cafeteria at the Memorial Hospital System in Houston justify the use of a large steam kettle with mixer assembly. The York (PA) Hospital turns out smaller batches of baked goods so the bake shop uses two 20-qt. (18.9 l) steam kettles with special drains to shield the bakers as they tilt the kettles to remove their contents.

## Cook in Deep Steam Kettles

| | |
|---|---|
| *Vegetables* | *Eggs, scrambled and* |
| *Rice* | *soft or hard cooked* |
| *Spaghetti* | *in the shell* |
| *Noodles* | *Soups of all kinds* |
| *Macaroni* | *Casserole* |
| *Dried* | *combinations* |
| *Beans* | *Cocoa or Coffee* |
| *Puddings* | *Chop Suey* |
| *Pie* | *Beef Stew* |
| *Fillings* | *Turkey a la King* |
| *Ice cream* | *Gravy* |
| *bases* | *Vegetables-fresh,* |
| *Poultry* | *frozen, loose pack,* |
| *Gelatin* | *solid pack* |

Two self-contained steam-jacketed kettles installed in the support station at Bob Burns Restaurant, Woodland Hills, CA, have a flush-to-floor draintrough in front of them with sectioned grates for easy removal.

To make it easy for foodservice workers handling either normal or large batches in steam kettles, the Loma Linda (CA) Hospital kitchens paid careful attention to proper working heights. (Counter models should always be set at heights that make it easy for workers to look in the kettles to check contents.) The kettle filler and the automatic water meter at the hospital are located conveniently between kettles.

There are many ways to handle the problems that can occur when pouring contents from steam-jacketed kettles. At the Middle Tennessee Mental Health Institute, Nashville, a portable receptacle with an adjustable spout allows any steam kettles to be drained and the liquid put into a floor drain without splashing or running on the floor. All steam equipment in the Tennessee hospital is wall mounted, and all outside openings are insect and rodent proof.

A self-contained, tilting table-top kettle can be installed on a counter or table top or on a support stand for convenient working height; it can be placed in any section of the kitchen where electricity is available. Kettles have 10-, 20-, and 40-qt. (9.4, 18.9 and 37.9 l) capacity; they are used to produce appetizers, bagels, fudge, icings, gelatin, melted butter, potatoes, rice, reconstituted foods, seafood, and stuffing. Cooking times are listed in the following table for 40-qt. (37.9 l) models:

## TABLE TOP STEAM KETTLE PRODUCTION TIME CHART*

| Product | Cooking Time* |
|---|---|
| Water (212°F.) (100°C.) | 8–12 minutes |
| Tapioca | 1 hour |
| Chocolate Pudding | 13 minutes |
| Glossy chocolate frosting | ½ hour |
| Chocolate syrup | ½ hour |
| German chocolate icing | ½ hour |
| Canned vegetables | 10 minutes |
| Frozen vegetables | 15–18 minutes |
| Onions (3 gal.) (11.3 l) | 5 minutes |
| Celery (3 gal.) (11.3 l) | 5 minutes |
| Minestrone soup | 45 minutes |
| Clam bisque | 1 hour |
| French onion soup | 2 hours |
| Cream of potato | 1 hour |
| Beef barley | 1½ hours |
| Beef noodle | 20 minutes |
| Split pea | 20 minutes |
| Chicken noodle | 20 minutes |
| Vegetable beef | 1 hour |
| Pasta (9 lb.) (4 kg) | 10 minutes |
| Spaghetti (10 lb.) (4.5 kg) | 8 minutes |
| Shells (10 lb.) (4.5 kg) | 11 minutes |
| Frozen ravioli (60 pieces) | 22 minutes |
| Brown gravy | 15–20 minutes |
| White cream sauce | 20 minutes |
| Cheese sauce | 15 minutes |
| Chili | 1½–2 hours |
| Ground meat (15 lb. (6.8 kg) browned) | 7 minutes |
| Spaghetti sauce | 1 hour |

*All cooking times submitted by Groen kettle users. Amount is 40 qt. (37.9 l) unless otherwise stated.

## WHAT SIZE KETTLES?

One suggested rule of thumb for estimating size of kettles allows about 8 lb. (3.6 kg) of meat or vegetables or about 4 lb. (1.8 kg) of poultry for each gallon of kettle capacity. These figures take shrinkage into account and leave a reasonable level below the brim of the kettle.

Another guide to kettle selection states:

- One 20-qt. (18.9 l) tilting table kettle (minimum) should be available for preparing small quantities of sauces, and gravies.
- One 30-gal. (113 l) kettle should be specified for each 600 meals.
- One 40-gal. (151 l) is needed for each 800 meals served during the peak period.

From El Camino Hospital comes this tested-in-operation recommendation: 50 gal. (189 l) for soup stock; 40 gal. (151 l) for stewing; 20 gal. (75.5 l) for vegetables; 10 and 20 qt. (9.4 and 18.9 l) for gravies and sauces.

Selection of kettle size must also be guided by the ability of workers to handle the masses of food required to fill kettles of the sizes being considered. Mechanical mixers now available with some kettles increase the amount of food which can be handled easily.

When sizable steamer capacity is required, using two smaller kettles instead of one large one adds flexibility. But the two smaller kettles take more floor space than a larger one.

Manufacturers have developed recommendations based on selected meal patterns in various institutions. This data is available for guidance in specifying equipment.

Further selection factors essential to satisfactory operation are suggested by experienced users of this equipment:

- Safety valves and pressure gauges.
- With self-generated steam models there will need to be automatic low-water cutout and a thermostatically-controlled cutout heat. Thermostats can be set to shut kettle off as product reaches desired temperature.
- Check kettle interior. Interior bottoms can be sloped to the interior front. The draw-off from the kettle interior (area at which food leaves kettle) is steam-heated up to draw-off valve to keep contents hot while kettle is being emptied. With this design, the model offers low working height, and heavy food can be drawn off without tilting or dipping.
- If self-generated steam models, need automatic low-water cutout and a thermostatically-controlled cutout heat.
- If tilting, require secure device for stopping at any degree of tilt.
- For stationary kettles provide tangent outlets that permit a straight flow and faucets that open completely in a straight line for ease of cleaning.
- Covers of large kettles should be hinged and balanced to stand open without tipping, and easily removable.

## Cook in Shallow Steam Kettles

| | |
|---|---|
| Braising Beef or Veal | Heart |
| Brisket, Flank Steak | Liver |
| Rump Roasts, Chuck | Kidney |
| Roasts, Short Ribs | Tongue |
| Roasting Pork-all cuts | Simmering large cuts |
| Pork Chops | of Meat |
| Roasting Ham | Corned |
| Roasting Lamb-all cuts | Beef |
| Swiss Steak | Stock |
| Fricassee of Chicken | Gravy |
| or Turkey | |

**Kettle Installation Musts**—Plan in advance to:
- Check steam supply.
- Provide water connection with hot and cold water and a swivel faucet for filling or cleaning.
- Protect faucets or other projections to prevent bumping.
- Check height of kettle against accepted working height standards. Locate counter models at heights easy for users to operate and see into.
- Arrange adequate, unhazardous drainage for kettles; grated gutters are a recommended drainage method.
- Allow sufficient room around kettles for uncrowded operation.
- Assure good ventilation in area.
- For self-generating gas-heated kettles, be sure there is sufficient supply of gas with excessive drafts eliminated. If direct flue connection must be made, a draft diverter should be utilized, properly adjusted to prevent "lifting off" of the flame on gas burner.
- For electric-heated kettles, be sure there is proper voltage and phase plus adequate supply of electricity to insure against fluctuating voltage.

Many accessories are available for use with steam kettles. Among them are the following: front-type food draw-off system, pan carry cart, cover-mounted automatic stirrer, strainers, thermostatic controls, lift-off cover, graduated measuring rod, draw-off tube, swing drain funnel, rotating baskets, water meter, support stand, and basket insert.

**Cook in Tilting Table Model Steam Kettle**

| | |
|---|---|
| *Eggs, scrambled, soft or hard cooked* | *Foods to be reheated* |
| *Vegetables, fresh and frozen, cooked in small amounts* | *Preparing jellied salads and desserts* |
| | *Heating canned foods* |
| *Cereals* | *Lobster and shrimp* |
| *Puddings, pie fillings, syrups, sauces* | *Sauces* |
| | *Pasta* |
| *Soups* | *Ground Meat Dishes* |
| *Stewed fruits* | *Poultry Items* |
| *Salad dressings* | *Stews* |
| | *Syrups and Glazes* |

## ENERGY SAVERS

Expand use of steam-jacketed kettles to perform tasks such as boiling water (make sure to heat only amount needed) or thawing frozen food (substitute for boiling water).

Check the energy evaluation charts available from some manufacturers to find out how steam kettles can be substituted for other kinds of cooking equipment.

Turn steam off when cooking is completed. Keep kettles covered; heating food to cooking temperature with the lid closed saves 5 to 10 percent of the heat needed per batch and reduces energy usage by 66 to 75 percent, according to Carol Michael, instructor, Department of Home Economics, Miami University, Oxford, OH.*

## SANITATION AND MAINTENANCE

The construction of steam-jacketed kettles—stainless steel with full or polished finish—simplifies cleaning. The base areas and location around them should be planned for equally easy cleaning. The kettle must be cleaned every time a different food is prepared, and also when no longer in operation. A step-by-step procedure to ensure quick, thorough cleaning has been worked out:

Whenever possible, turn the steam off before draining what you have been cooking. When the

*School Foodservice Journal, Feb. 1978.*

sides of the kettle are not hot, the food or liquid won't stick to the sides as the level goes down.

If there is not time to clean kettle immediately after use, fill it with water above the cooking line and turn on the steam to heat the water. This soaking will help later.

If step 2 was followed, open drain and let soaking water out; scrubbing with a very fine metal sponge or a brush. If the kettle is cleaned directly after cooking, swish water around inside the utensil to pre-rinse it.

Now close the drain and pour in a bucketful of hot soapy water. Dish machine detergent works well.

Using the soapy water, scrub the inside of the kettle thoroughly, including the underneath sides of the lids and hinges.

Using the same soapy water, scrub the outside of the kettle, including legs, frames, pipes; or counter tops and cabinet front pan support, if any. Rinse and wipe dry.

Open the drain, and as soapy water runs out, plunge a bottle brush in and out to clean drain pipe and valve.

Close drain; fill kettle about one-third full of water and heat it. Use this hot water to rinse the outside of the kettle; then swish it around to rinse the inside. Drain rinse water out and leave drain open until ready to use kettle again. Be sure kettle is thoroughly rinsed inside and out.

If small amounts of cooked food have been allowed to adhere to the inside of a steam-jacketed kettle, they may be soaked off with warm water and detergent or dislodged with a brush or very fine metal sponge.

## STEAM COOKERS

Cooking with a flow of steam directly over food marks the difference between the steam cooker or compartment steamer and the steam-jacketed kettle, where the steam is held between the jacket and the kettle and its heat is transferred to the food through the kettle.

Because the steam that flows over foods being cooked in a compartment steamer does not transmit flavors, several different items can be prepared in a steam cooker at the same time with-

**TYPES OF STEAM-JACKETED KETTLES**

| Capacity | l | Jacket Height | Mounting | | | |
|---|---|---|---|---|---|---|
| 1 qt. | (0.9) | 1/2 | TT | | | |
| 4 qt. | (3.8) | 1/2 | TT | | | |
| 5 qt. | (4.7) | 1/2 | TT | | | |
| 6 qt. | (5.7) | 1/2 | TT | | | |
| 8 qt. | (7.6) | 1/2 | TT | | | |
| 10 qt. | (9.4) | 1/2 | TT | | T | |
| 20 qt. | (18.9) | 1/2 | TT | | T | |
| 10 gal. | (37.7) | 2/3 | F | | T | |
| 20 gal. | (75.5) | 2/3 FULL | F | W | T | TW |
| 25 gal. | (94.4) | FULL | F | | | |
| 30 gal. | (113) | 2/3 FULL | F | | T | |
| 40 gal. | (151) | 2/3 FULL | F | W | T | TW |
| 50 gal. | (189) | FULL | F | | T | |
| 60 gal. | (226) | 2/3 FULL | F | W | T | TW |
| 80 gal. | (302) | 2/3 FULL | F | W | T | TW |
| 100 gal. | (377) | 2/3 FULL | F | W | | TW |
| 125 gal. | (472) | 2/3 FULL | F | | | |
| 150 gal. | (566) | 2/3 FULL | F | | | |
| 200 gal. | (755) | 2/3 FULL | F | | | |

F  = Floor Mounted
W  = Wall Mounted
T  = Tilting
TW = Tilting Wall Mounted
TT = Tilting Table Mounted

out intermingling flavors, if each item is placed in a solid pan. On the other hand, the super-heated liquid will increase the blending of flavors in items such as stews, where several ingredients are combined in one pan.

Compartment steamers provide varying pounds per square inch of pressure (PSI), depending on the model. They are generally divided into three types, depending on the amount of pressure required to operate them. There are atmospheric or zero PSI (O kg/cm²) steamers that have a maximum operating temperature of 212°F. (100°C). They are recommended for vegetables, seafood, and certain meats. These units can be stacked one on top of another; one model holds one 12 × 20 × 2½-in. (30 × 51 × 6 cm) pan, but will also handle a 12 × 20 × 4-in. (30 × 51 × 10 cm) pan. Light and sound systems signal when items are done. Pressureless or atmospheric steam cookers can also be used to defrost.

The chart on the next page indicates quantities and cooking times for one model.

## COUNT ON COMPARTMENT STEAMERS FOR HEAVY PRODUCTION

Compartment steamers are the type most often used for high-volume production. They generally have a maximum operating pressure of 5 PSI (.3 kg/cm²) and reach a maximum temperature of 228°F. (109°C). Some of the steam cookers in this category can utilize six 2½ in. (6.5 cm) or four 4 in. (10 cm) pans; come in semi-automatic and fully automatic styles. They are used for cooking vegetables, meats, poultry, fish, cereal products, eggs, fruit, and starch products. They have been called the workhorse of the steam-cooker line.

High-pressure compartment steamers, usually smaller than the 5 PSI (.3 kg/cm²) units, operate at a maximum of 15 PSI (1 kg/cm²) reaching a temperature of 254°F.(123°C). They offer speed in some types of food preparation because of their higher pressure and higher relative tem-

**SUGGESTED COOK TIMES FOR ATMOSPHERIC STEAMER\***

| Product | Quantity | Pan Size In. | Cm | Time |
|---|---|---|---|---|
| Green Beans, French Cut frozen | 10 lb. (4.5 kg) | 12 × 20 × 4 Perf. | (30 × 51 × 10) | 8 min. |
| Mixed Veg. frozen, (Peas, corn, lima beans, carrots, gr. beans) | 10 lb. (4.5 kg) | 12 × 20 × 2 Perf. | (30 × 51 × 5) | 6 min. |
| Broccoli, Spears, frozen | 8 lb. (3.6 kg) | 12 × 20 × 2 Perf. | (30 × 51 × 5) | 5½ min. |
| Brussel Sprouts, frozen | 10 lb. (4.5 kg) | 12 × 20 × 2 Perf. | (30 × 51 × 5) | 9 min. |
| Corn on the Cob, 3″ frozen cobbettes | 30 pieces | 12 × 20 × 2 Perf. | (30 × 51 × 5) | 6½ min. |
| Spinach, leaf thawed | 50 oz. (1.4 kg) | 12 × 20 × 2 Perf. | (30 × 51 × 5) | 2½ min. |
| Ocean Perch, frozen fillet | 1 lb. (453 gm) | 12 × 20 × 2 Perf. | (30 × 51 × 5) | 15 min. |
| Lobster Tail, frozen | 12 oz. (340 gm) per tail | 12 × 20 × 2 Perf. | (30 × 51 × 5) | 10 min. |
| Shrimp, frozen in shells (solid block) | 5 lb. (2.3 kg) | 12 × 20 × 2 | (30 × 51 × 5) | 7 min. |
| Rice, long grain, in scant 1½ qt. water | 4 lb. (1.8 kg) | 12 × 20 × 2 Solid | (30 × 51 × 5) | 20 min. |
| Eggs, hardcooked in shells, Refrigerated | 2 dozen | 12 × 20 × 2 Perf. | (30 × 51 × 5) | 10 min. |
| Eggs, hardcooked, broken into pan (no peeling shells!) | 2 dozen | 12 × 20 × 2 Solid | (30 × 51 × 5) | 12 min. |

Each cavity will handle a full size steam table pan 12″ × 20″ × 4″ (30.5 × 50 × 10 cm) deep (or shallower). ½ size pans may be handled singly or in pairs.

\*Groen Division, Dover Corporation

perature. They can be used for frequent cycling of food cooking, for blanching, and for reheating previously prepared food. These cookers may hold three 12 × 20 × 2½-in. (30 × 51 × 6-cm) pans or two 12 × 20 × 4-in. (30 × 51 × 10-cm) pans or combinations. These high-volume units are most often used in operations that must have large quantities of food ready at one time.

One of these speed cookers has a perforated plate designed to send steam jets onto frozen food to defrost it and heat it quickly. With the plate in place, the unit accommodates one standard 2-in. (15 cm) pan. With the plate removed, three pans can be used, but cooking time is longer.

Another speed cooker is designed to prepare small batches (2½ to 22 lb.) (1.1 to 10 kg) of frozen vegetables and other foods in continuous supply. Many establishments gain their "good vegetable" reputation by using this method.

An example of the food production that steam cookers offer is shown here for a model 25 in. (63.5 cm) high × 25 in. (63.5 cm) wide × approximately 34½ in. (88 cm) deep.

In another model that combines pressure and pressureless steam cooking, 100 percent hot, dry steam provides pressureless defrosting with pressurized quick cooking. The cooking starts only after the automatic pressureless defrosting cycle

| Food | Lb. Per Hour | Kg Per Hour | Servings Per Hour 5 to lb. (5/453 gm) | 8 to lb. (8/453 gm) |
|---|---|---|---|---|
| Fresh or frozen vegetables Short term cooking (7–8 min.) | 150 | 68.6 | 750 | 1200 |
| Fresh or frozen vegetables Medium cooking (10–12 min.) | 100 | 45.3 | 500 | 800 |
| Fresh or frozen vegetables Long cooking (14–16 min.) | 75 | 34 | 375 | 600 |
| Turkey (whole)* | 25 | 11.3 | 106 | 170 |
| Meats (beef or pork)* | 20 | 9 | 85 | 136 |
| Lobster | 63 whole | | | |
| Chicken (halves) Blanching only (3 pans) | 75 | 34 | | |
| Cook and brown (1 pan) | 16 | 7.2 | | |
| Casserole (12 × 20 × 2-in.) (30.5 × 50 × 5 cm) Pre-Browned | 6 | 2.7 | | |
| Heated only | 18 | 8.2 | | |

*15 percent average shrinkage indicated

## Items Most Often Prepared in Steam Cookers

Vegetables (including Potatoes)
Rice and Beans
Meat
Hard-Cooked Eggs
Poultry
Puddings,
Boston Brown Bread
Fish and Seafood
Soft-Cooked Eggs
Dumplings
Apples
Cereals, Pasta Products

is completed. When food is cooked a buzzer signals and the cooking signal light goes off. These cookers range from 12 to 36 in. (30.5 to 91.4 cm) wide and can cook quantities from one 3-oz. (85 gm) serving to 45 lb. (20.4 kg).

An 18 in. (45.7 cm) wide model will cook 7 lb. (3.2 kg) of frozen mixed vegetables in 1 minute or 18 defrosted lobster tails in 6 minutes.

Here are steam-cooker preparation times for several common menu items:

### Vegetables, Fresh

| | |
|---|---|
| Asparagus spears, medium | 2–2½ min. |
| Beans, green or wax | 2–3 min. |
| Cabbage, coarse shredded | 2–2½ min. |
| Corn-on-cob, small | 3–4 min. |
| Onions, sliced 1/4 in. (6 mm) | 3–4 min. |
| Potatoes, sliced 1/4 in. (6 mm) | 4–5 min. |
| Spinach, leaf | 1 min. |

### Vegetables, Frozen

| | |
|---|---|
| Beans, French-cut green | 1 min. |
| Broccoli spears | 1–1½ min. |
| Brussels sprouts, medium | 2½–4 min. |
| Carrots, baby whole | 2½–3 min. |
| Cauliflower | 1–1½ min. |
| Chinese pea pods | 1/4–1/2 min. |
| Corn, whole | 1/2–1 min. |
| Mixed vegetables | 1 min. |
| Peas | 1 min. |
| Yam patties, 2-oz. (57 gm) | 5–6 min. |

Zucchini, 1/4 in.
   (6 mm) slices            1–1½ min.

**Vegetables, Canned**

| | |
|---|---|
| Beans, green or wax | 1/2 min. |
| Carrots, baby whole | 1/2 min. |
| Potatoes, small whole | 2–2½ min. |

**Seafood, Fresh or Thawed**

| | |
|---|---|
| Clams, soft shell | 1½–2 min. |
| Crab legs or claws, cut into pieces | 3 min. |
| Lobster tails, 5-oz., (142 gm) halved or flowered | 3½ min. |
| Lobster, whole, 1–1½ lb. (453–679 gm) | 7–9 min. |
| Fish fillets | 1–3 min. |
| Shrimp, green, 10–12 ct. per lb. | 4 min. |

**Meat and Poultry**

| | |
|---|---|
| Beef, 1/2 in. (1.2 cm) cubes, separate | 30–35 min. |
| Chicken breasts, boned and rolled | 7–8 min. |
| Chicken wings (precook) | 2 min. |
| Spareribs (precook) | 12–15 min. |
| Wieners | 1½–2 min. |

**Eggs**

| | |
|---|---|
| Eggs, hard-cooked | 6½ min. |

(Also see Cooker-Timer Guideline chart on page 36.)

At Bob Burns Restaurant, Woodland Hills, CA, a 2-unit high-pressure steam cooker is mounted on a stainless steel shelf. The shelf is partially supported by a compact steam generator that operates the cooker. (See picture Chapter 3, Ovens.)

At the Foodservice Facility of the California Highway Patrol Academy, Bryte, cafeteria pans used for cooking in compartment steamers are also used for serving. All materials handling at the operation has been developed around a 12 × 20-in. (30 × 51 cm) module to simplify the system.

## STEAM COOKING SMALL BATCHES

In restaurants or other operations where patronage is steady all day, the small, high-pressure steam cooker is a better choice for fast preparation of small batches so that they are ready just a little ahead of service. Batteries of these are desirable for a varied menu.

Specially designed cookers prove particularly suitable for thawing where frozen convenience foods are used as individually reheated meals or are reheated in bulk. Cooking from thawed state cuts heating time in half, and yield is better because there is less dehydration.

Combination units of steam cookers and kettles are also used frequently in foodservice operations.

Locating the steam cookers is a matter of choice. If vegetables and poultry are to be blanched before french frying, a high-pressure steamer near the preparation area and adjacent to refrigeration is sensible.

For general cooking, either the main production area or a position behind the steamtable is the best location for steam cookers.

For reheating frozen prepared food, a backbar or work table adjacent to both refrigerator and freezer, and very near the serving counter or other service unit, such as the tray line, is certainly the choice location. Cookers using dry agitated steam for small batch vegetable cooking can be a merchandising plus behind cafeteria serving lines. Vegetables may be heated and served as needed.

Fish is most delicate—its flavor, texture, and shape most perfectly preserved—when it is steamed. Gourmet dishes such as fish in parchment (en papillote) and fish for an almost unbelievable variety of sauces are excellent when prepared in a steam cooker. They may be seasoned as usual before cooking.

Hard-cooked eggs can be cooked in the steamer in or out of their shells. If the eggs are intended for slicing or halves, they should be steamed in the shell. Fill pan to the top (but not above) and cook 5 to 6 minutes, starting at room temperature. Hold for 5 minutes before placing in cold water. Use a strainer.

If eggs are to be chopped for salad or sandwich mixtures or garnishes, they may be broken first into a solid pan and steamed that way. Oil pan to avoid sticking. They steam in less time and save about 4/5 of the labor of shelling after cooking.

## HIGH-SPEED STEAM COOKER—TIMER GUIDELINE

### Frozen Vegetables

*Minutes*

| | |
|---|---|
| 3½–5 | **Artichoke** hearts |
| 1 | **Beans,** baby lima, cut green, cut wax |
| 2–3 | **Beans,** Fordhook lima |
| 1–1½ | **Beans,** Italian |
| 3–4 | **Beans,** speckled butter |
| 1–1½ | **Beans,** whole green (ice side up) |
| 1/2–1 | **Broccoli** florets |
| 1–1½ | **Broccoli** spears (ice side up) |
| 2½–4 | **Brussels sprouts,** medium |
| 2½–3 | **Carrots,** baby whole |
| 2–2½ | **Carrots,** crinkle cut or sliced |
| 1–1½ | **Carrots,** diced |
| 1–1½ | **Cauliflower** |
| 1/2–1 | **Celery,** cut |
| 1/4–1/2 | **Chinese pea pods** |
| 1/2–1 | **Corn,** whole kernel |
| | **Mixed Vegetables** |
| 1/2–1 | **Far Eastern** (French cut beans, broccoli, onions, mushrooms) |
| 1 | **Italian** (zucchini, Italian beans, broccoli, onions, mushrooms) |
| 1/2 | **Normandy** (broccoli, cauliflower) |
| 1/2–1 | **Parisian** (broccoli, cauliflower, crinkle cut carrots) |
| 1 | **Regular** (peas, corn, carrots, baby lima beans, green beans) |
| 1/2–1 | **Roman** (broccoli, cauliflower, red pepper) |
| 1–1½ | **Scandinavian** (zucchini, green beans, onions, peas, carrots) |
| 1 | **Sicilian** (cauliflower, zucchini, Italian beans, onions) |
| 1/2–1 | **Tahitian** (broccoli, French cut beans, celery, red pepper, mushrooms) |
| 1 | **Peas** |
| 8–9 | **Peas,** blackeyed |
| 1 | **Peas and diced carrots** |
| 1–1½ | **Peas and pearl onions** |
| 1 | **Peas,** petite |
| 1–2 | **Pepper,** green diced |
| 4–4½ | *****Potatoes,** stew cut (frozen, dehydrated, cover with hot salted water) |
| 1–2 | **Squash,** crookneck, 1/4" (6 mm) slices (loosen) |
| 1–1½ | **Squash,** zucchini, 1/4" (6 mm) slices (loosen) |
| 1 | **Succotash** (corn, baby lima beans) |
| 5–6 | **Yam patties,** 2 oz. (57 gm) one layer in pan |

For cooking frozen vegetables in the Models 100-G and 10/G-12, add 1/2 to 1 minute onto the above cooking time.

### Thawed Frozen Vegetables

*Note:* These vegetables must be thawed and drained. Place in pan, separate for better steam circulation. One pkge.-Model 10; two pkges.-Model 20; 6 pkges.-Model 30.

*Minutes*

| | |
|---|---|
| 13–14 | **Collard greens,** chopped (add chopped ham) |
| 3–4 | **Okra,** whole |
| 2–3 | **Okra,** cut |
| 2–4 | **Spinach,** chopped |
| 2–4 | **Spinach,** leaf |
| 8–9 | **Squash,** mashed |

### Special Handling of Frozen Vegetables

*Note:* Place vegetables ice side up, flat in pan. Set timer for almost zero. When buzzer rings, open door and loosen with large fork. Close and set for full timer setting.

*Note:* 1. In half pan, use maximum of 2 frozen packages of vegetables laying flat on strainer.
2. Full pan will hold up to 4 packages of vegetables laying flat on strainer.

*Minutes*

| | |
|---|---|
| 1/2 | **Asparagus** cuts or sm. spears |
| 1–1½ | **Asparagus** spears, medium |
| 1½–2 | **Asparagus** spears, jumbo |
| 1 | **Green Beans,** French cut |
| 1–1½ | **Broccoli,** chopped or cut |

### Fresh Vegetables

*Minutes*

| | |
|---|---|
| 1–2 | **Artichokes,** whole-precooked. Bring to serving temperature. |
| 8 | **Artichokes,** Jerusalem, 1/4" (6 mm) slices, blanch to peel |
| 1–2 | **Asparagus** cuts and tips |
| 2–2½ | **Asparagus** spears, fresh, medium |
| 2–3 | **Beans,** lima, waxed, whole or cut green |
| 5 | **Beets,** diced, 1/2" (1.3 cm) |
| 4–6 | **Beets,** sliced 1/4" (6 mm) |
| 1 | **Beets,** whole-blanch to peel |
| 8–10 | **Beets,** young whole |
| 1–1½ | **Broccoli spears** |
| 2–2½ | **Cabbage,** coarse, shredded |
| 1½–2 | **Cabbage,** diced |
| 1–1½ | **Cabbage,** fine shredded |
| 1 | **Cabbage,** leaves to blanch (remove outer leaves, repeat) |
| 5–6 | **Cabbage,** wedge (4 oz. ea.) (114 gm) |
| 3–5 | **Carrots,** baby whole |
| 1–1½ | **Carrots,** diced |
| 2–3 | **Carrots,** sliced 1/2" (1.3 cm) |
| 2–3 | **Cauliflower** florets |
| 2–2½ | **Celery,** sliced (1/2" rings) (1.3 cm) |
| 2½–3 | **Celery,** sliced (1/4" rings) (6 mm) |

**TIMER GUIDELINE (cont.)**

**Fresh Vegetables (cont.)**

*Minutes*

| | |
|---|---|
| 3-4 | **Corn-on-cob,** small |
| 4-5 | **Corn-on-cob,** medium |
| 5-7 | **Corn-on-cob,** large |
| 1/2 | **Eggplant,** blanch to peel (keep in lemon juice) |
| 1/2-1 | **Eggplant,** sliced 1/2″ (1.3 cm) |
| 4-5 | **Kohlrabi,** sliced 3/8″ (1 cm) |
| 2 | **Kohlrabi,** blanch for peeling, remove heavy green skin |
| 5-6 | **Kohlrabi,** diced 1/4″ (6 mm) |
| 3-4 | **Mushrooms,** whole, small |
| 4-5 | **Mushrooms,** medium |
| 5-7 | **Mushrooms,** large |
| 5-6 | **Mushrooms,** 1/4″ sliced (6 mm) |
| 3 | **Okra,** whole |
| 2 | **Okra,** cut |
| 1½-2 | **Onions,** diced |
| 3-4 | **Onions,** sliced 1/4″ (6 mm) |
| 6-7 | **Onions,** sliced 1/2″ (1.3 cm) |
| 5-6 | **Onions,** whole (small, white) |
| 2-2½ | **Parsnips,** diced |
| 6-8 | **Parsnips,** whole, small |
| 1-1½ | **Peas** |
| 2-3 | **Peppers,** green diced |
| 1-1½ | **Peppers,** green halves |
| 1-1½ | **Potatoes,** thin sliced (no water added) |
| 4-5 | **Potatoes,** 1/4″ sliced (no water added) (6 mm) |
| 6-8 | **Potatoes,** 1″ cubed chunks (no water added) (2.5 cm) |
| 8-10 | **Potatoes,** new (red skin), small |
| 9-10 | ***Potatoes,** quarters, cover with hot salted water |
| 14-15 | ***Potatoes,** halves, cover with hot salted water |
| 20-25 | **Potatoes,** to bake (7-9 oz.) (199-255 gm). Wrap in foil. |
| 25-30 | **Potatoes,** to bake (9-11 oz.) (255-312 gm). Wrap in foil. |
| 15-17 | **Potatoes,** sweet, to bake (7-8 oz.) (199-226 gm). Wrap in foil. |
| 15-17 | ***Rice** 1 lb. (453 gm) rice/6-7 cups (0.7-0.8 l) hot salted water, stir. Cook, hold 5 minutes, drain, and rinse in cold water, then hot. Add melted margarine or oil if held before service. |
| 18-20 | ***Rice,** USDA 1 lb. (453 gm) rice to 6 cups (0.7 l) hot salted water, stir. Cook, hold 5 minutes, drain, and rinse in cold water, then hot. Add melted margarine or oil if held before service. |
| 25-30 | ***Rice,** Blend, long grain and wild. Add rice, seasoning packet, margarine to 2¼ |

*Minutes*

| | |
|---|---|
| | qts. (2.18) hot water, stir. (Use less than recommended amount of water.) Hold 5 minutes before service. Do not rinse. |
| 15 | **Rutabagas,** sliced 2″ (5 cm) cook, remove skin, then mash |
| 1 | **Spinach,** leaf |
| 10-11 | **Squash,** Acorn halves 1¼-1½ lbs. (567-680 gm) per half. Cook, remove skin, season and mash. |
| 4-5 | **Squash,** Acorn quarters (peeled) |
| 2-3 | **Squash,** Summer, sliced 1/2″ (1.3 cm) |
| 3-5 | **Squash,** Zucchini, sliced 1/2″ (1.3 cm) |
| 2-3 | **Squash,** Zucchini, sliced 1/4″ (6 mm) |
| 1 | **Tomatoes,** stewed (first blanch 1/4 min. for peeling) |
| 3½ | **Tomatoes,** whole (first blanch 1/4 min. for peeling) |
| 1 | **Turnips,** blanch to peel |
| 6-7 | **Turnips,** cubed 1″ (2.54 cm) |
| 4-6 | **Turnips,** sliced 1/4″ (6 mm) |
| 3-5 | **Turnips,** strips or diced 1/2″ (1.3 cm) |

**Canned Vegetables**

Vegetables must be drained before heating in pan with strainer.

*Minutes*

| | |
|---|---|
| 2 | **Beans,** Fordhook lima |
| 1/2 | **Beans,** green or wax |
| 1/2 | **Beets,** diced |
| 2-2½ | **Beets,** sliced |
| 2-3 | **Beets,** whole |
| 10-12 | **Cabbage,** red |
| 1/2 | **Carrots,** baby whole |
| 1½ | **Carrots,** sliced |
| 2½-3 | **Celery,** cut |
| 1/2 | **Corn,** whole kernel |
| 1/2 | **Mixed vegetables** (lima beans, carrots, green beans, peas, potatoes, celery, corn) |
| 1/2-1 | **Onions,** small whole |
| 1/2 | **Peas** |
| 1/2 | **Potatoes,** diced (rinse before cooking) |
| 2-2½ | **Potatoes,** small whole (rinse before cooking) |
| 10-12 | **Sauerkraut** |

**Meats (Fresh or Thawed)**

*Minutes*

| | |
|---|---|
| 30-35 | **Beef,** 1/2″ (1.3 cm) cubes (separate before cooking) |
| 45-50 | **Beef,** 1″ (2.5 cm) cubes (separate before cooking) |
| 5-10 | **Beef,** ground (separate). Break up cooked beef with wire whip. |

## Meats (Fresh or Thawed) (cont.)

*Minutes*

| | |
|---|---|
| 17–20 min/lb. | **Corned beef brisket** (2–4 lbs. (0.9–1.8 kg) each) |
| 7–7½ | **Franks** (4 oz. (114 gm) each), 2 layers only. |
| 1½–2 | **Hamburger patties,** (2 oz.) (57 gm), pre-cooked, stacked vertically on end in pan. |
| 4–5 | **Liver** (4–5 oz. slices) (114–142 gm). One layer in pan. |
| 1 | **Sausage,** small linked, pre-browned. |
| 4–6 | **Sausage,** (6 oz.) (170 gm), fresh linked, pre-browned. (Puncture with fork). |
| 5–7 | **Sausage,** Polish (6–7 oz.) (170–199 gm). (Puncture with fork). |
| 12–15 | **Spareribs.** Cook, add BBQ sauce and finish in oven or broiler. |
| 25–30 | **Spareribs,** country style. Cook; add BBQ sauce and finish in oven or broiler. |
| 30–45 | **Shortribs.** After cooked, drain and add gravy. |
| 1½–2 | **Wieners** (fresh or frozen). Two layers only. |

## Poultry (Fresh or Thawed)

*Minutes*

| | |
|---|---|
| 7–8 | **Chicken breasts,** boned & rolled (one layer) |
| 2 | **Chicken wings** (fill pan). Precooked as for frying, cool, batter and fry. |
| 3 | **Chicken wings** (fill pan). |
| 6–7 | **Chicken quarters** (fill pan). Precooked for frying, cool, batter and fry. |
| 7–8 | **Chicken quarters** (fill pan). |
| 6–8 | **Cornish game hens,** whole. Cook, then brush with paprika & butter-brown under broiler or in oven. |
| 10m/lb. | **Turkey,** double breasts (9–10 lbs). (4–4.5 kg) |
| 30–45 | **Turkey** halves. (10–12 lbs). (4.5–5.4 kg) |
| 3–3½ min/lb. | **Turkey,** whole (20–25 lbs.) (9–11.3 kg)./Model 30 only. |

## Seafood & Fish (Fresh or Thawed)

*Minutes*

| | |
|---|---|
| 3 | **Crab** claws (6 oz.) (170 gm) cut into pieces |
| 3 | **Crab** legs (8 oz.) (226 gm) cut into pieces |
| 1½–2 | **Clams,** soft shell |
| 2½ | **Clams,** Little Neck |
| 3 | **Clams,** Cherrystone |
| 4 | **Clams,** hard shell |
| 1–3 | **Fish** fillets (snapper, trout, etc.) One layer in pan. Time depends on thickness of fillet. |
| 3–5 | **Fish** steaks, 3/4″ (1.9 cm) thick (halibut, salmon or Swordfish), one layer in pan. |
| 7–9 | **Lobster,** whole (chicken), 1–1½ lb. each (453–680 gm) each. |
| 11–12 | **Lobster,** whole, 2–2½ lb. (0.9–1.1 kg) each. |
| 3½ | **Lobster** tails (5 oz.) (142 gm) halved or flowered add paprika |
| 6 | **Lobster** tails (5 oz.) (142 gm) whole, cook one minute less, add butter and paprika, place under broiler to brown. |
| 1/2–1 | **Scallops** (4 pieces/ounce) |
| 2 | **Shrimp,** green (26–30 count/lb.) (453 gm) |
| 3 | **Shrimp,** green (21–25 count/lb.) (453 gm) |
| 4 | **Shrimp,** green (10–12 count/lb.) (453 gm) |

## Eggs (Preferably room temperature)

*Minutes*

| | |
|---|---|
| 1/2 | ***Eggs,** poached—Use very fresh eggs. Drop in pan of hot salted or vinegar water; cook; Remove with perforated spoon. |
| 3 | **Eggs,** soft-cooked (no water). Hold hot 5 minutes before serving. |
| 6½ | **Eggs,** hard-cooked (no water). Hold hot for 8½–9 minutes before placing in cold water to shell. |

## Fruits

*Minutes*

| | |
|---|---|
| 1/2–1 | **Avocado,** Blanch for peeling. |
| 1 | **Grapefruit.** Blanch for peeling. |
| 1/2 | **Oranges.** Blanch for peeling. |
| 15 | **Pumpkin,** unpeeled, cut up. Cook, remove skin, then mash. |

*Do not use strainer.
Information courtesy of Hobart Food Equipment Company.

Scrambled eggs may be cooked soft in the steam cooker in solid steam table pans that have been coated with a thin film of butter. Poaching may also be done in the steamer. At the end of the cooking period, condensed moisture is simply poured off.

Spaghetti can be cooked in water in solid pans. If a few strands at a time are dropped into hot, salted water, and if all spaghetti is thoroughly wet before steaming starts, strands emerge separately.

To cook rice, add 1 lb. (453 gm) rice to 6 cups (1.4 l) hot, salted water. Drain and rinse in cold water. USDA recommends 1 lb. (453 gm) rice to 5 cups (1.2 l), hot, salted water; do not drain or rinse.

Other jobs that the steam cooker does well are: cooking fruit cakes, steamed puddings, sheetcakes and gingerbread; melting butter for sauces and batters (no browning in the steamer); blanching fruits and vegetables for easy peeling; defrosting frozen bread; freshening stale bread; loosening dried-on food before washing pans.

In one deli operation, large quantities of raw beef, ham, corned beef, and pastrami are prepared in a very efficient cooking battery that consists of a convection oven, a compartment steamer, and a hot-top range. Corned beef prepared in the compartment steamer is stored on pan racks in the walk-in cooler until needed. The operator reports that utilization of the compartment steamer reduces cooking time, enhances flavor, and allows the use of a less expensive grade of meat.

## COULDN'T WE STEAM COOK THAT?

Putting the question, ''Couldn't we steam cook that?'' to every menu item is especially advisable in light of the preparation advantages currently offered by this cooking method. Among the pluses a steam cooker can provide:

- Speed and efficiency through more "as needed" preparation, with minimal or no holding time
- Maximum preservation of color and texture
- High-level retention of nutritive food values
- Assurance of constant temperature cooking
- Energy savings from automatic operation of equipment (fuel used only when steam cooking unit is in operation); elimination of pot washing; reduction in floor space needed for food-preparation equipment; lowered air-conditioning costs; less skilled labor required; use of same pan for cooking and serving
- Expansion of menu possibilities
- Reduction in food shrinkage.

## VACUUM DRAWS STEAM INTO FOOD MASS

One type of high-pressure steam cooker permits dry steam to transfer its heat directly to the food to be cooked. To insure that steam is concentrated on the food, the steam is directed into the low-specific-heat, low-thermal-conductive stainless steel cooking compartment through multiple jets.

These jets, in turn, direct the agitated dry steam onto the contents of food pans. Food in the pans gets immediate latent heat from the steam to cook foods fast all the way through.

Fast cooking is assured since the jet directed steam (1) disperses the low temperatures around the food and (2) through rapid condensation of steam creates a vacuum in the food mass by which more steam is drawn into the food to speed heat transfer.

This equipment offers:

- Excellent color, flavor, texture, and aroma for foods prepared in it.
- Cooking times so speedy that frozen vegetables can be prepared in small quantities fast enough to match serving-line requirements.
- Foods in which only minimum liquid remains so that cooking can be done in solid pans to retain the soluble vitamins and mineral salts.

## AUTOMATIC DEFROST FOR FROZEN FOODS

For frozen foods this cooker is designed with a patented automatic defrost cycle and electronically delayed timer action that prevents either overcooking or undercooking. The timer that controls the cooking cycle will not start operating until after the product has been automatically defrosted.

Foods are cooked in a stainless steel compartment that holds one or more stainless steel pans.

Recommended for preparation in this equipment are fresh or frozen vegetables, seafood, rice, poultry, eggs, spaghetti, potatoes, custards, and individual frozen entrees portioned in bags.

These cookers are made with three different size cooking compartments in single or multiple compartment models. Compartments, depending on size, hold: 1/3 size pan; 1/2 size 5-in. (12.7 cm) pan; 2 full size pans 2½ in. (6.5 cm) deep or 1 full size pan 4-in. (10 cm) deep. Cookers are available as counter models and freezer base models.

In multiple compartment cookers, each compartment can be operated separately so that food items requiring different cooking times can be prepared side by side in the same piece of cooking equipment.

Door of cooking compartment is designed for easy cleaning and swing-out operation; remains tightly sealed until all the pressure is gone. The 15-min. electronic timer has time selections in 30-sec. intervals to match established cooking times.

An unorthodox but convenient steam cooker is one brand of braising pan. With a steamer attachment, the pan is capable of processing 3 full 12 × 20 in. (30 × 51 cm) pans simultaneously. Cooking is faster than in a conventional low-pressure cooker; it is comparable to the high-pressure speed cooker.

An energy-saving, manual steam-flow control is one important asset of a new single-com-partment, counter-top steam cooker. The unit has a 5-kw self-contained atmospheric steam generator that holds three 12 × 20 × 2½-in. (30 × 51 × 6 cm) counter pans or up to six 1-in. (2.5 cm) perforated pans. It also contains a built-in water conditioner to prevent lime build up. To help train employees to use it properly, operating instructions are available in English, French, and Spanish.

Another high-speed steam cooker operates with an internal pressure of 10 to 13½ PSI (0.6 to 0.9 kg/cm$^2$). Hot, dry steam in the cooking chamber assures 240° to 275°F. (116° to 246°C) heat for low-cost defrosting and fast cooking. Large-volume, 2-compartment models can be either vertical or horizontal; a 4-compartment installation is also possible.

## STEAM COOKER/DEFROSTER

Because today's foodservice uses frozen foods so universally, some steam cooker manufacturers now offer a compartment that converts to a pressureless cooker/defroster while the second compartment is preparing fresh food. Manufacturers provide detailed instructions that tell what items can best be prepared in each type of compartment.

Some examples of timer settings for pressureless steam-cookers are listed here:

**FROZEN PREPARED ENTREES***

**(Using Three Standard 2½-in. (6.4 cm) Steamtable Pans)**

| Item | Pan Size | Weight Per Pan | Pressureless Timer Setting |
|---|---|---|---|
| Lobster Tails 6–8 oz. (170–225 g) | 12 × 20 × 2½ in. Solid Pan (1/1-65 mm) | 7–8 lb. (3.2–3.6 kg.) | 10–12 min. |
| Shrimp, C.D.P. | 12 × 20 × 2½ in. Solid Pan (1/1-65 mm) | 16–20 lb. (7½–9 kg) | 4–5 min. |
| Shrimp, Green | 12 × 20 × 2½ in. Solid Pan (1/1-65 mm) | 16–20 lb. (7½–9 kg) | 5–7 min. |
| Bulk Pack Frozen** | 12 × 20 × 2½ in. Perf. Pan (1/1-65 mm) | 3½–4 lb. (1.6–1.8 kg) | 25–35 min. |
| Bulk Pack Defrosted** | 12 × 20 × 2½ in. Perf. Pan (1/1-65 mm) | 3½–4 lb. (1.6–1.8 kg) | 15–25 min. |

*Market Forge

**Use Pressure Timer and place entire pan in a perforated pan.

## STEAM COOKER PURCHASING POINTERS

The importance of good construction and design underlies this purchasing check list:

- Heavy duty gaskets
- Adequate safety devices
- Accurate pressure gauges
- Compartments fabricated to form one-piece body; entire interior of stainless steel
- Shelves or supports removable without use of tools
- Height at proper level to load and unload
- Local service readily available
- Equipment readily serviceable from front or sides.

Some models also offer automatic controls such as timers for each compartment. In these models, when food in the compartment is done, a bell rings or a buzzer sounds to notify the user. In other models, steam automatically shuts off and all steam and condensate is exhausted from the compartment when cooking cycle is completed. Another excellent feature in some models is that the door can be opened and food added after cooking has started.

Accessories available for compartment steamers include manual sliding shelves, low-temperature work station, heat exchange, pan slide adapters, stainless steel hose with hot/cold faucet, and steam table pans—solid or perforated.

When selecting steam cookers, consider the source and character of the steam. For the equipment to operate properly, reasonably dry steam of at least 5 PSI (0.3 kg/cm$^2$) for compartment-type and 12 to 15 PSI (0.8 to 1 kg/cm$^2$) for high-pressure cookers is necessary. Trap near reducing valve drains condensate. Equipment may generate its own steam or use a boiler located near the kitchen.

## MATCH COOKER CAPACITY TO REQUIREMENTS

Several factors must be considered to obtain cookers that match the operation's requirements. Working heights are especially important; lower ones are now available.

Cookers available from one manufacturer range from high-pressure units that will hold 3 12 × 20 × 2½-in. (30 × 51 × 6 cm) pans (producing about 72 portions) to 3-compartment low-pressure models with an 18-pan capacity. Other compartment steamers offer a capacity of six 4-in. (10 cm) pans. Small counter top models that fit in small space turn out about 30 to 35 lb. of food (13.6 to 16 kg).

Capacity data are useful as rules of thumb. The following guide is based on meals per hour:

**STEAM COOKING COMPARTMENT REQUIREMENTS**

| Meals Per Hour | Low Pressure (5 PSI) (0.3 kg/cm²) Compartment Steamers | High Pressure Steamer |
|---|---|---|
| 200–500 | one 2-compartment | one 3-compartment |
| 500–750 | one 3-compartment | three 4-compartments |
| 750–1000 | one 3-compartment or two 2-compartments | four 6-compartments |
| 1000–up | provide one 2-compartment combination per 500 meals/hour | provide one compartment for each 200–300 meals/hour |

## CHECK ON COOKING CHARTS

Charts with suggested times for steam cooking a wide variety of products are available and offer an excellent basis for working out steam-cooker production schedules. They are especially useful when matched with the specific equipment used in gathering the cooking data they contain. Since these charts are constantly being refined by the makers of steam cookers, operators should make sure the charts in use in their kitchens include the most up-to-date findings from steam-cooker time studies.

However, when one of the most convinced users of steam cookers emphasizes that cooking times may vary from day to day with a single vegetable, it is clear that suggested cooking times for this equipment must not be considered a final answer. Instead, the required time for some products must be determined by the individual institution, subject to variation as the quality, maturity, and size of the raw ingredients vary. In this operation, vegetables are given batch checks and steaming times are adjusted, as the finished product dictates, after taste test. A half-minute variation in steaming time in a high-pressure cooker improves quality of some finished products.

The chart on the next page provides detailed information and suggested cooking times.

## CONTAINER CHOICES

Scrutiny of container sizes for steam cookers will insure that those selected will:

- Match menu needs
- Minimize handling (usually serving size pans can be transferred direct from cooker)
- Permit suitable load size.

Choice of containers may be made from: "Baskets that are tall or flat, requiring only one or two to fit the compartment height; wide or narrow for one or two in the compartment width; and perforated or solid for products with or without liquid. Pans of serving size 2½ to 4-in. (6.5 to 10 cm) in depth, whether solid or perforated, may be obtained."

The number, type and size of container should be specified exactly. Keep in mind that smaller pan capacities permit more uniform distribution of steam within the compartment. Some steam cookers are designed to utilize 12- × 20-in. (30 × 51 cm) cafeteria pans and 18 × 26-in. (45.7 × 66 cm) bake trays.

## OPERATING INSTRUCTIONS

These easy steps for operating a 5 PSI (0.3 kg/cm²) dual compartment steamer are for a unit that can be used either as a pressureless steam cooker or as a steam pressure cooker:

### Pressure Cooking

Before loading the cooker be sure compartment is hot. If not, follow preheating instructions.

1. Slide pans of food into cooking-compartment pan supports.
2. Close cooking-compartment door and push down on latch handle to engage lock.
3. Place cooking-mode selector switch in pressure cooking (down) position.
4. Set 60-minute timer (bottom) to required cooking time. (See Test Kitchen Bulletin for cooking time.)
5. Turn off buzzer, which sounds to indicate cooking is complete, by setting timer dial to the off position.
6. Allow pressure to return to 0 PSI. Open door by pulling up on latch handle. Allow remaining vapor to dissipate before raising door to full open position.
7. Unload by sliding pans of food from pan supports.

### Operation

Before each initial operation of cooker and at any other time when cooking compartment is cold, a 2–3-minute preheating cycle is required.

1. Check steam supply to insure pressure is at cooker.
   a. Direct Steam—Turn on valve for external steam supply.
   b. All other units—Follow steam generator operating instructions on plate of control box inside cabinet base.
2. Close cooking compartment door and lock securely in place by pressing down on latch handle.
3. Place cooking mode selector switch in the pressure cooking (down) position.
4. Set 60-minute timer (bottom) to '3-minutes.'
5. Turn off buzzer, which sounds to indicate cycle complete, by setting timer dial to the off position.
6. Allow pressure to return to 0 PSI. Open door by pulling up on latch handle. Allow remaining vapor to dissipate before raising door to the full open position for loading.

### Pressureless Steam Cooking

Before loading the cooker, be sure compartment is hot. If not, follow preheating instructions.

**PRESSURE STEAM COOKING TIMER SETTINGS AND PORTIONS***

**Meat—Poultry—Fish**

| Item | Approx. Raw Weight Per Pan | Recommended 12" × 20" (1/1) Solid Pan | Number of Pans | Pressure Timer Setting in Minutes | Approx. Number Cooked 2 oz. (55 g) Servings Per Pan* |
|---|---|---|---|---|---|
| Chicken Cut-up | 8 lb. (3.6 kg) | 2½ in. (65 mm) | 1–3 | 18–25 | 15–20 2 oz. |
|  |  |  | 4–6 | 25–30 | Protein (55 g) |
| Chicken, 4 lb. (1.8 kg) Whole | 3 each | 4 in. (100 mm) | 1–2 | 45–55 | 25–30 2 oz. |
|  |  |  | 3–4 | 55–65 | Protein (55 g) |
| Fowl, 5 lb. (2.3 kg) or more whole | 2 each | 4 in. (100 mm) | 1–2 | 50–60 | 20–25 2 oz. |
|  |  |  | 3–4 | 65–75 | Protein (55 g) |
| Fish fillets | 3 lb. (1.4 kg) | 2½ in. (65 mm) | 1–3 | 8–12 | 12–15 2 oz. |
|  |  |  | 4–6 | 10–15 | (55 g) |
| Frankforts | 5 lb. (2.3 kg) | 2½ in. (65 mm) | 1–3 | 3–4 | 35–40 2 oz. |
|  |  |  | 4–6 | 4–5 | (55 g) |
| Hamburgers 3 oz. (85 g) | 5 lb. (2.3 kg) | 2½ in. (65 mm) | 1–3 | 12–14 | 20–25 2 oz. |
|  |  |  | 4–6 | 15–18 | (55 g) |
| Meatballs 1 oz. (30 g) size** | 6 lb. (2.7 kg) | 2½ in. (65 mm) | 1–3 | 18–22 | 20–25 2 oz. |
|  |  |  | 4–6 | 22–25 | Protein (55 g) |
| Meatloaf* | 15 lb. (6.8 kg) | 2½ in. (65 mm) | 1–3 | 35–40 | 50–60 2 oz. |
|  |  |  | 4–6 | 40–45 | Protein (55 g) |
| Pork Chops 4 oz. loin bone (115 g) | 6 lb. (2.7 kg) | 2½ in. (65 mm) | 1–3 | 25–30 | 24 2 oz. |
|  |  |  | 4–6 | 30–35 | Protein (55 g) |
| Sausage 1½ oz. (45 g) | 6 lb. (2.7 kg) | 2½ in. (65 mm) | 1–3 | 18–21 | 18–20 2 oz. |
|  |  |  | 4–6 | 22–25 | (55 g) |
| Turkey On Carcass | 20–22 lb. (9–10 kg) | 2½ in. (65 mm) | 1–2 | 100–120 | 50–60 2 oz. Protein (55 g) |
| Turkey Off | 10–12 lb. (4.5–5 kg) | 2½ in. (65 mm) | 1–3 | 50–60 | 55–65 2 oz. |
|  |  |  | 4–6 | 60–75 | Protein (55 g) |

*Market Forge

**Raw weight for Meatballs and Meatloaf includes hamburg and extenders and yields 2 oz. (56 g) protein plus extenders or 3 oz.(85 g) total portion.

1. Slide pans of food into cooking-compartment pan supports of pressureless steam cooker.
2. Close cooking-compartment door and push down on latch handle to engage lock.
3. Place cooking-mode selector switch in pressureless cooking (up) position.
4. Set the 10-minute timer (top) to required cooking time. (See Test Kitchen Bulletin for unit.)
5. Press pan selector button (1,2, or 3) to match the number of pans loading in cooker.

Note: To activate control circuit, first set the 10-minute timer, then push the pan selector button.

The button acts as a timer delay: 1 pan = 2½ min.; 2 pan = 3½ min.; 3 pan = 4½ min.

6. Turn off buzzer, which sounds to indicate cooking is complete, by setting timer dial to the off position.
7. Open door by pulling up on latch handle. Allow remaining vapor to dissipate before raising door to full open position.

8. Unload by sliding pans of food from pan supports, taking care to avoid hitting compartment opening.

## CLEANING STEAM COOKERS

A popular asset of today's steam cookers is one-step cleaning. Washing the cooking chamber with a mild detergent each day is all the interior cleaning required. Some manufacturers recommend putting ice in the chamber and turning on the unit to clean drain lines. Leave compartments dry and doors open after cleaning. Clean up spills, either inside or outside the cooker, immediately. Flush boilers at least twice a week to prevent corrosion; some models have boilers that flush daily. The American Gas Association recommends removing and cleaning shelves and supports. Gaskets should be cleaned and replaced when worn.

One question to decide early is whether units mounted on legs, with enclosed bases or pedestal, or wall mounting will fit best into the cleaning schedule.

## TILTING BRAISING/FRY PANS

The tilting braising/fry pan is an item originally imported from Europe but now offered by American manufacturers. Because energy-efficient steam is its heat source, the tilting braising/fry pan has become another important piece of cooking equipment in the on-going effort to save energy. American foodservices use the pans to cook everything from roux to fish, to meat, to egg foo yong, and a wide variety of other ethnic dishes.

### Cook in Tilting Braising/Fry Pan

| | |
|---|---|
| *Complete Breakfasts* | *Rice* |
| *Roasts* | *Sauces, Gravies* |
| *Stews* | *Vegetables, fresh* |
| *Ground Meat* | *and frozen* |
| *Dishes* | *Seafood* |
| *Steaks, Chops, Ribs* | *Chili* |
| *Potatoes* | *Taco Meat* |
| *Poultry* | *Crepes* |
| *Pasta* | |

Its usefulness is based on its large cooking surface and wide range of even temperatures, e.g., 100° to 425°F. (38° to 219°C). Adequate insulation on the front keeps working temperatures comfortable. The tilting braising/fry pan can be mounted on casters for use in more than one location.

The tilting braising/fry pan can cook ingredients from raw stage to completion. With lid in place, it can roast or bake. Some models, with optional equipment, can operate as high-speed steam cookers.

One tilting braising/fry pan, with thermostatic controls, shuts off automatically when the desired temperature is reached; it also keeps oil at proper temperature, and permits cooked items to be held at serving temperature for some time.

Fast, easy cleaning is another welcome feature of tilting braising/fry pans.

Tilting braising/fry pans have proven to be fast and easy to use, although they may necessitate some changes in food production methods. These rules of thumb offered by one manufacturer will help determine how to use the tilting braising/fry pan most effectively:

If the current recipe calls for oven finishing, cook the item in the tilting braising/fry pan by reducing time to one-half or two-thirds of that called for. When recipes call for quick browning or sauteing as in hamburgers, chicken or pancakes, use a temperature from 300° to 350°F. (149° to 177°C). A counter-balanced, stainless steel cover permits the pan to be used for smothered items or as a roaster.

When recipes call for simmering meat in liquid as in pot roasts, or stews, use a temperature of 200°F. (93°C)—unless you wish to drive off liquid rapidly, then go over 212°F. (100°C). As long as there is liquid in the pan there will be no additional cooking over 212°F. (100°C), so setting above that for these functions simply drives off liquid. The lower setting will prevent high shrinkage.

For browning and sauteing chicken, eggs, home fried potatoes and other sauteing—employ a temperature between 212°(100°C) and 280°F. (137°C).

One model, occupying only 36 in. (91.4 cm) of floor space 33 in. (83.8 cm) deep, braises 50 Swiss steaks in 15 min.; boils 1,000 4-oz. (114 gm) portions of oatmeal per hour; sautes enough

**TILTING BRAISING/FRY PAN TIME CHART**
**(Size 4 Braising/Fry Pan Used)**

| Product | Quantity | Cooking Time* |
|---|---|---|
| Steaks, 7 oz. (199 gm) minute | 26 | 5 min. |
| Scrambled Eggs | 2–3 cases | 5 min. |
| Grilled Cheese Sandwiches | 48 | 7–8 min. |
| Hamburgers | 60 | 5 min. |
| Hamburgers | 700 | 2 hrs. |
| Pancakes | 24 | 1½ min. per side |
| Chocolate Mousse | 200–300 portions | 15 min. |
| Noodles | 30 lbs. (13.6 kg) | 15–20 min. |
| Dumplings, Bohemian | 15 loaves (175 portions) | 10 min. |
| Chocolate Pudding | 850 8-oz. (226 gm) portions | 10 min. |
| Zucchini | 300–400 portions | 10–15 min. |
| Crabmeat Stuffing | 250 servings | 30 min. |
| Crepes | 250 (15–20 per batch) | 1 hr. |
| Veal, sauteed | 20 lb. (9 kg) | 25 min. |
| Chicken Breasts, boned | 120 lb. (54.4 kg) | 20–30 min. |
| Ribs, barbequed | 500 portions | 2 hrs. |
| Ground Beef, frozen | 55 lb. (25 kg) | 1 hr. |
| Taco Meat | 175 lb. (79.3 kg) | 1 hr. 10 min. |
| Refried Beans | 40 lb. (18.1 kg) | 2½ hrs. |
| Beef Ragout | 90 lb. (40.8 kg.) | 1¼ hrs. |
| Ground Beef Cheese Steaks | 500 portions | 1 hr. |
| Pepper Steak | 50 lb. (22.7 kg) | 1 hr. |
| Beef Tips | 50 lb. (22.7 kg) | 1 hr. |
| Chicken Cacciatore | 500 portions | 2 hrs. |
| Turkeys | 6 at 25 lb. (12.7 kg) each | 2 hrs. |
| Italian Beef Roasts | 200 lb. (90.6 kg) | 2¼ hrs. |
| Pot Roast | 90–100 lb. (40.8–45.3 kg) | 1¾ hrs. |
| Salisbury Steak | 350 portions | 1 hr. |

*All product cooking times submitted by Groen braising pan users.

vegetables for 200 orders of Chicken Cacciatore in 10 min.; stews 300 8-oz. (226 gm) orders in one load; grills 1,400 frankfurters per hour; simmers 18 gal. (68 l) of soup, meat sauce, or brown gravy; pan fries 50 orders of quartered chicken in 20 min.

## CONVERTING TO STEAM

Philip Bluefield of Bluefield Caterers in Baltimore prepares more than twenty different items in the tilting braising/fry pans. Bluefield Caterers use a steam assembly with the units that converts pans into top-speed steamers, each able to process three 12 × 20 × 4-in. (30.5 × 50 × 10 cm) perforated pans simultaneously. Steam production possibilities are indicated here:

| ITEM | QUANTITY | TIME | RESULTS |
|---|---|---|---|
| Sliced carrots (frozen) | 10 lb. 4.5 kg | 15 min. | Good color, firm texture, excellent taste. |
| Cut green beans (frozen) | 10 lb. 4.5 kg | 15 min. | Good color, firm texture, excellent flavor. |
| Whole, white, kernel corn (frozen) | 10 lb. 4.5 kg | 12 min. | Good color, firm texture, excellent flavor. |
| Broccoli Spears (frozen) | 8 lb. 3.6 kg | 13 min. | Good color, best way to cook broccoli |
| Potatoes cut, peeled (frozen) | 10 lb. 4.5 kg | 25 min. | Good flavor, good texture, no discoloring. |

Units are all equipped with pouring lips and self-locking tilt mechanisms for easy removal of stews, gravies, fat. Models are 36 to 37⅜ in. (91.4 to 95 cm) high to make operation easy. One group of models comes in these three dimensions and capacities: 24⅝ in. (7.7 cm) to back of pan × 24⅝ in. (7.7 cm) wide × 7 in. (17.8 cm) deep, and holds 18 gal. (68 l); 24⅝ in. (7.7 cm) to back of pan × 31⅝ in. (82.8) wide × 7 in. (17.8 cm) deep,

and holds 23.3 gal. (88.2 l); 24⅝ in. (7.7 cm) to back of pan × 42⅝ in. (108.3 cm) wide × 7 in. (17.8 cm) deep, and holds 30.8 gal. (116.6 l). Tilting braising/fry pans can either be floor or wall mounted. A table-top model is also available; it measures 18 in. (45.7 cm) wide × 24 in. (61 cm) to back of pan, is 7 in. (17.8 cm) deep, and holds 10 gal. (37.9 l).

## BRAIN TEASER—STEAM KETTLES

Have you learned all you should about steam kettles? Give yourself the following test and if you do not know the answers, go over the material a second time.

1. The space between the two bowls that form a steam kettle is filled with

   (Fill in) _____ which provides heat to cook the food.

2. Steam kettles come in several models. List 3 kinds:

   _____     _____     _____

3. Table model steam kettles hold from 10 to 20 qts.; floor or wall models can hold as much as: (Check one)

   20 gal. _____     200 gal. _____

4. These foods can be cooked in steam jacketed kettles: (Check right answers)

   Vegetables _____ Cakes _____ Macaroni _____ Roasts _____

   Pies _____ Soups _____ Beef Stew _____ French Fries _____ .

5. When cooking in steam kettles, learn how to operate: (Check right answers)

   Safety valves _____ Device for stopping pressure gauges _____ Kettles that tilt _____

   Covers of large kettles _____ .

6. To help in cleaning kettles, whenever possible, turn heat (Fill in) _____ before draining.

7. If you can't clean kettle as soon as you finish cooking, fill it with water above cooking line and turn steam on to heat water to (Fill in) _____ inside.

8. When it's time to clean kettle, open drain to let soaking water (Fill in) _____; then scrub with _____ or _____.

9. Outside of kettle (Check one)

   Should be cleaned _____     Should not be cleaned _____

10. Last step in kettle cleaning is: (Check one)

   Thorough rinsing inside and out _____ .
   Draining rinse water out _____

   *(For correct answers, see page 249.)*

## BRAIN TEASER—STEAM COOKERS

Have you learned all you should about steam cookers? Give yourself the following test and if you do not know the answers, go over the material a second time.

1. High volume compartment steamers or steam cookers are used in places that have to have most of their food ready

   (Check one): At one time _____, At different times _____.

2. These foods are most often prepared in steam cookers (Check right answers):

   Potatoes _____ Rolls _____ Scrambled Eggs _____ Poultry

   Puddings _____ Pies _____ Fish _____ Fried Shrimp _____.

3. Small high-pressure steam cookers are used to prepare (Fill in):

   Small batches of food just before service _____

   Large amounts of food _____ .

4. Food service operations may have (Check answer): Both kinds of cookers _____ ,

   Small-batch steam cookers _____ , High-volume compartment steamers _____ .

5. If you are cooking food in a steam cooker, be sure you know (Check answer): How safety devices work _____ , How to tell when food is cooked _____ .

6. Compartment steam cookers hold from 3 12 × 20-in. (30 × 51 cm) pans to (Fill in) _____ pans.

   Small counter top models turn out about ____ lb. (kg) of food.

7. Only one step is required to clean steam cookers. A daily washing of the compartment, including the shelves, with a mild detergent is all that has to be done, but spills either inside or outside should be (Fill in): _____

8. Containers for compartment steam cookers may be: *wide or narrow*; (Fill in) _____ or _____ , _____ or _____ .

9. In closing doors on steam cookers, follow directions carefully. Be sure latch is (Fill in) _____.

10. A type of steam cooker that concentrates dry steam directly onto food will not start cooking until frozen food has been (Fill in) _____ .

    *(For correct answers see page 249.)*

**BRAIN TEASER—TILTING/BRAISING/FRY PANS**

1. How does the tilting braising/fry pan save energy? _____
   _____ .

2. Name one way that thermostatic controls help in cooking with the tilting braising/fry pan. _____
   _____

3. Can oven recipes be used in a tilting braising/fry pan? (Check right answer)
   Yes ____ No____

4. How does operator remove contents of tilting braising/fry pan? _____
   _____

5. Safety in use of tilting braising/fry pan is insured by _____ _____

   or _____ _____ _____ _____ . (Fill in)

   *(For correct answers, see page 249.)*

**FIGURE   2.2**
Four 3-deck steamers contribute to the capability of Louisville's Commonwealth Convention Center to meet projected foodservice demands. Peak production is no problem with these high volume units available.

**FIGURE   2.3**
This pressurized steam cooker is designed to thaw frozen food first and then to build pressure for the cooking process. This eliminates any possibility of ice crystals remaining in the center of frozen foods when they come out of the
cooker.

**FIGURE 2.4**

One energy-saving idea resulting from the use of the tilting braising/fry pan at Garden City (Kans.) Unified School District No. 457 occurs in pudding preparation. After water in tilting braising/fry pan comes to a boil, pan is shut off, pudding ingredients are put in, and mixture comes to a boil again without any additional heat. Human energy is also saved by filling taco shells directly from mixture held in tilting braising/fry pan. Units are on casters and can also be used in serving lines for direct dish-up.

**FIGURE 2.6**

Fast easy cleaning is a popular feature of the 9 in.-(22.9 cm) deep tilting braising/fry pan in use at Kulinary Kitchen Catering, Evanston, Ill. With parties of 1500 and more to be served on occasion, it is important to be able to count on production of 36 lb. of lasagna sauce in 1 hr., 50 lb. (22.7 kg) of chili in 30 to 45 minutes, 90 lb. (40.8 kg) of beef ragout in 1 hr., or enough chocolate mousse for 200 to 300 in 15 min., with whipped cream added after mousse is removed from tilting braising/fry pan.

**FIGURE 2.5**

A time-saver in saute preparation for Italian and seafood specialties, the tilting braising/fry pan in use at Scordatos Restaurant, Hawthorne, N.J. helps produce food for 3500 to 4200 patrons per week. Among items sauted in it are onions, mushrooms, ground beef, veal for veal cacciatore, and crabmeat stuffing for stuffed flounder, shrimp, and clams.

**FIGURE 2.7**

Pie fillings are portioned directly into shells from this 20-qt. (18.9ℓ) tilting table-top steam kettle at West Essex (N.J.) Junior High School.

**FIGURE  2.8**
Bagels are boiled for 1 minute in this compact, 40-gal. (151ℓ) self-contained steam jacketed kettle at The Bagel Place, then baked in a revolving oven for 10 minutes. Boiling the bagels before baking partially cooks them, gives them their unique crust and shine, and kills the yeast to prevent rising. The Bagel Place, a full line delicatessen and bagel bakery in Toledo, Ohio, serves over 300 daily, yet occupies only 1150 sq. ft. (10683 dm$^2$) and seats 15. It bills itself as ''the most compact bagel bakery in existence.''

**FIGURE  2.9**
The main cooking battery at Doctor's Hospital, Tulsa, Okla. makes maximum use of steam equipment in providing 6825 meals per week. At lower left is convection steam unit, tilting braising/fry pan, and at lower right a steam kettle. A griddle, broiler, two fryers, an open burner range for holding and small quantity production of stocks, and a double convection oven complete the line. Line is protected by installation of automatic washdown and fire-controlled, grease extracting ventilating system.

**FIGURE  2.10**
Vegetable preparation for the 8500 meals per week served at the Sheraton St. Louis Hotel is done at this station. The two-compartment steamers are flanked by a steam-jacketed kettle and a heavy duty range oven.

**FIGURE 2.11**
The steam preparation area at York (Pa.) Hospital has one 80-gal. (302ℓ) steam-jacketed kettle and two 2-compartment steamers, all wall-mounted for easy cleaning.

**FIGURE 2.12**
Reliance on convenience foods to meet a large share of their menu needs led to the use of steam in providing the required 4114 meals per week for patients and cafeteria patrons at Doylestown (Pa.) Hospital. Shown here from left two 40-qt. (37.9ℓ) steam-jacketed kettles, two 20-qt. (18.9ℓ) kettles, a 2-compartment steam cooker and generator. A mobile tilting braising/fry pan (not shown) positioned behind the steam cooker has its own special floor drain. Shown in front of kettles are two removable sliding drainers. (See close-up at left.)

**FIGURE 2.13**
This high volume pressure steamer (see facing page) has a top compartment that can be converted to a pressureless cooker/defroster by flicking switch below first dial on control panel. Lower compartment is 5PSI (1kg/cm$^2$) pressure cooker that can cook 60 lb. (27.2 kg.) of fresh food at a time. Controls have clearly marked direction indicators and are easy to read.

**FIGURE   2.14**
Sliding drainer for steam kettles has been specially equipped with stainless steel mesh screens. Screens keep liquid from splashing on worker when kettles are emptied.

**FIGURE   2.15**
This cooking center at the Food Service Facility of the California Highway Patrol Academy, Bryte, Ca. clusters kettle mixer units. Mixer is hydraulically controlled. Control console for steam-jacketed kettle is at right.

**FIGURE   2.16**
Both compartments of this high velocity steam cooker/defroster are pressureless so door can be opened during either cooking or defrosting cycle. Cooking and defrosting can be done at the same time, each process taking place in a separate compartment. Cooking capacity is a full 45 lb. (20.4 kg) of frozen vegetables. Timer on control panel can be set for required cooking time.

**FIGURE   2.17**
To produce the 7500 meals per day currently required for the Houston, Tex. Memorial Hospital System, Southwest Unit, a centralized cook/chill production system was set up, designed to ultimately provide 12,500 meals per day. Hot food for the system is prepared in wall-mounted steam kettles with mixer assembly (shown here) as well as a conveyor steam cooker, fryer, and broiler.

**FIGURE 3.1**
The platform for the microwave ovens in the kitchens of Bob Burns Restaurant, Woodland Hills, Calif. was designed to provide a convenient working height for the ovens. Underneath the platform, stainless steel guides hold 18- by 26-in. (46- by 66-cm) bun pans used either for finished or ready-to-prepare products. This microwave/steam cooker combination is depended on especially for small batch work and a la carte orders.

# Chapter Three

# Ovens

In modern foodservice operations, ovens are used to bake; roast; braise; oven broil; oven fry; cook casseroles; reheat precooked, packaged, and chilled food items; and reconstitute frozen foods.

The general purpose ovens at the Foxfire, an Anaheim, CA, restaurant, are used for meat roasting and are located under the hot tops and open burners. (See picture, Chapter 1, *Ranges.*) Ovens are preheated at 350°F. (177°C) for 25 minutes. Roasts, seasoned with salt and cracked black pepper, are cooked at 350°F. (177°C) for 2¾ to 3¼ hr., depending on size. The prime rib holding oven is set at 140°F.(60°C); roasts are transferred from it to hot-food section in cook's dish-up station. Range ovens placed in the semi-exhibition entree cooking line at Foxfire are used for baked potatoes, lobster tails, baked shrimp, baked sole, and the featured special of the day.

At the Apple Tree Inn, Kansas City North, MO, hickory-smoked meats are stars on the menu. They are precooked in a wood-fired, revolving, hickory-smoke oven located in a separate room. Another popular specialty also comes out of the Apple Tree ovens—hot muffins, served to patrons by a strolling baker.

To pick the right oven for the job at hand requires knowing what to expect from each type, food production to be supplied, floor space available for ovens, operating costs, installation requirements, and availability of service.

## OPERATING OVENS TO SAVE ENERGY

Of special importance today is choosing an oven that makes good use of energy. Energy-saving ways with ovens listed in a timely article* include:

* Put product in an oven that is as close to the size of the product as possible.
* Preheat ovens only for bakery goods. Place other products in oven before turning it on. Adjust cooking time as needed.
* When preheating oven for baking, set dial only at desired temperature.
* Load ovens to capacity, allowing only 2-in. (5 cm) clearance for air circulation. Load ovens quickly to minimize heat loss.

*School Foodservice Journal*, Feb. 19, 1978.

- Keep oven production constant so ovens will have to be heated only once.
- To minimize door opening, use meat thermometers located outside ovens to check meat doneness.
- When using well-insulated oven, turn heat off a few minutes ahead of scheduled time and product will finish baking with retained heat.

Mary Respeliers, the manager of Nickerson Farms, Honey Creek, IA, saves energy by putting stickers on ovens to show the exact amount of preheating each needs; then she checks to make sure employees follow suggested timing.

## TYPES OF OVENS

As one expert writes, "Ovens come in so many shapes and sizes, vary so much in construction, and are so frequently altered or adapted for special purposes that it is very difficult to put them in proper categories." He offers these classifications:

- Standard heavy-duty ovens are engineered for use with 18 × 26-in. (46 × 66 cm) pans. Pie, cake, bread, muffin and similar pans should be of sizes to fit in multiples of the 18 × 26-in. (46 × 66 cm) dimension, e.g. one 17 × 23-in. (43.2 × 58.4 cm) meat pan or six 9-in. (22.9 cm) pie tins. As another example of deck capacity, a single deck can hold 60 lb. (27.2 kg) of meat or ten 1-lb. (453 gm) loaves.
- Restaurant range ovens are generally 12- to 15-in. (30.5 to 38.1 cm) high and intended for use with a 20- × 21-in. (50 × 53.3 cm) pan size base. Ovens which do not list capacities on that base, indicate usable backing area, or give maximum pan size should be checked. Oven size is not necessarily the same as baking area.
- Range and general purpose ovens have one-pan (18 × 26 in.) (45.7 × 66-cm) capacity.
- Deck or peel ovens have two-pan 18 × 26-in. (46 × 66 cm) (side by side) deck capacity. These ovens are direct fired with items baked on the hearth or oven bottom, or they have indirect, recirculating heating systems—sized from one bun pan to 70 per oven. They may be roasting or baking with roasting deck up to 17. in. (43.2 cm) high and baking deck 5- to 8-in.

(12.7 to 20.3 cm) high; these ovens are most often made up of three or four decks; each deck may be heated separately. By installing the necessary number of decks, the oven can bake, stew, roast, oven braise, and reconstitute at the same time, each in a separate compartment. A center shelf in a roast oven can provide two-deck bake oven flexibility.

### Bake Ovens

Bake ovens are best for baking. They have a cavity up to 8-in. (20.3 cm) high and because their cavity volume is low in relation to the product, they are more sensitive and more efficient than equivalent roast, range, or general purpose ovens, which have cavities 12- to 15-in. (30.5 to 38.1 cm) high and correspondingly greater volumes to be heated.

The higher cavity is necessary for large roasts and whole turkeys; but bake ovens will roast as well as roast ovens or general purpose ovens if the load fits, and they will bake better and faster.

Very few range or general purpose ovens will bake satisfactorily on the deck and the rack simultaneously without switching pans or varying times.

The most efficient and best performing standard ovens available are of the two-pan bake type; these are the preferred ovens unless the operation produces large beef roasts and turkeys for display.

### Oven Selection

Oven selection should be based on several factors. First, carefully analyze the job's requirements. Then thoroughly investigate the equipment available. More compact deck ovens are now being introduced to permit comfortable working heights. One 2-deck electric oven will hold three standard roast pans in two 14-in. (35.6 cm) decks, the same capacity as three conventional ovens.

## OVEN PURCHASING POINTERS

Oven purchasers should look for:

- Design that permits easy and thorough cleaning. If ceramic material is used, it should be

non-absorbent and sufficiently hard so it will escape injury during cleaning.
- Wiring or manifolds concealed.
- Easy access to all parts.
- All-welded construction of structural steel for durable rigid frames.
- Outside bodies of 16 to 18 ga. metal attached to solid frame support with durable finishes.
- Inner linings of 18 ga. rustproof sheet metal, reinforced to prevent buckling.
- Fronts all one-piece construction.
- At least 4 in. (10 cm) of nonsagging, rodent proof, spun fiber glass or other equally efficient insulation on all sides.
- Walls surrounding insulation tightly sealed to prevent entrance of moisture.
- Devices around doors to minimize heat loss. Handles that stay cool to the touch.
- Sturdy doors, preferably containing windows so contents can be viewed without opening door.
- Doors that can easily hold 150 lbs. (68 kg) in weight, counterbalanced for easy opening and closing and to prevent slamming. Hinges of the heavy duty type.
- Doors that open level with bottom of oven or deck so they can be used as loading platform.
- Durable heating units made of warp-proof alloys.
- Thermostatic control precise between 150° (66°C) and 550°F. (288°C).
- Signal lights to indicate when oven is on, timers, and outside indicating thermometers.
- Chambers vented, dampered, and with baffling required to direct the heat.
- System to conduct vapor out, preventing its flow back as condensate.
- Controls in front, easily accessible to workers.
- Where necessary, decks valved individually for steam delivered in even distribution. Traps and drains to prevent water from being blown into oven.
- Capacity to heat to 450°F. (232°C) in 20 min. plus good recovery ability and equally good cooling ability.
- Height of top and bottom decks suitable for comfortable loading and unloading.
- Window door or solid door—whichever will promote better performance in the specific installation.
- Suitable exterior finish.

- Two input-heat levels, one for top unit, one for unit below.
- Oven light.
- Oven insulated on all six sides.
- Oven cycling light.
- Electricity.
- Gas.
- Throttle-down instead of snap-off thermostats.
- Choice of 1-deck oven with single thermostat or 2-deck oven with one thermostat.

## COUNTER OVENS

One infrared, counter oven can serve as a back-up oven to increase productivity or as a primary source of heating and cooking to provide extra menu items. It will heat and cook frozen entrees, refrigerated entrees, fruits and vegetables, breads and pastries, desserts, eggs, and specialty foods. It measures 38⁹/₁₆ in. (97.9 cm) wide by 16¹/₁₆ in. (40.8 cm) high by 20½ in. (52 cm) deep. Its cooking speed is shown below for several food items when bulk packaged in 10 × 12-in. (25.4 × 30.5-cm), 12 × 20-in. (30 × 51-cm), or 10½ × 15½ in. (26.7 × 39.4 cm) foodservice pans.

| Product | Time (minutes) |
|---|---|
| Frozen Beef Burgundy | 30–35 |
| Frozen Precooked Lasagna | 42–45 |
| Refrigerated Precooked Salisbury Steak | 20–25 |
| Fresh Frozen Escalloped Potatoes | 18 |
| Frozen Rolls | 10 |
| Baked Alaska | 2½–3 |
| Fresh Cheese Omelet | 2½–3½ |
| Fresh Tortillas | 2 –2½ |

Another counter or table model is 34 in. (86.4 cm) × 14 in. (35.6 cm) × 19-in. (48.3 cm). Unit can hold one full-size steamtable pan.

At Hogate's, Washington, D.C.'s long-established seafood restaurant, refrigerated shrimp, oysters, rarebits, Newburgs, creoles, or oysters Rockefeller take only a few minutes to heat. One radiant heating, quartz oven has two radiant-plate heaters, covering top and bottom oven surfaces, which emit high-intensity infrared heat to penetrate all foods uniformly. A specially designed, insulated and air-cooled, stainless steel cabinet contains heat so the area around the unit remains cool.

Food in aluminum foil containers or wrappings can be reconstituted in this energy-saving unit. Food also browns during cooking.

## 3 STEPS TO DEPENDABLE OVEN OPERATION

Manufacturers have spent great effort to assure dependable oven performance once proper installation has been completed. As one service manager has found, most oven problems result from improper installations or use. For best results, ovens must be:

- Level, that is, the oven deck (or hearth) must be level, as well as the oven;
- Not overvented;
- Used properly with the best pans available.

He stresses that gas ovens must be rated properly for input with a flow meter after installation. They should be checked regularly by the correct methods for proper calibration. To alleviate installation/use problems, all gas 2-pan ovens are equipped with pressure regulators that solve the installation/use problems caused by incorrect Btu ratings.

To determine needed oven capacity, the operator or planner should analyze menu requirements and the time permitted to meet them. The production potential of one line of ovens may be calculated from the charts shown here:

**OVEN PRODUCTION POTENTIAL***

### 2-Pan Bake and Pizza Ovens

| External Dimensions | | | | | | Compartments' Internal Dimensions | | | | | | Capacities | | | |
|---|---|---|---|---|---|---|---|---|---|---|---|---|---|---|---|
| Width | | Depth | | Height w/legs or Base | | Width | | Depth | | Height | | 12-in. (30.5 cm) Pizza | 1-lb. (453 gm) Loaves | 9-in. O.D. (22.9 cm) Pie Tins | 18 × 26-in. (45.8 × 66 cm) Roll Pans |
| in. | cm | in. | cm | in. | cm | in. | cm | in. | cm | in. | cm | | | | |
| 54⅜ | 138 | 36 | 91.4 | 52 | 132 | 37¼ | 84.6 | 28½ | 72.4 | 8 | 20.3 | 6 | 20 | 12 | 2 |
| 54⅜ | 138 | 36 | 91.4 | 71 | 177 | 37¼ | 84.6 | 28½ | 72.4 | 8 | 20.3 | 12 | 40 | 24 | 4 |
| 54⅜ | 138 | 36 | 91.4 | 71 | 177 | 37¼ | 84.6 | 28½ | 72.4 | 8 | 20.3 | 18 | 60 | 36 | 6 |

*Based on pan sizes and strapping, giving deck loading of 3 lb. per sq. ft. (1.4 kg/9.3 m²). When pans and strapping require greater area, capacities will be reduced proportionately.

### 2-Pan Combination Ovens

| Basic Section External Dimensions | | | | | | Compartments' Internal Dimensions | | | | | | | | | | | |
|---|---|---|---|---|---|---|---|---|---|---|---|---|---|---|---|---|---|
| | | | | | | Bake | | | | | | All-Purpose | | | | | |
| Width | | Depth | | Height w/legs or Base | | Width | | Depth | | Height | | Width | | Depth | | Height | |
| in. | cm | in. | cm | in. | cm | in. | cm | in. | cm | in. | cm | in. | cm | in. | cm | in. | cm |
| 54⅜ | 138 | 36 | 91.4 | 66 | 167.6 | 37¼ | 84.6 | 28½ | 72.4 | 8 | 20.3 | 37¼ | 84.6 | 28½ | 72.4 | 12 | 30.5 |
| 54⅜ | 138 | 36 | 91.4 | 72 | 182.9 | 37¼ | 84.6 | 28½ | 72.4 | 8 | 20.3 | 37¼ | 84.6 | 28½ | 72.4 | 12 | 30.5 |
| 54⅜ | 138 | 36 | 91.4 | 70 | 177.8 | 37¼ | 84.6 | 28½ | 72.4 | 8 | 20.3 | 37¼ | 84.6 | 28½ | 72.4 | 12 | 30.5 |

| Oven Combination | Capacities | | |
|---|---|---|---|
| | 9" (22.9 cm) O.D. Pie Tins | 17" × 23" (43.2 × 58.4 cm) Meat Pans | 18" × 26" (46 × 66 cm) Roll Pans |
| 1 bake, 1 all-purpose | 24 | 2 | 4 |
| 2 bake, 1 all-purpose | 36 | 2 | 6 |
| 1 bake, 2 all-purpose | 36 | 4 | 6 |

Add 35 lb. (15.9 kg) to each section when corplate decks are used instead of air-cushion decks.

* See asterisk on facing page.

**OVEN PRODUCTION POTENTIAL\*** (cont.)

### 2-Pan All-Purpose Ovens

| Basic Section External Dimensions | | | | | | Compartments' Internal Dimensions | | | | | |
| --- | --- | --- | --- | --- | --- | --- | --- | --- | --- | --- | --- |
| | | | | Height w/legs or Base | | All-Purpose | | | | | |
| Width | | Depth | | | | Width | | Depth | | Height | |
| in. | cm | in. | cm | in. | cm | in. | cm | in. | cm | in. | cm |
| 54⅜ | 138 | 36 | 91.4 | 56 | 142 | 37¼ | 84.6 | 28½ | 72.4 | 12 | 30.5 |
| 54⅜ | 138 | 36 | 91.4 | 71 | 177 | 37¼ | 84.6 | 28½ | 72.4 | 12 | 30.5 |
| 54⅜ | 138 | 36 | 91.4 | 75 | 190.5 | 37¼ | 84.6 | 28½ | 72.4 | 12 | 30.5 |

| | Capacities | | | |
| --- | --- | --- | --- | --- |
| | 9" (22.9 cm) O.D. | 17" × 23"(43.2 × 58.4 cm) | 18" × 26"(46 × 66 cm) | 1-lb. (453 gm) |
| Oven Combination | Pie Tins | Meat Pans | Roll Pans | Loaves |
| 1 all–purpose | 12 | 2 | 2 | 20 |
| 2 all–purpose | 24 | 4 | 4 | 40 |
| 3 all–purpose | 36 | 6 | 6 | 60 |

Add 35 lb. (15.9 kg) to each section when corplate decks are used instead of air-cushion decks. *Based on pan sizes and strapping, giving deck loading of 3 lb. per square foot (1.4 kg/9.3 cm²). When pans and strapping require greater area, capacities will be reduced proportionately.

### 4-Pan Bake Ovens

| Basic Section External Dimensions | | | | | | Compartments' Internal Dimensions Bake | | | | | | | |
| --- | --- | --- | --- | --- | --- | --- | --- | --- | --- | --- | --- | --- | --- |
| | | | | Height w/legs | | Width | | Depth | | Height | | Deck | |
| Width | | Depth | | | | | | | | | | | |
| in. | cm | in. | cm | in. | cm | in. | cm | in. | cm | in. | cm | sq. ft. | m² |
| 54⅜ | 138 | 64½ | 163.8 | 52 | 132 | 37¼ | 84.6 | 57 | 144.8 | 8 | 20.3 | 14.5 | 134.9 |
| 54⅜ | 138 | 64½ | 163.8 | 71 | 177 | 37¼ | 84.6 | 57 | 144.8 | 8 | 20.3 | 29.0 | 269.7 |
| 54⅜ | 138 | 64½ | 163.8 | 71 | 177 | 37¼ | 84.6 | 57 | 144.8 | 8 | 20.3 | 43.5 | 57.7 |

| | Capacities | | |
| --- | --- | --- | --- |
| | 9" O.D. (22.9 cm) | 1-lb. (453 gm) | 18" × 26" (46 × 66 cm) |
| Oven Combination | Pie Tins | Loaves | Roll Pans |
| 1 4–pan bake | 24 | 40 | 4 |
| 2 4–pan bake | 48 | 80 | 8 |
| 3 4–pan bake | 72 | 120 | 12 |

### 6-Pan Bake Ovens

| Basic Section External Dimensions | | | | | | Compartments' Internal Dimensions Bake | | | | | | | |
| --- | --- | --- | --- | --- | --- | --- | --- | --- | --- | --- | --- | --- | --- |
| | | | | Height w/legs | | Width | | Depth | | Height | | Deck | |
| Width | | Depth | | | | | | | | | | | |
| in. | cm | in. | cm | in. | cm | in. | cm | in. | cm | in. | cm. | sq. ft. | m² |
| 73⅜ | 186.4 | 64½ | 163.8 | 51 | 129.5 | 56¼ | 142.9 | 57 | 144.8 | 8 | 20.3 | 22 | 204.6 |
| 73⅜ | 186.4 | 64½ | 163.8 | 70 | 177.8 | 56¼ | 142.9 | 57 | 144.8 | 8 | 20.3 | 44 | 409.2 |
| 73⅜ | 186.4 | 64½ | 163.8 | 70 | 177.8 | 56¼ | 142.9 | 57 | 144.8 | 8 | 20.3 | 66 | 613.8 |

| | Capacities | | | |
| --- | --- | --- | --- | --- |
| | 9" (22.9 cm) O.D. | 1-lb. (453 gm) | 1½-lb. (566 gm) | 18" × 26"(46 × 66 cm) |
| Oven Combination | Pie Tins | Loaves | Loaves | Roll Pans |
| 1 6–pan bake | 36 | 60 | 40 | 6 |
| 2 6–pan bake | 72 | 120 | 80 | 12 |
| 3 6–pan bake | 108 | 180 | 120 | 18 |

Information courtesy of General Electric Company.

## RACK DATA (PAN CAPACITIES SHOWN FOR SINGLE RACK)*

### Deep Convection II Cook-n-Hold Ovens

| No. Std. Racks | Std.-Rack Spacing in. | cm | No. Optional Racks | 11-Rack Spacing in. | cm | Rack Size in. | cm | 9 in. (22.86 cm) OD Pie Tins | #200 Pans | 18 in. × 26 in. (46 × 66 cm) Pans |
|---|---|---|---|---|---|---|---|---|---|---|
| 5 | 2.87 | 7.29 | 6 | 1.25 | 3.18 | 27.5 × 20 | 69.8 × 50.8 | 9 | 2 | 1 |
| 10 | 2.87 | 7.29 | 12 | 1.25 | 3.18 | 27.5 × 20 | 69.8 × 50.8 | 9 | 2 | 1 |
| 5 | 2.87 | 7.29 | 6 | 1.25 | 3.18 | 27.5 × 20 | 69.8 × 50.8 | 9 | 2 | 1 |
| 5 | 2.87 | 7.29 | 6 | 1.25 | 3.18 | 27.5 × 20 | 69.8 × 50.8 | 9 | 2 | 1 |

### Standard Convection II Cook-n-Hold Ovens

| No. Std. Racks | Std.-Rack Spacing in. | cm | No. Optional Racks | 11-Rack Spacing in. | cm | Rack Size in. | cm | 9 in. (22.86 cm) OD Pie Tins | #200 Pans | 18 in. × 26 in. (46 × 66 cm) Pans |
|---|---|---|---|---|---|---|---|---|---|---|
| 5 | 2.87 | 7.29 | 6 | 1.25 | 3.18 | 27.5 × 20 | 69.8 × 50.8 | 6 | 2 | 1 |
| 10 | 2.87 | 7.29 | 12 | 1.25 | 3.18 | 27.5 × 20 | 69.8 × 50.8 | 6 | 2 | 1 |
| 5 | 2.87 | 7.29 | 6 | 1.25 | 3.18 | 27.5 × 20 | 69.8 × 50.8 | 6 | 2 | 1 |
| 5 | 2.87 | 7.29 | 6 | 1.25 | 3.18 | 27.5 × 20 | 69.8 × 50.8 | 6 | 2 | 1 |

### Deep Convection Ovens

| No. Std. Racks | Std.-Rack Spacing in. | cm | No. Optional Racks | 11-Rack Spacing in. | cm | Rack Size in. | cm | 9 in. (22.86 cm) OD Pie Tins | #200 Pans | 18 in. × 26 in. (46 × 66 cm) Pans |
|---|---|---|---|---|---|---|---|---|---|---|
| 5 | 2.88 | 7.30 | 6 | 1.25 | 3.18 | 27.5 × 28 | 69.85 × 71.12 | 9 | 2 | 1 |
| 10 | 2.88 | 7.30 | 12 | 1.25 | 3.18 | 27.5 × 28 | 69.85 × 71.12 | 9 | 2 | 1 |

SPECIAL ORDER ONLY. (Racks/supports convert device to conventional convection oven.) Cavity accepts 16 compartmentalized baskets, each w/capacity of 10 individual school lunch foil packs.

### Standard Convection Ovens

| No. Std. Racks | Std.-Rack Spacing in. | cm | No. Optional Racks | 11-Rack Spacing in. | cm | Rack Size in. | cm | 9 in. (22.86 cm) OD Pie Tins | #200 Pans | 18 in. × 26 in. (46 × 66 cm) Pans |
|---|---|---|---|---|---|---|---|---|---|---|
| 5 | 2.87 | 7.29 | 6 | 1.25 | 3.18 | 27.5 × 20 | 69.8 × 50.8 | 6 | 2 | 1 |
| 10 | 2.87 | 7.29 | 12 | 1.25 | 3.18 | 27.5 × 20 | 69.8 × 50.8 | 6 | 2 | 1 |
| 5 | 2.87 | 7.29 | 6 | 1.25 | 3.18 | 27.5 × 20 | 69.8 × 50.8 | 6 | 2 | 1 |
| 5 | 2.87 | 7.29 | 6 | 1.25 | 3.18 | 27.5 × 20 | 69.8 × 50.8 | 6 | 2 | 1 |

*General Electric Company

## REVIEW OVEN RULES REGULARLY

At regular intervals, supervisors should review recommended operating procedures for their ovens with kitchen workers. The following are typical of the easy-to-follow instructions available from oven makers:

- In 2-deck single control sections, load the compartment that contains the thermostat element first. This is always the lower compartment.
- Always load each shelf evenly, spacing pans away from each other and away from the side of the oven.
- Never add material to a section after foods have started to bake—unbalanced baking will result.
- Open doors as seldom as possible. Shifting pans is unnecessary in most cases.
- For strong bottoms and light tops, heat oven to at least 25°F. (4°C) above baking temperature before loading. Turn control down to baking temperature after loading.
- For stronger tops, turn thermostat to 25°F. (4°C) above indicated recipe temperature for final 10 minutes of baking.

## CLEANING OVENS

Oven maintenance has been systematized. Here is the cleaning procedure for one type of gas oven:

Clean secondary air ducts and air entry ports semiannually.

Outside of black-finish ovens may be cleaned and kept in good condition with light oil.

Saturate a cloth and wipe oven when cold; wipe dry with a clean cloth.

On ovens with stainless steel exteriors, deposits of "baked-on" splatter, oil, grease, or light discolorations may be removed with any of several cleaners.

Heat-tint or heavy discolorations may be removed with stainless steel wool.

Apply cleansers when the oven is COLD. Always rub with the grain of the metal.

When necessary, use stainless steel wool. Apply only light pressure.

Shelves may be cleaned with a long-handled triangular scraper, such as that used for cleaning broiler grids. Shelves can be removed for scrubbing, if necessary, but avoid doing so, if possible, because they are hard to handle. After scrubbing, replace them in the oven to dry and heat the oven to 350°F. (177°C) with the doors open. Be sure deck hold-down clips are put back to prevent deck from warping.

On aluminized steel liners do not use wire brushes or steel wool or caustic solutions such as ammonia, lye, or soda ash. Do not use domestic oven cleaners as they will damage aluminum coating.

For cleaning painted oven interiors use cleaners recommended for aluminized steel linings. However, eventually the paint will wear away from the surface. When that happens, scrub surfaces with a wire brush and grease solvent, then refinish with heat-resistant aluminum paint available from the oven manufacturer.

Scrape all sugar, oil, or carbon deposits from valve and door handles and edges of doors daily.

Clean residue from beneath doors with small broom or brush, at least once each day. Brush out combustion chamber daily. Remove control-panel cover and clean control compartment at least monthly.

The AGA recommends the following procedures for cleaning gas ovens:

Remove boilovers and spills as soon as possible, before material has time to carbonize.

Every day wipe bottoms and linings of cooled oven with a damp cloth. Never throw water on oven decks to clean them. Guard against broken door hinges and cracks by cleaning crumbs and encrusted matter from opening area. Do not slam or stand on oven doors.

Once or twice a year check that the oven is level. Check for warped oven sides or bottom.

## CAUSES OF UNEVEN BAKING

When looking for uneven baking, remove goods from oven and inspect where light is uniformly distributed. Baking chamber light will make goods appear lighter near the light.

When investigating the possible causes for uneven baking, another manufacturer urges operators to remember the following:

Light or shiny pans will not absorb heat as fast as black, dull pans. Thin or worn pans will transmit heat faster than thick pans. Warped pans are frequently the cause of uneven baking. Some pans are flat outside of the oven but warp when exposed to the oven heat. Pans of different materials transmit heat at different rates.

Muffin tin cups should be flat across the bottoms so that all cups will contact the hearth to the same degree—otherwise light or underdone bottoms will occur.

When double pans are used as a convenience in loading or to catch spills from fruit pies, remember that the lower pan must lie flat in order to prevent an unevenly baked bottom. In some instances, using an under pan is not advisable because the under pan may reflect too much heat away from the container holding food to be baked.

## MECHANICAL OVENS

Revolving tray ovens control costs very well. They have flat trays suspended between two revolving spiders that rotate like a ferris wheel or merry-go-round. This entire assembly is housed in a porcelain or stainless chamber. The food is loaded on the trays as they appear opposite the door opening. Provision is made to prevent a blast of hot air from escaping when the door is opened for loading and unloading.

There are also rotating ovens in which shelves turn like "lazy susans," and traveling-deck ovens that move food products through on a conveyor belt.

A new infrared conveyorized oven cooks food by means of radiant heat from above and below as food passes through an open-end tunnel on a conveyor. The radiant heat in the cooking tunnel of each deck can be set up to 850°F. (454°C). There are separate controls for top and bottom temperatures. Cooking time for each deck is set by adjusting the conveyor speed so that food takes .8 to 99 minutes to move through heat tunnel.

There is no moving air in tunnel to remove moisture from food. Because radiant or infrared heat does not heat air, both ends of tunnel are open and heat loss from door closing is not a problem. Decks operate separately; during slow periods all but one deck can be closed off.

The following table shows examples of production possible in an infrared conveyorized oven:

## CONVEYORIZED RETURN OVEN CAPACITY*

### Round Pans

| Pans/Carrier<br>Diameter of<br>Pan | 12<br>6 in.<br>15.2 cm | 7<br>7 in.<br>17.8 cm | 6<br>8 in.<br>20.3 cm | 5<br>9 in.<br>22.9 cm | 3<br>10 in.<br>25.4 cm | 2<br>12–14 in.<br>30.5–35.6 cm | 1<br>15 in.<br>38.1 cm |
|---|---|---|---|---|---|---|---|
| 4 min. | 492 | 287 | 248 | 205 | 123 | 82 | 41 |
| 5 min. | 393 | 229 | 196 | 164 | 98 | 65 | 32 |
| 6 min. | 328 | 191 | 164 | 136 | 82 | 54 | 27 |
| 7 min. | 281 | 164 | 140 | 117 | 70 | 46 | 23 |
| 8 min. | 246 | 143 | 123 | 102 | 61 | 41 | 20 |
| 9 min. | 218 | 127 | 109 | 91 | 54 | 36 | 18 |
| 10 min. | 196 | 114 | 98 | 82 | 49 | 32 | 16 |
| 12 min. | 164 | 95 | 82 | 68 | 41 | 27 | 13 |
| 14 min. | 140 | 82 | 70 | 58 | 35 | 23 | 11 |
| 16 min. | 123 | 71 | 61 | 51 | 30 | 20 | 10 |
| 20 min. | 98 | 57 | 49 | 41 | 24 | 16 | 8 |
| 25 min. | 78 | 45 | 39 | 32 | 19 | 13 | 6 |
| 30 min. | 65 | 38 | 32 | 27 | 16 | 10 | 5 |

*Example:* A 5-minute product in a 10 in. (25.4 cm) pan would be cooked at a rate of 98 per hour per tier.
*See end of chart on facing page.

## CONVEYORIZED RETURN OVEN CAPACITY (cont.)

### 18 × 26-in. (46 × 66 cm) Sheet Pans

| Cook Time (Minutes) | Production Per Hour** | Cook Time (Minutes) | Production Per Hour |
|---|---|---|---|
| 5 | 32.5 | 17 | 9.5 |
| 6 | 27 | 18 | 9 |
| 7 | 23 | 19 | 8.5 |
| 8 | 20 | 20 | 8 |
| 9 | 18 | 25 | 6.5 |
| 10 | 16 | 30 | 5 |
| 11 | 15 | 35 | 4.5 |
| 12 | 13.5 | 40 | 4 |
| 13 | 12.5 | 45 | 3.5 |
| 14 | 11.5 | 50 | 3 |
| 15 | 11 | 55 | 3 |
| 16 | 10 | 60 | 2.5 |

**PRODUCTION FORMULA:

$$\frac{164 \times \text{number of pans per carrier}}{\text{cook time (min)}} = \frac{\text{production per hour}}{\text{per tier}}$$

*CTX Cooking Systems, Black Body Corporation

## HOW TO OPERATE CONVEYOR OVEN

Allow sufficient time for initial warm-up—45 minutes. For greatest energy savings, turn on one deck at a time starting with the bottom deck (No. 1) as this deck takes the longest to heat.

When resetting temperature, allow 10 to 15 minutes for heat to adjust.

Temperature settings should NOT vary more than 200°F. (93°C) between decks.

Top and bottom temperature settings on each deck should NOT vary more than 75°F. (24°C) (except 30°F. (−7°C) on deck No. 1).

Set temperatures progressively lower from upper to lower decks—highest temperature on highest deck, lowest temperature on lowest deck.

Temperature settings on the conveyor oven will normally be higher than for other methods of cooking because the controllers are sensing the heat source and not the air. Use the time and temperature chart supplied by manufacturer as guideline for food and pans.

These infrared conveyorized ovens offer the possibility of cooking different foods on the same deck and/or several decks set at a variety of times and temperatures. The decks on one model are numbered just like the floors of a building—the one on the bottom is No. 1. The food container is set on and removed from the carrier or conveyor belt outside the tunnel. Food should not be put into the tunnel or removed before it leaves the tunnel.

## CONVEYORIZED OVEN ON LOCATION

Souffles and fine wines are bringing people to Grape Expectations in St. Louis' Chesterfield Shopping Mall just to dine. Founders of Grape Expectations feel that souffles are so popular with their customers because they are difficult to make at home. Grape Expectations souffles are served in the European manner—with a center that is soft enough to act as a sauce for the outer portions.

Because souffles and quiches—two exceptional entrees—are made to order, a four-tier infrared conveyorized oven has been used in the system. The oven can cook four types of food at different temperatures simultaneously and produce a good version of each dish.

For example, one tier may have onion soup at 275°F. (136°C) for 2½ minutes; entrees at 675°F. (357°C) on another tier; 18-minute sweet souffles on the third, and 7½-minute quiches on the bottom. Each tier has its own timer.

"This conveyorized oven eliminates the greatest area of failure associated with souffles," according to Grape Expectations. "The products are not subject to shock from thermo changes or slammed doors. It's a first-in, first-out system, where items come out in sequence."

## MECHANICAL OVEN FEATURES

Mechanical ovens should provide these features:

- Increased capacity for baking and roasting.
- Several basic menu items can cook simultaneously in one piece of equipment.
- Oven construction that includes vent systems that assure needed moisture retention in completed products.
- Equipment that easily turns out casseroles to extend menu variety.

## ROTATING OVEN CAPACITY

| No. Trays | Tray Size In. | Cm | 2½-lb. (1.1 kg) Chickens | 25-lb. (11.3 kg) Ribs or 25-lb. (11.3 kg) Turkeys | 15-in. (38.1 cm) Pizza Per Hr. | 9-in. (22.9 cm) Cakes 9-in. (22.9 cm) Pies | 18 × 26-in. (46 × 66-cm) Bun Pans |
|---|---|---|---|---|---|---|---|
| 4 | 30 × 18 | 76.2 × 45.7 | 80 | 8 | 80 | 24 | 4 |
| 4 | 60 × 18 | 152.4 × 45.7 | 160 | 16 | 160 | 48 | 8 |
| 4 | 60 × 26 | 152.4 × 66 | 240 | 24 | 280 | 72 | 12 |
| 5 | 60 × 23 | 152.4 × 58.4 | 300 | 30 | 350 | 75 | 10 |
| 4 | 96 × 26 | 243.8 × 66 | 400 | 40 | 440 | 112 | 20 |
| 5 | 96 × 23 | 243.8 × 58.4 | 460 | 50 | 550 | 130 | 15 |

- Revolving tray ovens or rotating ovens that offer a working surface at normal working heights when pans are properly racked for loading and unloading. A bakery cart used to unload items of all kinds from the revolving tray oven markedly reduces the lifting required.
- Fuel use that decreases as oven load decreases so minimum load is economically feasible.
- Other equipment controls cooking by varying both temperature and time; control in a revolving oven is by time alone because the temperature is fixed at a level suitable for everything in the oven.

## WHERE TO LOCATE MECHANICAL OVENS

In determining need for mechanical ovens, location is an important factor. Most operators locate their first rotating oven in the bake shop area. The second oven is usually installed in the meat preparation area.

Other considerations that determine need:

- Kind and capacity of food output
- Time allowed to produce required output
- Space available
- Possibilities for simultaneous scheduling of menu items requiring same temperatures for baking or roasting

- Maximum peaks at present, and possible future needs (experts recommend projecting for 5 years).

## HOW MUCH WILL A ROTATING OVEN COOK?

To help estimate oven sizes, one manufacturer supplies a size information blank. When the operator fills out this form, the manufacturer can recommend size of oven needed. In the table above, capacity for one rotating oven is shown in terms of food production. These capacities are approximate per oven load. Capacities for 8- and 12-in. (20.3- and 30.5-cm) pizzas are proportionately larger.

The approximate capacity per oven load for two revolving oven models, holding 12 standard large steam table pans and 7 standard bun pans respectively:

| | |
|---|---|
| Turkeys, 25–30 lb. (11.3–13.6 kg) | 14 |
| Hams, average size | 28 |
| Prime beef, average | 14 |
| Chickens, average | 84 |
| Bread, 1½ lb. (679 gm) loaves | 35 |
| Pies, 9-in. (22.9 cm) | 35 |
| Danish pastry | 14 doz. |
| Pizza, 16-in. (40.6 cm) 7 per load or 56 per hr. (Field tests show that pizza is better baked at 500°F. (260°C) for 7 min.) | |

**MEASURE CAPACITY BY MEALS PER DAY***

Recommended sizes for revolving tray ovens have also been based on number of meals served per day from one kitchen:

| 18 × 26-in. (46 × 66 cm) Pan Capacity | Per Day | Oven Size | | Total Meals Per Day | Oven Size | | 18 × 26-in. (46 × 66 cm) Pan Capacity |
|---|---|---|---|---|---|---|---|
| | | In. | cm | | In. | cm | |
| 8 | 3300 | 6-96 × 26 | 243.8 × 66 | 450 | 4-60 × 18 | 152.4 × 45.7 | 30 |
| 8 | 3500 | 6-96 × 26 | 243.8 × 66 | 600 | 4-60 × 18 | 152.4 × 45.7 | 30 |
| 8 | 3800 | 7-96 × 26 | 243.8 × 66 | 800 | 4-60 × 18 | 152.4 × 45.7 | 35 |
| 12 | 4000 | 6-108 × 26 | 274.3 × 66 | 1000 | 4-60 × 18 | 152.4 × 45.7 | 36 |
| 12 | 4250–4500 | 8-96 × 26 | 243.8 × 66 | 1250 | 4-60 × 26 | 152.4 × 66 | 40* |
| 15 | 4800–5000 | 7-108 × 26 | 274.3 × 66 | 1500 | 5-60 × 26 | 152.4 × 66 | 42* |
| 18 | 5300–5500 | 9-96 × 26 | 243.8 × 66 | 1750 | 6-96 × 23 | 243.8 × 58.4 | 45* |
| 20 | 5800–6000 | 8-108 × 26 | 243.8 × 66 | 2000 | 4-96 × 26 | 243.8 × 66 | 48* |
| 20 | 6300–6500 | 9-108 × 26 | 274.3 × 66 | 2250 | 4-96 × 66 | 243.8 × 66 | 54* |
| 24 | 6800–7500 | 5-96 × 26 | 243.8 × 66 | 2500 | 4-108 × 26 | 274.3 × 66 | 2-25's |
| 24 | 7800–8500 | 6-96 × 26 | 243.8 × 66 | 2650 | 4-108 × 26 | 274.3 × 66 | 2-30's |
| 25 | 8800–9300 | 7-96 × 26 | 243.8 × 66 | 2850 | 5-96 × 26 | 243.8 × 66 | 2-35's |
| 25 | 9500–9800 | 7-108 × 26 | 274.3 × 26 | 3050 | 5-96 × 26 | 243.8 × 66 | 2-42's |

*Oven height and low kitchen ceiling may dictate combination of two smaller ovens instead.

*Note:* The makers of this chart note: Oven size recommendations are approximate and calculated for roasting, baking, and cooking. Due to so many variables, this chart should be used only as a starting point.

Accessibility of the oven has an important bearing on its use. In well-planned kitchens, operators report the following types of food are oven cooked:

**Entrees**

| | |
|---|---|
| Ham | Bacon |
| Turkey | Braised Vegetables |
| Barbecued Chicken | Souffles |
| Baked Potatoes | Chops |
| Beef Roasts | Roast Suckling Pig |
| Casseroles | Pork Roasts |
| Baked Tenderloin | Scalloped Vegetables |
| Baked Chicken | |

**Baked Goods**

| | |
|---|---|
| Rolls | Cookies |
| Pies | Sweet Rolls |
| Pastry | Bread |
| Layer and Sheet Cakes | Variety Breads |
| Custards | Meringues |
| Danish | |

## MECHANICAL OVEN PURCHASING POINTS

Factors to check when purchasing revolving ovens include:

- Sound construction
- Trays perfectly stabilized, with adequate facilities for leveling; trays should be firm, sway proof, tip proof at all stages of revolution
- Maximum of automatic controls
- Tray constructed properly to carry load
- Tray position indicator
- Adequate motor
- Exterior temperature
- Proper insulation
- Cleaning ease: access door, and easily-removed parts
- Most oven capacity in least space
- Exterior finish
- Opening properly located, easy to operate
- Maximum flexibility in heat-up, cool-down times

- Emergency hand drive for quick unloading in case of power failure
- Automatic and instantaneous motor shut off, alarm bell, and momentary push-button release or equivalent controls to prevent damage to oven caused by careless loading of trays
- Enough fuel capacity to bring oven temperature from normal room temperature to baking or roasting temperature speedily; in indirect-fired units a temperature increase of about 5 or 6 degrees (approximately 3 degrees on the C scale) per min.; semi-direct or direct-fired units, about 8 to 10 degrees (approximately 16 degrees on the C scale) per minute.

Ovens are an expensive investment, one that justifies extra effort spent in careful selection. Visit other operations to learn how their installations have worked out.

Install ovens in accordance with local building codes. Follow the manufacturer's recommendations carefully.

## MAINTENANCE PROGRAM

Oven maintenance is not complicated; however, regular maintenance should be scheduled. To assure trouble-free operation, one model's manufacturer suggests:

"Check oil level in speed reducer once a month and fill to the top of filler plug with 60 w steam cylinder oil or equivalent. Oil the electric motor once a month with light machine oil. The main shaft bearings require just enough lubricant to prevent rusting.

"Use No. 2 cup grease or equivalent once every 3 months. Do not force the grease into bearings, as this will break seal and cause them to leak. Do not use any lubricant on bearings inside the oven as they are designed to run dry."

Cleaning has become easier with changing designs, as one manufacturer points out:

"As time has gone by, each new year's model has meant a larger and larger cleanout door until finally we have practically the whole lower quarter of the oven removable so that a man or a woman can get inside the ovens and scour to his or her heart's content. The trays in these ovens are now removable by hand without tools and can

be taken to the sink for a scrubbing. We've even made the tray frames so they are removable to scrub also."

The better they are taken care of and the more they are used, the greater an institution's return on revolving ovens, according to experienced operators.

## MOVING AIR SPEEDS BAKING, ROASTING, RECONSTITUTION

The interaction between food and equipment development reached a high point in the convection oven. Convection or moving-air ovens meet the need for rapid reconstitution of frozen food items, rapid reheating of prepared foods, roasting, and baking.

Moving air in convection ovens continually plays on foods in the oven to speed heat absorption and reduce cooking time. The moving air prevents formation of the layer of insulating air that normally surrounds the food.

Convection ovens save energy because they use low baking temperatures and preheat food quickly. They range in size from counter units to large roll-in models. They may have multiple pan racks or shelves that can be spaced close together.

There are five types of convection ovens:

**Convection Ovens.** A motor-driven fan forces air circulation within the cavity. The rapid air circulation insures even temperature distribution to all parts of the oven and fast heat transfer to the food products.

Some models are practically airtight. Therefore, during roasting, when a pan of water is placed in the oven, moisture is drawn off the pan and the air inside the oven becomes saturated. Thus, with 100 per cent humidity in the air, very little moisture is drawn from the food.

Two operating procedures are stressed in the use of this oven: (1) put a pan of water in the oven when roasting meats; (2) remember that air must circulate to do a proper job, so do not crowd too many items on each shelf. Leave ample room around each item to be roasted or baked. Since heat is even on all sides, there is no need to turn pans of food around.

In one model, the oven chamber measures 18 in. (45.7 cm) high × 27 in. (68.6 cm) wide × 30 in. (76.2 cm) deep, and the burner output is 130,000 Btu per hour. Roasting capacity is three 65-lb. (29.4 kg) rounds of beef, eight 21-lb. (9.5 kg) ribs of beef and proportional amounts of other meats. The baking capacity, using five racks, is forty pies of 9-in. (22.9 cm) diameter.

The high heat permits effective reconstitution of frozen foods, and the use of the "on-" and "off"-type thermostat makes possible low-temperature meat roasting at 190°F. (88°C) to 225°F. (107°C).

**Thermionic Ovens.**  These are highly efficient electric directional bake or roast ovens with power blower and duct system that provides for low-velocity, high-volume air movement.

**Muffle Ovens.**  Combining features of a standard oven and a forced convection oven; designed to perform with the speed and efficiency of forced air convection or to operate as a standard oven; oven preheats quietly without fan; with a flick of a switch, it becomes a convection oven.

These ovens are available in three basic compartment heights: 7¼ in., (18.4 cm) 12¼ (31 cm) in., and 16¼ in. (42 cm). Ovens are sectional type; sections are 60 in. (152.4 cm) wide by 36 in. (91.4 cm) deep and are designed for stacking in any combination of heights. Up to three forced air convection sections may be added to existing ovens.

In models that are indirectly heated, the oven chamber is sealed when both oven door and damper are closed. The moisture retained in the sealed oven chamber provides an ideal roasting climate and an ideal baking climate for all except a few baked items.

The damper should be opened only under the following conditions:

- To cool the oven rapidly
- To dry the oven atmosphere
- To bake the following or similar items: cream puffs; eclair shells; patty shells; some baking powder biscuits
- If necessary to expel moisture or smoke just before opening door to unload.

Not all convection ovens use the damper method of expelling moisture or smoke. One model uses a fluttering-door method. The door of this oven flutters slightly as the moisture pressure builds up in the oven, thus expelling steam across the top of the door.

In one convection oven, the hot air that used to go out the vent is now captured and recirculated back into the oven, thus saving up to 40 percent of gas needed.

Many convection ovens have an automatic door switch that shuts off the fan as the oven doors open. This feature helps retain heat in the oven and maintain temperature during loading and unloading. In some units, if the oven needs to be cooled even more rapidly, an overload cool switch can be used to draw cool kitchen air into the oven while the doors are open. This switch can also be used to dry the oven atmosphere.

**Roll-in Rack Convection Ovens.**  The single roll-in rack convection oven has a heating element and fan housed outside the cooking area. Baffles placed on two sides of oven increase air movement created by the fan. Controlled air movement from two sides of the oven is designed to equalize velocity of hot air. Specially designed, graduated openings in baffles on two sides of oven—with the smallest openings closest to source of heat—distribute heat evenly.

An 18-shelf mobile oven rack makes it possible to roll the filled rack directly from preparation area into oven; after the food is cooked, the same rack can be pushed out of the oven to the serving area. To cook approximately 2,700 steaks per hour in this oven, operator should have second rack loaded with steaks ready to go into oven as soon as first rack of cooked steaks is ready to come out.

Actual changing of mobile racks takes only a few minutes. The 2,700 per hour rate (this will vary slightly depending on actual size of steaks) permits a total of 15 minutes each hour for loading and unloading. As the system smooths out, steak production could be increased.

Heat is said to vary no more than 4°F. (approximately 2.4°C) within this oven, no matter how foods are arranged on the shelves. Larger quantities of steaks, in demonstrations, have cooked faster than small quantities. When the forced hot air hits a great mass, it penetrates deeper and quicker and the cooking time is slightly less.

Dual temperature controls permit two different types of food to be cooked simultaneously at two different temperatures. Steam injection controls oven moisture content, speeds heat-up of frozen foods. Steam may also be used to clean the oven when the cooking process is completed.

**Slow-cooking Convection Ovens.** These ovens decrease meat shrinkage, save energy. One model maintains stable temperatures from top to bottom with an air system that directs air in cyclonic fashion to keep meat from drying out. The oven operates on 110/120 volt current and units can be stacked; when portable, oven can be moved to various locations.

Another unit is designed to roast meats at temperatures from 200° to 225°F. (93°–107°C). It uses air convection but requires that roasts be put in oven on wire grid and cook at temperature between 200°F. (93°C) and 225°F. (107°C). Oven automatically switches to "hold" when meat is done, thereby keeping meat shrinkage to around 7 per cent. This unit also can be used away from the main cooking area and may not require hood ventilation if health department regulations permit.

## PRELIMINARY STEPS IN CHOOSING CONVECTION OVENS

Take the following preliminary steps to select the convection oven that will perform best in your operation:

1. Estimate space available for oven or ovens.
2. Carefully analyze production requirements so oven capacity will match menu needs.
3. Investigate all equipment available; models include:

- compact convection ovens for counter, can also be mounted on built-in rack guides
- standard convection ovens for high-capacity baking, roasting, or reconstituting
- deep convection ovens—one model requires only 6 min. to preheat to 350°F. (177°C) and only 2100 watts to hold 350°F. (177°C)
- combination of standard cooking and low-temperature cooking and holding, or automatic holding ovens; in these ovens meat size

and doneness are interrelated with oven-cavity temperature and time.

A table is available that shows cooking times. With oven controls set at proper cook temperature and time, oven cooks first with full power, then with stored energy remaining in the cavity until meat is done. If meat is left in cavity when done, oven will automatically switch to a holding position.

A 36-in. (91.4 cm) deep oven offers the following typical production per section: at low temperature, 30-lb. (13.4 kg) rolled beef roast in 8½ hours at 200°F. (93°C); rare 20-lb. (9 kg) standing prime ribs in 4¾ hours at 200°F. (93°C). At higher temperatures, 550 3-in. (7.6 cm) sugar cookies in 15 minutes at 300°F. (149°C); 132 well-done hamburgers (5 per lb. (453 gm)) in 10 to 12 minutes at 400°F. (204°C). A 44-in. (111.8 cm) deep model can turn out 890 3-in. (7.6 cm) sugar cookies in 15 minutes at 300°F. (149°C).

4. Order equipment with proper fuel requirements (gas type or voltage).
5. Install equipment correctly, and make sure all personnel scheduled to use it understand its operation thoroughly.

Selecting equipment to match projected food production resulted in the choice of two roll-in convection ovens for the main kitchen of the Milwaukee (WI) Exposition and Convention Center. This kitchen provides all the food for the three buildings in the complex. System is equipped to allow product to be prepanned, placed on portable racks, and kept in walk-in unit until needed. Ovens allow portable rack to be rolled directly into oven without any product rehandling.

Rack-type convection ovens come in models large enough to roast as much as a ton of meat per load or bake up to 7,000 cookies per hour.

## PURCHASING POINTS FOR CONVECTION OVENS

Well-constructed ovens offer these advantages:

- Design that permits easy and thorough cleaning. Ceramic material should be nonabsorbent and hard enough to be cleaned without injury.

- Concealed wiring and manifolds
- All parts easily accessible for servicing
- Durable rigid frames of all-welded, structural steel construction
- Outside bodies of 16 to 18 ga. metal attached to solid frame support with durable finishes
- Optimum air circulation
- Inner linings of 18-ga. rustproof sheet metal, reinforced to prevent buckling
- Fronts all one-piece construction
- Sufficient nonsagging, rodent-proof, spun fiber glass or other equally efficient insulation on all sides
- Walls surrounding insulation tightly sealed to prevent entrance of moisture
- Devices around doors to minimize heat loss
- Handles that stay cool to the touch
- Sturdy doors, preferably containing windows so contents can be viewed without opening door
- Doors counter balanced for easy opening and closing and to prevent slamming. Heavy-duty hinges
- Doors that open level with bottom of oven or deck
- Easy cleaning
- Positive stop racks in convection-oven sections to prevent tipping when partially withdrawn
- Long-life motor
- Durable heating units made of warp-proof alloys
- Thermostatic control precise between 175°F. (79°C) and 500°F. (260°C)
- Signal lights to indicate when oven is on, timers, and outside thermometers
- Chambers vented, dampered, and baffled to direct the heat
- System to conduct vapor out of oven, preventing its flow back as condensate
- Controls in front, easily accessible to workers
- Sufficient racks for scheduled loads
- Type of mounting best suited to kitchen
- Dual-speed fan; high speed for frozen products and low speed for delicate baked goods
- Dual-wattage input—51 KW or half of that by flicking the switch.

To determine needed oven capacity, analyze menu requirements and the time that can be scheduled to meet them. The production potential of a line of convection ovens is shown on pages 66–67.

## ESTIMATES OF CONVECTION OVEN CAPACITY

Here is another run-down on the capacity of one convection oven:

- Reheats 88 frozen meals to hot in 20 minutes
- Cooks 150 lb. (68 kg) of beef at one time
- Cooks 120 lb. (54.4 kg) of poultry at one time
- Cooks 480 orders of two eggs each
- Bakes 6 18 × 26-in. (46 × 66 cm) pans of pastries
- Bakes 24 1¼-lb. (566 gm) loaves of bread
- Bakes 36 8 to 10-in. (20.3 to 25.4 cm) pies
- Bakes 75 casserole dishes
- Cooks 3 bushels (81.5 kg) of 80-count Idaho potatoes.

## HOW TO OPERATE MOVING-AIR OVENS

One manufacturer offers these easy-to-follow operating instructions:

1. If unit is electric, snap on power switch with door open; if unit is gas, snap on electric toggle switch with door open.
2. Convector fan may start operating with door open. If so, depress convector fan switch so that fan is operating only when door is closed.
3. Arrange shelf positions according to item to be baked or roasted. (Cooking chart on left panel of oven or oven recipe cards will give correct positioning.)
4. Close doors. Fan should come on, otherwise unit is not operating correctly. (Steps to be taken are further outlined in instructions.)
5. If unit is gas fired, turn main gas valve to BURNERS ON.
6. Preheat to desired cooking temperature and allow to cycle once to obtain even temperature throughout oven. With many foods, warm up is not necessary; eliminating this step saves considerable energy.

7. Oven is ready to cook and may be loaded when indicator light goes off. The load should be adjacent to oven to facilitate rapid loading so that doors will be open as short a time as possible.

8. If using the convection oven for long-term roasting of meats, fish, or poultry, place about a qt. (0.9 l) of water in a suitable container in the oven.

9. Close doors and set timer for desired cooking time.

10. Interior lights may be turned on or off as desired.

11. Bell will ring when cooking is completed. Oven is ready to unload.

12. If oven temperature is to be lowered, open doors with fan on, and lower thermostat to the desired temperature. Oven will cool rapidly. Fan may be turned on when doors are opened by depressing fan switch. The switch should be depressed again before resuming cooking. In some models, safety interlock door automatically shuts off blower and heating elements when doors are opened.

13. To turn off electric oven, turn oven thermostat and power switch off and leave doors

## COOKING CAPACITY FOR ROLL-IN RACK CONVECTION OVEN*

| Sheet Pans Per Oven Load | Item | Approximate Weight Per Piece | | Temperature Setting Degrees Farenheit | Celsius | Cooking Time Approximate Minutes | Shrink or Weight Loss | Degree of Doneness |
|---|---|---|---|---|---|---|---|---|
| 4–5 | Boneless Beef Rib | 12–14 lb. | 5.4–6.3 kg | 325 | 163 | 135–150 | 16% | Medium |
| 4–5 | Top Round of Beef | 14–18 lb. | 6.3–8.2 kg | 300 | 149 | 150–165 | 14–16% | Medium |
| 5–6 | Top Round Split | 7–8 lb. | 3.2–3.6 kg | 300 | 149 | 105–120 | 14–16% | Medium |
| 9 | Diced Beef (To Sear) | | | 375–400 | 190–204 | 12–15 | | Only Sear |
| 6 | Bottom Round Beef | 14–18 lb. | 6.3–8.2 kg | 300 | 149 | 150–165 | 14–16% | Medium |
| 9–11 | London Broil—1 in. | 1½–2 lb. | 679–905 gm | 450–475 | 232–301 | 8 | 6–8% | Rare–Med. |
| 8 | Sirloin Strip Roast | 8–10 lb. | 3.6–5.4 kg | 400–450 | 204–232 | 35–45 | 10–12% | Rare–Med. |
| 9–11 | Meat Loaf 3½–4 in. | 5–6 lb. | 2.3–2.7 kg | 300 | 149 | 75–90 | 10–16% | Well Done |
| 9–11 | Fresh Canadian Backs | 7–9 lb. | 3.2–4 kg | 300 | 149 | 50–55 | 14–16% | Well Done |
| 9–11 | Legs of Lamb (Boned) | 3–4 lb. | 1.4–1.8 kg | 275–300 | 134–149 | 75–90 | 8–12% | Well Done |
| 9–11 | Baked Pork Chops | 5 oz. | 142 gm | 325–350 | 163–177 | 20–25 | 20–22% | Well Done |
| 9–11 | Baked Chicken Halves | 1½ lb. | 679 gm | 275–300 | 134–149 | 25–30 | 20–22% | Well Done |
| 9–11 | Baked Chicken Quarters | 8–10 oz. | 226–283 gm | 275–300 | 134–149 | 25–30 | 20–22% | Well Done |
| 9–11 | Boneless Chicken Breast | 6 oz. | 170 gm | 275–300 | 134–149 | 25–30 | 20–22% | Well Done |
| 9–11 | Barbecue Chicken Half | 1 lb. | 453 gm | 400 | 204 | 20–25 | 20–22% | Well Done |
| 9 | Sirloin Steaks | 10 oz. | 283 gm | 450–500 | 232–260 | 8–10 | | Med. Rare |
| 9 | Delmonico Steaks | 8 oz. | 226 gm | 450–500 | 232–260 | 8–10 | | Med. Rare |
| 9–11 | Salisbury Steak | 5–6 oz. | 142–170 gm | 300 | 149 | 18–22 | 15% | Well Done |
| 9–11 | Hamburgers | 2½–3½ oz. | 71–99 gm | 400 | 204 | 5–6 | | Well Done |
| 9–11 | Fish Steak (Fresh) | 7–9 oz. | 199–254 gm | 325 | 163 | 16–20 | 14–16% | Well Done |
| 9–11 | Fish Steak (Formed) | 4–5 oz. | 114–142 gm | 350 | 177 | 16–20 | 18–20% | Well Done |
| 9–11 | Fresh Fruit Pies | 3–3½ lb. | 1.4–1.6 kg | 350 | 177 | 25–35 | | |
| 9–11 | Turnovers | 4–4½ oz. | 114–128 gm | 375 | 190 | 12–16 | | |
| 9–11 | Cream Puff Shells | 1–1½ oz. | 28–43 gm | 400–200 | 204–93 | 10–15 | | |
| 9–11 | Cookies (Variety) | 3 | | 325 | 163 | 4–6 | | |
| 9–11 | Sheet Cakes | 5–6 lb. | 2.3–2.7 kg | 325–350 | 163–177 | 25–35 | | |
| 9–11 | Roast Potatoes | Egg Size | | 350 | 177 | 25–30 | | |
| 9–11 | Baked Idahos | 8–10 oz. | 226–283 gm | 350 | 177 | 25–40 | | |
| 9–11 | Frozen Pre-Plates | 8–10 oz. | 226–283 gm | 350 | 177 | 25–30 | | |
| 9–11 | Bread Dressing | ½ Pans/ 5 lb. | 2.3 kg | 300 | 149 | 25–35 | | |
| 9–11 | Toast/Bread | | | 350 | 177 | 3–4 | | |
| 9–11 | Toast/English Muffins | | | 350–375 | 177–190 | 3–4 | | |

*See end of chart on facing page.

**COOKING CAPACITY FOR ROLL-IN RACK CONVECTION OVEN** (cont.)

**Frozen Food Products**

| Sheet Pans Per Oven Load | Item | Approximate Weight of Each Container | Temperature Setting/Degrees °F °C | Cooking Time Approximate Minutes | Capacity (Items per pan) |
|---|---|---|---|---|---|
| 9–11 | Frozen Fruit Pies 9 in. × 1½ in. (22.9 × 3.8 cm) | 3–3½ lb. (1.4–1.6 kg) | 350 (177) | 45–50 | 3 |
| 18 | Pot Pies—Individual | 7 oz. (199 gm) | 325 (163) | 25 | 15 |
| 9 | Casseroles—Covered | 10 oz. (283 gm) | 350 (177) | 45 | 15 |
| 9 | Casseroles—Refrigerator | 10 oz. (283 gm) | 350 (177) | 25 | 15 |
| 18 | Dinners—Individual—Covered | 14 oz. (396 gm) | 305 (152) | 20 | 4 |

| Baskets Per Oven Load | | | | | |
|---|---|---|---|---|---|
| 40 | School Lunch—Type A 5 in. × 6½ in. (12.7 × 16.5 cm) | 14 oz. (396 gm) | 305 (152) | 20 | |

| 12 in. × 20 × 2 in. Steam Table Pans Per Oven Load | | | | | |
|---|---|---|---|---|---|
| 18 | Vegetables—Covered | 228 Fl. oz. (6.7 l) | 325 (163) | 30 | |
| 18 | Potatoes Au Gratin—Uncovered | 228 Fl. oz. (6.7 l) | 350 (177) | 45 | |
| 18 | Scalloped Potatoes—Uncovered | 228 Fl. oz. (6.7 l) | 300 (149) | 45 | |
| 18 | Beef and Gravy—Uncovered | 228 Fl. oz. (6.7 l) | 350 (177) | 45 | |
| 18 | Beef Burgundy—Uncovered | 228 Fl. oz. (6.7 l) | 350 (177) | 25 | |
| 18 | Spaghetti and Meat Balls—Uncovered | 228 Fl. oz. (6.7 l) | 325 (163) | 40 | |
| 18 | Shrimp Creole—Uncovered | 228 Fl. oz. (6.7 l) | 305 (152) | 40 | |

*Crescent Metal Products, Inc.

open. To turn off gas oven, turn oven thermostat power switch and main gas valve off; leave doors open.

## FOLLOW DIRECTIONS FOR SHELF AND PAN ARRANGEMENT

These instructions for using one manufacturer's convection oven stress the importance of shelf and pan location: There are eleven tracks on the sidewalls of the oven. Six shelves are standard equipment; more may be ordered if you need them. Correct location of shelves is most important for satisfactory results. Locations are indicated with tracks numbered from the top down. The following table of shelf positions is for your reference:

**SHELF POSITIONS**

| | Meat | Baked Products |
|---|---|---|
| 1 Shelf | track 11 | track 5 |
| 2 Shelves | tracks 5, 11 | tracks 5, 8 |
| 3 Shelves | tracks 3, 7, 11 | tracks 3, 7, 11 |
| 4 Shelves | tracks 2, 5, 8, 11 | tracks 2, 5 8, 11 |
| 6 Shelves | tracks 1, 3 5, 7, 9, 11 | tracks 1, 3, 5, 7, 9, 11 |

Always put 18 × 26 × 1-in. (46 × 66 × 2.5 cm) pans in the oven lengthwise to allow for proper air circulation and obtain more uniformly-colored finished product. On the other hand, if two 12 × 20 × 2½-in. (30 × 51 × 6 cm) pans are used on one shelf, place one in front of the other to allow for better circulation. Other types of convection oven will take pans either way.

## FRUIT PIE PRODUCTION

Actual operation of convection ovens is easy, as outlined in this procedure for baking frozen or fresh fruit pies:

1. While the oven is cool, place racks in shelf positions 1, 3, 5, 7, 9 and 11 (a total of six shelves); racks are always positioned from the top.
2. Preheat oven to 400°F. (204°C).
3. While oven is preheating, place six 8 or 10-in. (20.3 or 25.4 cm) fruit pies on each of six 18 × 26 × 1-in. (46 × 66 × 2.5 cm) sheet pans (total—36 pies).
4. When the oven is preheated and pilot light goes out (signifying that oven has reached desired temperature) open doors and load oven with pies. (Note: be sure to place the sheet pans in the center of the oven with the 26-in. (66 cm) depth running from front to back.) Close doors. Loading time should be approximately 45 seconds.
5. Set timer at 400°F. (204°C) for 50 minutes for frozen pies; 45 minutes for fresh pies. Do not open doors during baking operation.

## LOADING RACK OVENS

Convection ovens have, as noted earlier, brought about the revival of the large roll-in rack oven. With one model now available, a complete meal for about 2,500 people can be reconstituted in one loading of this single-rack oven.

Frozen prepared foods can be loaded on special roll-in racks, nontoxic under elevated temperatures, and held in freezer until time for service. At serving time, loaded racks can be rolled directly from the freezer into the rack oven; preheat time is only 10 min. for one direct-fired oven. This oven comes in two sizes: (single) 5 ft. 10 in. (1.78 m) wide by 10 ft. 8 in. (3.25 m) deep by 8 ft. 3 in. (2.5 m) high—capacity 40 standard 18 by 26-in. (46 × 66 cm) pans properly spaced; (double) 9 ft. 4 in. (2.84 m) wide by 11 ft. 6 in. (3.5 m) deep by 8 ft. 3 in. (2.5 m) wide—capacity 80 pans. Again, ovens should only be preheated for foods that must go into heated cavity.

## CLEANING ELECTRIC CONVECTION OVENS

The importance of oven cleaning as an energy-saving measure was stressed by Carol Michael, Dept. of Home Economics, Miami University, Oxford, OH., in the *School Foodservice Journal*:

"Ovens should be kept clean. A carbon build-up on the lower edge of the door can prevent the oven door from closing tightly, allowing much heat to be lost. Once a year, have a service representative thoroughly inspect the entire oven for efficient operation. Most important, have the representative calibrate the oven thermostat to make sure it is heating normally.

"Follow the manufacturer's operating and cleaning instructions for proper convection-oven maintenance. The fan should be cleaned periodically because an accumulation of dirt restricts air delivery. Have motor checked once a year."

Directions for cleaning electric convection ovens are easy to follow; first be sure to turn power off. Typical are these instructions for removing and cleaning oven interiors of one counter model:

1. Remove bottom pan.
2. Lift out side baffles.
3. Lift out fan-venting baffles.
4. The fan wheel is fastened to the motor shaft with a cap and socket-type cap screw. Use an Allen wrench to remove the cap screw and slide the fan wheel off the motor shaft. The bottom pan and baffles are porcelainized steel and may be soaked in hot water and detergents or ammonia to remove grease. The fan wheel is balanced and must not be dropped or damaged.

Replace all removable parts very carefully after cleaning.

5. Wash oven exterior.

Directions for cleaning larger counter model and table and floor models:

1. Lift off air-deflection baffles mounted on inside of door and back of oven compartment.

2. Fan-venting funnel baffle—remove the screw near top of baffle and lift up and out. This baffle has a wire fan guard, which also may be removed if required.

All of these parts are stainless steel and may be cleaned with hot water with detergents or other recommended commercial cleaners. The same cleaning solution may also be used on the oven's interior walls.

The fan wheels on these models are held to the motor shaft with a washer and screw. Remove screw and slide fan wheel from shaft. Do not damage the balance wheel.

3. Wash oven exterior.

Non-stick and easy-to-remove oven linings are available in some convection-oven models to make cleaning easier.

### Tips on Convection Oven Operation

1. Bread, rolls, cakes, brownies, coffee cake, pie, and pastry squares bake easily and well in the convection oven.
2. Roasts, poultry, fish, sausages, hamburger patties, and baked stuffed pork chops are protein items that may be prepared in the convection oven.
3. Frozen prepared meals defrost and heat uniformly at 500°F. (260°C) in the convection oven in 20 to 30 minutes.
4. Load pies in oven on 18 × 26-in. (46 × 66 cm) sheet pans for ease of loading and to prevent overloading.
5. Standard 12 × 20 × 2½-in. (30 × 51 × 6 cm) pans should be placed one in front of the other for best results. 18 × 26 × 1-in. (46 × 66 × 2.5 cm) pans should always be put in lengthwise. This positioning allows 1½- to 2-in. (3.8 to 5 cm) space on both sides of the oven.
6. Use meat racks for roasting so that roasts will not sit in their juices.
7. Overloading the oven is the biggest single cause of nonuniform baking and roasting.
8. All pans should be centered vertically and horizontally in the oven for best results.
9. For best preparation, always put a partial load of food on the center shelves in the oven.
10. Reduce the moisture in your cake and bread recipes if your favorite recipe does not come out right.
11. The fans in most convection ovens will not operate when doors are open. Never load oven if fan is operating.
12. Do not use pans that are too deep; they will tend to produce poor color.
13. No need to put water in the oven for hamburgers because cooking time is so short.
14. If possible, take advantage of load control system that assures controlled top browning.
15. Always use commercial oven light bulbs in oven. Do not use home light bulbs or domestic oven light bulbs; they do not last and may shatter, spoiling an entire oven load of food.

### OPERATING ADVANTAGES OF MICROWAVE OVENS

The microwave oven permits the foodservice operator to prepare items in bulk during slack periods, chill, or freeze them—then as demand dictates, thaw, heat, or reheat the items—to fill patron orders as they arrive.

Other basic contributions of microwave ovens to foodservice include: (1) reheating single servings of precooked food; (2) complementing existing food heating equipment, especially during slow periods at the beginning and end of meal periods; (3) speedy defrosting (1 minute for a frozen steak) that eliminates over preparation; (4) eliminating bottlenecks in preparation and service; (5) decreasing labor costs through elimination of peak periods.

Menus that take advantage of microwave ovens can be broadened without added equipment by introducing food preparation procedures that previously would have been too time consuming. Preparation time saved through the use of microwave ovens could, for example, make it possible for some items requiring elaborate preparation—perhaps sandwich specialties—to appear on the menu. Menu variety can also be increased with the introduction of specialties that can be purchased in precooked form, then reconstituted to order in seconds.

Microwave ovens can be used to lengthen hours of operation. The late customer who wants pancakes can have them even though the cook has gone off duty. Pancakes can be cooked during off-peak hours, then refrigerated. Whenever an order is placed for them, it is a simple matter for the waitress to take the plate of cakes from the refrigerator, heat it for a few seconds in the microwave oven, and serve hotcakes with a fresh-made taste.

Increased seat turnover is another potential of this equipment. Normally a customer has to wait 10, 15, or 20 minutes after placing an order before the food is served. Using a microwave oven, many kinds of food can be served within 2 minutes after the order is placed. Multiplying the 8- to 12-minute speedup on turnover by the daily patronage gives an indication of volume that can be added.

Microwave ovens in hospital wards assure that patients get their hot foods hot while at the same time reducing the kitchen workload.

## PROFIT POTENTIAL OF MICROWAVE OVENS

Evaluation of higher costs for energy at Zum Zum, the fast counter chain featuring German-Bavarian wurst, prompted a revamping of menu items to include higher-priced entrees. Microwave ovens made it possible to offer the necessary newcomers to Zum Zum's menu.

Variations on the hamburger theme introduced in 1974–75 helped increase check averages to $1.40. By 1976–77, salads beefed up the check average to $1.85. Customers could choose shrimp Louis, cold meat or fruit platters, chef and Nicoise salads.

Casseroles, crepes and grilled sandwiches were added in 1977. "Customers expected these items to be served just as fast as hot dogs," as President Don Raleigh reported to *Institutions* magazine. "We were able to do this by using microwave ovens."

By equipping each unit with two microwaves, Zum Zum could serve appealing casserole choices such as chicken Chasseur, veal blanquette, and seafood cocotte. Other new headliners on the menu were pastrami, tenderloin, Reuben and Rachel sandwiches, plus chicken and seafood crepes. The microwave ovens have increased higher-priced items from 11 percent of luncheon-dinner covers to 40 percent since October, 1977. "We're hoping to increase this amount to 56 percent," Raleigh added.

"The biggest secret is the dish itself. It must be straight-sided and covered, with at least one-fourth of an inch (6 mm) between the food and the casserole lid, to allow for expansion.

"Crepes are also heated in the microwave in casserole dishes and then browned for 30 seconds in high-intensity ovens.

"Our microwave foods now account for one-third of our food items," claims Raleigh. "They are responsible for an even greater percentage of our sales.

"We have not had to add any personnel, even with our increased menu," Raleigh adds. "Labor costs are about 26 percent. We usually have ten employees on each of two shifts who handle approximately 2,000 customers each 13-hour day. Food costs stay around 32.5 percent."

## MICROWAVE OVENS OFFER PORTION, QUALITY CONTROL

At Beth Israel Medical Center in New York City, microwave ovens are used to reheat food in pantries on each patient floor. The ovens have made it possible to consolidate many small jobs into one larger, more efficient operation. As reported in *Foodservice Equipment Specialist* magazine, the result has been more effective supervision, greater freedom in operation, and more diversified use of kitchen staff.

As the cart of prepared food trays arrives at floor service station, under the floor dietitian's supervision, two people take the assembled trays from the cart, remove the entree, and put it into one of the three microwave ovens, where it is heated for 30–75 seconds.

When four entrees are heated, they are reunited with their trays, which are placed on a two-shelf truck and wheeled to the patients. Total serving time for each 38-bed section is a half hour.

"This system not only allows us to serve the patient a tasty, hot, nutritious meal, but also allows us much greater portion and quality control," says Ron Fread, Director of Food Services. "This in itself has decreased the total number of man hours required to serve each meal, and has created a sense of team work.

"The morale of our staff is fantastic," he proudly continues, "due mainly to the responsibilities which each individual member of the staff now has."

The chef has adapted his production procedures, and the cooks have altered their techniques, as it is no longer necessary to maintain large quantities of hot food for extended periods of time. More care goes into the cooking, and the microwave ovens are proving to be a quality-control tool for menu testing.

Several new "concept" salad bar restaurants on the West Coast use microwave ovens as their only cooking equipment. The ovens reheat quiche and soup, the only nonsalad items featured. Usually these dishes are made off premise. Salad restaurants are now being franchised in other areas of the country.

Two large-cavity microwave ovens are used to reheat Cantonese food specialties at Wu Ben's, Newport Beach, CA. Mandarin Duck, Shrimp Hawaiian, Sweet and Sour Pork, Lobster Cantonese, and Rumaki all get microwave oven treatment just before service to customers.

## HOW MICROWAVE ENERGY IS PRODUCED

Microwave heat is produced by short radio waves called microwaves; they belong to the same family of energy used in television and radar. Food is cooked in microwave ovens by the conversion of microwave energy into heat within the food. The energy is introduced by magnetron tubes that send their energy into the oven cavity.

These tubes transmit microwaves into the oven cavity at the speed of light. Because microwave energy causes heating to take place deep within the product and at the surface simultaneously, food production is extremely fast for suitable food items. However, microwaves lose half their energy after penetrating 3/4 in. (1.9 cm) into the food and then half of their remaining energy after penetrating another 3/4 in. (1.9 cm). Microwaves do the best job when food is not too thick.

Microwave ovens provide energy, which is converted into heat in a food product in the oven. The given amount of energy can be concentrated all on one item or diffused over several. The more quantity and bulk to be heated, the more time required to heat it.

The length of time it takes for microwave heat to bring foods to desired temperatures depends on (1) the temperature of the food as it goes into the oven, (2) the volume of the food item to be heated, (3) its moisture content, (4) the density of the item, and (5) the diameter of the item.

## TIME CONTROLS COOKING

To fit microwave food preparation into an existing operation, the first step is effective training of employees in this new concept of food preparation. Once the operating personnel have grasped the fact that time is of the essence, they can get optimum results from this equipment, whether it is used for special items or to prepare the full menu line. Since the thickness of food, its density, and moisture content affect the length of time required for microwaves to heat an item through, any time schedule set for microwave heating must allow for these variables.

Quick reheating from 40°F. (4°C) to serving of casseroles is shown on following page for one type microwave oven. Timer settings for another unit are on page 73, part of a very detailed list available from the manufacturer.

Where microwave ovens have been set up for use by patrons in vending operations, the machine can be coordinated with a limited menu; simple matching of label to control button makes operation easy, insures proper oven time for each item.

## TYPES OF MICROWAVE OVENS

The three types of microwave-oven operation most common currently:

- Reconstitution of refrigerated foods by vending-machine patrons.
- Reconstitution to order of frozen or refrigerated meals or menu items by foodservice personnel, either in the kitchen or at the point of service—hospital ward, counter, etc.
- Reconstitution of foods in bulk—frozen or refrigerated; either several casseroles, platter meals, or portions at one time, or reconstitu-

tion of bulk, prepared-ahead frozen foods for service to plates and trays.

The cook/package/chill food-production system at the Memorial Hospital System, Southwest Complex in Houston depends on two types of ovens to bring foods from the 30°F. (−1°C) temperature at which they are stored to the piping-hot point needed at time of service. On hospital floors, items are reheated in microwave ovens. Food to be served in the satellite hospital cafeterias is packaged in half-size foil pans and reheated in infrared ovens before going on service lines.

Microwave ovens can be conveniently located in very little space. At Doylestown (PA) Hospital, a microwave unit has been placed opposite the tilting braising/fry pan on a worktable overshelf.

One foodservice designer feels that when microwave ovens are located on nursing floors to reconstitute foods from chill or frozen temperatures, there should be one microwave oven for every fifteen patients.

A variety of microwave oven models are available to fill the requirements outlined on the preceding pages:

• Single cavity microwave oven—on counter, at waitress stations, in kitchen near food supply; small portable units also available for poolside or similar locations, or for truck operation using portable generator for power. Can deliver from 650 to 1300 watts, depending on model.

• High wattage output, usually 2-magnetron oven for reconstituting bulk items for steam table supply, heavy-duty defrosting, multi-plate and multi-container supply, and increased production at point of service.

## SYSTEM FOR FAST SERVICE RESTAURANT

The microwave oven installation selected by an individual food service must, of course, meet that operation's menu requirements. One system, suggested by a manufacturer to adapt the microwave oven to fast-service commercial restaurants, gives an indication of microwave potential:

"This system is suggested for coffee shops, chain-store restaurants, department-store restaurants, drive-ins, and highway restaurants, table service restaurants, and other similar installations where labor saving, speed of service, high seat turnover, and space economy are vital.

"Many of such foodservice operations are already supplied with commissary food, or use a considerable amount of prepared and partly prepared food. Most of them have menus or menu boards whose listings remain fairly standardized with the exception of a few daily changes in the

## CASSEROLES

*Heat covered from refrigerated temperature (Approx. 40°F.(41°C.))*
*1000 Watt or (120v) system*
*Usable space: 13 in. (33 cm) wide, 13 in. (33 cm) deep, 7⁹⁄₁₆ in. (18.6 cm) high.*

| Quantity | Item | Approximate Heating Time | Advance Preparation Instructions |
|---|---|---|---|
| 7 oz. (199 gm) | Baked beans with wieners | 70 secs. | Cut wieners in chunks and place around perimeter of container, leaving center depressed |
| 7 oz. (199 gm) | Beef stew | 75 secs. | Place bulk of product around perimeter of container, leaving center depressed. |
| 7 oz. (199 gm) | Chicken a la King | 65 secs. | Place bulk of product around perimeter of container, leaving center depressed. |
| 7 oz. (199 gm) | Curried franks and rice | 65 secs. | Place cooked rice in concave shape in bottom of container. Place sauce and wiener chunks on top of rice with wiener chunks toward edges of container. |
| 7 oz. (199 gm) | Meat loaf, tomato sauce or gravy | 75 secs. | Slice meat loaf into thin slices. Mask with tomato sauce or gravy. Keep center of food product slightly separated. |

## SELECTED TIMER SETTINGS FOR MICROWAVE OVENS*

| Refrigerated Items to Reheat | 208/240V | 120 Volts |
|---|---|---|
| | Approx. Time (Sec.) | |
| **SOUPS** | | |
| Clam Chowder (6 oz.) (170 gm) | 60 | 80 |
| Chili (8 oz.) (226 gm) | 90 | 120 |
| **SANDWICHES** | | |
| Ham & Cheese (4½ oz.) (128 gm) | 15 | 20 |
| Roast Beef (3 oz.) (85 gm) | 20 | 25 |
| Hamburger (4 oz.) (114 gm) | 30 | 40 |
| Reuben (4½ oz.) (128 gm) | 45 | 60 |
| **CASSEROLES** | | |
| Beef Stew (6 oz.) (170 gm) | 75 | 100 |
| Lobster Newburg (6 oz.) (170 gm) | 60 | 80 |
| Lasagna/Sauce (8 oz.) (226 gm) | 90 | 120 |
| Baked Beans/Franks (7 oz.) (199 gm) | 50 | 65 |
| Chicken a la King w/Rice (6 oz.) (170 gm) | 30 | 40 |
| Macaroni/Cheese (6 oz.) (170 gm) | 60 | 80 |
| **MEATS** | | |
| Prime Rib (Rare) (8 oz.) (226 gm) | 50 | 65 |
| Chicken Quarter (6 oz.) (170 gm) | 90 | 110 |
| Sausage Links (2 oz. (57 gm) Precooked) | 30 | 40 |
| **VEGETABLES** | | |
| Corn (4 oz.) (114 gm) | 20 | 25 |
| Baked Beans (4 oz.) (114 gm) | 25 | 35 |
| Peas (4 oz.) (114 gm) | 20 | 25 |

| Plated Meals & Misc. to Reheat | 208/240V | 120 Volts |
|---|---|---|
| ITEMS | Approx. Time (Sec.) | |
| Sliced Ham w/Raisin Sauce, Gr. Beans, Escalloped Pot. (7½ oz.) (213 gm) | 60 | 80 |
| Spaghetti w/Meat Balls (6 oz.) (170 gm) | 70 | 90 |
| Veal Parmesan (6½ oz.) (184 gm) | 60 | 75 |
| Pancakes (3) | 30 | 40 |
| Raw Idaho (8 oz.) (226 gm) Potato | 165 | 190 |
| Pre-Baked—75% (7-8 oz.) (199–226 gm) | 60 | 75 |
| **ITEMS TO DEFROST & COOK** | | |
| ITEMS | | |
| Fish Steak (4 oz.) (114 gm) | | |
| Defrost | 50 | 60 |
| Cook | 65 | 80 |
| Rainbow Trout (6 oz.) (170 gm) | | |
| Defrost | 50 | 60 |
| Cook | 60 | 80 |
| Lobster Tail (5 oz.) (142 gm) | | |
| Defrost | 60 | 75 |
| Cook | 60 | 75 |
| Steak (8 oz.) (226 gm) | | |
| Defrost | 75 | 90 |
| **BAKERY ITEMS TO REHEAT** | | |
| ITEMS | | |
| Rolls (Sweet & Dinner) (7 oz.) (199 gm) | 10 | 15 |
| Pie (Fruit) (5 oz.) (142 gm) | 20 | 25 |
| Cake (3 oz.) (85 gm) | 10 | 15 |
| Apple Strudel (3 oz.) (85 gm) | 10 | 15 |

*Hobart

hot food 'specials.' Customers are offered a choice of hot dishes, usually with a choice of accompaniments, although occasionally a menu for such an operation will ask that substitutions not be made.

"There are several possible alternatives for microwave oven systems in such operations: individual packs of meat and separate 'individuals' of vegetables, or bulk packages of meats and vegetables, or combinations of the two systems.

"Frozen bulk packs to be defrosted and heated can be installed in pantry serving units from which food is dished to order. Since bulk packs never hold more than 18 portions, only the minimum is defrosted and heated to keep ahead of actual need, and food is never kept hot for more than a few minutes before serving. Bulk containers for microwave heating must be of plastic, glass, paper, or permanent ware, providing the permanent ware does not have any metal core or metal decoration.

"Traffic in such restaurants always tapers off toward the end of a serving period at which time the operator can switch to heating individual portions or plates, possibly even from the frozen state as orders come in. If substitutions are not to be permitted on the plate, the contents of the entire hot part of the meal can have been frozen together in a single dish."

## SPECIAL USES FOR MICROWAVE OVENS

Operators using microwave cookery point to inherent advantages such as these:

For certain foods, 8-second cooking time for each ounce of food from refrigerated temperature to 150° to 180°F. (66° to 82°C) Colder foods may take 10 seconds per oz. (28 gm) if food is not more than 1/2-in. (1.3 cm) deep. Frozen food takes about twice as long to defrost and heat as chilled food.

- Speedy defrosting—best results achieved when foods are defrosted in microwave oven, removed from cavity, then put back into microwave for separate heating to preferred service temperature.
- Reheating in small batches to assure short steamtable holding time.
- In hospitals, service of late trays and hold trays simplified because they can be made up at any time and served when they are called for. Even more important for hospitals is the possibility of introducing convenience-food systems utilizing microwave ovens at nourishment stations.
- Slack-time preparation of frozen foods for quick reconstitution during rush period.
- Use as back-up equipment to prevent running out of baked potatoes, casseroles, vegetables.

- Possibilities of featuring hot rolls, breads, and desserts.
- Minimal food waste.
- Increased menu variety.
- Lower labor costs.
- Portion control with consequent lower food cost.
- Inherent economy, as no power is wasted in microwave cooking.

## WHAT TO LOOK FOR IN PURCHASING

Easy operation is a feature of all units. Push buttons start oven heating for timer-controlled interval and opening door automatically shuts off heat.

To insure successful experience with a microwave installation, foodservice operations should look for these features in microwave ovens:

- Easy access to filter
- Possibility of separate power circuit if required by buyer
- Regulated supply of power
- Ease of maintenance
- Timer system with choice of controls, dial or push button
- Provisions for cooling
- Easy-set timer
- Safety provisions
- Signal system.

## SAFETY RULES

Safety for users of microwave ovens and the workers that service them is a primary concern with all manufacturers. Be sure to observe these safety rules:

- Follow manufacturer's instructions for recommended operating procedures.
- Before installation, check oven for evidence of shipping damage.
- Equip compartment doors with special interlocks that shut off the microwave generator automatically whenever the latch is opened. Hinges may contain additional switches. Never tamper with locks.

- Have door seal and a choke absorber for the machine to reduce microwave emission in the opening considerably below values specified as safe by U.S. government standards. (Standards for the microwave oven were established by the U.S. Dept. of HEW in The Performance Standard for Microwave Ovens 42CFR78-212 of the Dept. of HEW, 5 mw for the lifetime of the oven, 1 mw at point of acquisition by the customer). Never insert objects through door grill or around door seal.
- Keep metal containers out of ovens.
- Have automatic, thermal shut off to prevent fire. "No load" provisions are important to preserve life of tubes that provide the heat energy in microwave ovens. Employees should be aware of the damage that can be done to tubes through improper operation. Never operate an empty oven. If the tube is located in cavity, a paper cup half-filled with water will provide ample protection for some models if turned on when cavity is empty. In one model, automatic safety switches prevent damage to the tube if unloaded oven is turned on.

Users of microwave ovens should always (1) switch oven off before opening the door; (2) stay at least an arm's length away from the front of oven while it is on; (3) not operate damaged oven. No one except a qualified service person should try to adjust or repair a microwave oven.

Careful installation assures satisfactory operation of this equipment. One manufacturer offers these tips for his company's microwave unit:

1. Place the microwave oven on a table or stand so that user will have easy access to the cavity (cooking compartment).
2. Place unit where it will be protected from dirt, overhead leaks, or other possible sources of contamination.
3. This microwave oven is designed so that the filter will be kept clear. Do not permit filters to be obstructed. Restricting the air flow through the oven will reduce efficiency and, in some instances, may cause fuses to blow. Units may be installed in a line behind a false front, if desired.
4. Sufficient power is mandatory; most units now operate on 120 volts.

5. Make sure the area in front of the microwave oven is large enough so that the people using it will not block traffic. Swing-up doors in one model keep door from using aisle space and also get door out of way of operator during loading and unloading.

## MICROWAVE OVEN OPERATING PROCEDURES

To operate this type of microwave oven:

1. Push on button. Green light will come on. After a 5-second warm up, buzzer will sound, and oven is ready for continuous use.
2. Lift up door, place covered food in oven, closing door firmly. It must latch properly or the unit cannot be turned on.
3. Touch correct timer "touchplate" (seconds)—a small red light signals that plate is activated and a larger red light indicates oven is operating.
   or: Turn optional dial timer (minutes) to desired setting and touch plate. (To permit repeat setting, dial timer remains set).
4. When buzzer sounds (red lights go out), open door, remove food. If more time is needed, repeat Step 3.
5. At end of serving period, push off button and wipe oven clean.

Note: Whenever the door is opened, the cooking cycle will stop. To restart, close door firmly, and again touch proper plate.

Servicing some microwave ovens is made easy by a split outer case, which allows easy access to all electronic components. These units also have a special guard that protects the magnetron tube from destructive reflected energy.

## CLEANING PROCEDURES

Since dirt reduces oven efficiency, microwave ovens are designed to be cleaned easily. Employees should always keep in mind that oven-cleaning routines have to be followed carefully; comprehensive booklets of cleaning directions available from manufacturers for their ovens are good guides to follow.

Remove all grease, spatters, and spills from the cooking compartment. If left in the compartment, they will continue to cook on subsequent cycles until they become charred. After charring, they will continue to absorb microwave energy, cutting down efficiency, and may cause dish or shelf breakage. If the inside of the unit becomes spattered, wipe it with a paper towel or wash it out with a soft sponge or cloth dipped in warm water containing a mild detergent. To clean oven shelf, one manufacturer recommends placing a damp rag over oven shelf, turning oven on for 10 seconds, then wiping clean.

It is important to keep the door enclosure area and gasket free from grease build up. If not properly cared for, microwaves can leak. Filters on some models may also require cleaning. The splatter shield may be removed occasionally for thorough cleaning.

In many units, the shelf is built in. However, if the shelf is removable, remove the shelf from the compartment as often as necessary to keep the unit clean. Wash the interior surfaces of the compartment using a soft cloth dipped in warm water and mild detergent. Make sure that no food particles accumulate in the shelf supports. Rinse the surface with clear water and dry them with a soft cloth.

Wash the shelf with soap and water. Avoid harsh abrasive cleaners that will scratch the surfaces of the shelf and result in discoloration.

## SETTING UP TIME CHART

The production possibilities of the microwave ovens vary with the wattage capacity of the ovens. Typical heating times for products in microwave ovens have been charted by manufacturers of the equipment. However, operators who wish to develop a heating time chart for items served in their own operations can do so, using this procedure:

1. Determine portion size and shape and select suitable container. Set times for similar foods listed in time chart prepared by manufacturer.
2. Place each menu item scheduled for microwave heating in the oven in exactly the same portion size and shape in which it is to be served.

3. At the end of the cycle see if the food is at serving temperature, approx. 185°F. (85°C) If it is not, put it back and heat a little longer. Repeat until desired temperature is obtained, keeping track of time for each heating of item. Use a probe-type food thermometer.

With one unit that has push-button controls, it is possible to have manufacturer's technician readjust cooking times to meet needs of specific foodservice operation.

## BEST TO DEFROST FIRST

In a systematic production schedule, foods can be defrosted a day ahead, in a thawing refrigerator, in amounts to meet anticipated demand. In addition to the advantage of being ready, thawed foods require less energy to reach serving temperatures. Thawed items can be held safely at refrigerator temperatures for at least another day or two, if necessary.

If the needed amount of food is underestimated, follow the microwave system of defrost-rest-heat, described on pages 77 and 78.

It is generally known by now that microwave ovens will not crust and will not brown, except in the case of large meat products that require 10 or more minutes cooking time. While this is a disadvantage for some products, it is a distinct advantage for reconstituting frozen foods or prepared-in-advance products such as mashed potatoes. After a short period under the broiler or on the grill to prebrown, many items can be quickly finished in the microwave oven.

Microwave production works best if the cross-section or depth of food is not more than 2 in. (5 cm).

## "MUST" MATERIALS FOR PACKAGES, CONTAINERS, DISHES

Because microwave energy's effect on food is diminished and distorted if food is placed on metal containers, packaging must be of (1) plastic (polystyrene and polyethylene have proved successful); (2) glass or paper (plasticized paper containers are being made for use in microwave ovens); (3) permanent ware, providing dishes do not have a metal core or metal decorations.

Use this test to determine whether a container is suitable for microwave cooking:

Place a cup filled with water on or in dish to be tested. Place in microwave oven and set time for 1¼ minutes. When cup or dish has been in oven the allotted time, make these checks:

- If water is warm and dish is cool, dish can be used for cooking in microwave oven.
- If water is lukewarm and dish slightly warm around the edge, dish may be used to heat foods that require only a short period of time in a microwave oven.
- If the dish is quite warm or hot, and the water is cool, the dish should not be used because the dish is absorbing the microwaves. Its material could cause dish to break or prolong cooking time for food placed in it.

Specify appropriate container materials for all purchased foods, as well as those prepared on premises, that will be heated in microwave ovens. When products to be put in microwave ovens are prepared off premise, heating directions on the cover of the package speed operation.

## CHECKS FOR COMBINATIONS

Methods of presentating combination platters have been worked out so that all items will heat to the optimal state within the same period in the microwave oven. Recommendations based on manufacturers' research are now available for many combinations.

One manufacturer suggests this advance preparation:

For a platter containing a 6-oz. (170 gm) club steak, a 6-oz. (170 gm) baked potato, and 2 oz. (57 gm) of Brussels sprouts—"Presear steak to desired degree of doneness. Be sure that fat rim on steak is well charred. Place steak, with fat rim facing outward, on perimeter of plate. Cut prebaked potato into halves and place on perimeter. Place Brussels sprouts toward plate perimeter but slightly inside. Heat covered but permit steam to escape."

For a platter of meat balls (6-oz.) (170 gm), sauce (2 oz.) (57 gm), spaghetti (2 oz.) (57 gm) and broccoli (2 oz.) (57 gm)—"Place 3 meatballs, 2-oz. (57 gm) each, around perimeter of plate. Put some sauce over each meat ball. Place spaghetti in center of plate and divide broccoli evenly, placing at opposite ends of plate along edge. Heat covered but permit steam to escape."

For a platter of 4 oz. (114 gm) of sliced roast pork with 1 oz. (28 gm) gravy, 2½ oz. (71 gm) rice pilaf and 2½ oz. (71 gm) whole kernel corn—"All are easily-heated items and should be arranged evenly around perimeter of plate. Heat covered but permit steam to escape."

## ARRANGING FOOD ITEMS ON PLATE

When assembling combination platters such as roast beef, parslied boiled potatoes, and buttered Brussels sprouts, make sure there are no edges or thin slices of food overhanging the cooking container (stay within the well of the plate). Microwaves are emitted in a steady flow and heat thin edges far more rapidly than thicker food sections.

Some of the uncooked and raw foods that may be prepared in a microwave oven include: thin-sliced bacon, lobster tail, salmon steak, halibut steak, swordfish steak, brook trout, Idaho potatoes, and almost all vegetables.

Frozen items may be quickly defrosted by preheating in the microwave oven, then after a short period outside the oven, they may be returned to the microwave oven to be heated to serving temperatures. Defrosting possibilities in a 120 V. oven include: 8-oz. (226 gm) club steak—40 sec. (Heat for 20 sec. Turn product over. Heat for additional 20 sec.). 8-oz. (226 gm) lamb chops (2)—40 sec. (Place chops in container with bones against each other. Heat for 20 sec. Turn chops over and heat for additional 20 sec.) 8 oz. (226 gm) rainbow trout—40 sec. (same method as club steak above). Vegetables in pouch—50 sec. (heat for 50 sec. Remove from oven. Flatten and shape package. Allow product to rest 1 to 2 min.). All of the above items should be covered while heating.

To both defrost and heat in the microwave oven, allow a rest period, determined by the size of the item, between the defrosting and the heating operations to permit any last ice crystals to defrost completely. When time permits the defrosting of frozen foods far enough in advance of cooking time, place the food in the microwave oven for 3 seconds per oz. (28 gm). Then remove the food from the oven and let it stand at room temperature to finish defrosting.

Vegetables or other foods packaged in individual, plastic cooking pouches can be heated right in the bags. Be sure to puncture the top of the pouch before placing it in microwave oven. This lets steam escape during the heating process and prevents the bag from building up too much steam pressure.

To heat precooked entrees or casseroles faster in the microwave, cover them with a plastic banquet cover or an inverted paper (unwaxed) or china plate before slipping them into the oven. The steam created during the heating also helps to warm the food. Again, be sure to leave a vent for some of the steam to escape. Bread, pastry, and breaded products are an exception; they should be heated uncovered at low power.

## RAPID WARM UP FOR SANDWICHES

Sandwiches scheduled for rapid warm up in the microwave oven should have fillings that are fully precooked. Pretoast and cool the buns, then assemble and wrap sandwiches in open-end or perforated bags. As they are ordered, place them in the oven. Sandwiches heat very rapidly, so be careful not to overheat. Sliced meats on buns heat best if heaped on lightly with bulk of meat toward edge of bun.

The microwave oven cannot sense whether food placed in it has a temperature of 70°F. (21°C) or 40°F. (4°C). If 40 seconds of heating is needed to bring a portion from 70°F. (21°C) to 135°F. (57°C), then more time will obviously be needed to heat from 40°F. (4°C) to 135°F. (57°C). The variables in microwave heating are all dictated by the food item; its temperature, density, weight, and moisture content significantly affect the heating time needed.

## BRAIN TEASER—DECK AND REVOLVING OVENS

Have you learned all you should about ovens? Give yourself the following test and if you do not know the answers, go over the material a second time.

1. In modern kitchens ovens are used to: (a) _____

   (b) _____ (c) _____

2. Bake ovens have lower ( ) or higher ( ) cavities than roast ovens. (Check the right answer).

3. Roast ovens must have larger opening or cavity to cook (Fill in) _____ _____

   _____ _____.

4. In two-deck ovens, compartment which contains thermostat should be loaded (Fill in)

   _____ _____ This is always the lower compartment.

5. When putting pans in deck ovens, load shelves evenly and place pans away from (Fill in)

   _____ and also away from _____

6. List three ways to save energy when using oven:

   (1) _____ (2) _____ (3) _____

7. You can recognize a revolving tray oven because inside it are trays that go round like a (Fill in)

   _____

8. Revolving ovens are used to cook: (List three food items)

   (a) _____ (b) _____

   (c) _____

9. Food is loaded into revolving ovens on trays as they appear opposite door opening. Openings are

   arranged to keep (Fill in) _____ from coming out.

10. List 3 reasons why revolving ovens are easy to clean: (a) _____

   (b) _____ (c) _____.

   *(For correct answers, see page 250)*

## BRAIN TEASER—CONVECTION OVENS

1. What was the convection oven designed for? _____

   _____

2. How does it operate to lower cooking time? _____

   _____

3. Because air must circulate if the convection oven is to operate properly, it is important to: (Check right answer.)

   a. Put pans close together _____

   b. Leave room around each pan _____

   c. Turn pans of food frequently _____

4. A multi-shelf mobile oven rack can be loaded with food in preparation area, rolled into rack convection oven and when foods are through cooking in the oven, the rack can be rolled out and on to serving area. True ____ False ____ (Check answer)

5. List six foods that can be prepared in a convection oven.

   _____  _____  _____

   _____  _____  _____

6. Shelves in convection oven (need to be carefully arranged) (can be put in any way) (Cross out wrong answer.)

7. In convection oven with fan that operates while oven is on, be sure fan is on "off" when oven is being loaded with food. True ____ False ____

8. It is important that foods to be loaded into oven be placed near the oven so that doors_____

   _____(Complete sentence.)

9. What kind of light bulbs should be used in convection ovens?_____

   Why?_____

10. What is the biggest single cause of uneven baking?_____

    _____(Fill in.)

*(For correct answers, see page 250)*

## BRAIN TEASER—MICROWAVE OVENS

1. Name two ways a microwave oven can be used. _____

   _____

2. Microwave heat is produced by short radio waves called microwaves. These waves are also used in _____ (Fill in.)

3. Microwave energy produces heat inside and on the surface of the food at the same time. This (speeds up) (slows down) cooking. (Cross out wrong answer.)

4. What is the controlling factor in cooking food in microwave ovens? _____

5. It takes how much more time to cook 10 lb. (5.4 kg) of the same food in a microwave oven than it takes to cook 1 lb. (453 gm)(Fill in.)_____

   _____

6. List three food items that can be cooked in microwave ovens:_____

   _____

   _____

7. Name one way in which microwave ovens are made safe to operate:_____

   _____

8. Food particles cannot be left in a microwave oven because_____

   _____(Complete sentence.)

9. Since dirt reduces their efficiency, microwave ovens have been designed to be (easy) (hard) to clean. (Cross out wrong answer.)

10. Which of the following containers cannot be used when heating food in microwave ovens? Plastic _____ Glass _____ Paper _____ Metal _____ (Check right answer.)

    *(For correct answers, see page 250)*

**FIGURE   3.2**
When Marshall Field & Co., Chicago's landmark department store, "went suburban" with foodservice locations, they chose 10 radiant heat quartz ovens to reconstitute the frozen items to be featured on the shopping center menus. These were foods that had been successfully frozen for retail sale for many years, and the quartz oven in the downtown kitchen proved successful in bringing them up to serving temperature. Entrees are usually packed in 1/3-, 1/4-, and 1/2-sized aluminum foil steam table pans.

**FIGURE   3.3**
Roast duck, a specialty of the Louisville, Ky. Hyatt-Regency Hotel, is prepared in convection ovens. See-through doors make it easy to check roasting progress.

**FIGURE    3.4**
Roll-in rack for this convection oven is 32¾ in. wide by 27⁷⁄₁₆ in. deep by 59¹³⁄₁₆ in. high (832 mm by 697 mm by 1520 mm). Oven has a 60-minute timer and switches that provide either high or low heat in either compartment.

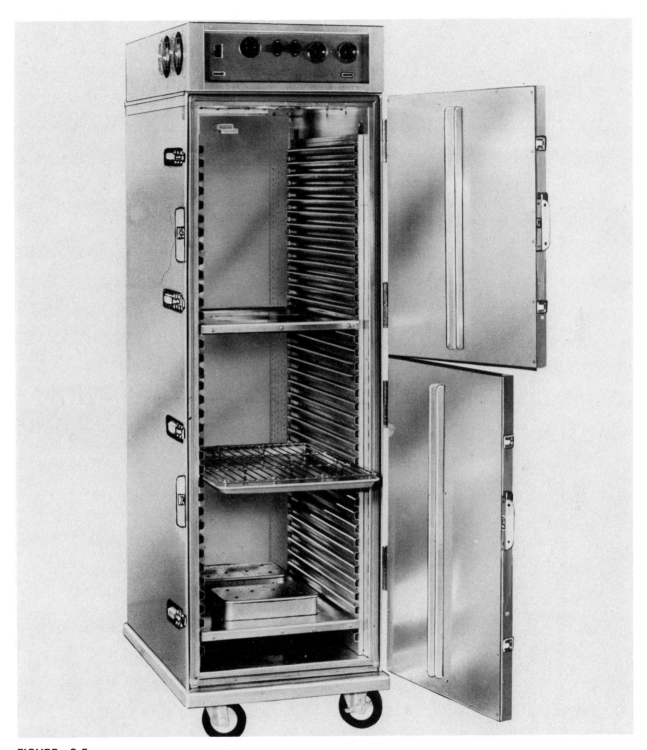

**FIGURE   3.5**
Mobile convection oven cabinet takes less than 6 ft. (182.9 cm) of floor space, provides temperature range from 150° to 350°F. (66 to 177°C). Recommended for slow cooking, roasting, and baking, with research on slow roasting indicating that a 5 to 7 percent reduction in meat shrinkage is possible. Oven cabinet is 23¼ in. (59 cm) wide by 33½ in. (85 cm) deep by 81¾ in. (207.6 cm) high and has spaces for 37 18- by 26-in. (46- by 66-cm) pans.

**FIGURE   3.6**
This gas bake and roast oven in Atlanta's Admiral Benbow Inn provides fine dining menu items for the luxurious entertainment areas as well as the restaurant and coffee shop.

**FIGURE   3.7**
Self-basting potato cakes, shaped in 3-oz. (85 gm) triangles, cook and brown in 5 minutes in quartz oven at Arby's Restaurant, Edmonds, Washington. The oven's radiant plate heaters covering top and bottom oven surfaces emit high intensity infrared heat that penetrates all foods uniformly.

**FIGURE   3.8**
Four double deck convection ovens are basic to meeting production demands at the Commonwealth Convention Center in Louisville, Ky. Banquet food for 3000 to 400 with menus featuring Coquilles St. Jacques or Breast of Chicken Mornay with Peach Cardinal are frequently served. Ovens are also flexible enough to operate satisfactorily for groups in the 100 to 1000 range. Complete foodservice for 5000 patrons at one time was the goal set for the Center which is designed for middle-sized conventions in the 5000 to 9000 range.

**FIGURE  3.9**
The ovens at the rear of this picture are designed for roll-in operation. Modular pans are stacked on racks prior to baking. The Food Service Facilities of the California Highway Patrol Academy, Bryte, Ca. has adopted a 12- by 20-in. (30- by 51-cm) model for all use to minimize handling.

**FIGURE 3.10**
Double convection ovens back up Doctor's Hospital's foodservice goal of preparing all pastry and bread products from raw to done on-premise. The bakery area in the Tulsa, Okla. hospital is also equipped with a tilting kettle, reach-in refrigerator, open burner unit, mixer on stand, and sink. Baked items for nearly 7000 meals per week come out of this compact area.

**FIGURE   3.11**
Roasts and baked potatoes are produced from this support station at Bob Burns Restaurant. Two even heat-top ranges with ovens beneath them and a convection oven with a holding oven under it provide items for 225 patrons who lunch from 11:30 to 2 P.M. and 350 who dine from 7 to 9:30 P.M.

**FIGURE 3.12**
These three ovens enable bake shop production to meet needs of 450-seat cafeteria and 567 bed hospital (34,000 meals per week) at Memorial Hospital System, Houston.

**FIGURE   3.13**
A rotary oven turns out the on-premise baked items so welcome at York (Pa.) Hospital. This well-equipped bake shop has its own range with two open burners and a hot top, and two tilting steam kettles.

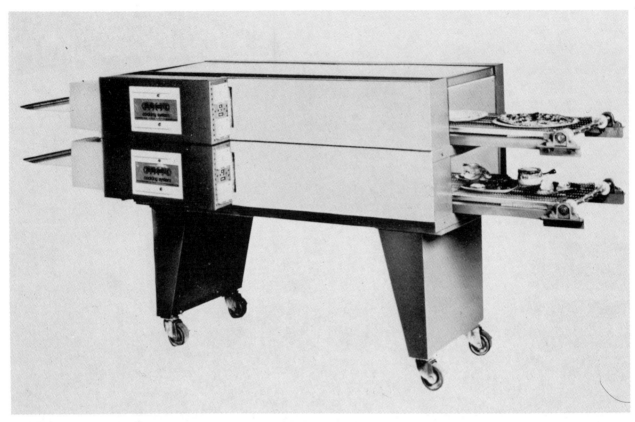

**FIGURE   3.14**
This in-line conveyorized infrared oven moves food in a straight line through the heat tunnel. Tunnel can be narrow or wide depending on items to be cooked in it. Additional decks can be stacked on the oven. A wide in-line model is available with 1 to 6 decks.

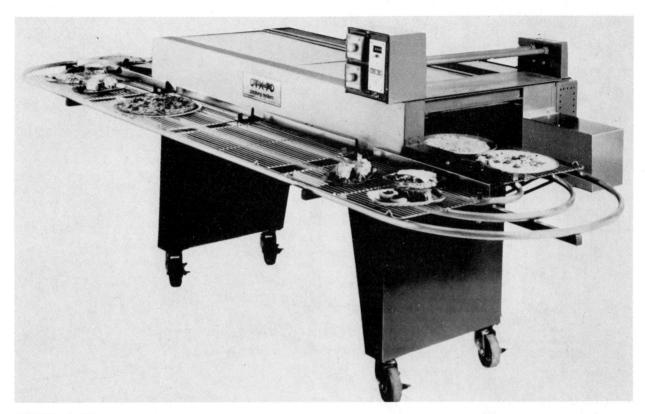

**FIGURE   3.15**
In a return conveyorized infrared oven the food moves in a loop around the oven, passing through a heat tunnel at the back. This permits flexible loading or unloading as pans may be taken off or put on at any point on the conveyor outside the heat tunnel. Additional decks or tiers can be added as menu changes require.

**FIGURE  4.1**
Griddle on semi-exhibition entree cooking line at Foxfire Restaurant, Anaheim, Ca. is part of a pleasant and safe environment. Glazed, earth-toned tile provides an attractive background for griddle activity. A well-maintained exhaust-ventilating system in the hood has coated, flush-mounted, removable filters. Filters are cleaned weekly. Hood is also easy to clean since it has a smooth, highly polished, stainless steel interior and flush-mounted, vapor-proof lights. Grease-collecting receptacles are removable for easy cleaning, and the nozzle above the griddle is part of a dry chemical fire control system.

# Chapter Four

# Griddles and Grills

A key question faced by foodservice operators today is how to turn out food fast enough to satisfy patrons in a hurry or to keep up with the high-volume kitchen production schedules that must be maintained. The answer: the griddle.

For the griddle to fill the needs of the operation, these factors must be considered:

- proper capacity
- choice between mobile and built-in models
- motion- and space-saving patterns of operation
- opportunities for energy saving

## SAVING ENERGY AT THE GRIDDLE

Energy-saving use of griddles requires these procedures: (1) heat only the area of the griddle needed for product to be prepared; (2) choose lowest setting possible for satisfactory product; (3) cover the surface as completely as possible to keep heat from being wasted and from going into the room where it may add to worker discomfort; (4) keep griddle clean.

A new method of conducting heat across a griddle surface provides the entire surface with uniform heat and will cook products evenly at temperatures up to 400°F. (204°C).

The heat-pipe principle involves heating liquid under vacuum beneath a 12-gauge stainless steel surface. The heated fluid vaporizes, condenses under the griddle surface, and then falls back to the evaporator.

Wherever food is placed it creates a cold spot that causes a low-pressure area. Then the hot vapor immediately rushes to that spot allowing instant heat recovery.

This design reduces energy needs by 30 to 40 per cent. A solid-state touch control panel also saves energy by permitting unit to be turned down to "warm" or "off" during slow periods. The control panel is composed of solid-state electrical modular parts so if problems occur, replacement is easy, with minimal delays in production. Users report that even though eggs cook faster on the surface, meat cooks at lower temperatures for less shrinkage and juicier products.

Fuel saving is also significant with a griddle equipped with four precision thermostats and multiple elements. The operator can use 1/4, 1/2, 3/4, or entire surface, saving power on parts of griddle not needed. This griddle comes in the following size:

| DIMENSIONS (WIDTH-DEPTH-HEIGHT) | OUTPUT | VOLTAGE | WATTAGE |
|---|---|---|---|
| 36½ × 29⁹⁄₁₆ × 8 in. (92.7 × 75 × 20.3 cm) | 975 burgers/Hr. | 208 or 230 | 16.0 KW |

A larger model with 2 × 6 ft. (5 × 15.2 cm) of griddling surface has eight precision thermostats that control 1/8, or any multiple, of the solid, ½-in. (1.3 cm) thick, leakproof, polished steel top. Each control has its own signal light. This griddle can turn out more than 102 griddle cakes or 133 hamburgers per loading, an hourly output of 1,950 burgers.

The griddle can be a constant help in providing the cooked-to-order items that patrons translate as "somebody cares." It is the key to breakfast business in wide-ranging operations where a trained operator working off a clean griddle turns out bacon and eggs to King Customer's taste.

Garnishes from the griddle help to create merchandised features in many dining rooms; in others, the menu flexibility that is a by-product of this equipment brings in off-hour volume.

## TELLING GRILL FROM GRIDDLE

There is no spectator sport with more appeal than watching food cook. To capitalize on the pleasure the public is known to derive from the sight, sound, and smell of menu items being prepared, more and more foodservice operations are spotlighting their griddle and grill units. Existing equipment is being moved to more attention-getting positions in some operations while others are adding new units to capitalize on the merchandising plus of short-order cooking.

In any discussion of griddles and grills, the first challenge is apt to be "define your terms." Generally the griddle is described as a flat-top appliance, usually heated from beneath by gas or electricity, with a cooking surface ranging from 7 in. (17.8 cm) wide by 14 in. (35.6 cm) deep up to 69 in. (175.3 cm) wide by 24 in. (61 cm) deep.

The grill is a cooking unit similar to a griddle except that food cooks on top of a griddle, whereas the grill has two heated surfaces. Food placed between the two surfaces cooks simultaneously from top and bottom in a grill.

Because of the close construction relationship between griddles and grills, many of the findings reported here apply to both pieces of equipment, so, except where information is specific to the grill, the term griddle will be used.

What kind of food production can be expected from a griddle? Any answer to that question must recognize that the production possibilities of the griddle depend more on the efficiency of the operator than is the case with any other piece of foodservice equipment.

## HOW MUCH CAN THEY COOK?

However, as a yardstick for relating equipment to need capacity, manufacturers list such peak-time potential as the following:

| Griddle Surface | Potential Output |
|---|---|
| 18 × 20 in. (45.7 × 50 cm) | 160 eggs or 240 hamburgers per hour |
| 24 × 36 in. (61 × 91.4 cm) | 720 4-oz. (114 gm) hamburgers per hour |
| 18 × 42 in. (45.7 × 106.7 cm) | 120 griddle cakes or 600 hamburgers or frankfurters per hour |
| 24 × 48 in. (61 × 122 cm) | 1080 4-oz. (114 gm) hamburgers or 2160 4-in. (10 cm) diameter pancakes |
| 646 sq. in. (4168 cm²) | of griddle space, 675¼ lb. (114 gm) hamburgers per hour |
| 864 sq. in. (5574 cm²) | of griddle space, 1020¼ lb. (114 gm) hamburgers per hour |

Griddle capacity has also been translated from inches to numbers of food items that can be accommodated. A 24-in. (61 cm) griddle with a surface area of 432 sq. in. (2787 cm²) is capable of handling 32 hamburgers, 30 eggs, or 12 4-oz. (114

**GRIDDLE CAPACITY***

One manufacturer of griddles has charted the food capacity of three models as:

| Food | Capacity | | |
|---|---|---|---|
| | 24" × 36" (61 × 91.4 cm) | 32" × 36" (81.3 × 91.4 cm) | 32" × 72" (81.3 × 182.9 cm) |
| Hamburgers [4-oz. (114 gm) servings, 3½-in. (8.9 cm) diam.] | 48 | 60 | 120 |
| Beef Tenderloins [5-oz., (142 gm) 1-in. (2.5 cm) thick] | 36 | 45 | 90 |
| Minute Steaks [4-oz., (114 gm) ½-in. (1.3 cm) thick] | 18 | 22 | 44 |
| Bacon [22 to 32 slices per lb. (453 gm)] | 6 lb. (2.7 kg) | 7½ lb. (3.4 kg) | 16 lb. (7.3 kg) |
| Pork Sausages [1½-oz. (43 gm) servings, 3½-in. (8.9 cm)] | 45 | 56 | 112 |
| Fish Cakes [2-oz. (57 gm) servings, 3½-in. (8.9 cm)] | 45 | 56 | 112 |
| Fried Eggs | 45 | 56 | 112 |
| Griddle Cakes [4-in. (10 cm) diam.] | 32 | 40 | 80 |
| Fried Potatoes (servings) | 15–18 | 20–25 | 40–50 |
| Ham Steaks [1 lb. (453 gm) tenderized, 1/2-in. (1.3 cm) thick] | 18 | 22 | 44 |
| Liver [3-oz. (85 cm) slices, 3/8-in. (1 cm) thick] | 27 | 35 | 70 |
| Fried Onions (servings) | 60 | 75 | 150 |

**PRODUCTION POTENTIAL***

**Drop-in Griddles**

| Overall Body Dimensions | | | | | | Grid Surface Dimensions | | | | | | Temperature Range | |
|---|---|---|---|---|---|---|---|---|---|---|---|---|---|
| Width | | Depth | | Height Above Top | | Width | | Depth | | Area | | | |
| in. | cm | in. | cm | in. | cm | in. | cm | in. | cm | sq. in. | sq. cm | °F. | °C |
| 24¹³⁄₁₆ | 63 | 23½ | 59.7 | 1/4 | 0.6 | 22⁵⁄₁₆ | 56.7 | 17¹⁵⁄₁₆ | 45.6 | 400 | 2600 | 200–450 | 93–232 |
| 24¹³⁄₁₆ | 63 | 29½ | 75 | 1/4 | 0.6 | 22⁵⁄₁₆ | 56.7 | 23⁵⁄₁₆ | 59.2 | 533 | 3465 | 200–450 | 93–232 |

**Typical Production**

| Preheat Time (Minutes to 350°F. (177°C)) | Hamburgers (2½ oz., (71 gm) 3½" (3.8 cm) diam.) | | Pancakes (4"(10 cm) diam.) | | Minute Steaks (4-oz. (226 gm), ½"(3.8 cm) thick) | | Fried Eggs | |
|---|---|---|---|---|---|---|---|---|
| | Qty./ Load | Qty./ Hour | Qty./ Load | Qty./ Hour | Qty./ Load | Qty./ Hour | Qty./ Load | Qty./ Hour |
| 8 | 32 | 480+ | 21 | 260–320 | 12 | 145 | 30 | 450+ |
| 8 | 42 | 630 | 36 | 450–550 | 16 | 192 | 40 | 600 |

*General Electric Company

gm) minute steaks at one time. A fast preheat, high-production unit with a 1663 sq. in. (10810 cm²) griddle surface can produce the following hourly quantities: 2400 + 2½ oz. (71 gm), 3½-in. (8.9 cm) diam. hamburgers (120 per load); 900 + 4-in. (10 cm) pancakes (80 per load); and 700 + 4-oz. (114 gm) 1/2-in. (1.3 cm) thick minute steaks (48 per load).

The two charts above also indicate how much griddles can cook.

In estimating griddle production rates, remember that the operator has to perform three operations to cook each item: loading, turning, and unloading. Capacity to turn out 1080 hamburgers an hour means the operator must perform 3240 cooking operations in 3600 seconds. These do not include picking up plates, folding rolls, or similar dish-up tasks.

In addition to griddle capacity, there are other features to investigate when considering a griddle:

- Type of metal; shape
- Attractive appearance if visible to customers
- Ease of installation
- Drainage run positioned so that scrapings can be moved out of the way as rapidly as possible with minimum motion and effort
- Rate of heat introduction, retention, and recovery adequate for speedy production
- Ease of cleaning
- Minimum maintenance.

To obtain adequate griddle capacity for an operation, two small griddles or a large griddle and a sandwich grill may prove satisfactory.

## TRENDS IN INSTALLATION

Two installation trends have been reported: (1) the use of built-in equipment in small to medium size operations (the sanitation advantage of built-in equipment is generally recognized); (2) where high production must be scheduled, the almost universal requirement that equipment be placed on mobile stands, so it can be rolled out from walls or from underneath the canopy for thorough cleaning.

Special modifications in griddle design are also increasing, such as requests for special location of the grease trough, a special shelf attached to the front of the griddle, or a special temperature control that permits toasting buns on a griddle.

A successful part of planning for one labor-efficient restaurant featuring Mexican foods is the use of the grill or griddle in tortilla preparation. Flour tortillas are the staple of much of the menu at Ninfa's Tacos Al Carbon, Inc., Houston. They are rolled and grilled at one end of the cooking and serving line, then supplied hot to the various serving stations as needed.

At the Bob Burns Restaurant, Woodland Hills, CA, the entree cooking line contains a variety of equipment to meet the needs of a diversified menu. Among the units is a built-in griddle with a refrigerated base. The refrigerated base has self-closing drawers as an aid to fast griddle performance.

## PRESS SPEEDS BURGER COOKING

A device to speed griddle cooking of quarter-pound burgers has been developed and use-tested in Tastee Freeze units. It is a hand-held press with heat ducts that penetrate the patties. Shaped like a plasterer's trowel, the press is made of sandwiched aluminum, approx. $5 \times 11 \times 1/4$-in. ($12.7 \times 28 \times 0.6$ cm) thick. It works through insertion of stainless pins into the burger. Cooking time is reduced from the former 4½ to 5 min. to 90 seconds.

In a test run, each unit had three presses connected to a timer that signalled the operator when to turn the patties and when to remove them. Reported energy savings ranged from 10 to 15 per cent. In addition, it was found that most grill thermostats could be reduced by 25° to 50°F. (4° to 10°C).

The size and shape of the press can be varied to fit different types of foods and griddles. For example, a 26-in. (66 cm) press can handle five burgers at a time. However, burgers smaller than quarter-pounders (114 gm) cannot be cooked with this device because they are too thin.

The press is also useful for other boneless meats—bacon takes 45 to 60 seconds without turning; link and pattie sausages approximately 30 to 45 seconds without blanching. A thawed breakfast steak can be ready in about 90 seconds per side.

The press can cook frozen meats faster without defrosting than they normally take after thawing, so handling, staging, and shrinkage are reduced. A frozen quarter-pound (114 gm) burger takes about 55 seconds on each side.

The press is always left standing in direct contact with the grill so that it is always ready to go. It must be preheated for 20 minutes before initial use.

Carefully planned methods that speed griddle use have been successfully developed in many operations. One hamburger chain has evolved a griddle set up that helps the company meet its goal: Serving three customers completely, including making change, every two minutes.

Proper controls are essential to good griddling. In small units, one thermostat may control the entire griddle, permitting a temperature range of 200° to 450°F. (93° to 232°C) A signal light indicates unit is on and when it reaches desired temperature. Where surface is sectioned, individual thermostats can control each section, using the same type of signal lights.

## INSTRUCTIONS INCREASE GRIDDLE OUTPUT

These detailed instructions have increased griddle output of fast-selling items at the White Spot Drive-Ins, Vancouver, B. C.:

### Preliminary Preparation

1. Cut Grade A, boneless beef chucks in 3-in. (7.6 cm) pieces.
2. Use suet in the proportion of 1 lb. (453 gm) suet to 5 lb. (2.3 kg) lean beef.
3. Combine lean beef and suet and mix well.
4. Grind only once through a 3/16 plate on food chopper.
5. Mold hamburgers in automatic machine using 1/4-in. (6 mm) plate, making 6 patties per lb. (453 gm) (As each patty is molded, it drops on a piece of wax paper separating the patties.)
6. Refrigerate until ready for cooking.

### Final Preparation

7. Place patty on hot griddle and cook until juices show on the surface of the hamburger.
8. Turn patty over to finish cooking.
9. Once the patty is browned, season with White Spot's special seasoning.
10. Prepare bun. While patty is cooking, split bun and toast.
11. Place each bun half on griddle, face up. Dress each half with White Spot's special seasoning.
12. On one half, place hamburger.
13. If ordered, top hamburger with cheese, onion, sauteed mushrooms, bacon, or lettuce and tomatoes.
14. Top with the other half of the toasted bun.

15. Cut bun in half. Garnish with a long slice of dill pickle.
16. Place bun on serving plate and serve at once.
17. If there is any delay in the bun being picked up, keep piping hot under infrared quartz lamp on counter.

## MULTIPLE PATTY FLIPPER

In addition to time-saving instructions, special equipment has been devised in some operations to speed output. In McDonald hamburger operations, a multiple-patty flipper turns 36 hamburgers at once.

Pancake production has been speeded in a university foodservice where one worker pours batter onto the griddle and a second worker turns the cakes.

The White Tower Management Corporation has determined the most efficient rotation methods, and adheres strictly to these methods to keep production on their griddles at the optimum. The Stouffer organization achieves griddle control via recipes. Recipes for griddle items specify both the temperature for cooking and the amount to be cooked to obtain maximum capacity.

Sectioning the griddle and requiring employees to adhere strictly to the section set up save time and energy as heat can be carefully related to product. One section of the griddle can be reserved for hotcakes, one for bacon and ham, and one for potatoes. No other food is cooked in these sections to assure proper heat control and cooking for each food at all times. In one hamburger operation, the tops and bottoms of buns are each cooked at a separate temperature.

Operations with fairly limited production needs are specifying rotary grills that cook food items to required degree of doneness. In some models, blade then moves finished item into pan.

### Roving Griddles

Portable griddles in the residence halls at Northern Illinois University in DeKalb get maximum use. The movable griddles are located under the hood in the kitchen when used for frying heavy items such as steaks and chops. This position makes it convenient for the cooks to transfer browned items to the rotary oven. At breakfast and lunch time the griddles are moved into the cafeteria line to fry eggs, pancakes, french toast, and sandwiches to order. A hood is provided for them in this location also.

## GRIDDLE TIMES, TEMPERATURES

Proper temperatures and proper timing need to be worked out for the most frequently cooked items. Griddle operators should observe these recommendations suggested as a guide until the operation's own rates are set:

### SUGGESTED COOKING GUIDE FOR GRIDDLE ITEMS

| Food | Control Set | Time in Minutes |
|---|---|---|
| Hamburgers | 350 F.(177C) | 3.4 |
| Cheeseburgers | 350 F.(177C) | 3.4 |
| Cheese Sandwich | 375 F.(190C) | 3.4 |
| Ham Salad Sandwich | 375 F.(190C) | 3.4 |
| Frankfurters | 325 F.(163C) | 2.3 |
| Minute Steak—medium | 400 F.(204C) | 3.4 |
| Club Steaks—inch thick, med. | 400 F.(204C) | 3.5 |
| Ham Steaks | 375 F.(190C) | 3.4 |
| Beef Tenderloin | 400 F.(204C) | 3.4 |
| Boiled Ham | 375 F.(190C) | 2 |
| Corn Beef Patties | 350 F.(177C) | 2.3 |
| Bacon | 350 F.(177C) | 2.3 |
| Canadian Bacon | 350 F.(177C) | 2.3 |
| Sausage Links | 350 F.(177C) | 3 |
| Sausage Patties | 350 F.(177C) | 3 |
| French Toast | 350 F.(177C) | 2.3 |
| Pancakes | 375 F.(190C) | 2 |
| American Fries | 375 F.(190C) | 3.4 |
| Potato Patties | 375 F.(190C) | 3.4 |
| Scrambled Eggs | 300 F.(149C) | 1.2 |
| Hard Fried Eggs | 300 F.(149C) | 3 |
| Soft Fried Eggs | 300 F.(149C) | 2 |
| Sunny-Side-Up Eggs | 300 F.(149C) | 2 |

When cooking temperature over 350°F. (177°C) is required and griddle needs to be heated, set thermostat 25° (15°C) below desired temperature for first 10 minutes, then reset for desired temperature for remainder of cooking time. This procedure is suggested because, on the first cycle, griddles overshoot temperature and the initial low setting will save heat.

## CLEANING AND MAINTENANCE

Set a routine for cleaning and maintenance. Griddle cleaning is a daily procedure, performed by the griddle man in most operations. The time involved in griddle cleaning is more easily accepted when compared with the time required to wash the number of pots and pans that would otherwise be used. A material—silicone spray—has been developed that holds a griddle surface and reduces cleaning requirements.

Be sure to remove completely the protective grease that covers a new griddle. If heat is applied before this rust-preventative coating is removed, the griddle may be permanently discolored.

### Seasoning Prevents Sticking

Griddles must be correctly "seasoned" so foods will not stick during cooking. "Seasoning" means covering griddle surface with a partially carbonized fat coating that will keep foods from sticking. Griddles must also be reseasoned after cleaning.

The preferred procedure for "seasoning" a new or clean griddle: (1) set griddle at 375°–400°F. (190°–204°C); (2) pour special griddle-seasoning fat on surface; (3) let fat heat till it smokes; (4) wipe griddle surface; (5) pour on second coating of fat; (6) heat fat till it smokes; (7) wipe down. Griddle is now ready for use.

### Never Strike A Griddle Surface With A Spatula

Removing all carbon from griddle between each batch is done most easily with a very sharp spatula. However, workers should be trained never to strike the griddle surface with the edge of a spatula. Most griddle surfaces can be nicked or damaged by a blow from the edge of a spatula.

### Cleaning Routine

One operation, that sets "hospital-clean" griddle standards, demands that every morning the griddle look as if it had just come from the factory. The routine includes cleaning, scouring, and bleaching. Griddles are cleaned while still warm, then allowed to cool before being scoured and polished. The first thing in the morning they are washed with soap and water, then bleached, and a very light coating of oil is applied.

One manufacturer of gas griddles advises this daily cleaning procedure:

1. Make sure griddle surface is warm, not hot. About 150° to 175°F. (66° to 79°C) is recommended.
2. Remove large loose particles with a spatula.
3. Pour special griddle cleaner on surface adjusting the amount used to the size of the griddle: a 24-in. (61 cm) griddle requires 1/2 cup (0.1 l); 36-in. (91.4 cm), 3/4 cup (0.2 l); 48-in. (122 cm), 1 cup (0.25 l); 60 to 72-in. (152.4 to 182.9 cm), 1½ cup (0.36 l).
4. Spread over surface with a cloth. Let stand 5–10 min.
5. Wipe or scrape into drain trough.
6. Sponge surface with enough water to remove all residue.
7. Wipe surface dry with cloth or sponge.
8. Grease surface with cooking fat and proceed with cooking.

The daily cleaning of electric griddles is outlined as follows:

After each use, scrape surface with a stiff metal spatula. Daily, wipe chrome surfaces with damp, slightly-soaped cloth; pay special attention to switches and thermostat. Empty and clean grease receptacles and drip tray. Keep temperature lower during periods of little use.

In addition, users of electric griddles are advised once every week to use pumice or griddle stone over surface. Clean with the grain of the metal while surface is warm; avoid steel wool because it may get in the food or scratch the surface. Wipe cord and plug with dry cloth to prevent too much grease absorption.

## Quarterly Check Up

At Northern Illinois University, DeKalb, the preventive maintenance person checks such things as fuses, thermostats, switches, and controls four times a year. This person checks each grill on campus monthly for items such as level-cooking surface, condition of cooking surface, and heating units.

## MENU ITEMS FROM THE GRIDDLE

Suggested menu items to schedule for griddle production include:

- Stuffed Lamb Patties made of lean ground lamb mixed with bread crumbs, salt, pepper, marjoram or rosemary, beaten eggs, and milk. Use a no. 16 scoop to portion patties. Place a thin slice of tomato and one of onion on each patty top the stack with a second patty. The edges of the two patties are pressed together and the stuffed patties are grilled 10 minutes per side.
- For a Neptune Burger, prepare tunaburger mixture to be shaped into patties in a hamburger molder. Mix flaked tuna, slightly beaten egg yolks, fine bread crumbs, melted shortening, salt, and pepper. Portion with a no. 12 scoop, shape patty, and cook on griddle until delicately browned. Canned salmon, codfish flakes, or other fish may be alternated with tuna.
- Schedule chops for browning on the griddle during slack periods; bake in the oven in time for meal service.
- One-half inch (1.3 cm) slices of canned corned beef hash can be speedily served from the griddle.
- Canadian bacon will not curl on the griddle if five small slits are made around the edges before cooking.
- American-fried potatoes are reputation-building when 1 tbsp. (0.015 l) cream per portion is added to cooked, sliced, and seasoned potatoes before griddling.
- A popular French toast formula reads: 1 loaf bread, 3 eggs, 1/2 tsp. (3 gm) soda, 2 cups (0.5 l) milk combined for dipping.
- Peaches prepared on a griddle make an excellent accompaniment for meat and poultry items. If canned wedges are used, they should be well drained. If fresh peaches are used, 1/4-in (6 mm) crosswise slices work best.
- A quick trick for Western sandwich makers—pour egg mixture on large griddle and cut it into sandwich-size portions when turning.
- Pineapple slices are an excellent griddle item. Remove canned pineapple from can and drain. Peel and slice fresh pineapple and hold in sugar after cooking.

- Fish portions from the griddle gain luxury appeal from a topping of spicy tomato sauce filled with flaked lobster.
- Apple rings sprinkled with brown sugar and cinnamon and then cooked on the griddle add color to meat entrees.

## Promotable Pancakes

Pancake appeal continues to set new records. Here are several tips that will keep quality high:

If pancakes are raw inside, the griddle temperature was too high. If they are tough, too light in color, or leathery in taste, look for one of these causes—temperature too high; cooking period too short; cooking period too long and temperature too low; pancakes turned more than once during cooking period; batter improperly prepared.

If pancakes stick to griddle surface, the surface may have been (1) improperly seasoned, (2) too lightly greased, or (3) incorrectly cleaned.

For best results, do not stack pancakes after cooking. Steam between pancakes makes them soggy and spoils flavor. Overlap pancakes instead for better taste, texture, and customer appeal. If necessary, stack only long enough for quick serving.

When preparing pancakes with berries or fruit in the batter, you may need to grease griddle more heavily.

Use only fresh, good quality butter, because pancakes have such a mild flavor that they may be ruined by strong butter. Whipped butter may be flavored with syrup, honey, or ground fruit.

For a hearty pancake, add shredded dried beef to pancake batter (4 oz. (114 gm) beef for each lb. (453 gm) of dry pancake mix). Offer a tangy cheese sauce as accompaniment.

Sausage pancakes with cinnamon-applesauce are made by adding cooked sausage bits to pancake batter and substituting sausage fat for usual shortening. Offer hot, cinnamon-flavored applesauce as a topping.

Apple pancakes are a popular pork accompaniment. For each lb. (453 gm) of pancake mix, add 3/4 qt. (339.8 gm) peeled and chopped apples, 2 tsp. (12 gm) cinnamon, and 2 tbsp (28 gm) sugar.

## Good Grilled Sandwiches

When preparing cheese sandwiches to be grilled, spread with butter that has been kept at room temperature. Cheese for sandwiches can be held at room temperature up to 4 hours. Sprinkle oregano over cheese for unique flavor.

A good mixture for grilled ham-salad sandwiches combines 1/2 cup (114 gm) mayonnaise, 1/2 cup (114 gm) sweet-pickle relish, and 1 lb. (453 gm) ground meat.

For a novel, yet substantial, grilled sandwich, arrange thin slices of turkey or chicken on a slice of bread, dip avocado slices in lime juice, sprinkle with salt and pepper, place on sandwich and cover with second slice of bread. Dip sandwich in egg batter and grill in melted butter until brown.

Put oregano-sprinkled slices of mozzarella cheese between slices of Italian bread; dip in egg-milk; grill.

**BRAIN TEASER—GRIDDLES**

1.  Heat for griddles usually comes from (above) (below) flat top. (Circle right answer.)

2.  Food cooked on a grill is placed between two surfaces and heat comes
    from _____ and _____ to cook both sides at once. (Fill in right answer.)

3.  Griddles are often located (where people can watch them) (out of sight). (Cross out wrong answer.)

4.  Griddle output has been increased in many operations by: (Place check after right answers)

    a.  Special instructions _____       e.  Sectioning surface of griddles _____

    b.  Use of steam kettle _____        f.  Following recipes _____

    c.  Special equipment _____          g.  Time control _____

    d.  Dividing griddle jobs between      h.  A mixer _____
        workers _____

5.  Temperature and cooking times for griddle items (are not important) (should be carefully followed).
    (Cross out wrong answer.)

6.  Griddles should be cleaned (daily) (monthly). (Cross out wrong answer.)

7.  Why should griddles be seasoned? _____

    _____

8.  When should griddles be seasoned? _____

    _____

9.  Name four foods that are often cooked on a griddle.

    _____  _____  _____  _____

10. When a scraper is used to clean the griddle, why should the worker be careful never to strike the
    griddle with the edge of the scraper?_____

    _____

*(For correct answers, see page 250)*

**FIGURE   4.2**
There are two groupings of equipment like the above at the Louisville (Ky.) Convention Center to produce food for separate banquets scheduled at the same time. Equipment includes heavy duty gas range fry top with elevated broiler and open burner unit with ovens underneath. Fry kettle is positioned at left of range equipment and refrigerator is at right.

**FIGURE  4.3**
Production is increased when items to be grilled are kept in refrigerated or storage freezer drawers below hot-top unit as shown here. Drawers should be sized to hold enough raw product for peak periods.

**FIGURE 4.4**
In the front cooking line at the Red Onion Restaurant, Huntington Beach, Ca. there is first a drop-in grooved griddle and next a conventional griddle. Tacos at the Red Onion are made individually and cooked on the griddle, said to provide superior texture. Alongside the conventional griddle are two dry heat wells that hold the red and green hot sauces that accompany many of the Red Onion's Mexican specialties.

**FIGURE  4.5**
Open 14 hours a day, the Food Service Facility of the California Highway Patrol Academy at Bryte serves 11,000 meals per week. Mobile equipment permits flexibility of operation. Here counter is set up for breakfast with roll-in griddles in position for speedy production of breakfast favorites.

**FIGURE 5.1**
The test of a deep fat fryer, according to one manufacturer, is the quality of its output of french fried potatoes. Proper training of employees is important in keeping the equipment operating at its peak. At Burger King, well-trained employees turn out peak production of high quality french fries at installations like the above. The landing space at right, with seasoning and bagging supplies stored conveniently beneath it, pays off in high employee productivity.

# *Chapter Five*

# Fryers

Fried foods—French fries, fried chicken, fried shrimp, and the new fried favorites such as mushrooms, zucchini, and almost any other type of vegetable—remain favorites year after year in all types of foodservice, as noted in *Restaurants & Institutions'* menu census. Response to the census also shows good fried foods are nearly always identified with eating away from home. Providing product consistency of these ever-popular items to match customers' expectations is a continuing challenge.

Manufacturers of both frying equipment and shortenings are working to help operators achieve maximum consistency with minimum effort. Such technological innovations as fryer computers, highly refined fats, and all-in-one frying units have helped cater to customer taste without sacrificing product quality, while keeping labor costs in line.

## FROM STAPLES TO SPECIALTIES

Although the basic tasks of fryer production are such staple menu items as fried chicken, fish and seafood, potatoes, croquettes and doughnuts, a growing number of operations are adding gourmet specialties to their fryer schedules.

Wherever such specialties have been developed, they have met with an enthusiastic reception. Often they are the kind of dish that creates word-of-mouth advertising, enabling a host or hostess to introduce a guest to a memorable food item not usually encountered when eating out.

Checking fryer schedules against the menu may reveal a gourmet potential that can be capitalized on profitably. One gourmet item that has been especially successful is French-fried mushrooms.

## FRYER SELECTION

Whether fryer production is to be backbone-of-the-menu, epicurean, or, preferably, to cover both areas, the same basics of fryer selection apply. Proper selection and operation of deep-fat fryers assures the necessary output of quality, deep-fried items that have such appeal for Americans in all patron categories.

A 5-point formula for estimating number of fryers required is based on these factors:

- Approximate number of patrons served in peak hour
- Percentage of those patrons ordering fried food
- Average portion size of regularly scheduled, deep-fried items
- Weight of total quantity to be fried per hour
- Weight divided by 12 (batch every 5 min.) to determine how many ounces (grams) need to be fried at one time to maintain hourly output.

With these data in mind, decide whether one or two or more small units will best save energy.

When determining the type of fryer that will do the best job, the location should be worked out to allow enough space for satisfactory loading and unloading. The most common complaint encountered in one survey of fryer operators was "not enough space."

## LANDING ARRANGEMENTS FOR FRIED FOODS

Landing arrangments described included stainless steel pans; a long table, sometimes stainless, sometimes heated; stainless steel pans with weep holes to drain off excess oils; large bowl in ring stand that can be pulled up to fryers.

One manufacturer has provided a combination work surface, landing area, and storage unit in a cabinet provided separately or in a battery with adjacent fryers. It provides both drain and storage areas and has proven a very practical answer to the space problem.

Two specialties of the Foxfire Restaurant, Anaheim, CA—a Monte Cristo sandwich and flavorful steakhouse fries—are prepared in a fryer with adjacent stainless steel work surface that is a feature of the semi-exhibition entree cooking line.

Kotschevar and Terrell in their book, *Food Service Planning*, recommend:

"Fryers should be arranged with work space around them. End-of-the-line location is best. Free movement is hampered when they are located between a tall oven and other cooking equipment, such as a broiler (Fryers should never be located next to open burners.)

"A landing area at least 2 ft. (61 cm) wide should be provided next to the fryer for supplies awaiting frying and for foods removed from the fryer. This may be a mobile table or cart."

Working surface for fryer operation is especially important. One well-planned arrangement at the Red Onion Restaurant, Huntington Beach, CA, speeds production of one of their popular Mexican specialties. Two fryers mounted in one cabinet have a stainless steel worktable attached on the right to provide necessary working surface at a convenient level. Tortillas to hold guacamole are formed and deep-fried at this station. The corn tortilla is pressed down into a round holder, much like an oversized soup ladle, and deep-fried to a golden brown. When done, the tortilla retains its cup shape.

## HOW MANY FRYERS?

Once location has been determined, estimate the number of fryers needed based on work load anticipated in the specific operation. One manufacturer offers this 6-step estimating method:

- Determine approximate number of patrons served in peak hour.
- Estimate usual percentage of patrons who order any kind of deep fried foods. (Average is 1½ servings per customer; an operation specializing in fried foods would probably require 2½ servings per patron.)
- Estimate average portion size in fried items regularly scheduled. (French fries are usually served in 3-oz. (85 gms) portions; other food items in larger amounts.)
- Determine weight of total quantity to be fried per hour.
- On basis of a batch every 5 minutes, divide weight by 12 to determine how many oz. (gm) will have to be fried at one time.
- Use manufacturer's recommendations for amount of fat required for amount of food estimated. In modern fryers, fat capacity or fat weight has little relationship to product or load weight. (Fat requirement is more a factor of input and efficiency when potatoes are the

product and is more closely related to surface area when frying breaded items.)

Often two or more small fryers will prove most economical where peak periods alternate with slow periods because they offer more flexible frying capacity and potential energy savings.

According to one expert, "Fryers should fry from 1½ to 2 times their weight of fat per hour. Fryer requirements for some short-order operations are sometimes based on a load of 1/2-lb. (266 gm) of fried potatoes per seat per hour."

Since a basket load of frozen French fried potatoes requires the most heat to cook, fryers are rated by the number of pounds of potatoes per hour they will cook. As a guideline, 100 lb. (45.4 kg) of potatoes per hour is considered a very high output for a 16-in. (40.6 cm) wide fryer that holds 40 to 50 lb. (18.1 to 22.7 kg) of shortening. Obviously, an extremely large fryer can cook more than 100 lb. (45.4 kg) of potatoes per hour, but it will take much more space, use more shortening, and so forth.

High volume producers of French fries usually want a fryer to cook 100 lb. (45.4 kg) of potatoes per hour, in a minimum amount of space. A 16-in. (40.6 cm) fryer, with a shortening capacity of 40 to 50 lb. (18.1 to 22.7 kg), that can be powered with either gas or electricity, has been designed solely to cook potatoes.

Just as it is costly to use a 5 ton (4.5 metric ton) truck for a light hauling job, so it is more expensive to use a high Btu or kw fryer for a relatively light frying job. Also, with many foods, cooking capacity is more dependent on fryer area than on power input or even pounds of fat to pounds of food ratio. Capacity needed at a production rate that will maintain desired cost ratio, with special attention to energy costs, should be a basic determinant in fryer selection.

## FIVE TYPES OF FRYERS

Fryers break down into these five types:

- Conventional restaurant types, ranging from a small 11 × 11-in. (28 × 28-cm) kettle to a 24 × 24-in. (61 × 61-cm) size with corresponding fat capacities of 15 to 130 lbs. (6.8 to 59 kg). Models may be free-standing or built-in fryers in single or multiple units. They may be light duty, 20-in. (51-cm) deep, or heavy duty, 25 to 27-in. (63.5 to 68.6-cm) deep. They must be installed on stands designed to keep working heights comfortable.
- Semi-automatic, high-production model turns out continuous-portion batches via conveyor. Each batch is discharged as it is completed, while other batches continue to cook.
- Automatic fryers that completely control the frying cycle from the time the operator pushes the time button. When button is pushed, a cycle is set in motion that automatically lowers basket into frying fat, fries food to serving state, then raises baskets to drain position. One 14¾ × 23⁹/₁₆ × 13 (37.5 × 59.8 × 33 cm) fryer has an output of 300 2-oz. (57 gm) servings of preblanched French fries per hour; other models offer output of 480 and 600 2-oz. (57 gm) servings per hour. A kettle 15 in. (38 cm) wide × 17 in. (43.2 cm) deep turns out 6 lb. (2.7 kg) of breaded fried chicken every 8 minutes or 2½ lb. (1.1 kg) of fried shrimp in 3 minutes.
- Counter models at small end of size range are excellent where space is limited or as auxiliary fryers.
- Pressure fryers are equipped with tightly sealed lids that permit moisture given off in cooking process to build up steam pressure within fry kettle; moisture stays within fried product though coating continues crisp. The pressure also tends to force heat into the product and reduce cooking time, thus saving energy. Pressure fryers are used primarily to prepare chicken.

The pressure seals in the food's natural juices and seals out shortening. It also tumbles the food in the oil to insure thorough, even cooking.

At the end of the cooking cycle, a buzzer sounds to indicate food is ready to be removed from fryer. When buzzer sounds, pressure automatically is released from the cooking well through an exhaust system. A special locking mechnism on cover prevents operator from opening fryer until pressure is released.

A ratcheting handle easily attaches to basket of cooked food. Operator only has to place the handle in the basket slot, push down, and the handle and basket snap together as one piece

making it easy to remove the basket and empty
its contents. No hot pad or mitts are required to
unload this unit.

## Automatic Fryer Controls

One two-basket, counter-model fryer has automatic electric controls, which include timers and
basket-lowering and raising units. Holding space
alongside its baskets form part of unit. Here fried
products are held under quartz heat lamps. The
24¹³/₁₆ × 23½ × 26½-in.  (63 × 59.7 × 67.3  cm)
unit cooks 30 lb. (13.6 kg) potatoes raw-to-done
per hour or 25 lb. (11.3 kg) of chicken.

## SELECTING FRYER FUEL

The late Warner Kerzmann, in the equipment
course outline he prepared for Northwood Institute, Midland, MI, which was published in *Foodservice Equipment Specialist*,* summarizes the
basics of selecting fryer fuel:

> Electric fryers, because the heat source is in the
> fat, have a heat transfer efficiency approaching
> 100 percent. New gas fryers under test conditions
> range from slightly above 40 percent to about 65
> percent efficient. The efficiency rating can
> decrease radically if ventilation conditions are
> not ideal, or if the heat transfer system compo-
> nents are not replaced when needed.

Kerzmann also pointed out:

> There are essentially three sizes of fryers on
> which most comparisons are based. The first is
> the light-duty electric counterline type with
> dimensions of approximately 20- by 20- by 9-in.
> (50- by 50- by 22.9-cm), fat capacity of 15 lb. (6.8
> kg), input of 6 kw, and a production of approxi-
> mately 25 to 30 lb. (11.3 to 13.6 kg) of potatoes
> per hour.
>     Floor model units are approximately 20 in.
> (50 cm) wide by 36 in. (91.4 cm) deep or heavy-
> duty counter models approximately 20 in. (50
> cm) wide by 25 in. (63.5 cm) deep, with an input

*"The Industry's First Textbook," by the late Warner
Kerzmann, originally published in *Foodservice Equipment
Specialist* magazine, Chicago, IL 1978.

of 12 kw, and a production of approximately 60
lb. (27.2 kg) of potatoes per hour.
    The third standard is the drive-in type,
either gas or electric, approximately 14 to 15 in.
(35.6 to 38.1 cm) wide, 30 to 36 in. (76.2 to 91.4
cm) deep, and 14 to 31 in. (35.6 to 78.7 cm) high,
not including legs. These have a gas input of
100–150,000 Btu or an electric input of 20 to 22
kw, and production capacity between 100 and
150 lb. (45.4 and 68 kg) per hour.

**Computer Control.**   Computer-controlled fryers
come in capacities ranging from 15 to 60 lb. (6.8
to 27.2 kg). A built-in, solid-state computer control continuously monitors and adjusts fryer
cooking time to compensate for fat temperature
changes, thereby providing proper heat input for
desired "doneness" of the specific load. Load size
can vary. To fry different foods, operator only has
to adjust the computer "doneness" dial. Computer is preprogrammed for a wide range of foods.

A separate computer available for most existing units permits independent right and left
basket operation. Lights signal when power is on,
when right or left basket is operating, and if probe
fails.

These fryers shut themselves off if a new load
has been fried for 30 minutes; time can be extended to 2½ hours. They preheat to 350°F.
(177°C) in 6 minutes and only 485 watts is required to hold the temperature.

## PURCHASING CHECKPOINTS

When looking at fryers, be sure the following
points meet your specifications.

- accuracy of temperature control to save energy
  through exact timing for product to be fried
- heat input—high rate saves energy since less
  fat needs to be heated
- speed of recovery
- automatic operation
- economical use of fat
- flavor protection
- ease and safety of use; proper working heights
- cleaning ease
- sturdiness
- design
- usable dimensions

- signal light, timers
- type—counter, free standing, or built in
- drain facilities
- basket construction.

Choose among options available on fryers, such as covers, casters, extra tank (lift out), single basket, basket lifts, computerized controls, or legs.

In some fryers designed for operations that bread fried items, provision is made for crumbs or other sediment to collect in an area below the heat source where the fat is cooler. In this cold zone, the fat does not circulate so sediment or crumbs keep from charring and spoiling food flavor.

Chicken submerged in hot shortening on a 3-tiered rack can be deep fried at a rate of 75 lb. (34 kg) per hour in one unit now available. Load is automatically raised at end of cooking cycle. Average frying time is 11 minutes per load of 15 lb. (6.8 kg) or 6 chickens. A simmer/fry cover reduces cooking time to save energy and to keep chicken moist.

Three counter-fryers recessed into the top are an important element in the entree cooking line at Bob Burns Restaurant, Woodland Hills, CA. The battery of equipment chosen for the line supplies all dishes on the restaurant's varied menu. Refrigerated bases under the fryers keep food items at hand for the speedy production required at restaurant's peak periods.

## FRYER INSTALLATION

Once fryers have been purchased follow this pre-installation advice: "Although this equipment is insulated and designed to put a maximum of heat into the food, adequate ventilation should be provided, preferably with a hood.

"In installing gas fryers, never make a direct flue connection between the flue of fryer and vent flue unless a flue diverter is used—and sometimes this is not satisfactory. Venting into a hood is preferable.

"Be sure there is sufficient clearance between doors and openings to move equipment into the kitchen. When installing a battery of fryers, assemble all fryers in line. Equipment must

be leveled front to rear and right to left (preferably by use of spirit level.)"

The necessary electric connections should be provided for electric fryers.

An example of a tailored-to-operation fryer installation is the custom-fabricated set up at Scottie's Fish'n Chips, West Toledo, OH, designed to serve 2,000 meals a week:

"Construction is of stainless steel, inside and out. We used four 24 × 24-in. (61 × 61 cm) fat containers and built bodies of four 29-in. (73.7 cm) wide fryers, making the total width of these units 116 in. (294.6 cm).

"We also constructed two 20-in. (50 cm) wide batter bins with covers, which fit between three of the four fryers. These enable the cooks to dip the fish in batter in the bins alongside the fryers, and then place the fish directly into the fry baskets. This saves manpower and unnecessary steps in the operation.

"Alongside one fryer we built a sink with a drain outlet. Above the fryers are two warming ovens, built into the backsplasher, to keep orders hot until picked up by the waitresses.

"Total width of the installation is 178 in. (452 cm) The fryers and batter bins are 34 in. (86.4 cm) from the floor to the top, providing a good working height."

Atop the entire battery is a specially constructed hood (made locally). Actually, it is a hood within a hood; the outer hood brings in fresh air, and the inner hood draws air from the fryer area. Thus the installation literally uses its own air and does not draw on the air in the dining area. This is said to cut the operator's air conditioning bills in half.

## SOLVING PEOPLE PROBLEMS

Wendy's utilizes a cold-soaking method to clean fryers. A special, nontoxic cleaning agent is added to the drained-out fryers.

Because the vats are boiled out only at the end of the week, Wendy's frying operation provides a safe, cool, and less energy-consuming environment for employees—one result of the ongoing training and research program at Wendy's International, headquartered in Columbus, OH.

Director of Research and Development Dave Treadway and Director of Training Philip Pappas have developed a training program designed to provide quality product in their high-volume operations. They had found that most of their problems with frying equipment were caused by the people who operated the fryers. Therefore, they are now training the store managers to operate, test, maintain, and clean the units to improve product quality and to insure consistency of items that come from fryers.

## FRYER CLEANING

### Fry Kettles Lift Out

Modern deep-frying equipment is designed for easy cleaning; in many instances kettles lift out for washing. Directions for equipment care are easy to follow; for example, these simple but effective cleaning instructions for gas frying equipment:

- Clean fry pot before using.
- Close all valves and fill with hot water. Add a strong detergent or special fryer cleaning agent and boil water for 20 minutes. Brush inside using a bristle brush (never use steel wool).
- Flush with clean water to which vinegar has been added. Dry with cloth.

The American Gas Association recommends that the fryer and filter fat in a commercial filter be drained daily. They also advise that the following routine be carried out weekly:

- Wash kettle with hot alkaline solution.
- Rinse thoroughly with clear water and 1/2 cup (0.1 l) vinegar.
- Dry kettle with cloth, not by heat of burner.
- Replace fat before lighting gas burner.
- (Note: When using solid fat with (1) tube-type fryers, pack fat around tubes; (2) open-pot fryers, set on melt cycle.)

### Removing Burned-on Grease

If the fryer has been allowed to become coated with burned-on greases, follow these procedures:

- Drain completely. Refill with water.
- Heat to boiling point.
- Add special fryer-cleaning agent.
- Boil for 30 minutes.
- Turn burners off.
- If possible, leave solution in fryer overnight.
- Brush with bristle brush until clean.
- Drain and flush with clean water to which vinegar has been added.
- Dry with cloth.

A similar cleaning routine for electric fry kettles reads:

- Turn power switch to "off."
- Remove frying baskets and grasp element lift handle to lift elements from the frying pot.
- Grasp basket supports and rotate outward to left and right of fry kettle respectively.
- Install drainer accessory to fryer. Prime as directed and empty frying fat from frying pot into a suitable container.
- Using a rag or other suitable insulation, grasp frying pot handles to pull frying pot up and out of the appliance shell. Frying pot should then be washed in the sink as you would any other pot or container.
- Replace original frying pot (or duplicate pot) into fryer shell; lower heating elements; rotate basket supports inward until they snap into position. Refill frying pot with liquid or solid fat.

### Removing Carbon

To clean heating elements:

Carbonization will eventually discolor the heating elements and frying pot. To remove, periodically (once a month or oftener, as required) fill the frying pot with water and a good commercial fry-kettle cleaner. Turn fry kettle off and let stand overnight.

The next day raise the elements, remove frying pot and empty. Replace pot and fill with clean water plus vinegar or other neutralizing agent.

The special cleaning agents that have been developed for deep-fat fryers help to speed cleaning. Some fryer manufacturers offer swing-up, self-cleaning elements that automatically burn off any carbonization, then turn themselves off.

## FAT FOR THE FRYER

Fats or oils for deep frying must possess different physical qualities than those used for bakery or general purposes.

Hard fats pack with difficulty into deep fat fryers and usually have high melting points. Solid frying compound placed over electric elements or gas tubes can cause burn outs or melt welds where fat is missing. Solid fat should be melted before being put in fryer. Semisolid or liquid products are easier to handle since they are packed in cans and can be poured directly into the kettle. No melting is necessary. Constant research and new product developments are creating liquid frying agents with long life and minimum decomposition.

The frying compound must have excellent stability to withstand the rigors of frying. A frying agent with much free fatty acid, will break down quickly. Butter, chicken, or other animal fats are a poor choice for frying; they contain high amounts of free fatty acids. One definition of an acceptable frying fat or oil states: It can be heated above 300°F. (149°C) without catching fire or smoking excessively; its taste and odor are acceptable, and it solidifies below body temperature.

When a frying agent is heated to a high temperature, it will give off a thin, bluish-white smoke. Smoking indicates that the fat is decomposing because of action of heat. The fat level in the fryer should cover coils completely. If coils are not covered, 25 percent of the energy entering the fryer may be lost.

## Foods That Cause Fat Breakdown

Food containing large quantities of moisture, such as raw potatoes, quickly break down fats in frying. Sediment from flour, crumbs or other food particles will speed the breakdown process.

Salt also encourages breakdown; foods should not be salted over fat. Even the high copper content of oysters may cause deep-frying fats to break down more quickly.

A checklist of characteristics to look for in a frying agent includes the following:

- Good color
- Neutral flavor
- Low flavor transfer
- Low absorption in foods fried in it
- Good stability
- Develops appetizing, golden brown, crisp surface
- High smoking temperature
- Resistance to rancidity development
- Resistance to gumming or polymerization
- Produces foods of uniform quality.

Most fryers take only 5 to 7 minutes to preheat from room temperature to 350°F. (177°C), the usual temperature for frying. Be sure not to set thermostat above desired frying temperature; this practice does not speed preheating, but does waste energy. Do not preheat fryers too far ahead of scheduled use; for maximum energy saving follow manufacturer's recommendations.

When the kettle is not in use, turn down the heat to prevent unnecessary breakdown of fat. Some operations install several small fryers rather than one large one; during slow periods only one kettle is used.

Strain the fat frequently to remove sediment; straining or filtering can double the life of your frying fat. Use several thicknesses of cheese cloth, a special filter bag, or a fat-filtering machine.

Straining is done at a temperature around 200°F. (93°C). If you use a filtering machine, fat may be filtered at a temperature of 350°F. (177°C). If sediment still remains, cool the fat to below 200°F. (93°C). and sprinkle it lightly with water, allowing the water to carry down fine particles of burnt material to the bottom. Pour or siphon the clear fat from the water sludge. Be sure to add new fat after straining or filtering.

Careless placement of new fat in the hot fryer seriously burns the fat. To prevent this problem, if using hard fat, melt and pour it into the fryer before applying heat, then raise the temperature gradually.

## Taste Test Fat Daily

The operator of a fryer should taste the fat once a day to determine its condition. Next to cleanliness, the best way to assure successful deep-fat frying is to select a quality frying compound and control its turnover rate. Because controlled turnover preserves the life of frying fat and diminishes breakdown, it is important to understand the process. Slow turnover in fat consumption is also recommended by manufacturers who point out that adding 15 to 20 percent of new frying compound daily helps reduce breakdown.

## What Fat Turnover Means

"Fat turnover" is the amount of fat used each day in comparison to the kettle capacity. That the loss of fat in the fryer is due to its being boiled off into the air is a misconception. Even though a minute portion is lost in this manner, the main reason that fat disappears is absorption. All foods retain 10 to 40 percent of the fat in which they are fried. For example, 100 pounds (45.4 kg) of French fried potatoes will absorb 8 to 11 pounds (3.6 to 5 kg) of fat and 100 pounds (45.4 kg) of dredged food will take up to 10 to 20 pounds (4.5 to 9 kg) of fat, depending on the food.

Some manufacturers advise a total daily fat turnover, if possible. This means that if a kettle holds 25 lb. (11.3 kg) of frying fat, and if 25 lb. (11.3 kg) of fresh fat can be added in small portions throughout the day to replace the used fat, there is a one-to-one turnover. To maintain as rapid a turnover as possible, install a fryer of proper capacity to suit the operation.

Avoid introducing excessive moisture to the frying fat by draining items before putting them in the fryer. Draining raw, wet foods, such as French fried potatoes, before placing them in the fryer conserves energy and assures safer operation.

## 10-Point Program Preserves Frying Fat

Since fat care is basic to good deep frying, kettle users are urged to adopt this 10-point program designed to preserve fat and produce the finest fried foods:

- Choose a fat that does not break down quickly.
- Take care to avoid scorching fat. Scorched fat is broken-down fat; it speeds up the deterioration of all the fat in the kettle. Melt fat before putting in kettle or at least melt sufficient fat

to cover tubes or elements, then add plastic shortening. Where melting fat outside kettle presents problems, use liquid or semiliquid shortening.
- Do not fry foods at temperatures above those recommended. The higher the fat temperature the more rapid the rate of fat deterioration.
- During short intervals between frying, lower the heat. Do not keep heat on for long periods between batches. If metal basket is left in fat, between frying periods, heat will not be required to warm basket when frying starts.
- Keep fat clean. Strain or filter daily or at the end of every shift. Fryers are available with built-in filtering systems that allow the operator to filter a fryer in 3 to 4 minutes. In some situations, filtering the shortening 3 to 4 times a day will double its life.
- Maintain thermostats in good calibration.
- Size appliance to meet peak demand precisely; fry to capacity to minimize fat absorption and need for fat replenishment.
- Do not overload baskets. Fill only two-thirds to minimize cooking time and save energy.
- Add at least 15 percent fresh fat to your kettle daily, even if you must ladle out some fat and use it in gravy to make room for the added fat.
- Keep your equipment clean.

## NEW IDEAS FOR FRIED FOODS

Fried foods are popular at all thirteen of the Manufacturers Hanover Trust Company's employee facilities. Replacing older fryers with highly productive new units has facilitated preparation of more types of fried foods—fried chicken, French fries, veal cutlets, shrimp, clams, Chinese egg rolls, and Jamaican meat pies.

Variety is a requirement for any employee foodservice operation, especially in a city such as New York with many ethnic food tastes to satisfy.

Menus at each MHT location are basically the same, but slight variations have been incorporated to accommodate the employee mix at each bank, for each location has a higher concentration of one of the ethnic groups.

Since the installation of the new fryers, which feature a melt cycle and an effective filter system, the operations have saved as much as one hundred dollars a day in shortening and labor costs.

**DEEP-FAT FRIED FOODS COOKING GUIDE**

The following are suggested cooking times and temperatures for the various foods shown. The tables are presented as a guide only, since many variables will affect the frying times such as the initial temperature of the food, the size of the food pieces, and the amount of food. Large pieces require a longer frying time and lower temperature than small pieces. If the fry kettles are overloaded, the frying temperatures may drop so low that a much longer frying time will be necessary to cook the food than is recommended. Under such conditions the foods may become fat soaked and unappetizing. It is important for the fry cook to determine what amount of food may be added to the fry kettle without causing an excessive drop in temperature.

*POTATOES*

The following table is based on a load ratio of one pound of potatoes for every six pounds of fat.

| *French Fries* | *Size* | Temperature Setting °F. | °C | *Frying Time in Minutes* |
|---|---|---|---|---|
| Raw-to-done | ⅜ in. (1 cm) cut | 350 | 177 | 5–6 |
| Blanched, only | ⅜ in. (1 cm) cut | 350 | 177 | 2½–3 |
| Browned, only | ⅜ in. (1 cm) cut | 350 | 177 | 2½–3 |
| Raw-to-done | ¼ in. (6 mm) cut | 350 | 177 | 5 |
| Blanched, only | ¼ in. (6 mm) cut | 350 | 177 | 2½ |
| Browned, only | ¼ in. (6 mm) cut | 350 | 177 | 2½ |
| Raw-to-done | ½ in. (1.3 cm) cut | 350 | 177 | 7 |
| Blanched, only | ½ in. (1.3 cm) cut | 350 | 177 | 3½ |
| Browned, only | ½ in. (1.3 cm) cut | 350 | 177 | 3½ |
| Commercially-treated | ⅜ in. (1 cm) cut | 350 | 177 | 5–6 |
| Frozen, Fat-blanched | ⅜ in. (1 cm) cut | 350 | 177 | 2½–3 |

SEAFOODS

| | | °F. | °C | Minutes |
|---|---|---|---|---|
| Frozen Breaded Shrimp | | 350 | 177 | 3–4 |
| Fresh Breaded Shrimp | | 350 | 177 | 3 |
| Frozen Fish Fillets | | 350 | 177 | 4 |
| Fresh Fish Fillets | | 350 | 177 | 3 |
| Fresh Breaded Scallops | | 350 | 177 | 4 |
| Breaded Fried Clams | | 350 | 177 | 1 |
| Breaded Fried Oysters | | 350 | 177 | 5 |
| Frozen Fish Sticks | | 350 | 177 | 4 |

CHICKEN

| | | °F. | °C | Minutes |
|---|---|---|---|---|
| Raw-to-done | | 325 | 162 | 9–11 (2¼–2½ lb. size) |
| Croquettes | | 350 | 177 | 3–4 |
| Turnovers | | 350 | 177 | 5–7 |
| Precooked, Breaded | | 350 | 177 | 3–4 |

| MISCELLANEOUS | Temperature Setting °F. | °C | *Frying Time in Minutes* |
|---|---|---|---|
| Breaded Veal Cutlets | 350 | 177 | 3–4 |
| Breaded Onion Rings | 350 | 177 | 3 |
| Precooked Cauliflower | 350 | 177 | 3 |
| Precooked Eggplant | 350 | 177 | 3 |
| Breaded Tamali Sticks | 350 | 177 | 3 |
| Fritters | 350 | 177 | 3 |
| French-toasted Sandwiches | 375 | 190 | 1 |
| Yeast-raised Doughnuts | 375 | 190 | 1 |
| Hand-cut Cake Doughnuts | 375 | 190 | 1½ |
| Glazed Cinnamon Apples | 300 | 149 | 3–5 |
| Corn-on-the-cob | 300 | 149 | 3 |

## FRYING GUIDE FOR UNIT WITH 28-LB. (12.7 KG) SHORTENING CAPACITY*

| Food | Temperature Setting °F. | °C | Time (in min.) | Capacity/Load (all models) lb. | kg |
|---|---|---|---|---|---|
| French-Fried Potatoes ⅜ inch (1 cm) strips (raw-to-done) | 375 | 190 | 6–9 | 6.1 | 2.8 |
| Potato Chips, thin slices | 350 | 177 | 3–4 | 1.94 | 880 gm |
| Fish Fillets, 5″ × ½″ (12.7 × 1.3 cm) | 365 | 185 | 3–4 | 8.8 | 3.9 |
| Shrimps | 375 | 190 | 2–3 | 5.58 | 2.53 |
| Oysters and Clams | 395 | 201 | 2–3 | 3.7 | 1.7 |
| Chicken, 2-lb. (906 gm) size quartered [8 oz. (226 gm) serving] | 325 | 162 | 12–13 | 7 portions** | |
| halved [1-lb. (453 gm) serving] | 325 | 162 | 12–16 | 7 portions** | |
| Croquettes | 365 | 185 | 3–4 | 8.8 | 3.9 |
| Fritters, fruit, vegetable or meat 2½″ (6.4 cm) diameter | 375 | 190 | 4–5 | 30** | |
| Doughnuts, 2½″ (6.4 cm) diameter | 375 | 190 | 2–3 | 30** | |
| French Toast, 4″ × 4″ (10 × 10 cm) slices | 325 | 162 | 2–3 | 12** | |
| Turnovers, fruit, vegetable or meat [4″ × 2½″ (10 × 6.4 cm] | 375 | 190 | 3–4 | 18** | |

*General Electric Company
**Capacities given are limited by energy available to maintain continuous frying temperature, except those marked with a double asterisk (**) in which case capacity is limited by surface of the item in preparation.

## FRYING GUIDE FOR UNIT WITH 15-LB. (6.8 KG) SHORTENING CAPACITY*

| Food (Frozen) | Temperature Setting °F. | °C | Capacity/ Load lb. | kg | Minimum Suggested Time/Load (Minutes) | Capacity Per Hour** lb. | kg |
|---|---|---|---|---|---|---|---|
| French-Fried Potatoes ⅜ in. (1 cm) | 350 | 177 | 2.5 | 1.1 | 4 | 30 | 13.6 |
| Fish Fillets 4-oz. (114 gm) Cod | 350 | 177 | 2.5 | 1.1 | 4.5 | 27 | 12.2 |
| Shrimp 12/14 | 350 | 177 | 2.5 | 1.1 | 3.5 | 33 | 15 |
| Chicken 4–6 oz. (114–170 gm) serv. | 350 | 177 | 2.0 | 0.9 | 9 | 12 | 5.4 |

*General Electric Company
**allows for handling time between loads

Here are more good frying tips from operators:

- When breaded foods are prepared, strain fat frequently.
- Load fry baskets to one-half, never more than two-thirds full.
- Never salt foods directly over the fat. Salt in the fat reduces its life.
- Discard fat as soon as it tends to bubble excessively before food is added or when gummy film collects on the frying baskets or heating elements.

- Raw, wet foods, such as potatoes and oysters, should be drained or wiped dry before frying to extend the life of the fat.

## SETTING FRYING TIMES

As a guide to developing standard frying times, manufacturers have worked out frying times for many foods items. The frying guide charts were prepared from their findings. However, before trying these frying times, check out the following variables:

- Temperature recovery rate of the fryer
- Amount of food to be fried at one time
- Temperature of food to be fried (frozen; thawed)
- Size and shape of food pieces.

The Eatery, White Flint Mall, Kensington, MD, wanted to make sure that foods were fried at the correct temperatures and for the correct length of time. Therefore, this operation has placed cards on the walls above the fryers listing the frying temperature and time for all items they serve so no guesswork is necessary.

## BREADING

To provide crisp, protective coverings for food exposed to frying temperature, bread products to be fried. Uniform coating is of extreme importance. Cracks or breaks in the surface or incompletely breaded spots often cause the product to burst or split under heat. Batters serve the same purpose; take similar care to assure that the item to be fried is completely covered by the batter.

### Tips for Better Breading

These sixteen tips for better breading and frying are listed by one breading-mix manufacturer:

1. Have foods to be fried at room temperature.
2. It is more efficient to dip with one hand and bread with the other.
3. Follow general breading directions carefully.
4. For extra crunchy crispness and added weight, dip in batter and breading, then batter and breading again.
5. When double dipping, as described above, add 1 to 2 minutes extra frying time.
6. When frying foods with high moisture content, be sure to allow foods to "rest" after breading. Set aside for 2-3 minutes, then recover with breading mix. This "setting time" insures a perfect seal. (For onion rings; oysters; shrimp; scallops; fish fillets.)
7. Choose frying shortenings carefully—hydrogenated shortening, corn and peanut oils are less likely to break down at high temperatures.
8. Melt shortening in fryer at 200°F. (93°C) and then turn heat to proper frying temperature.
9. Tailor the temperature to the product.
10. Fry similar-sized pieces together.
11. Do not overload the fryer—pieces should not touch.
12. Drain fried products on absorbent paper before serving.
13. Clarify shortening often—filter at least once a day.
14. Store oils in cool place—shortening in light-proof container.
15. Discard rancid shortening or shortening that foams or smokes excessively.
16. Keep shortening temperature below smoking point to minimize frying odors.

## BRAIN TEASER—FRYERS

1. What food items are usually deep fried? (List four.)

   _____  _____  _____  _____

2. Fryers need to be located where there is plenty of space to _____ baskets full of fried foods after they are lifted out of fryers. (Fill in.)

3. There are four types of french fryers. Name two. _____ _____ .

4. A fryer that has become coated with grease needs _____

   _____ (Complete sentence.)

5. To keep fryer from becoming coated with grease, _____

   _____ (Complete sentence.)

6. When fat smokes, it is a sign that it is decomposing. What causes this? _____

7. When fry kettles are not being used, heat should be (left on high) (turned down). (Cross out wrong answers.)

8. Fat turnover means _____
   (Complete sentence.)

9. Excessive moisture in foods to be fried uses extra heat and causes temperature to drop. What should be done to keep this from happening?_____

   _____ .

10. Foods in the fryer (can) (cannot) be salted while they are frying. (Circle right answer.) Give reason why your answer is right. _____

   _____ .

*(For correct answers, see page 250.)*

**FIGURE   5.2**
Tortilla chips are prepared in these fryers located on the support cooking line at the Red Onion Restaurant, Huntington Beach, Ca. A stainless steel table mounted at left of fryer was fabricated to the height needed for the two plastic containers which receive the tortilla chips after they are fried and drained. Filled containers are taken to the waitress stations where they are portioned into wicker baskets for table service.

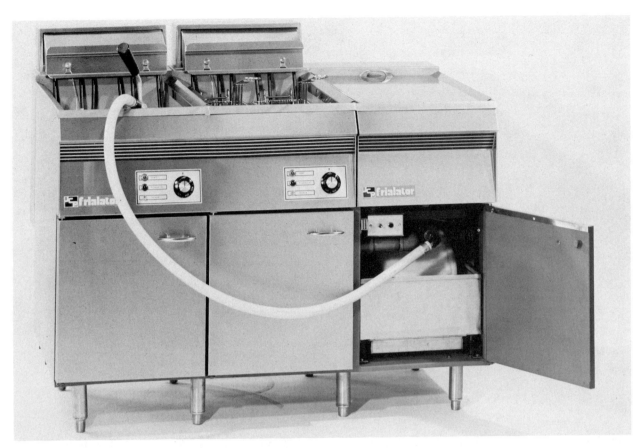

**FIGURE   5.3**
A built-in filter in a matching cabinet makes the job of filtering the cooking oil easy, fast, and safe. One filter can service up to five fryers operating in a single battery.

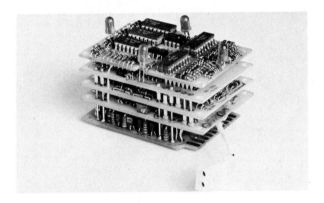

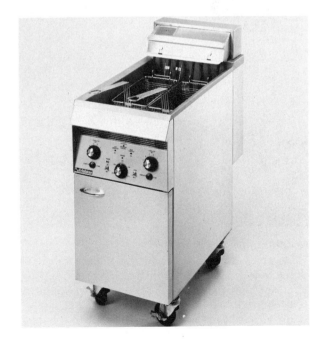

**FIGURES   5.4 and 5.5**
Built in computerized controls enable today's modern fryers to practically think for themselves. The fryer can automatically monitor and adjust frying time to control doneness on two loads which may be fried at different times and temperatures. It may be programmed for as many as six different products. The "brain" is a small plug-in unit, (see picture above).

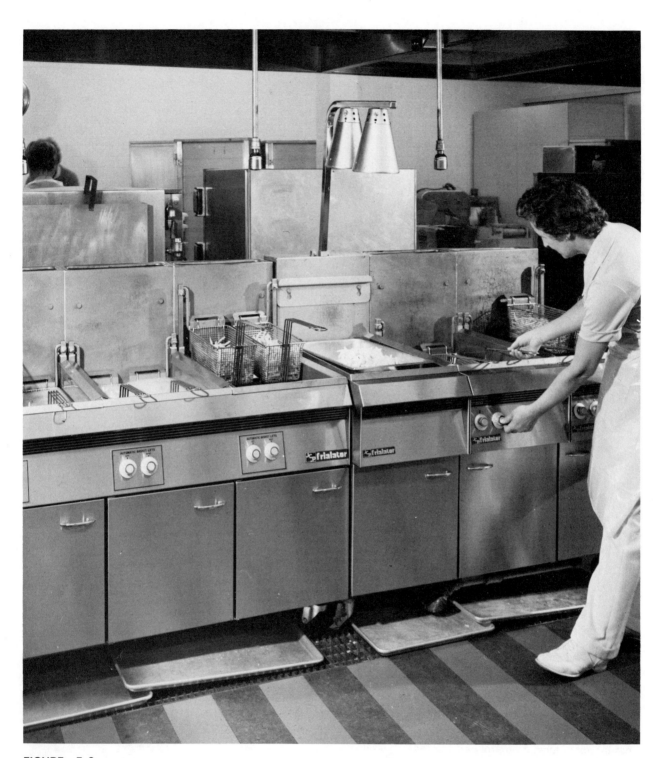

**FIGURE   5.6**
This battery of five fryers being used to cook french fries includes a built-in filter (third unit from right) which services all the fryers through interconnecting piping. The filter unit includes a well on top designed to hold a 12- by 20-in. (30- by 51-cm) cafeteria pan into which the fries are dumped. Overhead heat lamps keep them warm. Each fryer is equipped with two timers, one for each basket, and with automatic basket lifts which raise the fries out of the cooking oil as soon as they are done. This battery can cook 500 lb. (227 kg) of frozen french fries per hour.

**FIGURE 5.7**
The flexibility of half- and full-size fry kettles combined in a single cabinet allows every foodservice operator to order the combination of frying equipment that is exactly right for his or her needs. For example, with this unit, both the full- and half-size fryers may be needed to meet peak period demand. During off-peak periods the half size fryer may keep up with demand, allowing the full size fryer to be shut down to save fuel costs.

**FIGURE   5.8**
Fried specialties are high volume items at the California Highway Patrol Academy in Bryte. To meet demands of 11,000 meals per week two units, each holding two fryers, are cantilevered (wall hung). They are part of one of the hexagonal cooking centers used to save steps and eliminate cross traffic in the Academy kitchen.

**FIGURE   5.9**
Increased efficiency for the chef or fry cook was designed into the station at Columbian House, Bolingbrook, Ill. A reach-in freezer within arm's reach of the fryers keeps product flow speedy and constant. Landing space between first and second fryer and beyond third is a further assist in keeping pace during peak production periods.

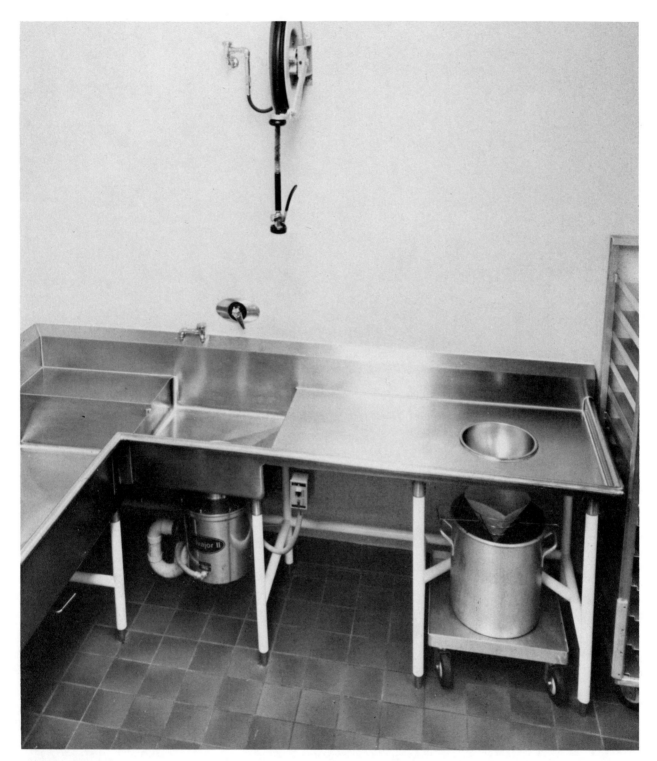

**FIGURE   5.10**
Mounted into the right hand drainboard of the utensil washing area in the Apple Tree Inn is a strainer/filtering device in which the specially seasoned shortening is strained and filtered into a portable container for easy return to the fryer station where it can be reused. Container is on portable dolly of correct height, and rails of base are formed to hold container and dolly in correct position.

**FIGURE 5.11**
At lower left in above picture is a freezer base kept stocked with shrimp and raw french fries at the Apple Tree Inn, North Kansas City, Mo. Top of freezer is used to process shrimp before it goes into fryers. Next to freezer is the portable fry stand which holds two deep fat fryers separated by a flat holding area. Finished items are held under heat lamp for brief period. Unit on wheels can easily be moved for speedy cleaning.

**FIGURE  5.12**
Four gas fryers assure speedy service of fast food items at the Catfish Restaurant in Houston, Tex.

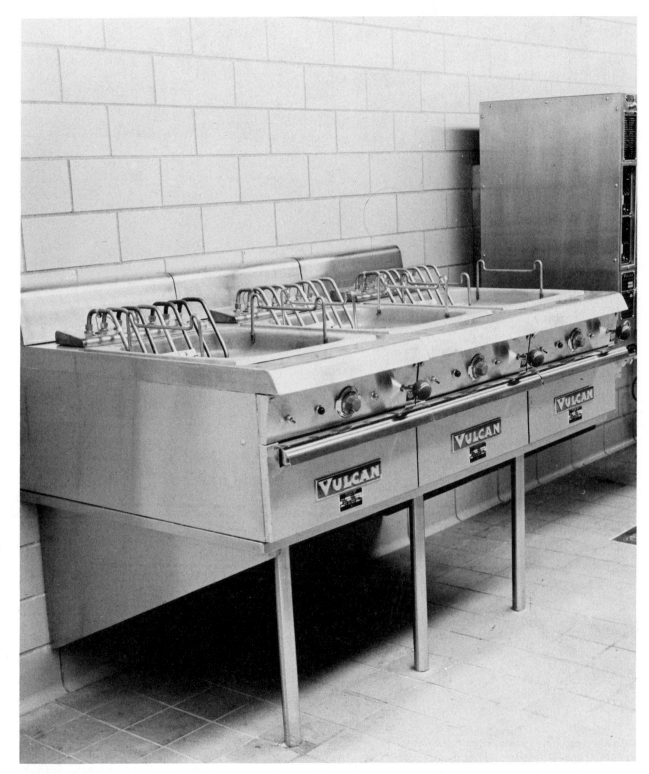

**FIGURE   5.13**
To help in meeting menu needs at Manteno (Ill.) State Hospital for 18,000 meals per day, three electric fryers were installed.

**FIGURE 6.1**

The semi-exhibition entree cooking line at the Foxfire Restaurant, Anaheim, Ca. features an infrared overfired broiler mounted above the back half of the grooved griddle. The combining of these two appliances provides flexibility and speed in the production of steaks. Located under the hood, it has also proved to be one of the most direct solutions to the air-pollution problems facing the foodservice industry. It is here that filet mignon, petite filet, tournedos of beef, brochette of beef, and special seafood steaks are prepared. The reach-in refrigerator at the end of the line holds items scheduled for broiling. The wall-mounted infrared overfired broiler is used as the final step for glazed crepe suzettes, crunchy topped casseroles, glazed stuffed shrimp, glazed filet of sole, and glazed omelets.

# *Chapter Six*

# Broilers

Some people believe the American love of broiled meat goes back to memories of frontier campfires with meat from the day's hunt sizzling above the flames.

Many people relive these memories regularly in their own backyard, where the family "chef" does the broiling. Taking advantage of this habit, Caesar's Restaurant, Westville, NJ, allows backyard-broiling enthusiasts to prepare the hoagie of their choice on one of the establishment's four broiler-griddles.

Because broiled foods have a special hold on the American public, broiling is frequently an eye-catching activity in exhibition cooking areas. To be sure of maximum broiler payoff, operators should (1) review purchasing checklists carefully before making a final broiler choice, (2) train workers thoroughly in the best way to use the broiler after it is installed, and (3) shorten the distance between broiler and point-of-service as much as possible to maintain broiled items at peak quality right up to fork point.

Proof of the American public's enthusiasm for broiled meat is the continual increase in these orders, even though broiled items are frequently the highest priced foods on the menu. Matching the American consumption of broiled foods is the variety of equipment now available for preparing them.

Whatever the operation's requirements, manufacturers say there is bound to be a broiler model that will meet them. Because the line of broilers is so extensive, foodservice operators are urged first to spend time determining just what they want a broiler to do and then to take the time to find a broiler that does just that.

## WHAT A BROILER IS

A good working definition of the broiler confines it to equipment that cooks food by high heat, usually direct, or by radiant heat. In another definition, broiling is said to be the process of cooking a piece of meat in its own juices without using fat (as in frying). The faster the cooking the better, in terms of maximum juiciness retained and minimum shrinkage.

## THREE BROILER TYPES

One expert classifies broilers into these three general types:

- Horizontal or overhead heavy-duty broilers (electric, conventional gas, or infrared gas)
- Char or underfired broilers
- Specialty broilers.

These broilers all have radiant heat sources over 1000°F. (538°C), grid or rack temperatures up to 1500°F. (816°C) when preheated, and ambient (broiling area) temperatures of 600°F. (316°C) to 1500°F. (816°C) with the grid preheated in a raised position.

How well a broiler can sustain these conditions under load; how much flexibility and control is available for different products; and degrees of doneness and finish are important operating features.

When selecting a broiler the individual operator should consider these factors:

1. Quantity and kind of broiled food to be served
2. Available floor space
3. Gas or electric fuel
4. Overhead or char broiler
5. For overhead gas broilers, broiling heat can come from flames moving across ceramic or from gas coming down through holes in ceramic (common to infrared units).

### CAPACITIES FOR ONE LINE OF CHAR BROILERS

| Dimensions | | | Capacity |
|---|---|---|---|
| in. | cm | cm | |
| 30¼ × 33¾ | 76.8 × 85.7 | | 24 12-oz. (340 gm) sirloin strips; 30 lamb chops; 20 chicken halves; 36 hamburgers (2 oz.) (57 gm) |
| 48¼ × 33¾ | 122.6 × 85.7 | | 42 12-oz. (340 gm) sirloin strips; 56 lamb chops 36 chicken halves 65 2-oz. (57 gm) hamburgers |

### BROILING CAPACITY— UNDERFIRED ELECTRIC BROILER

| | Hamburgers | | Strip Steaks |
|---|---|---|---|
| Load | | Per Hour | Per Hour |
| 36 | | 350–750** | 100–250 |
| 18 | | 175–375** | 50–125 |

**Depending on thickness, temperature and degree of cooking.

### CAPACITY AND COOKING TIME GAS BROILER APPROX. 18 × 32 in. (45.7 × 81.3 cm)

| | | Steaks | | | | | Toast, | | | | | Hot |
|---|---|---|---|---|---|---|---|---|---|---|---|---|
| | | T-Bone | Club | Chops | Hamburgers | Chicken | Rolls | Bacon | | Liver | Lobster | Cakes |
| No. of Pieces | Inside | 6–7 | 10 | 18–22 | 18–22 | 6 | 18 | 2 lb. (906 gm) | | Depends on size | | |
| | Top | | | | 30 | | 28 | 3 lb. (1.4 kg) | | | | 16 |
| Time (Minutes) | Rare | 4 | 2–3 | | | | | | | | | |
| | Medium | 5 | 3–4 | | | | | | | 3 | 15–18 | |
| | Well-Done | 6 | 4–5 | 3–4 | | 14–17 | | | | | | |
| | Inside | | | | 1½ | | 12–20 secs. | 30–45 secs. | | | | |
| | Top | | | | 3 | | 1 | 1–1½ | | | | |

**CAPACITY AND COOKING TIME COUNTER BROILER***

| Dimensions | | | Steaks T-Bone | Club | Chops | Hamburgers | Chicken | Toast, Rolls | Bacon | Liver | Lobster | Hot Cakes |
|---|---|---|---|---|---|---|---|---|---|---|---|---|
| | No. of Pieces | Inside | 6–7 | 10 | 18–22 | 18–22 | 6 | 18 | 2 lb. (406 gm) | Depends on size | | |
| | | Top | | | | 30 | | 28 | 3 lb. (1.4 kg) | | | 16 |
| 33 × 18 in. (83.8 × 45.7 cm) | | Rare | 4 | 2–3 | | | | | | | | |
| | | Medium | 5 | 3–4 | | | | | | | | |
| | Time in Minutes | Well-Done | 6 | 4–5 | 3–4 | | 14–17 | | | | | |
| | | Inside | | | | 1½ | | 12–20 secs. | 30–45 secs. | | 3 | 15–18 |
| | | Top | | | | 3 | | 1 | 1–1½ | | | |

*Magikitchen Equipment Corporations

## EQUIPMENT CAPACITY

Some idea of broiler capacity is indicated in the preceding charts and in these production figures:

- From one unit with 3.3 to 5.0 sq. ft. (3066 to 4645 cm) available broiler space, 75 to 100 lb. (34 to 45.4 kg) of fish or meat medium broiled per hour, depending on available broiler space.
- From a broiler with a capacity of 48 3½-in (8.9 cm) 2½-oz. (71 gm) hamburgers, 960 burgers per hour; with broiler capacity of 24 hamburgers (size as above), 420 per hour.
- From a broiler that can handle 24 8 × 3 × ½-in. (20.3 × 7.6 × 1.3 cm) New York strip steaks, 200 per hour; with broiler capacity of 9 steaks, 90 per hour.

## CHAR BROILERS

Horizontal, heavy-duty broilers are quite flexible in handling such items as casseroles or fish, but char broilers are limited primarily to steaks and chops. And they offer showmanship possibilities plus aroma appeal. Often they are located where customers can watch the dramatic performance.

Originally, gas-fired char broilers used char rock—either broken pieces of ceramic or ceramic briquettes—supported on bars over burners and heated by flame from the burners. Excessive smoke and flames from fat that dripped from broiling food (drains for excess fat were not available) led to the design features found in most of today's gas char broilers.

A closely spaced, sloped grid has grooves on each bar that funnel some of the fat to the front. Some new units have char rock; others use iron radiants. In some gas-fired char broilers, a fan creates a flow of air just above the radiants and results in lighter, less acrid smoke and less flaming.

These broilers are available in multiple sections of almost any length and broiling area. In one model, each foot of broiler width is individually controlled.

Because much smoke is given off during the cooking process, these broilers must be installed under an efficient exhaust hood. Due to the inherent flame characteristics of char broiling, the exhaust filtering systems should be no closer than 48 in. (122 cm) above the surface of the broilers.

In most electric char broilers, broiling may be done directly on the elements, on elements clamped to an iron grid, or on a grid close to the elements. These broilers provide marking and a char-broiled appearance, but they give off less aroma, food broiled on them has less char flavor, and there is little flaming.

One electric char broiler has three different heat areas on the top grid: hotter at the back for rare meat, cooler in front for well-done, and medium heat in the middle. Operator only has to learn proper positions to assure customer satisfaction.

## BRANDING BROILED ITEMS

Branding is an important consideration in broiler selection. Intense infrareds produced by today's broilers not only maintain grid-surface temperatures and minimize heat recovery time but also generally assure good branding. Round bars used in some grids provide a very pleasing brand mark and generally are not likely to char or severely burn the brand on the meat. This is especially helpful if the chef is not particularly experienced in the use of the broiler.

One electric counter broiler has been designed so that meat drippings falling on heated blocks ignite them and produce flame that char broils. This broiler uses only the energy of flaming meat fats to produce the charcoal effect and flavor. Heavy-duty models are available with grate surfaces 30½-in. deep × 22½-in. wide (77.5 cm deep × 57 cm wide) and 15½-in. deep × 22½-in. wide (39.4 cm deep × 57 cm wide), with six individually-controlled broiling sections for large or small orders. A 3-section unit is also available.

## HORIZONTAL HEAVY-DUTY BROILERS

Char broilers generally tend to be slower than horizontal heavy-duty broilers, which share certain characteristics, such as:

- An overhead or top radiant-heat source
- An adjustable grid mechanism that can be raised or lowered, and rolled in and out
- A ventilating system that retains heat in the broiling compartment while effectively clearing the smoke and moisture produced by broiling.

The conventional horizontal gas broiler has overhead heat from conventional bar-type gas burners that heat ceramic radiants to approximately 1500°F (816°C). In many models excess heat is vented into a finishing or au gratin oven above the broiler that maintains a temperature of up to 200°F. (93°C). The broiler is best suited for producing a variety of cooked-to-order broiled items.

Broiler design innovations are constantly being introduced to save energy, simplify operation and maintenance, and speed production. One new infrared gas broiler has a patented burner system that operates without fan, filter motor, or electrical components. With no moving parts to service or replace, this unit also offers fast pre-

heating, uniform heat distribution, and instant recovery. The broiler has a finishing oven above the broiler chamber and a full-sized, controlled range oven below.

## INFRARED BURNERS

In horizontal, heavy-duty gas broilers classified as infrared, the gas burns either in a ceramic brick that has a number of small holes or between special metal wings. These intense infrared rays not only reduce broiling time, but also increase the overall efficiency, reduce gas consumption, and provide for a more cost effective broiler. Cost effectiveness—high production with fuel economy—tends to be a story most people are interested in today.

## BROILER PRODUCTION

High-production broilers equipped with infrared burners may be mounted on top of one another since secondary air in these burners is supplied at input point of primary air. Infrared gas burners will preheat in 30 seconds and may be turned off, or at least turned down, when not in use. Tests show that infrared broilers cook 1-in. (2.5 cm) sirloin steaks in only 2 min. broiling time per side for rare and 2½ min. per side for medium.

A single broiler 14½ × 21½-in. (36.8 × 54.6 cm) can produce 340 2½-oz. (71 gm), 3½-in. (9 cm) diameter hamburgers per hr., loaded 24 per grate, or 80 8 × 3 × ½-in. (20.3 × 7.6 × 1.3 cm) strip steaks, loaded 9 per grate.

One high-production electric broiler 36½ × 29⁹⁄₁₆-in. (92.7 × 75 cm) delivers 760 hamburgers or 180 New York strip steaks per hour.

One infrared broiler has an au gratin oven with an attainable minimum temperature of 610°F. (321°C). The broiler measures 34-in. (86.4 cm) wide × 41¼-in. (104.8 cm) deep × 68⁵⁄₈-in. (174.3 cm) high. Other broilers in this line include a single deck, free-standing broiler 36-in. (91.4 cm) wide × 38³⁄₈-in. (97.5 cm) deep × 60-in. (152.4 cm) high and a free-standing, 2-deck model recommended where space and production requirements dictate its use. The broiler is 36-in. (91.4 cm) wide, 33³⁄₈-in. (84.8 cm) deep and 72½-in. (184.2 cm) high.

These broilers are heated by four fast radiant burners, which become "glowing" hot, projecting infrared heat down over broiling grid. The all-metal burners develop temperatures on the burner surface of more than 1600°F. (871°C), with grid temperatures of approximately 600°F. (316°C) to 800°F. (427°C). These burners have several layers of nickel chrome wire mesh to provide uniform heat distribution and long burner life. The units have high-medium-low heat control valves.

A stainless steel housing above and to the rear of the grooved griddle at The Red Onion Restaurant incorporates an infrared broiler. This elevated broiler, which covers the rear half of the griddle, speeds cooking of steaks and hamburgers on The Red Onion's mostly Mexican menu.

Counter models and broilers with finishing ovens powered by infrared burners are also available. The performance of infrared broilers can be gauged by one model that will preheat in less than 60 seconds and broil a 1-in. (2.5 cm) thick sirloin steak to medium rare in 5 minutes. This capacity can be maintained indefinitely since the burners are primarily air burners and are equipped with blowers to supply primary air.

After breakfast is over, a roll-in broiler takes the place of the roll-in griddle on the serving line at the Food Service Facility, California Highway Patrol Academy, Bryte.

At Doylestown (PA) Hospital the broiler in the cooking line is also on casters and has an electric cord set that speeds clean up of the area.

## ELECTRIC CHAR BROILERS

Electric broilers come in standard and heavy-duty models. Standard model electric broilers may be backshelf, counter top, on oven or cabinet base in modular overfired models, or mounted on a convection-oven base. They may have infinite heat controls; in some cases, when double stacked, the top unit can be adjusted for use as a finishing oven.

The standard electric char broiler offers advantages such as these:

- Special element that provides broiling heat immediately

- Radiant heat from above and conducted heat from below
- Inside grill adjustable 2½ to 5½ in. (6.4 to 14 cm) from radiant heat by turning dial on front panel
- Unit can be turned off during slow periods
- One movement opens door, pulls out griddle for quick and easy loading
- Polished cast iron griddles.

The heavy-duty electric char broiler has an adjustable grill similar to the one described above. It also features:

- Individually-controlled, separate heat elements for top griddle and broiler
- Two individually-controlled elements permit preparation of different orders simultaneously to speed customer service
- Polished cast iron griddle surface
- Some have modular design with two separately-controlled broiling sections to permit custom preparation of different foods at the same time
- Recessed controls with signal light that glows when either element is on
- Removable grease tray that directs grease into a 7-qt. (6.6 l) removable water pan.

## MARKS OF BROILER DISTINCTION

Armed with production and space information, the foodservice operator should survey horizontal heavy duty gas broiler models with an eye to the following characteristics:

- Proper concentration and direction of radiant heat to assure efficiency and low operating cost.
- Warp-resistant heating units of radiant ceramic or alloy materials.
- Broiler linings of durable, reflective materials.
- Units that heat to broiling temperatures in about 10 minutes or infrared broilers that require only 30 seconds to preheat.
- Variable temperature controls.
- Separate switches or turnoffs.
- Flues adequate to remove smoke, odors, and combustion products.

- Drip shields to keep drippings from floor.
- Air drafts designed so they do not affect flames or cool foods.
- Bodies of 16-gauge or heavier sheet steel, rigidly enforced with sturdy angle support.
- Rugged grids easy-to-adjust over distances 1½ to 8 in. (3.8 to 20.3 cm) from heat source.
- Easily pulled out grids with safety stop locks.
- All parts and areas accessible for easy cleaning and servicing. Broilers are often set in a battery with other broilers or pieces of equipment and placed under and attached to special hoods. Broilers do require servicing. Much expensive labor is needed if the unit must be freed from the ventilation system and pulled out of the battery. Particularly in these setups, front accessibility for service repair is essential.
- Arrangements for catching grease and drawing it into receptacle for easy disposal.
- Charcoal-broiler beds of heavy construction.
- Loading and unloading possible away from heat zone.
- Broilers installed as part of the cooking line may be (1) the same height as the range tops and equipped with a standard high shelf; (2) integral, with an overhead oven that is heated by the burners in the broiling compartment below—the overhead oven can increase broiler capacity when used as a warming compartment, a precook chamber, or a finishing oven; (3) mounted on a conventional, range-type oven and may also have an overhead warming oven.

Other factors contribute to successful heavy-duty electric broiler operation:

- Flame-free, smoke-free atmosphere
- Heat applied simultaneously to both sides of meat in some models
- High production of broiled items
- Broiling temperature reached in seconds and broiling efficiency maintained in peak hours during repeated, capacity grid loading
- Reduced broiling time—as much as 40 percent on many of the broiler products
- Intensity of heat established at time of installation, so finish, color, or doneness of broiled surface is controlled as operator desires
- Efficient use of fuel
- Increased broiling capacity in same floor space.

Charts showing typical production and a production guide appear below and on pp. 113 and 114.

**TYPICAL PRODUCTION (MEATS AT ROOM TEMPERATURE)***

**Standard Broilers**

*1-Broiler Section (all models) 22½ in. wide × 22¾ in. deep (56.7 cm wide × 56.8 cm deep)*

| PRODUCT | SERVINGS PER HOUR |
|---|---|
| Beef Tenderloin (7 oz.) (199 gm) | 285 |
| Lobster Tails (8–12 oz.) (226–340 gm) | 200 |
| Chicken (Broiler halves) | 30 |
| T-Bone Steak (12-oz.) (340 gm) | 106 |

*2-Broiler Sections (all models) 23½ in. wide × 22⅜ in. deep (59.7 cm wide × 56.7 cm deep)*

| PRODUCT | SERVINGS PER HOUR |
|---|---|
| Beef Tenderloin (7 oz.) (199 gm) | 570 |
| Lobster Tails (8–12 oz.) (226–340 gm) | 400 |
| Chicken (Broiler halves) | 60 |
| T-Bone Steak (12 oz.) (340 gm) | 212 |

*Drop-in Char Broilers*

COOKING CAPACITY (MEATS AT ROOM TEMP.)

| GRID COOKING AREA | | TRAY CAP'Y | | 3½" (8.9 cm) Dia., 2½ OZ. (71 GM) HAMBURGERS | | 8" × 3" × ½" (20.3 × 7.6 × 1.3 cm) NEW YORK STRIP STEAK | | GRID PREHEAT TIME (FROM COLD START) |
|---|---|---|---|---|---|---|---|---|
| In. | cm | (Qts.) | Liters | Max. Per Hour | Max. Per Load | Max. Per Hour | Max. Per Load | |
| 16 × 16 | 40.6 × 40.6 | 5 | 4.7 | 260 | 16 | 75–85 | 12 | 4 min. to 400°F. (204°C) |
| 16 × 32 | 40.6 × 81.2 | 10 | 9.4 | 520 | 32 | 150–170 | 24 | 11 min. to 650°F. (343°C) |

**TYPICAL PRODUCTION (MEATS AT ROOM TEMPERATURE)\* (cont.)**

**Standard Broilers**

*Backshelf Broiler*

| EXTERNAL DIMENSIONS | | | | | INTERNAL DIMENSIONS | | | | |
|---|---|---|---|---|---|---|---|---|---|
| *Height to Broiler Top* | *Width* | *Depths to Front of Handle* | *Depths Front to Back Panel* | *Vertical Travel of Handle* | *Broiling Compartment* | | | *Grid Area* | |
| | | | | | W | D | H | W | D |
| in. | 35⅝ | 36 | 22¾ | 16½ | 6 | 24 | 15 | 4 | 21¼ | 15 (Extension—10¼) |
| cm | 90.5 | 91.4 | 57.8 | 41.9 | 15.2 | 60.9 | 38 | 10 | 54 | 38 (Extension—26) |

| WEIGHTS (LB./KG) | TYPICAL BROILING TIMES (MINUTES) "MEDIUM DONE" FROM ROOM TEMPERATURE UNLESS OTHERWISE SHOWN |
|---|---|

| *Time to Preheat to Cherry Red* | *Ship* | *Net* | *Rib Steak 1" (2.5 cm) Thick 1½ lbs.* | *Club Steak 1" (2.5 cm) Thick 1½ lbs. (680 gm)* | *Porterhouse 1" (2.5 cm) 1½–2 lbs. (680-905 gm)* | *Porterhouse 2" (5 cm) Thick 3-3½ lbs. (1.4-1.6 kg)* | *Sirloin 1" (2.5 cm) Thick 2½-3½ lbs. (1.1-1.6 kg)* | *Sirloin 2" (5 cm) Thick 5-5½ lbs. (2.3-2.5 kg)* | *Tenderloin 1" (2.5 cm) Thick* | *Rib Chops ¾" (1.9 cm) Thick 2-3 oz. (57-85 gm)* |
|---|---|---|---|---|---|---|---|---|---|---|
| 15 min. | 235 106.6 | 165 74.8 | 12–14 min. | 12–14 min. | 14–16 min. | 30–35 min. | 14–16 min. | 30–35 min. | 12–14 min. | 14–15 min. (well done) |

*Broilers for Counter, Cabinet, or Modular Use*

TYPICAL PRODUCTION (ALL MODELS) GRID AREA: 25½ IN. WIDE × 27½ IN. DEEP (65.8 CM WIDE × 71.8 CM DEEP)

| *Food Product* | *Servings Per Hour* |
|---|---|
| Beef Tenderloin, 7 oz. (199 gm) | 368 |
| Beef T-Bone, 12 oz. (340 gm) | 136 |
| Beef Sirloin Strip, 12 oz. (340 gm) | 136 |
| Lobster Tails, 8–12 oz. (226–340 gm) | 258 |
| Chicken (Broiler Halves) | 39 |

**Broilers With Convection Oven Base**

*Broiler Sections*

DIMENSIONS

| Inches | cm | Product | Servings Per Hour |
|---|---|---|---|
| 26½ wide × 23¼ deep | 67.3 wide × 59 deep | Beef Tenderloin (7 oz.) (199 gm) | 285 |
| 30¾ wide × 29¼ deep | 78.1 wide × 74.2 deep | Lobster Tails (8–12 oz.) (226–340 gm) | 200 |
| | | Chicken (Broiler halves) | 39 |
| | | Beef T-Bone (12 oz.) (340 gm) | 136 |

\*General Electric Company.

**INFRARED BROILING GUIDE***

| Namp No. | Type Product | Thickness In. | cm | Weight Oz. | gm | Meat Temp. F. | C | Valve Setting | **Rack Pos. | Rare | Med. Rare | Med. | Med. Well | Well |
|---|---|---|---|---|---|---|---|---|---|---|---|---|---|---|
| 180 | Strip Loin Steak (Ctr. Cut) | 1½ | (3.8 cm) | 16 oz. | 453 gm | 40° | 4° | High | 2(d) | 4 | 6½ | 9 | 10½ | 11½ |
| 180 | Strip Loin Steak (Ctr. Cut) | 1½ | (3.8 cm) | 16 oz. | 453 gm | 40° | 4° | High | 3(d) | 4½ | 7 | 9½ | 11 | 12 |
| 180 | Strip Loin Steak (Ctr. Cut) | ¾ | (1.9 cm) | 12 oz. | 340 gm | 40° | 4° | High | 3(d) | 3 | 5 | 6¼ | 7 | — |
| 190 | Beef Tenderloin (Ctr. Cut) | 2 | (5 cm) | 8 oz. | 226 gm | 40° | 4° | High | 3(d) | 5½ | 8 | 10 | 12 | 14 |
| 412 | Pork Chop | 1 | (2.5 cm) | 8 oz. | 226 gm | 70° | 21° | High | 3(d) | — | — | — | — | 9 |
| 232 | Lamb Chop | 1¼ | (3.2 cm) | 7 oz. | 199 gm | 70° | 21° | High | 3(d) | — | 5½ | — | 8 | — |
| 184 | Butt Steak (End Cut) | 1 | (2.5 cm) | 10 oz. | 283 gm | 70° | 21° | High | 3(d) | 2½ | 4½ | 6 | 7 | 7¾ |
| | Lobster Tail (Preboiled) | — | — | 10 oz. | 283 gm | 70° | 21° | High | 3(d) | — | — | — | — | 2½ |
| | Ground Chuck Steak Patty | (Approx. ½) | (Approx. 1.3 cm) | 4 oz. | 114 gm | 70° | 21° | High | 3(d) | — | 5 | 7 | 8 | — |
| | Ground Chuck Steak Patty | (Approx. 1) | (Approx. 2.5 cm) | 8 oz. | 226 gm | 70° | 21° | High | 3(d) | — | 6 | 8 | 10 | — |

**Doneness was based as follows:**

Rare—deep red center
Med. Rare—lighter red center
Med.—deep pink center
Med. Well—light pink center
Well—brown center

*Note:* Broiling tests performed at Loft Restaurant, South Bend, Indiana on April 25, 1978. Lower deck of broiler (each grid 24½-in. wide × 27½-in. deep), (62.2 cm wide × 70 cm deep) 2-grid gas-fried, Total Btu per hour—154,000

*South Bend Range Corp.
**2(d)—2nd down
  3(d)—3rd down

## SPECIALTY BROILERS

Among specialty broilers are conveyor broilers, which have a continuous belt with a heat source above and below. Belt can be timed to produce varying thicknesses, degree of doneness, and range of menu items.

In vertical broilers the item to be broiled is held in a hinged wire grid alongside or between the heat sources, which may be charcoal, gas, or electric. Most common is heat on either side, and if heat is supplied by charcoal or char rock, they are held in a basket or grid arrangement.

The combination broiler/griddle has one set of burners to supply heat for both the broiler and the frying griddle that forms the top of the broiler.

This type of construction prevents this equipment from handling large-volume frying and broiler load simultaneously. The use of ceramic radiants improves performance but can affect griddle operation adversely in these combinations.

These broilers are designed for small kitchens with limited space and low volume. They may be used in range batteries or as separate, freestanding units.

### Salamander

The salamander or elevated broiler is a miniature broiler mounted above the top of a heavy-duty range (usually closed or hot top) or above a spreader plate as part of the back shelf assembly.

Salamanders also have a special function: to finish or glaze sauced dishes, au gratin items, or foods that do not require high broiling temperatures.

Features of the salamander include:

- Many similar to qualities found in heavy-duty broilers, including ceramic radiants
- Grid only 1.6 to 2.8 sq. ft. (1486 to 2601 cm²)
- Requires no floor space
- May be mounted in pairs on special stands or legs
- Often used as auxiliary broiler for preparation of short orders during slow hours when other broiling equipment is shut down
- Capacity adequate for entire broiling load in small operations serving small quantities of broiled food. Be sure chosen model can produce broiled items of satisfactory quality.

## BROILER INSTALLATION

Having selected a broiling unit with the greatest potential for the given situation, the purchaser must be sure the selection can be installed properly.

Among installation recommendations:

- Location near refrigerator and serving trays for fast production
- Fire-resistant location
- On level area
- With adequate hooding and venting systems since excessive, insufficient, or improperly-applied ventilation can cause too much heat loss, smoking, or loss of au gratin oven heat.

## TESTING BROILED MEATS

Much is said about using forks for broiling. Actually, as one authority points out, a fork is an awkward tool, even for steaks and chops. Tongs work better and give a better "feel" for doneness. A spatula or turner is necessary to turn ground meat patties and fish properly.

Most broil chefs judge doneness by the "feel" or the resilience of the meat, which varies with the grade, temperature, and cut; being able to judge this accurately every time is an acquired skill and/or natural talent.

Broiling times in charts vary with broilers, grade of meat, and other factors; are generally suggested as a guide rather than an absolute standard.

"Rare" is different in the South than in New York, and individual operators must work out the standards that are most satisfactory in their own locality.

## TIPS FOR BETTER BROWNING

Also remember that fat content of a cut is directly related to the crust or finish of a steak. Fatless cuts, such as filets, commonly are dipped in oil or marinated before broiling.

The lower the meat grade the less fat so lower grades are often dipped, marinated, or thawed in oil for better crust or finish. Some operators brush combinations of butter or oil and liquid browning on meat before broiling.

Filet mignon and other lightly fatted meats may be brushed with butter or garlic butter before broiling or when first placed over the fire to give a more even browning and prevent excessive surface charring.

## KEEPING BROILERS CLEAN

Broiler-cleaning routines are easy to follow, whether broilers are horizontal overhead or char underfired.

### Horizontal Overhead Broiler

1. Wipe the outside of the broiler every day with a cloth dampened in water that contains a noncaustic cleaning compound. Rinse, dry, and polish the outside of the broiler with a soft cloth.
2. To clean the inside of the broiler, be sure to use a cloth that is not too wet. Wring it well to prevent getting water inside the broiling compartment. Go over the inside surfaces of the broiler with a damp cloth.

3. If food has burned on the inside of the broiler, scrape it off with a long-handled scraper or brush. Do not use cleaners that will mar or scratch the lining on the inside of the broiler.
4. Remove the pans that catch grease from the broiler. Empty them and wash them with a mild solvent. Be sure to dry these pans thoroughly, then put them back under the broiler. Now the broiler is ready to use again.

### Char Underfired Broiler

1. Lift off the grids that rest on top of the char broiler and wipe them clean with a damp cloth. Wash drip shields. Under the grids are baffles. Take these out next and wipe them clean with a damp cloth.
2. Clean heat source for the char underfired broiler with a scraper (or wire brush, if particles of food have burned on.) Next wipe with a rag dampened in detergent and water.

3. Remove and empty drip trays and wash with detergent and water. Dry thoroughly and put them back under the broiler.
4. Where charcoal briquettes are used for broiling, all ashes and burned matches should be cleaned out from the pilot area. Also clean ashes out of the fire box with a vacuum cleaner or brush. Finally, wipe the outside of the broiler with a cloth dampened in water that contains a noncaustic cleaning compound.

## BROILER MAINTENANCE

The American Gas Association recommends that burners be kept clean and openings and air shutters be checked regularly to make sure they are clear. Burners also should be checked for adjustment by a gas company service representative, as needed.

**BRAIN TEASER—BROILERS**

1. Broiled foods are very popular even though they are usually the (most expensive) (cheapest) items on the menu. (Cross out wrong answer.)

2. What are the three kinds of broilers? (1.) _____ (2.) _____

   (3.) _____

3. Charbroilers are used mostly for_____(Fill in.)

4. The salamander broiler is usually located _____
   (Complete sentence.)

5. Infra-red burners are used in broilers to add_____(Fill in.)

6. What tools work best for turning steaks and chops?_____

7. How do most broiler chefs tell when meat is done?_____

   _____

8. Is "rare" meat the same everywhere in the country? (Yes) (No) (Cross out wrong answer.)

9. Since no fat is used in broiling, meat has to have fat in it to brown well during broiling. If meat does not have enough fat, what can be done to make it brown better?_____

   _____

10. When you clean the inside of a broiler, be sure to wring your cloth out hard as you should NEVER

    _____(Complete sentence.)

*(For correct answers, see pages 250–251.)*

**FIGURE   6.2**
At Jam, Inc., an Ogunquit, Me. restaurant, they broil steaks on the top grid of a charbroiler like the one shown here. At the same time, with the same heat, they cook bluefish on the lower salamander rack. At Benetz Inn, Quakertown, Pa., a 500-seat restaurant with a staff of 35, they broil steaks, hamburgers, and shishkebobs on a similar unit. There the salamander is used to brown baked onion soup and other specialties, such as Mornay and au gratin dishes. The lower salamander rack, utilizing waste heat thrown down from the top broiling surface, provides an extra, fuel-free cooking area and energy savings in both establishments.

**FIGURE   6.3**
Designed to provide 12,500 meals per day in the near future, Houston's Memorial Hospital System, Southwest Unit selected a conveyorized broiler as a component of its cook/package/chill system of food production.

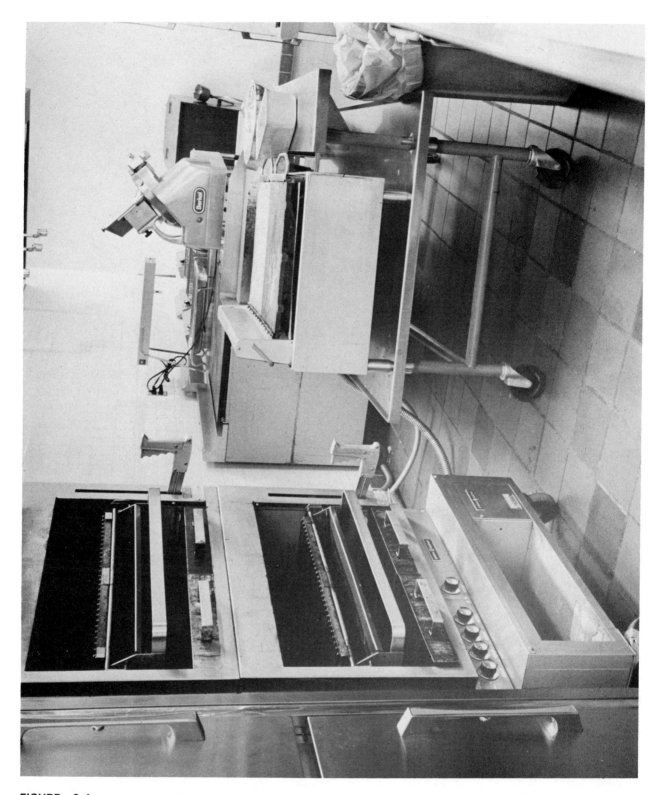

**FIGURE   6.4**
''Put it on wheels'' was the request made by the management when ordering equipment for Chicago's Columbian House Restaurant. Broilers roll out easily at clean-up time.

**FIGURE   6.5**
Two high volume, overfired infrared broilers at left in picture plus two adjacent wall-mounted salamanders (small overfired broilers) take care of the broiling requirements at Bob Burns restaurant, Woodland Hills, Ca. The small broilers are used for glazing and au gratin work at the restaurant, noted for its Scottish specialties.

**FIGURE   6.6**
Three double deck, infrared broilers are an important part of the main cooking battery at Louisville's Commonwealth Convention Center. They are essential to the food facilities designed to serve from 75 to 5000 people at one time with menus that range from beverages and canapes to full banquets.

**FIGURE 6.7**
Banquets held at the Lexington (Ky.) Convention Center are served from this supplementary or warming kitchen. Char broiler at lower left in picture plays important role in preparation of banquet entrees.

**FIGURE   7.1**

A waitress pick-up station visible to patrons was designed to maintain the atmosphere of a quiet country inn at the Foxfire Restaurant, Anaheim, Ca. Among the chief contributors to the atmosphere are the copper and crinkle-glass food warming lamps that contrast effectively with the dark stained wood. Antique copper covers the service shelf with copper and brass cooking utensils decoratively arranged above it. The wood doors below provide refrigerated and unrefrigerated storage space for waitress pick-up.

# Chapter Seven

# Infrared Food-Warming Equipment

Infrared food-warming units now come in many styles unlike the time not so long ago when the infrared lamp was the order of the day. At first, diverse lamp styles were introduced to heighten the merchandising effectiveness of the units. Today infrared lamps are available in a dazzling array of styles and in a variety of models as well.

Employing tungsten or nickel-chromium resistors within bulbs, tube, or rods, the infrared devices generate radiant energy rather than actual heat. Radiant energy maintains or creates heat only in the objects it strikes. The air around or between the lamp and product is not heated so it is possible to use the lamps very imaginatively. They turn up anywhere the need for a "spot" of heat can be combined with attractive display: on serving counters, carving stations, pickup areas, and buffet lines.

For very short-term needs, infrared lamps are often the best solution. They maintain an acceptable level of heat and are flexible. In addition, the lamps attractively spotlight the product, bathing it in a warm glow of light that highlights the color of the food on display.

Now infrared is also being used in both standard and portable models, with or without showcase lights. Keeping decor in mind, one portable food warmer for a 12 × 20-in. (30 × 51-cm) pan is available in rust, olive, and gold.

A wide selection of overhead models designed to heat areas of varying sizes is also available. Flexible mounting arrangements permit units to hang, stand, suspend, move, or be placed in tandem or dual positions to fit desired layout. Scientifically designed to provide a wider heat pattern, these overhead heating units can cover a large area with uniform heat that will keep food hot without cooking it.

Standard units come in 24-in. (61 cm), 36-in. (91 cm), and 48-in. (122 cm) lengths. A pilot light indicates that the unit is on; heat can be adjusted from high to low; a reflector and element guard assure safe use of quartz or metal element. Lights that focus on food are also available.

Factory-assembled units can be mounted side by side with 4-in. (10 cm) space between units. Two or more food-warmer models can be joined together to form one continuous housing up to

12-ft. (3.5 m) in length, with each unit individually controlled. Units longer than 12-ft. (3.5 m) are also available.

## ACCESSORIES ADD FLEXIBILITY

Accessories offer extra flexibility: tubular posts for mounting on counter tops; overhead suspension cord and plug set; stainless steel pan and wire trivet; remote infinite heat control for field installation at a remote location.

The function of infrared food warmers is to maintain safe and satisfactory serving temperatures for loose food, particularly French fries, and for plated foods waiting for pick up. Minimum safe holding temperature for most cooked foods is 140°F. (60°C), and it is desirable to hold most meats and vegetables between 140°F. (60°C) and 150°F. (66°C). Above 150°F. (66°C) additional cooking takes place. With energy costs of continuing concern, some operations have found that switching from incandescent heating lamps to quartz infrared lamps has reduced total energy consumption significantly. For maximum energy saving, take care to avoid excessive air circulation or drafts that decrease a unit's efficiency.

The universal interest in food warmers has provided the volume potential needed to justify wide-ranging research and development of models to meet every kind of demand. Reflectivity and its relation to the unique traits of radiant heat rays have been studied to develop fully all the advantages of the many characteristics of infrared rays and their penetrating qualities.

Vegetables especially get criticism when on-the-plate temperatures are tepid. A serving of carrots loses 20°F. (12°C) of heat in less than a minute after leaving the stove. Popped immediately under an infrared warmer, carrots remain at stove temperature.

Optimum temperatures for food on buffets, smorgasbords, and cafeteria counters can also be maintained with infrared warmers. One model can hold one to four steam-table pans of food.

Infrared warming lamps can also be mounted on carts designed for roving tableside service or dining room display of roast beef or other specialties.

## WIDE RANGE OF MODELS

Some food products such as pizza, require heat from below as well as from above. Most bottom-heat warmers use an electric element under a base to generate sufficient heat. This type of equipment is also designed to be as attractive and versatile as possible and to emphasize the unit's display capability. Many operators are choosing models that combine bottom-heat with infrared lamps.

When infrared and bottom-heat are combined, most products can be held safely for up to 30 minutes with minimum deterioration.

Models range from hanging bulbs to metal tubes under hoods—either stationary or hanging—to table models in a variety of sizes.

One manufacturer's line includes an infrared heater and roll warmer; a swing-away fish-and-chips warmer; mounted dual swivel hoods; and top heating units with two metal sheath infrared heating elements.

In these food warmers, the infrared-producing filaments are housed in lamps, tubes, or rods. These elements are described by one manufacturer of an extensive line of food warming equipment:

Infrared lamps: these are essentially the same as lamps or bulbs for illumination, the principal difference being that of filament temperature.

Since the production of light is not the objective, infrared is designed to operate at low filament temperature, resulting in much less light and more radiation than lamps for lighting purposes.

Operating with a cooler filament temperature means longer bulb life—in excess of 5,000 hours. These may be 250 or 375 watt lamps.

## TYPES OF TUBES

**Infrared Tubes.** Infrared producing tubes contain a filament within a sheath of quartz, tempered glass, or metal rod. Though infrared radiant energy is produced from these materials, the difference is in their efficiency—the amount of radiant energy produced from the amount of wattage it takes to operate the unit.

**Quartz Tubes.** These tubes are formed by fusing together tiny natural quartz crystals. Quartz is like glass in appearance but with properties that enable it to provide up to 20 times greater concentration of energy than is possible by other infrared sources.

This material will withstand higher temperatures and has greater resistance to thermal shock (ability to withstand quick extreme changes in temperature without cracking or breaking) than glass.

The natural properties of quartz enable a tube of shorter length and smaller diameter to produce as much, or greater, radiant energy than a larger open glass tube. This advantage permits better designed units which are more convenient to install.

**Glass Tubes.** Certain types of glass have been produced for specific uses; their composition can be changed to meet unusual requirements. Such tubes obtain heat resistance and basic properties through special processing that begins with normal glass from which practically all constituents, except silica, have been removed. In one unit designed for infrared application, the result is comparable to quartz properties and performance within certain temperature ranges. It will operate over the complete infrared wave length range and tubes can be colored red for warm visual effect.

### Handle with Care

All glass tubes must be handled with care. During cleaning avoid any pressure that might tend to bend or break the tube.

The most important factor in housing a filament in a glass tube is to use a sheath that will permit the greatest amount of infrared energy transmission.

**Metal Rods.** These rods consist of a sheath of stainless steel or nickel alloy for housing the filament. Though it is the least efficient of the tube-type infrared sources, it is almost unbreakable, easy to clean, and has a long life.

## WHERE TO INSTALL

Since the infrared food warmer is designed to supply only enough warmth to keep the heat from leaving the food, it should be located so that the radiating heat covers just the area the food will occupy—approximately 10 to 18 in. (25.4 to 45.7 cm) above the food. Variations in height will depend on the type of unit and the amount of heat required. Infrared units should not be used over a combustible material.

The attractiveness of infrared warmer design contributes to good showmanship in modern foodservice operations. Infrared warmers create a favorable impression where food is exposed to public view, particularly where lamps are used, since they spotlight the food in a warm glow. Using these lamps in open serving shelves provides a dramatic effect. In many operations, lamps are styled to serve as an effective element in the interior design.

Heightening the merchandising possibilities of infrared food warmers is a model with a mirror background to set off food held under four infrared bulbs in a stainless steel housing. The device stands 28¼-in. (71.8 cm) high, 27¼-in. (69.2 cm) wide and 24½-in. (62.2 cm) deep and has guide rails 4¾-in. (12 cm) high. The mirror is angled to give maximum reflection and there is 20¼-in. (51.4 cm) between the shelf and the bulbs.

Installing these units is easy since they are plug-in devices, which can be connected to the nearest 110-volt ac outlet.

## SAFETY FOR OPERATORS

This equipment assures safety for its operators by the 10- to 18-in. (25.4 to 45.7 cm) distance maintained between the food and the infrared source. Only actual physical contact with the source will burn skin.

Safety of foods held under lamps depends on proper use of the holding device. Holding equipment should never be used to reheat products. FDA (Federal Drug Administration) rules and common sense both dictate that most products must be maintained at 140°F. (60°C) to prevent contamination.

Past abuses have prompted the FDA to require thermometers in warming cabinets so operators using infrared lamps must have a product thermometer handy.

## TIPS ON USE OF FOOD WARMERS

Many operators with steam tables are adding overhead infrared lamps to their units. One operator has found that an overhead infrared rod keeps gravies on the steam table from "skinning."

In one Minnesota operation, a red infrared lamp casts an order-building glow over roasts set up to be carved to customer's order.

Pastries and fried products keep well with only infrared heat since there is no moisture to be absorbed by the product and this method of heating tends to keep food surface crisp.

Where peak production makes close oven scheduling necessary, a roast removed from the oven can be set on an ordinary table and kept warm for quite a long period by placing infrared units over it.

Units may be hung from the ceiling directly over the serving counter or they can be built in or rest on the serving counter.

Infrared can keep French fries hot and crisp for as long as 25 minutes. It holds chicken, shrimp, fish, oysters, French fries, hors d'oeuvres, croquettes, and breaded meats hot and crisp for an hour.

Air conditioning does not cool foods kept under a warmer and, by the same token, the infrared rays do not heat up air-conditioned interiors.

Dishes, if held no longer than one hour under infrared lamps, will feel warm to the touch but will not be too hot to handle. No breakage occurs as a result of the use of infrared for warming.

Oven-hot apple pie can be held topped with a slice of cheese under the infrared lamp and the cheese will soften slightly so that it cuts more easily when the pie is served.

## BRAIN TEASER—INFRARED FOOD-WARMING EQUIPMENT

1. Infrared food-warming equipment keeps food hot with radiant heat. How does radiant heat save energy? _____

2. Name two types of infrared food-warming equipment now available._____

3. Minimum safe hold temperature for most cooked food under infrared is (circle correct answer) 0°F (−18°C) 500°F. (260°C) 140°F. (60°C)

4. Which of the following conditions will occur if there are drafts near infrared warming units? (Check right answer) Lower temperature of food being held _____ Raise temperature of food being held _____

5. Which of the following products would require bottom heat as well as overhead heat to keep temperature at proper level? (check right answer) Salad _____ Pizza _____

6. In cleaning glass tubes from infrared food-warming units what should be avoided?_____

7. How are infrared units installed?_____

8. Does infrared food-warming equipment add heat to air conditioned interiors? (check right answer) Yes _____ No _____

9. How do these units affect plates holding food under them?_____

*(For correct answers, see page 251.)*

**FIGURES  7.2 and 7.3**
Pictured above and on the facing page are two areas profiting from a quartz tube food warmer installation at Bob Burns Restaurant, Woodland Hills, Ca. An elevated shelf is used to mount the tubes which reflect down on one side to the waiter/waitress pick-up shelf (see pictures). Flanking the food warmers on either side are open areas for cold food pick-up. On the opposite side from the waiter pick-up section is the chef's finishing table. This is located across from the cooking line and also supplied by the support cooking line. After menu items are plated for service, the chef places them under the tube to maintain just-cooked temperatures until waitress pick-up.

**FIGURE  7.4**
At left in picture two infrared heat lamps are used to create a self-service station for waiters on the salad and pantry pick-up counter of the Apple Tree Inn, Kansas City North, Mo. At this white tablecloth restaurant, where the design goal was creating a feeling of going into someone's home, french fried croutons and apple fritters are popular salad accompaniments. Infrared heat lamps keep products at serving temperature while orders are assembled for the 3200 meals per week served there.

**FIGURE 8.1**
The slicer for the support cooking line at Bob Burns Restaurant, Woodland Hills, Ca. is placed on a separate table. Table is well located between the walk-in refrigerator and the cooking line.

# Chapter Eight

# Specialty Equipment

Any successful effort at holding down costs starts with a close look at the many tasks required to prepare foods for the menu. The next step is to investigate equipment available to speed their performance.

If a job is being done repeatedly by hand, it is time to look at specialized equipment to learn if a machine can do the job at less cost. Make sure the cost of the energy required to run the machine is included in any cost comparison of machine production and manual labor.

Many foodservice operations have found that the purchase of specialized equipment has added new cooking style to the menu, giving an operation extra volume that rapidly writes off equipment cost and justifies increased energy costs. Sometimes a piece of special equipment offers better quality control or the dividend of an unexpected second use. Each use helps to reduce cost written off against each of the other jobs the equipment performs, thus helping to justify the new acquisition.

## HOW TO TELL WHAT IS NEEDED

When considering a piece of specialized equipment, several questions should be answered:

*Will this equipment fill a potential need in the particular foodservice? Is the specialized performance of the equipment suitable for the task to be performed?*

*Does the volume of requirement for the equipment justify investment in the piece of equipment, and especially important, the cost of the energy to operate it?*

*Since many items of specialized equipment are relatively new, has there been sufficient experience and record of its efficient and troublefree performance; is there good service for the device available? (A very fine device can become a problem, and even a practical impossibility, if there is no convenient, prompt, and effective service at reasonable service charges.)*

*Is there a good chance that the need for the device is likely to continue, or is it more likely that the type of item it produces will be simply a fad whose demand may diminish or disappear before investment in the device is amortized?*

Whether or not a piece of special equipment is economically justified probably can be estimated best on the basis of these factors:

- Capacity of equipment
- Normal production requirements for it
- Peak production requirements for it
- Energy cost
- Labor time it will release; use dollar estimate to evolve ratio to equipment cost
- Profit on new volume its use may add.

## HOW MUCH SPACE?

The next piece of crucial information for many purchasers of special equipment is how much space it will take. The search for space-saving installation and use of this equipment has paid off in (1) more compact design, (2) emphasis on the use of vertical space, and (3) installation in out-of-the-way places. Much of the equipment available for special jobs can now be wall mounted.

Often several pieces of specialty equipment will be located in one section. In the Sheraton St. Louis Hotel kitchen, such an arrangement places milk and hot chocolate dispensers, ice cream freezers, coffee makers, toasters, and hot-soup holding sections out of direct traffic flow.

Start a check of the special food production jobs in your operation. For each, recheck the specially designed equipment now available to avoid overlooking the cost advantages of specialty equipment. Keep in mind that specialty equipment selected to make labor more productive should be simple, versatile, and safe.

## SLICERS DO MANY FOOD TASKS

Helping to maintain the high productivity of the kitchen of the Foxfire Restaurant, Anaheim, CA., is a conveniently located slicer. The slicer is in an area where turkey and ham are prepared for the Monte Cristo Sandwiches, a favorite menu fea-

ture. Slicer also keeps supply of triangle tips available for French Dip Sandwiches. (See picture, Chapter 1, Ranges)

However, slicers pay their way in many preparation tasks beside slicing meat for sandwiches. Salad and vegetable preparation areas make maximum use of them. Tomato slicers that produce uniform slices quickly can be operated by hand or electrically, depending on the production needed. Models offer blades set for $3/16$ –, (5 mm) $1/4$ – (6 mm) or $3/8$ – (1 cm) in. slices. Some units occupy approximately $11\frac{1}{2} \times 18$-in. (29.2 × 45.7 cm) of counter space and are less than 10-in. (4.5 cm) high. Another unit 13-in. (33 cm) high requires $16\frac{1}{2} \times 13\frac{1}{2}$-in. (41.9 × 34.3 cm) of counter space.

Tomato slicers can also be used for cooked potatoes, hard cooked eggs, and for bananas, cored pears, peaches, mushrooms, sausage, peppers, pineapple, bakery products, meatballs, and boned meat. Do not leave wrappings on products to be sliced. A power-drive attachment that will more than triple the speed of one slicer is also available.

Safeguards for workers operating these machines have been carefully designed. Safety switches and guards keep workers clear of recessed blades. One manufacturer has prepared a complete training kit, which can be purchased for slicer-operator safety training and certification. Clear explanations with accompanying pictures introduce the worker to the machine, its operation, and the safety devices built into it. Striking posters warn against unsafe practices and list proper methods for operating slicers. A certificate to be awarded to workers who complete the training course is also included in this excellent, inexpensive training kit.

### How to Clean Slicers

Cleaning is important. Instructions for one slicer call for spray rinsing and drip drying, or running the parts through the dishmachine. On another model, loosening one thumb screw disassembles unit for easy cleaning. Blade and pusher assemblies can be lifted out and run through dishmachine.

Automatic models require more comprehensive cleaning procedures. The training kit described above gives illustrated, detailed cleaning and sanitizing instructions. Regular lubrication of the knife adjustment screw every time the slicer is cleaned is also recommended.

Every model should be cleaned daily, or oftener if not used constantly, as bacteria will develop from bits of food clinging to the machine.

Preventive maintenance of slicers requires a little reading and planning. One service technician recommends writing down manufacturer's instructions regarding time for periodic lubrication, correct lubricant, and maintenance of the equipment. This information should be kept handy for easy reference. Lubricating parts reduces friction and prevents the motor from overheating. Some parts of the slicer need to be lubricated once a year. If not enough maintenance information is available in printed form, ask the manufacturer or service technician to supply what is needed.

## CUTTERS OR CHOPPERS

Cutters or choppers are used to prepare fresh or cooked fruits, vegetables, and other cooked foods. Chopping is done in a bowl with a revolving blade. The bowl and cutting or chopping parts are lightweight and easy to remove for necessary cleaning. The outside of one unit wipes clean with a damp cloth. Its manufacturer's suggested cleaning routine for the interior states:

To clean food cutter, turn off switch. Wait until knives stop. Turn handle and swing up cover, lift up and off. With the left hand, turn knife shaft until blades are horizontal. With the right hand, unscrew large black knob, pull off knife assembly. Remove comb by lifting off locking stud. Grasp bowl with both hands and turn clockwise, lift up and off. All these parts may be washed in hot, soapy water, rinsed, and dried.

Safeguards incorporated in one model keep it from operating until cover is down and locked in place.

Attachments make it possible to use another model as a dicer, slicer, or shredder. Meat grinders or choppers are also available that use a different mechanism from the cutters and choppers described above.

## CUTTER/MIXERS

Cutter/mixers offer high production possibilities for bread and other doughs and batters, and for vegetables, salads, bread crumbs, chopped cheese or potatoes, chopped sausage, hamburgers, meat loaf, and salad dressings and similar items.

The cut/mix or other specified attachment when placed in bowl prepares ingredients to shape desired if proper running time is used. Because equipment operates at high speed, it is better to cut time too short and restart the machine than to let unit run too long.

A clear bowl cover on one model makes it easy to check contents. Electronic interlocks make it impossible to start the machine when the cover is open or bowl is tilted. The base is heavy enough for vibration-free operation, even with heavy doughs. A pour-through mixing baffle makes it possible to add liquids while the cutter/mixer is running. The cutter/mixer can be operated either continuously, or for short on/off periods. Start and stop buttons are clearly marked. Units are sized to handle either 30 or 45 qt. (28.2 or 42.3 l) maximum.

### Speedy Cleaning for Cutter/Mixer

Cleanup is fast, too. Usually all removable parts can be put through the dishmachine. The bowl and cover can be cleaned with water and detergent, rinsed, and wiped dry. Cleaning time can be saved by scheduling products in sequence so that small amount of product left in the machine will not affect the next product that goes through. One such recommended sequence:

1. Prepare bread crumbs. Empty bowl and wipe out any particles.
2. Prepare tossed salad. Empty bowl and wipe out any particles.
3. Prepare mayonnaise. Scrape bowl.
4. Prepare cole slaw. Scrape bowl.
5. Prepare ham salad. Scrape bowl.
6. Prepare meat loaf.

Proper sharpening of the blades of a vertical cutter/mixer, food cutter, or slicer is critical to prevent the food being handled in it from being bruised. Oversharpening or sharpening blades to a thin edge will dull them more readily. A maintenance program should be set up to insure that sharpening is done regularly and properly.

## TOASTERS

One approach to estimating needed toaster capacity stresses slices per minute rather than slices per hour to bring home the fact that peak service demands are measured in minutes. For this reason, toasting equipment capable of handling peak, rather than average, loads is essential to an efficient foodservice operation.

No one cares very much about service delays in off-peak periods, this expert points out, but if the operation is slowed down during busy periods by inadequate toasting equipment, the user can sustain a very real and expensive loss. He urges that toasting equipment requirements be guided by the rate of service required during the breakfast rush.

### How Many Toasters?

Arthur W. Dana, food operations consultant, suggests the following esimates as a guide to the amount of toasting equipment needed:

*For college, university and hospital cafeterias, hospital patient assembly lines where the largest demand is at breakfast.*

Toasting capacity needed equals number of diners served per minute per station times average number slices per person (this may be 1 slice for women, 2 slices or more for men)

equals 5 persons per minute times 2 slices per person

equals 10 slices per minute

equals 3 4-slice toasters (a fourth for emergency)

large conveyor-type toaster.

The same equipment could handle:

6 persons per minute times 2 slices per person equals 12 slices per minute.

7 persons per minute times 1¾ slices per person equals 11 slices per minute.

8 persons per minute times 1½ slices per person equals 12 slices per minute.

*For hospital assembly line:*

At one slice per person for hospital patients and an assembly speed of 6 a minute, a small size conveyor-type toaster or two 4-slot units (the extra two slots as a safety factor if elements burn out during peak needs) would be adequate.

*For toasted sandwiches in public restaurants:* Average sandwich maker's speed:

2 sandwiches or 4 to 6 slices (club sandwiches) a minute. Perhaps two 4-slice toasters for each station or an operation might get by with one 4-slice toaster if sandwiches are not primary business.

*For breakfast toast in hotels and public restaurants:*

Maximum counter seat turnover determines production required.

4-slot unit equals 4 slices per minute. Conveyor toaster equals 6, 9, 12, 16, or 18 slices per minute.

Or use seat turnover and/or number of waitresses to estimate toaster requirements for meal period service.

### Improving Production

New equipment should be purchased if present toast production could be improved with toasters that:

- Take minimum space
- Are designed to offset any fluctuations in heat supply or compensate for heat buildup; operate on low energy
- Offer wide range color control (all shades of toast from light to dark)
- Turn out uniform product regardless of number of slices or how long in use.
- Unload easily
- Permit economy of operation during periods of intermittent toasting.

### Automatic Advances for Toasters

One automatic electric toaster comes in 4, 6, 8, 10, and 12-slot capacities. A stainless steel unit with durable components requires minimum maintenance. Elements are protected and easily

**POP-UP TOASTERS\*\***

| Description | Toaster Output (Slices/Hour) | | | KW Rating | Bread Slot Width (In.) | Product Openings (cm) |
|---|---|---|---|---|---|---|
| | Light Setting | Medium Setting | Dark Setting | | | |
| 2-slice bread w/cord set | 225 | 175 | 110 | 1.35 | .69 | 1.8 |
| 4-slice bread | 450 | 350 | 220 | 2.70 | .69 | 1.8 |
| 4-slice bread w/cord set | 450 | 350 | 220 | 2.70 | .69 | 1.8 |
| 6-slice bread | 675 | 525 | 330 | 4.05 | .69 | 1.8 |
| 8-slice bread (2 CT24's with 1 tiered stand) | 900 | 700 | 440 | 5.4 | .69 | 1.8 |
| 16-slice bread (4 CT24's with 2 tiered stands) | 1800 | 1400 | 800 | 10.8 | .69 | 1.8 |
| 2 whole muffins (4 halves) | 135 | 115 | 60 | 1.79 | .97 | 2.5 |
| 4 whole muffins—8 halves 2 CT20's w/1 tiered stand | 270 | 230 | 1.20 | 3.58 | .97 | 2.5 |
| 8 whole muffins—16 halves 4 CT20's w/2 tiered stands | 540 | 460 | 240 | 7.16 | .97 | 2.5 |
| 2 whole buns (4 halves) | 225 | 175 | 110 | 1.79 | 1.28 | 3.3 |
| 4 whole buns—8 halves 2 CT22's w/1 tiered stand | 450 | 350 | 220 | 3.58 | 1.28 | 3.3 |
| 8 whole buns—16 halves 4 CT22's w/2 tiered stands | 900 | 700 | 4.40 | 7.16 | 1.28 | 3.3 |

\*For most four-slice bread toaster installations, the CT24 (or CT25) 3-pole 120/208, 120/240 volt unit will be used. Units will operate on 120/208V or 120/240V 3-pole. CT24 can be operated on 120V, 2-pole by use of a jumper supplied with device. Specify voltage when ordering.

\*\*General Electric Company.

replaced. When toast is ready, toaster shuts off automatically and keeps toast warm until needed.

An energy-efficient toaster with solid-state controls that automatically adjust toasting time to compensate for surrounding temperatures and voltage fluctuations is now on the market. The 4-slice model of this commercial pop-up toaster produces 380 medium slices per hour.

In the chart above, one line of pop-up toasters provides the output.

## Conveyor Toasters

For large-volume, continuous toast production, either electric or gas conveyor models are available.

One heavy-duty, motor-driven, electric conveyor toaster features front and rear delivery, easy-to-use front controls, permanently lubricated motor, sheathed elements, and easy-to-clean brushed stainless steel finish. Since all components can be reached simply by removing the right side panel, toaster can be serviced easily. It is 17½-in. (44.5 cm) wide × 15-in. (38 cm) deep, and 30¾-in. (78.1 cm) high.

The variable-speed option on this unit is recommended for operations that serve a variety of toasted products such as English muffins, bagels, and other items whose longer toasting time would otherwise require sending them through toasting cycle twice. Since conveyor speed can be controlled with the variable-speed option, these products only need to pass through toasting cycle once.

In the toast position, the unit will deliver the first two slices in 54 seconds, then additional slices every nine seconds—for a total production cycle of 800 slices per hour. Five minutes after switching from toast to bun position, the machine starts to toast bun halves, bagels, or English muffins.

One horizontal conveyor toaster can toast up to ten slices per minute. A color-sensing system maintains degree of brownness set for bread, buns, bagels, and English muffins throughout the run.

This toaster continues to operate with only slightly reduced production if one element burns out since power is supplied by multiple heating units. Machine measures 17½-in. (44.5 cm) wide × 22½-in. (57.2 cm) deep by 16¼-in. (41.3 cm) high. An energy-saving thermostat automatically adjusts amount of power as toast production varies.

Electric conveyor toaster can be mounted on the wall over sandwich-preparation area. An independent on/off switch controls the top and bottom heaters; turning the bottom switch off converts the toaster to a bun warmer. Horizontal conveyor belt permits easy loading of buns or bread slices up to 2-in. (5 cm) thick. Speed at which conveyor is set determines color of toast.

## Bun-Only Toasters

Bun-only toasters come in standard models that produce either 826 standard 3½-in. (9 cm) bun halves per hour or larger units that toast 1100 per hour. Standard unit has an 11-in. (27.9 cm) wide conveyor that holds three 3½-in. (9 cm) bun halves or two 5-in. (12.7 cm) buns side by side. A wider conveyor opening is optional for thicker buns. When the toaster is used on mid-heat setting, energy use can be reduced to 1500 kw per hour.

Gas toasters that can toast up to 1200 slices of bread per hour can also toast buns at the flip of a switch. Because heat input automatically matches load, there is less wasted energy, and no warm-up time needed if toasting is only done periodically.

They also offer:

- Easy loading
- Automatic operation
- Easy-to-clean stainless steel construction
- For bread or bun toasting, one- or two-side toasting that can be selected by a switch.

- Front or rear delivery for either toasted bread or buns
- A sensing system that automatically regulates flame to toast products to desired degree of brownness
- Mounting on 4-in. (10 cm) legs, with cord and NEMA (National Electrical Manufacturers Assoc.) 5–15 plug supplied
- Natural gas regulator included wherever natural gas has been specified.
- Pilot flame that automatically ignites burners
- Fail-safe device that assures automatic cutoff of gas if flame goes out.

The unit is 22-in. (55.9 cm) wide × 15-in. (38 cm) deep.

The American Gas Association recommends that this cleaning procedure for gas toasters be carried out daily: When the toaster is cool, clean the outside surface. Remove trays and wash thoroughly in warm water and dry. Keep chain and frame clean. Remove excess crumbs with soft brush. Clean steel surfaces with damp cloth and all-purpose cleaning compound.

## Bread for Toasting

What bread makes the best toast? One equipment manufacturer offers this answer:

Use bread of good quality with uniform texture and grain. If bread is too coarse, heat will penetrate too quickly and make toast too dry. If bread has heavy streaks of dough, such as those caused by careless mixing, these will remain white when the rest of the slice is browned.

Use a loaf approximately 4½ in. (11.4 cm) square, of even shape, because an uneven loaf often has uneven texture. For best toast, store the bread at least 24 hours, and up to 48 hours, but do not slice it too long before toasting.

If sliced bread must stand, stack it evenly, keeping top and bottom crusts in place so the cut surfaces are not exposed to the air and thus become dried on one side. Place a dry cloth over the bread; a wet one will cause uneven moisture distribution. Do not cut off the crusts before toasting because the exposed edges dry quickly and are apt to burn black before the rest of the slice is properly browned.

## Toast-Based Dishes

Some seldom featured toast-based dishes collected in a booklet published by one maker of toasters:

Ham and Poached Eggs—Dip toast in hot cream, sprinkle with tiny squares of boiled ham, and place two poached eggs on top. Garnish with a sprig of parsley. The dish is a delicious addition to the breakfast menu.

Creamed Asparagus—Heat asparagus tips in prepared white sauce and season with salt, black pepper, and paprika. Serve on hot buttered toast and sprinkle with either grated hard-cooked egg yoke or Parmesan cheese.

Fried Ham and Relish—Dip pieces of toast in soup stock, place slice of fried ham on top, and in center of ham place a spoonful of India relish.

Slice Tongue Rarebit—Place sliced tongue on hot toast and cover with rarebit sauce. Serve with horseradish-beet sauce on lettuce leaf.

Aristocrat Dinner Sandwich—Place thin chicken slice on trimmed toast. Spread with creamed Roquefort and brown lightly. Serve with a citrus slice salad (1/2 slice of grapefruit topped by 1/2 slice of orange) on facing sides of sandwich.

## Waffle Bakers

Often adding waffle-based items to luncheon, dinner, and late-night menus will make breakfast waffle production more profitable since equipment gets maximum use. High-production waffle-baking equipment also can be justified more quickly when waffles are featured throughout the day's menus.

Waffle bakers now come equipped to:

- Turn out crisp, golden-brown, light, fluffy waffles every time
- Take batter on treated non-stick grids
- Utilize automatic temperature control to maintain best baking temperature; turn baker off when waffle is done
- Signal when waffles are done
- Control final product through settings for light, medium, or dark
- Signal with bell timers
- Limit batter overflow through grid design

- Take minimum space because of compact design
- Be easily cleaned
- Use minimum energy

One unit that turns out two 7-in. (17.8 cm) waffles, using 1650 kw power per hour, measures 19¹⁵⁄₁₆-in. (50.6 cm) wide × 13½-in. (34.3 cm) deep × 8½-in. (21.6 cm) high and has timers operated electrically or mechanically.

Two factors affect waffle baker requirements:

1. Average baking time per iron (one model cites 6 min.)
2. Number of units in operation. Waffle bakers come in single units that can be arranged in batteries that combine up to six units.

## Volume-Building Waffle Ideas

Waffle ideas for round-the-clock service to build volume include:

### Breakfast

| | |
|---|---|
| *Cinnamon Waffles* | *Waffles with Sausage* |
| *Jelly Waffles* | *Marmalade Waffles* |
| *Sugar Waffles* | *Waffles with Fresh* |
| *Waffles with Eggs* | *Berries* |
| *Waffles with Ham* | *Buckwheat Waffles* |

### Lunch

| | |
|---|---|
| *Honey Waffles* | *Waffles, Chicken a la* |
| *Raisin Waffles* | *King* |
| *Chicken Waffles* | *Souffle Waffles* |
| *Waffles with Ham* | *Waffles a la Mode with* |
| *Chocolate Waffles* | *Fruit* |
| *Waffle Shortcake* | *Honey and Nut Waffles* |

### Dinner

| | |
|---|---|
| *Cheese Waffles* | *Waffles with Sausage* |
| *Waffles with Steak* | *Gelatin Waffles* |
| *Waffles with Ham* | *Waffles with Sole* |

### After Theater

| | |
|---|---|
| *Welsh Rarebit Waffle* | *Waffles with Chicken a* |
| *Lobster Newburg* | *la King* |
| *Waffles* | *Shrimp Newburg* |
| *Tomato Waffles* | *Waffles* |
| *Waffles with Ice Cream* | |

## EGG COOKERS

The cook in an "early morning fog" can no longer spoil the day for breakfast customers. Eggs the way they want them become an automatic procedure with today's timing, boiling, poaching, and frying equipment. These cookers may be heated by electricity or steam, with timers operated electrically or mechanically.

For boiling eggs, 2-, 3-, and 4-bucket models are available. Each bucket holds from one to six eggs at a time. At the end of a preset period, the eggs are automatically raised out of the boiling water. Timing is in half-minute steps, with a 6-min. limit.

Electric units are the most popular; however, steam and gas units are also available.

There is now a combination series for poaching and cooking. It is electrically heated and mechanically timed, with a maximum timing cycle of 15 minutes. The largest unit poaches as many as 12 eggs at a time and cooks 24. It can also be used for heating individual portions of frozen convenience foods. The units are furnished with individual egg-poaching cups.

### No Guesswork Equipment for Fried Eggs

The guesswork goes out of egg frying too with the use of multiple egg fryers on standard griddles. These units cut labor costs as well, since they eliminate movement between preparation table and griddles.

Stepped-up fried egg production is easily possible with multiple egg fryers; through the use of 16 fryers on 8 standard grills, as many as 384 eggs are fried in 2 min. at 325°F. (162°C).

Multiple egg fryers are made in four sizes: 9-, 12-, 16-, and 20-cup units, each unit holding two eggs. They operate as follows:

Eggs are broken into cups held in a rack either at a preparation spot away from the griddle or after rack has been placed on griddle. Breaking eggs before fryer goes onto griddle makes individual inspection possible before cooking and consequently reduces waste.

Any kind of fat can be used on griddle. Eggs go through rings on rack onto 300°F. (149°C) grill as flick of the finger tilts cups to gently place eggs on the griddle top. Rings keep each 2-egg portion separate. This procedure produces sunny-side-up eggs in approximately 2½ minutes.

For "over easy" eggs, a stainless steel sheet slides over the rings after the eggs are positioned on the grill. Frying time is reduced by approximately one-half minute when steel sheet is used. It can also be used to prepare omelets in the same manner in 2½ to 3 minutes.

## HOT DOG COOKERS

The common worry that all food sold in public places is soon going to taste the same certainly does not apply to hot dogs. However the public wants hot dogs, there is a machine that makes it easy to fill the request—whether for broiled, rotisseried, boiled, steamed, or fried.

In addition to speeding the cooking process, much of this equipment offers the "watch 'em cook" appeal that increases impulse buying. There are rotary cookers that are used on buffet tables where the moving elements provide an eye-catching focal point.

Nor are hot dogs just hot dogs any more. They are featured as hot dogs with chili dog sauce, double dogs, hot dogs with cheese sauce, hot dogs with barbecue sauce, foot-long dogs, or the Reuben dog (a hot dog with sauerkraut) to name some of the many variations. Popular as fast food carry-out items, in student unions, and at events where snacks are in demand, hot dogs and their accompanying buns can both be prepared in the same unit.

The standard model of such a unit will hold 56 dogs in rotating cradles or 54 dogs on rotating spikes. Dogs cook in 12 to 15 minutes; bun warmer holds 40 buns. The bun warmer is said to freshen stale buns, yet keep them from getting soggy, so it is possible to use day-old buns. A larger model will hold 84 dogs in cradles; has 60-bun warming capacity. Controls are easy to read and use.

The device can be cleaned easily: no tools are required and unit comes apart in 15 seconds. Soaking removes any off odors.

For franks with barbecue flavor, one grill is designed with fast-heating rollers that turn the hot dogs over and over at a slow, even speed that permits self-basting. These grills come in two sizes:

23½ × 13½  (59.7 × 34.3  cm)  holds  21 franks; turns out 420 per hour.

37 × 13½ (94 × 34.3 cm) holds 35 franks; turns out 700 per hour.

## Use Cooking Process as Hot Dog Merchandiser

The eye-arresting value of moving food-preparation equipment is featured in a hot dog cooker designed for counter display. The machine uses rollers to cook franks evenly. Rollers continue to revolve on whole surface of the machine even though frank cooking is confined to partial area during slack periods.

A conveyor in one machine broils hot dogs at the rate of 175, 350, or 400 per hour. To operate the unit, raw franks are loaded on a chute inside a glass door to start the broiling process. After broiling, the frank is delivered to heated holding position from which it easily can be served. Centrally located heating elements reduce broiling time.

One hot dog steamer has only to be plugged in wherever snackers are gathered. It takes 1 sq. ft. (929 cm²) of counter space and holds up to 100 standard hot dogs in see-through cylinder at correct serving temperature. Its stainless steel hinged lid, divided storage rack, and compartment of high-impact, clear plastic are all removable for easy cleanup. Inside "well" holds 2 qt. (1.9 l) water.

Counter griddles are used for preparing hot dogs in many operations. Where separate thermostats offer sectional control, hot dogs can be a frequent menu feature. Signal lights indicate griddle temperature for easy checking by counter personnel busy with other tasks. For larger griddle production of frankfurters, units can be installed in batteries sized to whatever capacity is needed.

## DOUGHNUT FRYERS

Extra production for coffee breaks or take-home sales is a bonus that comes with the purchase of special doughnut-frying kettles.

Doughnut kettles turn out doughnuts that are fried uniformly because heat is distributed evenly throughout the fat. The frying process can be automated by means of an adjustable thermostat, which can be set to the proper frying temperatures.

In one model, a special light indicates when proper temperature has been reached. Thermostat maintains this temperature automatically as long as the kettle is turned on. Batches can be turned out continuously.

A portable doughnut machine that turns out 16 doz. doughnuts per hour takes only 16 in. (40.6 cm) of counter space. Two fry screens and a detachable drain tray simplify continuous production; new batch can be frying while previous batch drains.

Another compact, portable counter-top model automatically fries, ices, and/or glazes both yeast-raised and cake doughnuts in one continuous operation at the rate of 40 doz. per hour. It measures 49-in. (124.5 cm) wide × 25-in. (63.5 cm) high × 25-in. (63.5 cm) deep.

Correct dough temperature is essential to good doughnut production. Temperature should be maintained between 75° (24°C) and 80°F. (27°C) by using water of proper temperature. If dough temperatures are too high, doughnuts will lack volume and be misshapen; if too cold, doughnuts tend to stay under the fat too long, fry too slowly, and tend either to crack open or to form ball doughnuts, absorb excess fat and lose volume.

## Locating Doughnut Fryer Screen

What is the proper location of the screen below the fat surface during doughnut frying? The best location for the screen is 2 to 3 in. (5 to 7.6 cm) below the fat surface while the dough is being dropped. The distance should be adjusted so that the doughnuts rise with the top side up just as the dough came from the cutter. Most frying kettles are from 6- to 8-in. (15.2 to 20.3 cm) deep. Put screen in to reduce depth of grease.

If screen is too near the surface, dough may stick on the screen and delay in rising, which may cause a heavily crusted or cracked doughnut, low in volume and screen marked.

If screen is too deep in fat, the doughnut frequently turns over while rising. Cracked and crippled doughnuts nearly always result.

To prevent doughnuts from sticking to the drainer screens in open-kettle frying, keep the drainer screens clean so that doughnuts will break away quickly and rise promptly to the surface. Clean carbonized or dirty screens with a wire brush and a mild solution of hot washing soda to remove all adhering material to which the dough will stick.

## SANDWICH GRILLS

Crunchy hot sandwiches are epicurean items that command higher prices and offer higher profits. It is easy to make more sandwich sales by merchandising higher-priced toasted selections when sandwich grills are convenient for quick preparation. These grills can turn out six sandwiches every 60 seconds in a compact $18^5/8 \times 15^5/8$-in. (47.3 × 39.7 cm) space. Other models turn out four to nine sandwiches.

Grills are designed not to mash or crush sandwiches; in some instances they have dials to set for correct cooking time and temperature. Simultaneous top and bottom grilling eliminates turning. Models with nonstick finish are available.

Temperatures are adjustable from 150° to 450°F. (66° to 232°C). A signal light glows red until grid has been preheated; it flashes on when current is needed to maintain temperature.

Sandwich grills have multiple uses. Bun toasting, meat cooking, ham and cheese melts can all be prepared on the sandwich grill. One model is also suggested for quickly heating up frozen waffles and similar ready-to-serve products.

Up to 600 sandwiches per hour can run through on two conveyors in a gas sandwich broiler 60 in. (152.4 cm) wide × 23 in. (58.4 cm) deep × 26 in. (66 cm) high. Meat traveling on one conveyor is broiled on both sides while buns toast on second conveyor. Simple rheostat-controlled conveyor drive governs broiling of different meats.

A smaller model, 22 × 13 × 33-in. (55.9 × 33 × 83.8 cm) utilizes revolving grills to broil up to 300 sandwiches per hour. Both unload cooked sandwiches automatically through chute from front or side.

## SPAGHETTI COOKER

This specialized spaghetti producer has two sections—one for cooking and reconstituting, another for rinsing and storage. The system also allows large-volume operators to add storage space.

The cooking section is equipped with a stainless steel cook pot, swing-away water filler, automatic (timed) basket lifter, stainless electric heaters, and a quick opening drain valve. When the timed cooking cycle is completed, the spaghetti basket is automatically raised.

The storage section consists of a stainless steel storage tank where the starch is rinsed from cooked spaghetti, using the swing-away water filler on the cooking section. The spaghetti is then portioned into individual cups provided with the unit; a total of 48 cups can be held in the storage tank at one time. Unsold spaghetti can be kept in the refrigerator overnight.

When orders are received, the preportion serving cups (one to nine at a time) are placed in the cup rack and lowered into the heated water (cooking) side of the machine. Only 30 sec. are required to reconstitute. Up to 500 individual servings of spaghetti can be reconstituted per hour.

The manufacturer points out that spaghetti has the highest profit margin of all menu items and, therefore, deserves extra emphasis and proper preparation.

This unit is not limited to spaghetti production only; it can cook all kinds of pasta, and has even been used to boil eggs for sandwich preparation. The unit is available with a cooker and rinse/storage tank, or the cooker only, or rinse/storage tank only.

## CHAFING DISHES AND HIBACHIS

Could your foodservice benefit from the introduction of an elegant, excitingly produced menu item?

Dishes flamed at table, as one maker of chafing dishes points out, "have an endless fascination for the restaurant guest. They please and flatter and give the chef an unlimited opportunity for showmanship. One should remember, however, to stay within the limits of tasteful showmanship and not to abuse that art of flame by extravagance, which is in violation of the basic principles of fine cooking."

Hibachis—small oriental heaters—when used for hors d'oeuvre preparation at the table, especially during the cocktail hour, also prove their worth.

It is easy to add a flaming dessert or Steak Diane at dinner, or to feature swiss fondue or oyster stew for late evening. Special equipment to simplify each of these glamorous preparations is available.

A rechaud lamp—the heating unit for much tableside preparation—now has been introduced with two burners. The extra burner only needs to be ignited for cooking; for heating or for holding hot food the traditional one burner is quite adequate.

Color too adds a new excitement to chafing dish design in high-style combinations of steel, copper, and brass.

Designers have remained practical in their approach to this equipment, however. Typical of its multiple-use potential is a 3-in-1 combination chafing dish that may be used as a rechaud for Cafe Diable preparation and as a chafing dish.

Swiss fondue preparation units help to capitalize on the continuing popularity of this late evening favorite. Fondue pots for use on chafing dish frames and special fondue sets are both available.

Oyster stew equipment makes service during the "r" months easy to merchandise profitably.

With a special Cherries Jubilee set, there is a "specialtie de la maison" air for the tableside service of many flaming dishes. Try these flamed specialties from the Colony Restaurant, New York City:

## Recipes for Tableside Cooking

**Veal Scallopinis Flambees Madere.** Saute veal scallopini and arrange pieces so they overlap slightly on buttered silver platter. Place on a rechaud in front of guests and flame with Madeira. Add a ribbon of light Madeira sauce and heat, but do not let sauce boil or the scallops will be toughened.

**Steak au Poivre Burgundy.** Cover steaks on both sides with crushed white peppercorns. Sprinkle with salt and cook to the desired degree of doneness without blackening the pepper. To the pan in which steaks were cooked add a few finely chopped shallots and some good red Burgundy. Reduce liquid and swirl in some butter off the fire. Transfer sauce to a sauce dish.

Place steaks on platter in front of guest and flambe with marc. Transfer steaks to serving platter and pour some of the Burgundy sauce over them. Serve with pommes soufflees or gaufrette potatoes.

**Spring Chicken Saute Champagne.** This is said to be a simple dish to prepare and delicate in flavor:

To a young chicken, cut in serving portions, add salt and pepper, butter, chopped shallots, onion, and bouquet garni. Add champagne, cover and simmer for 20 min. Transfer chicken to a silver timbale. Reduce sauce, add cream and veal stock, and cook until sauce is a fine consistency. Strain through a chinois (fine sieve) and add mushrooms. Whisk in a few pieces of butter and correct the seasoning.

To serve: arrange the chicken in the timbale on a rechaud and flame with fine champagne. Add the sauce and bring it just to a simmer to allow the flavors to blend. Serve with a timbale of rice creole, asparagus tips, stuffed artichoke bottoms, and buttered petits pois.

Here is George Oddoux's recipe for Peaches Jubilee:

**PEACHES JUBILEE**
*Yield:* 6 servings
**Ingredients**

| | | |
|---|---|---|
| Canned Peach Halves | 6 | (6) |
| Peach Syrup | 2 cups | (0.5 l) |
| Orange Marmalade | 2 oz. | (57 gm) |
| Rum Flavor Extract for Flaming | 1 oz. | (28 gm) |
| Vanilla Ice Cream | 1 pt. | (453 gm) |

**Method**

Heat peach halves with syrup and marmalade in crepe suzette pan over a rechaud. Pour rum flavor extract for flaming over peaches and ignite, spooning sauce over peaches. Serve in individual dessert dishes containing one scoop ice cream. Place peach half on side of ice cream and spoon on flaming sauce before serving.

## CHINESE COOKING EQUIPMENT

Chinese food in all its regional varieties continues to win converts among American restaurant patrons. What undoubtedly accounts for the growing enthusiasm for Chinese food is the variety of uniquely different seasonings and flavors used in dishes from the many regions of China. These regional distinctions create a deliciously diverse cuisine.

A line of commercial Chinese kitchen equipment is now being manufactured for professional chefs who want to produce authentic Chinese dishes. The equipment has been designed to suit the regional cooking variations among different kinds of Chinese menus.

## How the Chinese Kitchen Operates

The routine in a kitchen preparing Chinese food has been given full consideration in the development of this line of equipment. Each order is assembled, then handed over to the chef who prepares the food over high heat at a rapid pace. When the dish is finished, the chef quickly places it on platter on serving shelf in front of the range, then prepares cooking utensil for next order.

Long-handled fry pans or woks are cleaned with water and brushes only; no detergent is used. Water is easily available for the chef from a swing faucet and easily drained into the gutter at the back of the cooking unit. Within seconds, a cooking utensil can be ready to prepare the next order. Rinse water runs through gutter to slop sink with a strainer that retains solids for disposal via waste system. Backsplash returns any badly aimed water to gutter.

Chinese cooking equipment, designed to produce high cooking temperatures to sear food without overcooking, saves cooking energy and cooking time. Gas-fired units come in standard chamber sizes: 12-in. (30.5 cm), 14-in. (35.6 cm) 16-in., (40.6 cm) 18-in., (45.7 cm) and 20-in. (50.8 cm) (All but the 12-in. (30.5 cm) size are certified by the American Gas Association). A thick wall insulates the range top and body against the intense cooking heat with a 2-in. (5 cm) thick, refractory brick lining in every fire chamber. The 1900° (1038°C) to 2100°F. (1149°C) cooking temperatures needed for fast searing of meats or quick steaming of vegetables are quickly developed. One swing faucet is located over each cooking chamber in multi-chamber units.

An extension backsplash with gutter allows the slop sink to be located at either end when two ranges are joined. Ranges come in 2-, 3-, and 4-chamber units and can be paired to provide a unit up to 12 chambers long. In paired units, the slop sink is sometimes put between ranges with a soup-stock range installed in front of it. Stock-pot ranges can produce from 10 to 40 gal. (38 to 151.4 l) of soup and keep it simmering for service.

To prepare Chinese foods for an approximately 100-seat dining room with a normal carry-out service, one 2-range and one 3-range unit can be combined with a stock-pot range between the two units. This set-up permits two chefs to work at the two ranges. A soup-stock bowl can also be inserted in one cooking chamber in a multi-chamber range.

Gas-fired smokehouse units are available in 3-, 4-, and 5-burner models for preparing Chinese-style spareribs, pork tenderloin, and Peking Duck.

## PIZZA STACK AND COUNTER OVENS

A specialty food item with across-the-board popularity is within the reach of foodservice operations of all sizes. Equipment for producing it efficiently in a wide range of capacities makes fast-selling pizza—an item especially good for take-out—easy to fit into food production schedules. The pizza oven has been called the most common adaptation of the oven for a specific product.

Pizza production is being speeded today not only by specially designed pizza ovens but also by an adaptation of a soda fountain system for assembly.

One special pizza oven utilizes genuine brick hearths 2-in. (5 cm) thick for even baking, delicious hearth-baked flavor, texture, and aroma. It comes in three sizes with varying capacities. The large model, with baking chamber measuring 36-in. (91.4 cm) wide by 28-in. (71.1 cm) long by 6-in. (15.2 cm) high, has a pan baking capacity of twelve 12-in. (30.5 cm) pizzas or six 16-in. (40.6 cm) pizzas and will turn out eight 12-in. (30.5 cm) or five 16-in. (40.6 cm) pizzas every 4 minutes at a baking temperature of 625°F. (329°C). Smaller models are sized to turn out seven 12-in. (30.5 cm) or two 16-in. (40.6 cm) pizzas every 4 min. Units can be stacked to provide working height 46-in. (116.8 cm) from floor. Stacked models will double capacities listed.

## Pizza Oven Recovery Rates

In another pizza oven model—available in 1, 2 or 3 sections—rugged steel oven liners coated with molten aluminum offer fast preheat and during bake off send heat into pizza pans at a rapid rate. This oven also allows direct pizza baking on the decks themselves without sticking. Decks have capacity of 6 12-in. (30.5 cm) pizzas per deck; decks are 37½ in. (952.5 cm) wide by 28¾ in. (73 cm) deep. Necessary baking temperatures can be maintained with less power, thus reducing operating costs.

Signal lights, automatic temperature dials, and manual oven timers provide controls needed to meet uniform operating standards. An entire oven deck can be removed through door opening without any alteration in oven door or front.

Pizza production is most efficient when ovens offer high recovery rates since the baking period is only a matter of minutes so the door is constantly being opened for loading and unloading.

Stackable, in-line or return conveyor ovens are also available for high-volume pizza production. They can cook all types of pizza up to 18-in. (45.7 cm) in diameter. Each deck operates independently with its own time control for the variable-speed conveyor. The units have top and bottom radiant-heat elements with separate temperature controls. Time controls the cooking. In-line units are loaded and unloaded at either end. Return conveyor units carry items out of oven around to unloading point on side. Heat remains inside with either model. Models can both be stacked five decks high. (For picture, see Chapter 3, Ovens.)

### PIZZA PIE DOUGH

Heat hot enough to melt shortening.

5 lb: (2.3 kg) water (variable, depending on absorption of the flour used)

Add 4 oz. (114 gm) shortening. Add and start mixing 10 lb. (4.5 kg) bread flour, 4 oz (114 gm) salt.

Dissolve the following ingredients, add, and mix with the dough until it cleans away from the sides of the bowl. (In cases of stronger flour, the dough may be mixed for 1½ to 2 min. after the clean-up stage has been reached):

1 lb. (453 gm) water
3 oz. (85 gm) yeast

Allow the dough to come to a full rise. The full rise may be determined by inserting your hand approximately 4 in. (10 cm) into the dough and removing it quickly. If the dough recedes, it has come to a full rise and should then be punched and permitted to set for 1/3 the time necessary for the dough to come to a full rise. The dough is then scaled into desired-sized units, rounded up, and rested for 15 to 20 minutes.

Roll the rounded pieces out to a thickness of approximately 1/4 to 3/8-in. (6 to 10 mm) and round out to size of the pans in which the pizza is to be baked. Cover with oil, chopped peppers, chopped onions, anchovies, salt, grated cheese, and tomato sauce (see directions below). Proof slightly and bake at approx. 450°F. (232°C) Baking time will depend upon the size of the units being baked. For large units, it may be well to bake the pizza at slightly lower temperatures.

### ITALIAN PIZZA FORMULA

Peel ripe red tomatoes and break in to small pieces. To peel tomatoes, have a kettle of boiling water handy, drop the tomatoes in for a moment, remove them, and the skins will slip right off. Then cut out the stem part and the core and break the rest in little pieces.

Next, mix in with the tomatoes enough grated Parmesan cheese to obtain a good cheese flavor. This cheese is available by the pound at a baker's supply company or wholesale grocery. The strength of the cheese varies among batches so the amount required changes. Taste while adding to be sure of proper amount. Mixing the cheese with the tomatoes prevents it from burning during baking.

One way to use this sauce in finishing off pizza: Cover rolled-out pizza dough with the tomato-cheese mixture and finish off with strip anchovies. Break the anchovies into small pieces and distribute them evenly over the pan. Bake in a 425°F. (218°C) oven after giving some proof. Grated or finely chopped onion may also be added, if desired. Italian sausage or mushrooms may be used instead of anchovies.

## SPECIALTY BROILERS

Limited space no longer needs to limit the service of broiled hamburgers, steaks, or chops, as broiler dimensions are being reduced. One electric broiler unit equipped with four drawers—two for broiling, each independently controlled, and two that serve as food warmers—fits into a space 24 × 16½ × 15½ in. (60 × 41.9 × 39.4 cm). The unit broils six hamburgers or the equivalent in steaks, chops, chicken, or fish in each drawer. A timer controls the broiling cycle and a bell rings when patties are ready to serve. Smoke and odors are consumed and excess fat drains into easily-removed grease drawer.

Branching out from a successful carry-out chicken business. Chicken Royal in Oak Park, MI, installed a counter broiler so that hamburgers, steaks, and chops could be added to their menu. Customer demand for these quickly broiled specialities definitely has justified the investment.

## Small Automatic Electric Broiler

To meet the broiling needs of small chain operators, independent franchisees, diners, and specialized food outlets, a small automatic electric broiler has been designed. Its special heating system creates a compact cooking chamber that conserves energy and reduces venting requirements. The conveyor belt and cooking chamber are virtually self-cleaning, as fat is consumed by high heat in unit.

Models can be selected that broil fresh hamburger patties sized 8 oz. (226 gm) to 1 lb. (453 gm) at the rate of either 750 or 1,000 per hour. Frozen patties the same size can be produced at the rate of 575 and 750 per hour. The capacity for 4 to 1 lb. (453 gm) fresh patties is 450 and 720; frozen patties the same size, 325 and 540.

There is also a 14-in. (35.6 cm) conveyor broiler with a built-in bun toaster. It can turn out 1,000 8 to 1 lb. (453 gm) fresh patties or 750 frozen patties per hour. Capacity for 4 to 1 lb. (453 gm) fresh patties is 720 per hour and frozen 540 per hour. Capacity for bun halves per hour is 1500.

## CHEESE MELTERS

As meat prices climb and more ethnic specialties that use cheese are introduced on menus, the cheese melter has become an essential device in an expanding number of foodservice operations. Cheese melters were adapted from salamanders on the West Coast where they are used for Mexi-

can cuisine and for melting or browning cheese toppings on a variety of dishes.

In one installation, the Red Onion Restaurant, Huntington Beach, CA, cheese melters with multiple shelves are located above the work table at the end of the cooking line. They are used to finish off enchiladas and chili rellenos.

Cheese melters are useful in four production areas: (1) they melt the cheese used to top special dishes or casseroles, as well as on cheese-topped sandwiches; (2) they brown or crisp au gratin dishes, duchess potatoes, casseroles, and meringue pies; (3) they warm filled crepes, gravy, rolls, pastry, or other dishes ready for service; (4) they toast cheese and bread toppings, sliced breads, or hamburger buns.

One electric model reaches full operating temperatures as soon as food is put on the rack and shuts off as soon as food is removed. This saves energy in two ways; (1) minimum use of power and (2) minimum heat added to kitchen air. Rack can be adjusted to four cooking positions, each of which provides a different degree of heat—from warm to high. The large openings on this melter make loading easier and reduce spills. Counter, wall-mounted, and pass-thru models are available.

## Heat Sources for Cheese Melters

Another cheese melter is part of a heavy-duty gas griddle/cheese melter. The griddle gets its heat from the cheese melter located beneath it. Shelf with easy-to-grip handle holds items in cheese melter. Unit on legs is available in 31-in. (78.7 cm) and 42-in. (106.7 cm) widths.

An electric counter model cheese melter, which can be installed on legs for easy cleaning, has a 3-position food rack. It comes in either 24-in. (60 cm) or 36-in. (91.4 cm) widths. A removable drip pan makes clean up quick. All these units are stainless steel for fast exterior clean up.

A specialized salamander for convenient production of cheese specialties also has eye appeal. It is wall mounted in 24-in. (60 cm) sections, each of which is powered by a 20,000 Btu gas burner. A maximum installation has a total length of 120 in. (304.8 cm) and 5 shelves.

At the Red Baron Restaurants, Seattle, Alaska King Crab sandwiches build business. In just 40 seconds, the cheese is bubbling and the sandwich is ready to serve straight from the broiler in an attractive ramekin. Here is the recipe:

2 oz. (57 gm) crab meat
1 English muffin, split, toasted and buttered
3 oz. (85 gm) canned cheese sauce

Place bottom half of muffin in center of ramekin, cut top half in two and place on either side of bottom half. Heap crab meat in center and pour cheese sauce over it. Place under broiler or in cheese melter until heated through and cheese sauce bubbles.

## BARBECUE MACHINES

In barbecue or rotisserie machines, reflected infrared heat sears in juices, reduces shrinkage to the minimum, and gives a most delicious barbecue flavor to finished poultry and meats.

Most barbecue machines have spits inserted from the side to hold poultry or meats; however, an available counter, window, or back bar model features a "lazy susan" with hooks that suspend poultry, ribs or roasts. One model 30-in. (76.2 cm) wide × 23-in. (58.4 cm) deep × 48-in. (121.9 cm) high will barbecue 21 chickens on 7 hanging racks, 20 ribs on hooks or varying numbers of roasts and turkeys.

There are also 5-spit gas and electric barbecues with warmers below and glass doors with a special swing-away feature that makes loading and unloading easier. A 7-spit, high-volume model has interior illumination to attract patron attention. There are also 12- and 14-spit models.

Combination rotisserie and warmer models are also available. Rotisserie holds 30 chickens or equivalent; warms 50 to 60 chickens or equivalent. Make sure that chickens or other barbecued items are not held in warmer for more than three hours.

The base of the hot food pickup counter at the Apple Tree Inn, North Kansas City, MO., is equipped with a heated, barbecue rib holding unit.

Some machines are equipped with infrared warmers that keep food platters at 150°F. (66°C) with minimum dehydration for three hours. Food should not be kept in the warmer longer than that. These warmers make barbecued food easily available for self-service take out.

### Selecting Barbecue Machines

Points to check when selecting an infrared barbecue machine:

- Degree of visibility; for take out, maximum visibility of cooking foods is an effective tool to stimulate impulse buying
- Simple installation
- Easy operation
- Easy cleaning
- Durable construction
- Adequate insulation
- Infrared heat to provide fast, thorough barbecuing
- Compliance with sanitary and electrical codes
- Warm-up cabinet available
- Minimum maintenance
- Accessories included, such as spit for chickens, rack for frankfurters
- Safe loading area
- Easy-loading design
- Economical use of current
- Adequate precautions against breakdown
- Provisions for operation at less than capacity.

Barbecue machine installation and operating instructions such as the following, emphasize the operating ease:

"When you get your new infrared barbecue machine, the first and most important thing is to have a licensed electrician see that it is installed properly with adequate electric power. The machine will not work properly without adequate electric power of the required voltage.

"After mounting chickens, ribs, beef, or whatever is desired to be cooked on spits, firmly so that they will not flop, and with the weight as nearly balanced as possible, turn on the heat and start the motor. Always leave the heat on until done.

"It is urgently recommended that an internal meat thermometer be used to tell when done. One cannot tell accurately any other way. The thermometer should be used until the proper timing is established under the conditions in which you are operating. There are several factors that vary the cooking time—line voltage, size, and temperature of products when put into the barbecue machine."

## Cleaning Barbecue Machines

Daily cleaning of barbecue machines is recommended. Where foil is used to line machines, change it regularly when soiled or darkened.

In cleaning, avoid the use of cold water on hot heat-treated glass; use vinegar and water for glass, after it is cooled and use steel wool gently to clean rods. To simplify the daily cleaning job, one manufacturer suggests keeping an extra set of spits and skewers. Every night one set is soaked for easy cleaning.

## Barbecue Instructions

Detailed operating instructions for several barbecued items have been developed by a rotisserie manufacturer:

**Spareribs.**    Mount ribs on spit like a figure "S." Sprinkle lightly with special seasoning. Put into rotisserie, turn on heat and motor, and cook until done. Remove from rotisserie and paint with barbecue sauce immediately while hot.

**Barbecue Beef.**    Mount on spit, sprinkle lightly with special seasoning. Put into rotisserie, insert the internal thermometer and cook until the thermometer reads the desired doneness: rare, medium, or well.

**Turkeys.**    Use turkey-holder assembly, holding turkey firmly, balancing the weight with the weight balancer. Put into rotisserie. Always use internal thermometer to tell when done: 185°F. (85°C)

## How to Barbecue Chicken

Probably the largest single barbecued item is chicken. The easy-to-follow directions for preparing this popular item assure its uniform quality. One machine maker recommends this procedure:

"Take eviscerated chickens with feet and neck removed, dust with salt and paprika; take clean spit, hold at comfortable angle with roller end downward and

"Slip over spit a single prong with the points facing you, push it down to 2 in. (5 cm) of the roller, then tighten the thumb screw tightly.

"Take the first chicken, legs first, push the spit through so that the legs are confined between the prong wire and the spit.

"Slip a double prong over the spit and push it all the way down in such a position that each of the prong wires pierces the wings; then tighten the thumb screw.

"Slide second chicken over the spit and be sure that the legs are way down and in between the spit and the prong wire; again slide a double prong on to the spit down until the prong wires pierce the wings, and then tighten the thumb screw. This you repeat until you get the four chickens on; on the end use a single prong with the prong points away from you, and push down until they completely pierce wings, then tighten the thumb screw.

"We recommend that you preheat this barbecue machine. When you have strung the four chickens, or the amount required, you may then pull the rack out and mount the spits on the racks; repeat this with as many spits as you choose to use. Also remove and keep out of the machine any spits which do not have meats or poultry on them.

"Single prongs are used on both ends and double prongs are used in the middle. Be sure to see that legs and wings are secured.

"Better results are obtained if the bottom spits are changed with the upper spits after a half hour's run, as heat travels up, barbecuing the upper spit's load faster, also gravity pulling the juices downward gives more basting to the lower spits, and the upper is dependent on its own basting.

"For best results and easy care, line the back of the cabinet under the heating rods, with aluminum foil, which can be replaced at the discretion of the operator. The machine stays cleaner and a clean machine cooks quicker and better."

## BARBECUE COUNTER DISPLAY

One counter-display rotisserie can produce more than 400 hamburgers per hour. It is thermostatically controlled and requires no venting or exhaust system. A drum-type electric rotisserie can barbecue 8 chickens in two hours and requires only a space 27-in. (68.6 cm) high, 24-in. (60 cm) wide and 21-in. (53.3 cm) deep. Self-leveling

cradles that hold chickens, chicken parts, roast beef, spareribs, hamburgers, and hot dogs are easy to load.

There are also 3- and 5-spit barbecue counter models with 15- and 25-chicken capacities.

## DISPLAYS FOR FOOD

Salad and dessert sales soar when specialties are properly displayed. New developments are constantly improving display equipment and its merchandising potential.

The salad bar itself can be a decorative element, dressed up with containers of unusual design to attract patrons. Even the "sneeze guard" can be an attention getter. (See pictures p. 143G).

A portable salad bar island holding a 12-in. × 20-in. (30 cm × 51cm) pan has a removable cover and a "sneeze guard." The island can be used to entice patrons at their tables thus gaining extra salad sales.

A decorative food-carousel display server has been designed for hors d'oeuvres, cold foods, and salads. The ice tray maintains temperature, and the "sneeze guard" has been incorporated in unit. The server adds a note of color since it comes in amber, horizon blue, fern green, or clear.

Moving displays for corn-on-the-cob, meat pies, fruit pies, or turnovers are paying for themselves in many operations with increased sales and speedy service at just-right temperatures. Units are available that fit in either 1 or 2 sq. ft. (929 or 1858 cm²) of counter space.

One corn-on-the-cob display unit dips hot ears in a pan of dressing that seals in heat and adds to patron appeal. Safety glass doors permit either front or back loading. The rotating corn holder has eight 15-in. (38.1 cm) wire racks, detachable for easy cleaning in dishmachine.

Stationary, refrigerated display cabinets that present chilled desserts and salads at the point of perfection are volume builders too. Decorative exteriors and lighted interiors spotlight specialties that increase check averages.

## BRAIN TEASER—SPECIALTY EQUIPMENT

1. Which of the following should NOT be put through slicers? (Circle wrong answer.) Tomatoes, hard-cooked eggs, cooked potatoes, meat with bone in it, sausage, bread.

2. Why is it easy to clean cutters or choppers? _____

3. Why should cutting time be set for shorter period in cutter/mixer? _____

4. Toasters that can toast buns can also toast: (Check right answer.) Bagles ____ English muffins____ Chicken legs____

5. Waffle bakers pay their way when waffles are served. (Circle right answer.)
   Once a week   Every day   All through the day

6. Can hot dogs and buns both be prepared in the same unit? (Check right answer.) Yes ____ No ____

7. Portable doughnut fryers are (large) (small) pieces of equipment. (Cross out wrong answer.)

8. Sandwiches being grilled have to be turned over. (Check right answer.) Yes ____ No ____

9. How is starch rinsed from cooked spaghetti when using spaghetti cooker?

10. Which of the following can be used for tableside cooking? (Circle right answers.) Chafing dish
    Fry kettle  Hibachi  Fondue pots  Steam-jacketed kettle

11. Why must cooking equipment for Chinese food operate at high heat?

12. Why is a rapid heat recovery rate important in pizza ovens? _____

13. Can a small foodservice operation offer broiled items? (Check right answer.) Yes ____ No ____

14. Why is a cheese melter important where Mexican menus are served? _____

15. Barbecue machines should be cleaned: (Check right answer.)
    Daily ____ Weekly ____ Monthly ____

16. Displaying salads and desserts (increases) (holds down) sales. (Cross out wrong answer.)

    *(For correct answers see page 251.)*

**FIGURE 8.2**

An automatic doughnut machine keeps up with demand at York (Pa.) Hospital. From machine to doughnut fryer is a short trip with the production set-up in use there.

**FIGURE   8.3**
This one-chamber unit is part of a line of Chinese cooking equipment. Designed to produce high cooking temperature that sears food without overcooking, unit fits in easily where space is limited and provides an extra wok for steaming, frying, stir cooking, or other preparation necessary for Chinese food. Units are also available in 2-, 3-, and 4-chamber models.

**FIGURE   8.4**
At Columbian House Restaurant, Bolingbrook, Ill., the slicer is placed on a mobile stand so it can be easily moved into the cook's area when required.

**FIGURE  8.5**
The food cutter, mixer, and slicer are installed on a table 30 in. (76.2 cm) high so that the equipment can be operated easily by kitchen employees at Doylestown, Pa. Hospital since the majority are women. Vegetable slicer and meat chopper attachments are stored on the table undershelf. Grater and shredder plates and chopper knives are accommodated on a special frame between the table legs. Beaters, whips, and other mixer attachments are stored on a mixer attachment rack that is installed on inclined tubing sections welded to a horizontal member supported by the adjacent work table overshelf uprights.

**FIGURE   8.6**
Toaster is used to complete take-out orders and preparation as required for other menu items at this cook's finishing and waitress pick-up table at the Red Onion Restaurant, Huntington Beach, Ca.

---

**FIGURE 8.7**
Part of the chef's finishing table at Bob Burns Restaurant, Woodland Hills, Ca. are these centrally located toasters. They can be used to finish hot items from hot table on left or cold items from cold section on right.

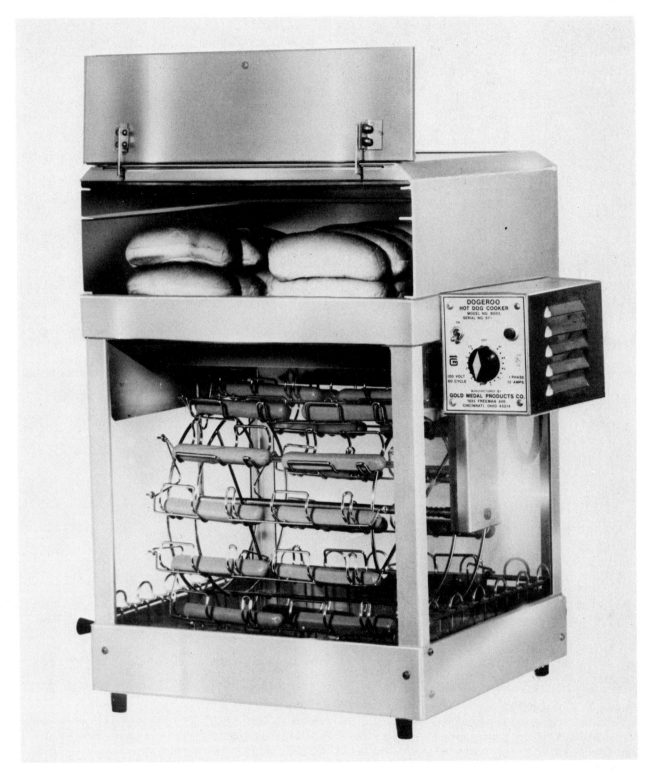

**FIGURES   8.8a and 8.8b**
Size of this rotating hot dog cooker, 20½ in. (52 cm) wide by 24 in. (60 cm) high by 15½ in. (39.4 cm) deep, makes it adaptable for many locations. Lighted red and white sign installed under bun warmer helps merchandise product. (See picture at left.)

**FIGURES   8.9a and 8.9b**
In planning the salad bar set-up at Foxfire Restaurant, Anaheim, Ca. special consideration was given to high standards of sanitation and practical maintenance. Lucite is used to retain ice in beds; lucite retainers can be removed for cleaning. Two see-through bowls hold salad greens. The height of the decorative sneeze guard is adjustable. (See picture.) Copper pan below the adapter plates is provided with an indirect drain. The goose-neck fixture at left was installed for convenient washing of the copper pan. Stainless steel adapter plates form the pan for the ice bed which is in two sections for ease of handling. Stainless steel clips secure adapter plates to mounting flanges. Lids on plate chiller at left in picture are removable to make cleaning of chiller easier.

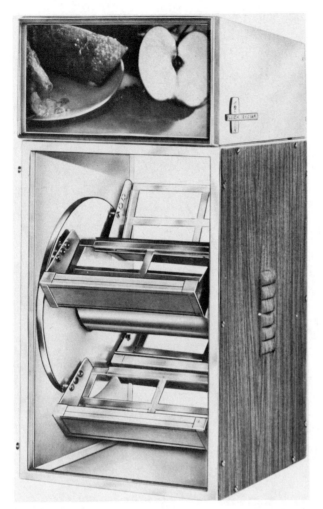

**FIGURE   8.10**
Rotary food merchandiser for meat and fruit pies or turnovers comes in either 12½ in. (31.8 cm) or 22 in. (55.9 cm) width. Dishwasher-proof racks are easily detached. A see-through plastic shield, also easily removed for cleaning, serves as sneeze guard; it is an optional accessory.

**FIGURE 9.1**
Adjustable, heavy duty wire shelving in one storage area at Chicago's McCormick Place is used primarily for canned goods storage. Space above top shelf allows extra room for miscellaneous supplies used in the convention center's foodservice operations.

# Chapter Nine

# Storage

## RECEIVING VITAL TO FOODSERVICE SUCCESS

With costs of all goods needed for foodservice operation continually rising, good receiving and storage practices are vital to "hold the line" on costs.

Receiving and storage areas should be designed to make it easy to follow cost-saving receiving and storage procedures. Loading docks should have heavy-duty materials and easily-cleaned surfaces. Good storage areas require good ventilation, good lighting, dry conditions, easily washed interiors, and proper temperatures for goods to be stored. Carefully calculate distance between receiving and storage; often shortening distances reduces costs.

Keeping receiving and storage areas clean, with goods shelved neatly, should be the first rule. Other essential control measures include tight procedures with planned follow up; arrangements that make unloading easy; storage areas set up for speeding inventory, proper rotation, and safe preservation of foods held.

Taking in and taking care of the supplies needed by a foodservice operation are major responsibilities. When properly planned and carried out, receiving and storage guarantee a good start for the preparation and service that are keys to an operation's success.

## RECEIVING SYSTEM

The lower level of the building that houses Victoria Station in Universal City, CA, provides receiving facilities for the operation. Three walk-in refrigerators, a walk-in freezer, liquor storage, and dry storage are adjacent to the loading dock. Supplies go to a rough preparation kitchen where a disposer handles the sizable amount of waste. An elevator is centrally located to ease transportation of food to the main level. A can-washing facility is located at the loading dock.

Supplies are brought from a raised dock area through a large security door at Sam Houston, Jr. High School, Irving, TX. In a classic straight-line flow of materials, supplies then move through receiving, past the manager's office, directly into either dry or refrigerated storage in the kitchen.

Goods are received at the loading docks on the main level for the foodservice department of the Milwaukee (WI) Exposition and Convention Center and Arena. The products are then transported to the second floor by a service elevator. There they are weighed in the elevator vestibule and trucked to one of the four storage areas—refrigerated and frozen foods; dry goods and paper products; linen and uniforms; alcoholic beverages.

The size and capacity of the storage areas were predicted on the basis of demand purchasing. Foodservice has to be available for groups ranging in size from 50 to 6,000 and for menus from a simple buffet breakfast to a five-course banquet. The majority of food and beverage purchases are dictated by the menu requirements of the scheduled events. With the possible exception of paper products and some frozen food, no large inventories are maintained.

**Alcoholic Beverages Storage.** Storage of alcoholic beverages is separate from all other storage functions. Within the area set aside for liquor stores there is:

- Secured bottle storage.
- Dry storage for condiments.
- Refrigerated beer and wine storage.
- Facilities for batch preparation of premixed cocktails.
- Storage space for portable bar and beer units.

The movement of food items flows from the storage facilities through the hot and cold production areas, to the plating stations.

To insure product control, fresh products are checked and weighed before they enter the storage area at Ninfa's Taco Al Carbon, Inc., Houston. Some products are processed before entering the refrigerator or freezer.

In the storage area, issue doors have been located between walk-in areas and near the dry-storage unit to provide the right quantity of product for each preparation period.

Meats and produce are processed for cooking and all finished product is placed in the working side of the walk-in cooler, ready for use.

The story of storage at Trueblood Hall, Southern Illinois University, Carbondale, cer-

tainly deserves an "A" for these important elements:

- Conveniently located areas—pantry near main kitchen; bake shop has own refrigerator and pantry; dishwashing room is in direct line to serving area for storage of clean dishes; all kitchen walk-in boxes are within 10 to 14 ft. (304.8 to 426.7cm) of work tables.
- Canned goods storeroom holds three months supply of canned goods, enough for meals for a whole term. The same room also stores detergents, paper goods, and dry food.
- Delivery trucks can drive into covered storage area to unload. All merchandise is stored on raised platforms to make cleaning easy.
- Dry storage for kitchen area held in large room with glazed tile walls, quarry tile floors, and shelves of stainless steel. Kitchen refrigerators have quarry tile floors, aluminum walls and ceilings, stainless steel shelving.

There is growing use of the module in storage and preparation planning. At San Diego, Calif. International Airport, an 18-in. (45.7 cm) module is used for all storage and preparation of food items.

All racks, refrigerators, and refrigerator drawers are based on this 18-in. (45.7 cm) module—18- × 26-in. (46- × 66-cm) pans are used for dry storage; special 18- × 24-in. (46- × 60-cm) stainless steel wire baskets are used for produce storage; 12- × 18-in. (30- × 46-cm) steam table pans for all other storage.

All products—fried, broiled, or griddled—in the coffee shop service kitchen are stored in 12- × 18 × 4-in. (30- × 46 × 10-cm) deep steam-table pans, two pans to a drawer section below cooking units. Additional products are stored in adjacent refrigerators on channel slides. When a drawer unit is emptied, a full one replaces the empty, and the empty pan is washed and is ready to go back into service as soon as needed.

## RECEIVING AREA

The receiving area is called the vital first step in the food handling operation by Joseph Laschober in "A Short Course in Kitchen Design." His approach to this area follows:

- The receiving area must be given careful consideration during design. Equipment and materials selected for use in this area must be able to withstand the hard-duty nature of work performed in the receiving and trash disposal process. At the same time, sanitation features must be considered to prevent contamination of foodstuffs.
- The receiving dock is a concrete platform high enough to afford easy unloading of trucks making deliveries. The standard height for the dock is 30 to 36 in. (76.2 to 91.4 cm) Smaller operations, where many deliveries are made in panel trucks, may find a lower height more practical. To achieve the 6-in. (15.2 cm) height difference, a ramp is provided for a portion of the dock. The ramp is on the street level, allowing panel trucks to back up to a 36-in. (91.4 cm) dock next to a trailer.

But some operations, such as Foxfire Restaurant, Anaheim, CA, do not need a raised dock because most delivery vehicles that supply them are equipped with hydraulic lifts.

A roof should be provided over the dock to afford weather protection for trucks being unloaded. The exact height and dimensions of the roof will depend on the size of trucks expected.

Cleanliness of the surface of the dock should be insured by means of a hot and cold water hose located nearby. A floor drain in the dock will aid in scrubbing down.

## EQUIPMENT FOR UNLOADING GOODS

When goods are being unloaded on the receiving dock, some means must be provided for conveying them to their proper location inside the building. Flat-bed trucks, two wheel hand trucks and gravity and "live" roller conveyors are all used for this purpose. The selection of equipment for use in a specific operation will depend upon the size and quantities of goods being delivered.

Ideally, storage areas should be located on the same level as the receiving dock. Where this is not possible and storage facilities are located on another level such as the basement, a live belt conveyor should be considered. If a belt conveyor is to be used, a reversible system should be specified. This will allow the conveyor to be used again in removing goods from storage.

## Scales

In connection with receiving procedures, it is often necessary to determine the exact weights of items being delivered. A scale, portable if possible, should be located on or near the dock.

The most common scale used for this purpose is the simple platform type. Generally mounted on wheels, this scale has a basic weighing range of 100 lb. (45.4 kg) This range can be extended, by adding extra counter-weights, to 1000 lb. (453 kg) The measured weights are read from a slide-bar arrangement.

The deluxe commercial scale offers many desirable features in return for its higher cost. The basic weighing range of 1/4 oz. (7 gm) to 250 lb. (113.4 kg) or 1/2 lb. (226 gm) to 500 lb. (226.8 kg) can be extended to 800 lb. (362.9 kg) with the addition of a tare beam.

This scale is read directly from a dial face. Some models include a device to print the measured weights automatically on invoices, special tickets, or roll tapes dispensed by the machine. These scales should also be specified with stainless steel weighing pans 27 × 30 × 6-in. high. (68.6 × 76.2 × 15.2 cm.)

## Data on Doors

Frequently the trash and can storage room has doors opening onto the receiving dock (for further details, see Chapter 13, Waste Handling). The balance of the receiving area includes the receiving office, employee time card racks, and bulletin boards. These items should be located in the area adjacent to the back door and dock.

Mr. Laschober also stresses the importance of receiving and storage area doors that offer security and are large enough for goods to be transported easily through them. Door openings and door heights should be large enough to take care of all loads.

An interesting approach is to have side-hinged (24 in. (60 cm) high) transom doors, which can be locked separately from the lower doors. When an extra high piece of equipment is moved from the dock into the kitchen, the high doors are opened, allowing a 5 ft. (152.4 cm) wide by 9 ft. (274.3 cm) high opening.

## PROTECTING STORED ITEMS

The storeroom is the supply bank for every institution. It is the source of supplies for every department, holding items until they are needed in preparation or service. These stored supplies represent a big investment and are the equivalent of cash. To assure maximum protection, supplies are best issued by requisition only, with the storeroom kept locked when the person in charge is not there.

Probably no department shows up the efficiency of the operation—or the lack of it—as much as the storeroom. This department should get high marks for good housekeeping at all times. It should be as well arranged and run as any supermarket, even though it is very much smaller in scale.

When the storeroom becomes so overcrowded that one finds cartons of breakfast foods, tins of cooking oil, shortening, or cases of canned goods, stored on the floor in an adjacent corridor or in any other available wide-open area, necessary precautions cannot be taken to protect the items or to insure control.

Whenever goods are purchased that are not needed for consumption within a short period of time, the buyer should consider the many cost factors that increase the original cost of such purchases. Some of these are the interest on the money invested; insurance; cost of storage; labor, and possible loss due to shrinkage, deterioration, and even spoilage. When these are added up, the buyer may change his or her mind about extra ordering.

Controlled buying and efficient storage procedures with proper facilities will save the food-service operator many dollars.

## RECEIVING PROCEDURES

The receiving of supplies is one of the most vital functions in the whole food operation. Proper receiving means more than merely counting the number of pieces, packages, and cartons received; it embraces essential procedures without which the food operation may lose thousands of dollars over a period of time.

The receiving clerk should be a well-trained person, capable of checking all food supplies on receipt for quantity, weight, quality, size, and/or count. Only in this way can one make sure that the goods received are as specified.

Unless such a thoroughly trained person is in charge, the receiving clerk should check the order for weight, count, and/or size and then the food-service manager or dietitian should check the items for quality.

A scale capable of weighing the supplies is a "must" in every receiving department. Many varieties of scales are available—portable ones that are limited in capacity and floor scales built to handle heavier loads (see Chapter 10, Scales).

### Duties of Receiving Clerk

In some operations, before looking at the invoice, the trained receiving clerk checks and weighs the supplies, and writes the quantity, weight, size, and/or count of each item on a printed form reserved for this purpose. Only then does he compare his figures with those on the invoice.

In other operations, the quantities and weights of all items are checked and compared with those on the invoice. In both cases any shortages are promptly reported to the dealer who then issues a credit slip, which later should be attached to the invoice. Meanwhile, the deduction is written in pencil on the invoice.

Any item returned to a supplier should be accompanied by a special printed form. On this slip write the item, quantity, and reason for its return. Have this slip signed by the receiving clerk and the delivery man, then deduct the item in pencil from the invoice. Later a credit slip should be sent by the dealer.

The invoice is now ready to be stamped with an indelible stamp and signed by the receiving clerk. One copy is given to the delivery man, the other one is kept on file.

The procedure outlined above is the correct one to follow before any invoice is OK'd and signed. But in operations where the receiving procedures are lax and no one person is responsible for receipt of supplies, the invoice is often OK'd by the chef or supervisor without checking the delivery. Naturally, the operation may pay dearly for such unbusinesslike procedures, for even dealers can make mistakes.

As the proper checking procedures do take time, it is advisable for the buyer to specify times for deliveries. Dealers will endeavor to follow such a schedule as nearly as possible. In this way, one delivery man will not be kept waiting while the order from another company is being checked. However, the cost of gasoline is making it much more difficult to schedule deliveries on such a tight schedule. Foodservice operators may well have to adjust their own procedures to accommodate to delivery problems that are likely to continue.

### Checking in Supplies

After accounting for the items that have been delivered, the next step is to check the price of each item on the invoice to make sure it is the same as that on the purchase order form. The extensions are checked either by the receiving clerk or the bookkeeping department.

A purchase record that itemizes purchases is a sound business procedure. Enter the date, vendor, brand and description, amount purchased, unit cost, and total cost in the purchase record book from the invoices, after the latter are approved for payment.

Businesslike storeroom procedures and continuing care in checking incoming supplies and invoices, together with up-to-date records, pay good dividends.

### WHAT MAKES A GOOD STOREROOM

Storage areas for two types of food, dry and refrigerated, should be planned with care. All too often in the original planning of the food establishment, little attention is paid to dry storage space, which is delegated to any left-over area.

Thus, it is not unusual to find the storeroom encumbered with uninsulated hot water pipes, water heaters, refrigerator compressors or condensing units, and other heat-producing devices. Or, the storeroom may be separated from the heating plant by only an uninsulated wall.

Under these conditions, it is almost impossible to keep the dry storage area at the desired temperature, i.e., 40° to 70°F. (4° to 21°C). Higher temperatures generally have a damaging effect on the food supplies and may lead to spoilage. Ideally, no piece of equipment that requires the care and attention of an engineer or maintenance man should be located in the storeroom.

But whatever the space allotted, the storeroom should be well-ventilated, well-lighted, dry, and clean. Proper circulation of fresh air carries off odors, inhibits the growth of molds, and prevents condensation on walls, ceiling, equipment, and food. For good lighting, use 2 or 3 watts for each square foot of floor area.

The walls of the storeroom should be constructed of material that can be washed easily. The floor should be heavy concrete.

Temperature control is important in the storeroom. Try to keep the area at a comfortable room temperature. In no case should the temperature be allowed to rise above 80°F. (27°C). Some operations will find it necessary to install an air conditioner to maintain the proper temperature.

### HOW MUCH SPACE FOR STORAGE?

The amount of space required for dry storage will depend on the type of operation, the menu, volume of business, purchasing policies, frequency of deliveries, and similar factors. On the basis of two-weeks supply of staples, some authorities consider that under normal conditions, minimum space requirement for an operation is ½ sq. ft. (465 cm²) per meal served daily. Others estimate that the minimum space required for an operation seating 150 is 15 × 8 sq. ft. (13,935 × 7432 cm²).

A good rule of thumb for estimating needed dry storage area is to take the meal load for the heaviest day anticipated and divide by two. This figure will equal the number of square feet needed for a storeroom in an average establishment for a 30-day supply of dry foods and supplies. For two-weeks storage, reduce the area by one half.

### SHELVING

Metal is the ideal material for storeroom shelves. Wherever possible the shelves should be adjustable. To prevent waste space, carefully calculate the depth between the shelves. Inside the storeroom, three shelving materials are common: wood, formed steel, and wire.

## Shelf Specifications

Wood shelving is normally built to the designer's specifications. An ideal height for the first or lowest shelf is 36 in. (91.4 cm) above the floor. This spacing will allow large cans, bags, or bins to be placed on the floor under the shelving.

The first shelf can be 24 in. (60 cm) deep. The depth of the upper shelves may range from 15 to 21 in. (38.1 to 53.3 cm). A clear 16-in. (40.6 cm) space between all shelves will accommodate two rows of No. 10 cans or three rows of No. 2½ cans.

Standard, prefabricated warehouse shelving can be used effectively in the storeroom. These units come in varying widths and heights. A common size is seven shelves high and 36 in. (91.4 cm) wide. This equipment is strong and durable. Shelf spacing can be adjusted easily.

Another common type of shelving is made of heavy chrome-plated wire. Standard units come in sections 12 or 18 in. (30.5 or 45.7 cm) wide and 36 or 48 in. (91.4 or 122 cm) long. Various shelf depths can be obtained by bolting sections together. Spacing is adjustable to a 7-ft. (213.4 cm) height.

It is now possible also to plan shelving requirements in advance because modular units have been designed to store common items without overhang or waste air. These typical sizes may be helpful:

No. 10 cans, 4 deep . . . . . 21-in. (53.3 cm) wide shelf
2 deep . . . . . 14-in. (35.6 cm) wide shelf
Dish and glass racks
20 × 24-in. (50.8 × 60 cm) . . 21-in. (53.3 cm) wide shelf
Gallon jugs, 2 deep . . . . . 14-in. (35.6 cm) wide shelf
Cafeteria pans
18 × 26-in. (45.7 × 66 cm) size . . . 21-in. (53.3 cm) wide shelf
12 × 20-in. (30.5 × 50.8 cm) size . . . 21-in. (53.3 cm) wide shelf
No. 2 cans, 6 deep . . . . . 21-in. (53.3 cm) wide shelf

Mobile shelving units are also available that can be adjusted to match fixed shelving. Goods can be stored in quantities that match common recipe requirements and can be rolled from storage to preparation areas.

All goods should be arranged in an orderly manner on the shelves, with every item in the same consecutive order as it appears on the inventory form to facilitate inventory taking.

## STORING BULK ITEMS

Bulk supplies in cartons, bags, or case lots, such as cartons of breakfast foods, bags of flour and sugar, large cans of salad oil and drums of shortening, should be stored on platforms or pallets 8 to 10 in. (20.3 to 25.4 cm) off the floor. Elevating bulk supplies makes cleaning easy, prevents damage from water or accumulated soil, and discourages the breeding of vermin. The pallets may be loaded directly from the delivery truck, thus eliminating the unnecessary work of rehandling the supplies.

Platforms for storing root vegetables may be from 8 to 15 in. (20.3 to 38.1 cm) off the floor. Such items as cereal products, dried peas and beans, are usually stored in galvanized cans equipped with tight-fitting covers, and rollers or dollies. Each can is labeled with the name of its contents.

## WHAT MAKES A GOOD BUY

A "par" storeroom inventory means a controlled inventory closely matching the needs of the operation. To many operators the amount of inventory to carry is almost a jigsaw puzzle. Without any minimum or maximum requirements set for each item, there is always the fear of running out of necessary supplies. This fear frequently results in overbuying, a particularly costly process in times of inflation.

Sometimes too great an attempt is made to take advantage of every bargain that is offered. All such good buys should be analyzed carefully against potential interest forfeited on the money spent for the bargain, and the energy costs of storing foods that must be refrigerated or held in storage freezers. Even the costs for space and supervision of foods held in dry storage may add too much to the purchase price.

## FIGURING SIZE OF INVENTORY

The type of operation, the menu, the clientele, the volume of business, the purchasing policies, and the frequency of deliveries will all influence the total amount of inventory to carry. A "par" inventory for each item should be established that tells the minimum quantity below which the item should not fall, and the maximum above which it should not go. For example: Bottles catsup—12 minimum; 48 maximum.

Based on the volume of business, many operators believe that the stock should be turned over three or four times monthly. For the average operation, under normal conditions, an estimate can be figured on the basis of the monthly cost of the food served. This cost is then averaged over a three or four month's period with a percentage added based on the rate of inflation. Twenty-five percent of this figure will represent a fair estimate for the amount of inventory that should be carried.

Many operators find it useful to keep a perpetual inventory, which is reconciled monthly with the physical inventory. A perpetual inventory acts as a buying guide, minimizes dead items, controls overbuying, prevents underbuying, and furnishes a record of past performance for future use. It gives immediate information on the purchase date of each item, the vendor, brand purchased, cost, the amount on hand after the last issue, and the "par" inventory.

Only if the perpetual inventory is kept up-to-date can it be of real value, as the information must be available when needed. Otherwise, keeping a perpetual inventory becomes a nuisance and only an "accounting motion," as the real benefits have been nullified.

### First-in First-out

"First-in and first-out" should be the guiding principle in all inventory keeping, that is, the supply of the item first received should be issued before the newer shipment is used.

In some operations, price marking of all case goods and containers is advantageous. The cost per case or per dozen may be marked on the carton with a colored crayon. When the case is opened and the containers placed on the shelves, the unit price is stamped on the end of the container—as in a supermarket. This system makes it easier to cost the requisition and also furnishes a way to tell similar items of different prices from each other.

## HOLDING SEMI-PERISHABLES

During the past 100 years—since the development of modern canning methods—tremendous strides have been made in lengthening the storage life of food. Manufacturers and processors have created hundreds of packaged food products that will withstand months and even years of storage, while retaining a high degree of quality. These are semi-perishables.

Foodservice management is fortunate to have such a wide variety of semi-perishables. These products have greatly simplified purchasing and storage problems, and have made it possible for even remotely located establishments to serve varied and nutritious menus.

Yet, although the foodservice/lodging field spends billions of dollars on these products annually, little advice on storing them properly is available. The inference, which popular opinion has followed, is that there are few if any rules or limits in handling semi-perishables. As one food expert has remarked, "Raw and perishable products may be handled with care and speed, but as soon as the product is put in a can or box, the idea begins to prevail that 'now we need not worry any more.'"

Another problem in storing semi-perishables is the fact that the buyer rarely knows the exact age of the products when he buys them. Thus it is difficult to tell precisely how long they can be stored.

Almost all foods—with the possible exception of salt and sugar—undergo chemical deterioration immediately after they are processed. This deterioration continues during their whole life until they are consumed.

Even though it may be possible to store a semi-perishable food for years before it is completely spoiled, it may not be practical for a high-quality foodservice operation to keep the item for more than a few months, and maybe not that long.

In even a few months, under average storage conditions, a semi-perishable food may have lost enough flavor, color, texture, or nutritive value to be below the desired standards. As in the case of nutrient loss, this deterioration may not be easily detected.

The charts on the following pages suggest practical, not maximum, limits for storage. They are based on the advice of food technologists, food processors, and storage experts. However, even these should be considered as outside limits for storage of these items. Stay well within them and in the long run you will get better value from purchasing and be able to serve patrons better, more nutritious food.

## THREE KINDS OF SPOILAGE

All foods are subject to spoilage from micro-organisms, chemical change, and infestation under certain conditions. Of course, semi-perishables are much less susceptible to microbial spoilage than fresh foods.

### Microbial Spoilage

Microbial spoilage is the action of bacteria, yeasts, and molds. Canning, drying, pickling, smoking, and salting are all designed to protect foods from microbial action; if these processes are carried out properly, there is little danger from spoilage. Of all types of microbial spoilage, bacterial action is the only one known to be a frequent cause of illness.

### Infestation

Infestation can occur in any food, semi-perishables included. Roaches, flies, and rodents must be considered dangerous because they are disease carriers. Organisms such as weevils, which fre-

quently develop in grain products, are not usually injurious. Technically speaking, the food can be reconditioned (insects removed), but it is much wiser for a foodservice operation to consider such food as spoiled rather than take the chance that the reconditioning might not be complete.

### Chemical Spoilage

Chemical spoilage covers many changes that may occur in even the most stable of semi-perishables. Something the food technologists call "browning reaction" may affect dried fruits and vegetables, fruit juice concentrates, jams, jellies, powdered milk, certain canned vegetables, meats, and many other foods. It darkens the color, may change the flavor, and reduce nutritive value.

The fats in foods are subject to deterioration or rancidity during storage. Chemical changes may alter the texture of preserved foods, creating either toughness or softness. The color pigments in products may change or be lost entirely, bringing about undesirable changes in appearance. Remember that chemical change also includes loss of vitamins.

## STORAGE REQUIREMENTS

*Temperature* is undoubtedly the most important factor in storage. At prolonged periods high temperatures encourage bacterial and mold growth, and insect infestation. They increase the rate of chemical change, rob flavor, and may even affect the keeping qualities of containers.

For example, in canned goods excessive temperatures during storage accelerate the action of acids in the foods, that, in turn, bring about pinholing in the cans, blackening of the interiors, and hydrogen swells.

Temperatures that are too low can cause damage also. The texture of canned foods may break down after they have been subjected to freezing temperatures. Emulsions in such products as mayonnaise and prepared mustard may be destroyed. Also avoid sudden changes in temperature that will create excessive condensation in

**DRY STORES CHART**

| Products | Cool Storeroom | Refrig. | Humidity | Signs of Deterioration | Notes |
|---|---|---|---|---|---|
| **BAKING STORES** | | | | | |
| Baking Powder | 8–12 mo. | | Max. 60% | Caking. | If stored too long, will lose leavening power. |
| Chocolate, baking | 6–12 mo. | 2 yr. | Max. 60% | Mold, mustiness, loss of flavor. | Keep away from strong-odored products. |
| Chocolate, sweetened | 2 yr. [not over 65°F. (18°C)] | | Max. 60%; not over 50% optimum | Mold, sugar bloom on surface, stale flavor, webbing. | Store off floor, away from walls; refrigerate in hot weather; more expensive grades keep longer due to better quality raw materials, higher fat coatings. |
| Chocolate Milk | 6–12 mo. | 1 yr. | Same as above | Same as above. | |
| Cornstarch | 2–3 yr. | 3–5 yr. | Max. 60% | Caking, foreign, musty odors. | Same as above. Begins losing some flavor after one month. |
| Tapioca | 1 yr. | 2 yr. | Max. 70% | | |
| Yeast, dry | 18 mo. | 3 yr. | | | Keep away from strong-odored products. |
| Baking Soda | 8–12 mo. | | Max. 60% | Caking. | |
| **BEVERAGES** | | | | | |
| Cocoa | 1 yr. | | Max. 85% | Caking, infestation (will occur if left uncovered for long). | Keep away from strong-odored products. Will become rancid in high temperature. |
| Coffee, ground (vacuum packed) | 7–12 mo. | 12–18 mo. | Max. 60% | Loss of flavor. | Store off floor and away from walls and strong-odored products. |
| Coffee, ground (not vacuum packed) | 2 wk. | 1 mo. | Max. 60% | Loss of flavor, foreign odors. | |
| Coffee, instant | 8–12 mo. | 3 yr. | Max. 85% | Caking, loss of flavor. | Caking tends to occur at high temperatures as well as in dampness if container leaks. Cakes are usually reclaimable. |
| Tea Leaves | 12–18 mo. | 3–4 yr. | Between 50% and 80%; 75% optimum | Loss of sweet aroma, absorption of foreign odors, mold, mustiness, dried-out leaves, infestation. | Store off floor away from direct sunlight and strong-odored products. High-temperatures and less than 50% humidity both tend to dry it out. |

**DRY STORES CHART (cont.)**

| Products | Cool Storeroom | Refrig. | Humidity | Signs of Deterioration | Notes |
|---|---|---|---|---|---|
| **BEVERAGES (cont.)** | | | | | |
| Tea, instant | 8–12 mo. | 3 yr. | Max. 85% | Loss of flavor, caking. | Avoid high temperatures and excessive dampness as either condition will cause caking, particularly if container is not completely sealed. Gradual flavor loss over course of a year at room temperature. |
| Carbonated Beverages | Indefinitely | | | | |
| **CANNED GOODS** **(Note: Following information is based on general tolerances.)** | | | | | |
| Fruits (in general) | 1 yr. | 4 yr. | Max. 60% | Softening, fading color, loss of flavor, can bulge, leakage, pin holing. | Good idea to specify "current pack only" or "last year's pack not acceptable" when buying canned fruits and vegetables. Keep away from direct sunlight, especially in warm climates, as solar radiation can easily push temperature inside cans above 100°F. (38°C) and considerably shorten storage life. Use well-ventilated area. (See other suggestions in text.) |
| Fruits, acid types, i.e., citrus, berries, sour cherries | 6–12 mo. | 3 yr. | Max. 60% | Same as above, but particularly pin holing due to acid action. | Same as above. Acid factor reduces storage life. |
| Fruit Juices | 6–9 mo. | 3 yr. | Max. 60% | | Same as above. |
| Meat, Poultry, Seafood (in general) | 1 yr. | 2–4 yr. | Max. 60% | Same as above. Crystals may form in canned crabmeat. They are not harmful, but annoying and thus quality is reduced. | Same as above. Temperatures above 90° F. (32°C) hasten deterioration appreciably for these products. Freezing affects texture, particularly of those containing vegetables. Those containing tomato, or other high-acid sauces have slightly reduced storage life. |
| Pickled Fish, Fish in Brine | 4 mo. | 12 mo. | Max. 60% | Mold and off odor. | If mold or off odor develop, discard product. |

**DRY STORES CHART (cont.)**

| Products | Cool Storeroom | Refrig. | Humidity | Signs of Deterioration | Notes |
|---|---|---|---|---|---|
| **CANNED GOODS (cont.)** | | | | | |
| Smoked Fish, light smoking sauce | This is a highly-perishable product. | | | | |
| Smoked Fish, heavy smoking | 1 mo. | 2–3 mo. | | Mold and off odor. | If mold or off odor develop, discard product. |
| Dried Fish | 1 mo. | 2–3 mo. | | Same as above. | Same as above. |
| Soups (including bouillon cubes and dehydrated soup mixes) | 1 yr. | 3–4 yr. | | | Avoid freezing (most canned vegetables freeze at 25°F. (−4°C)) and all sudden changes in temperature (to minimize condensation). Keep away from direct sunlight (explained under fruits). |
| Vegetables (except high-acid ones) | 1 yr. | 4 yr. | | Softening, fading color, loss of flavor, can bulge, leakage, pin holing. | |
| Vegetables, high acid, i.e., tomatoes and sauerkraut | 7–12 mo. | 2–3 yr. | | Same as above, but particularly pin holing due to acid action. | Same as above. |
| **CONDIMENTS, FLAVORS, & SEASONINGS** | | | | | |
| Mustard, prepared | 2–6 mo. | 1 yr. | | Gas bubbles, brown surface color, sulfur-like odor. | Affected by direct light as well as prolonged storage at high temperatures. Continual flavor loss, to some degree, from time of manufacture, so should be used as soon as possible. |
| Flavoring Extracts | Indefinite | | | | Never refrigerate. |
| Monosodium Glutamate | Indefinite | | | | |
| Salt | Indefinite | | Max. 60% | | Caking will occur in humid conditions, but has no lasting effect on quality. |
| Sauces (hot pepper, soy, steak, Worcestershire) | 2 yr. | 2–3 yr. | | Separation of ingredients, off odors, color change. | Affected by long exposure to light (color change); should never be frozen. |

**DRY STORES CHART** (cont.)

| Products | Cool Storeroom | Refrig. | Humidity | Signs of Deterioration | Notes |
|---|---|---|---|---|---|
| **CONDIMENTS, FLAVORS, & SEASONINGS** (cont.) | | | | | |
| Spices, Herbs, Seeds, whole | 2 yr. to indefinite | | | Fading color in herbs, loss of aroma. | In whole form, the flavor and aroma of spices are protected by cell structure. Bay leaves and other herbs lose bright color within a year. |
| Spices, Herbs, Seeds, ground (except paprika) | 1 yr. | 2 yr. | Max. 60% | Loss of aroma, faded colors, caking. | Keep off floor, away from outside walls. Reseal containers quickly after each use. Purchase in moderate quantities, replace frequently. |
| Paprika, Chili Powder, Cayenne, Red Pepper | 1 yr. | 1 yr. | Max. 60% | Fading color, infestation. | Keep away from direct light. During summer in hot climates, may be wise to refrigerate to guard against infestation. |
| Seasoning Salts | 1 yr. | 2 yr. | Max. 60% | Caking. | Very hygroscopic and once solidly caked, they are usually unredeemable. |
| Vinegar | 2 yr. | 3 yr. | | Presence of "mother" or vinegar "eel," evaporation or infestation. | Both "mother" and "eel" are signs of improper manufacturing, however, "mother" may also indicate storage troubles (usually loose caps) as may evaporation and infestation (fruit flies). |
| **DAIRY FOODS & CHEESE** | | | | | |
| Cheese, hard types (cheddar or American), particularly natural | | 1 mo. (32°F.) (0°C) 2 wk. (45°F.) (7°C) | | Drying out, "oils off," moldiness. | Needs tight wrapping. Store away from strongly-odored products. |
| Cheese, Soft types, e.g., cream, cottage, Limburger | | 1–2 wk. | | Drying out, "oils off," moldiness. | Needs tight wrapping. Store away from strong-odored products. Soft cheeses tend to change |

## DRY STORES CHART (cont.)

| Products | Cool Storeroom | Refrig. | Humidity | Signs of Deterioration | Notes |
|---|---|---|---|---|---|
| **DAIRY FOODS & CHEESE (cont.)** | | | | | |
| | | | | | body characteristics undesirably when stored at freezing temperatures. Storage life under refrigeration is shorter than for hard cheeses because texture allows spoilage agents to enter easily. Mild types, in particular, are potential sources of food poisoning if storage is prolonged or improperly handled. |
| Cheese Spreads | 1 yr. | | | Surface darkening, off flavor, odor, mold. | Those with wine have slightly longer storage life. All spreads become perishable once opened. |
| Cream, powdered | 4 mo. | 6 mo. | | Stale or tallowy odor, separating of butterfat. | Best refrigerated. |
| Milk, condensed | 1 yr. (if ave. temp. not more than 60°F. (16°C) 2 mo. at 70°F. (21°C) | 1 yr. | Max. 60% | Darkening, thickening, change in flavor, "sandiness," swelled cans (from fermentation). | Swelled cans should be discarded. |
| Milk, dry, non-fat (regular and instant) | 1 yr. | 2 yr. | Max. 35%, containers not hermetically sealed. | Flavor changes, lumping and darkening. | Extra grade (moisture 4% in regular, 5% in instant) in hermetically-sealed tins or glass keeps longer, but foil-laminated or polyethylene bags are also good. |
| Milk, dry, whole | 10–12 mo. | 2 yr. | | Darkening, stale flavor, rancidity. | |
| Milk, evaporated | 1 yr. (if ave. temp. not more than 60°F. (16°C) 2 mo. at 70°F. (21°C). | 1 yr. | Max. 60% | Darkening, separation of cream layer, gelling (due to changes in the protein). | Milk that has gelled should not be used because this condition could be due to a defective can as well as to protein changes. |

**DRY STORES CHART (cont.)**

| Products | Cool Storeroom | Refrig. | Humidity | Signs of Deterioration | Notes |
|---|---|---|---|---|---|
| **FATS & OILS** | | | | | |
| Butter | | 1 mo. (35°–45°F.) (2°–7°C) 6–9 mo. (0°F.) (–18°C) | Max. 55% | Absorption of foreign odors, rancidity. | The sweeter the cream used in making the butter, the longer the product will keep. Use double the normal wrapping (or airtight moisture-proof containers) for freezer storage. |
| Margarine | | 1 mo. (35°–45°F. (2°–7°C) 3 mo. (0°F.) (–18°C) | Max. 55% | Stale flavors, rancidity, surface darkening, mold, foreign odors, oil separation. | Keep away from strong-odored products. Aluminum wrapping offers additional storage protection. Higher quality products keep longer. |
| Salad Dressings (inc. mayonnaise) | 2 mo. (max. at 60°F. (16°C); optimum is 50°F.) (10°C) | 2 mo. | Not a factor. | Rancidity, off color, separation of oil from water. | Avoid direct light or sunlight and sudden temperature changes. |
| Salad Oil | 6–9 mo. | | Not a factor. | Rancidity (odor similar to old lard or grease). | A light high grade oil will keep better. |
| Shortenings, vegetable | 2–4 mo. | 1 yr. | Not a factor | Rancidity, absorption of foreign odors. | |
| Shortenings, animal fat (lard, etc.) | | 2 mo. | Not a factor | Rancidity, absorption of foreign odors. | Should be refrigerated; very perishable at room temperature; more perishable than vegetable shortenings at room temperature because softer (harder the fat, the longer the storage life). |
| **GRAINS & GRAIN PRODUCTS** | | | | | |
| Cereal Grains (for cooked cereal—any type) | 8 mo. | | Below 40% | Mold; webbing, infestation; musty, stale or free fat odor. | Store off floor away from walls. Be especially careful to keep them away from all strong-odored products as they act like a sponge for odors around them, the same is true of dampness. As one expert put it, "Cereals are best |

**DRY STORES CHART** (cont.)

| Products | Cool Storeroom | Refrig. | Humidity | Signs of Deterioration | Notes |
|---|---|---|---|---|---|
| **GRAINS & GRAIN PRODUCTS** (cont.) | | | | | |
| | | | | | when first made and thereafter deteriorate a little bit each day." In excessive heat or humidity they may not last more than a month. |
| Cereals (ready-to-eat) | 6 mo. | | Max. 60% | Loss of crispness and development of a toughness, mold, webbing, infestation, rancidity. | Essentially the same as for cereal grains, above. |
| Cornmeal | 8–12 mo. | | Max. 60% | Rancidity, mold, infestation, caking. | Essentially same as above. |
| Flour, bleached | 9–12 mo. | 2 yr. | Max. 60% | Infestation, caking, mustiness. | Essentially same as above. Low temps. (32°–43°F.) (0°–6°C) best protection against infestation. Refrigerating may be necessary in very hot climates. |
| Flour, whole grain | 2–4 mo. | 4–6 mo. | Max. 60% | Rancidity, infestation, caking, mustiness. | Essentially same as above. Since whole grain flours retain the oil-bearing wheat "germ," they are more susceptible to rancidity than bleached flour. |
| Macaroni, Spaghetti, and all Pastas | 3 mo. | | Max. 60% | Mold, infestation, checking, mustiness. | Essentially the same precautions as for other cereal grains, above. If pastas are subjected to sudden changes in temperature, they may check, that is, develop fine cracks that will cause disintegration in cooking. |
| Prepared Mixes | 6 mo. | 12 mo. | Max. 50% | Infestation, stale odor, discoloration, loss of baking performance. | Temperature particularly important: above 70°F. (21°C) may reduce life to 2–3 mo. |
| Rice, parboiled | 9–12 mo. | | | Infestation, color change (to yellowish), rancid odor. | Same general precautions as for other grains. |

## DRY STORES CHART (cont.)

| Products | Cool Storeroom | Refrig. | Humidity | Signs of Deterioration | Notes |
|---|---|---|---|---|---|
| **GRAINS & GRAIN PRODUCTS (cont.)** | | | | | |
| Rice, brown or wild | | 6–9 mo. | Max. 50% | Rancid odor, infestation. | Refrigeration is required because these products still have the dark outer covering which is more prone to rancidity and absorption of foreign odors than the rest of the kernel. |
| **SWEETENERS** | | | | | |
| Sugar, granulated | Indefinite | | Max. 60% | | Caking will occur in humid conditions, but has no lasting effect on quality. |
| Sugar, confectioners' | Indefinite | | Max. 60% | | Same as above, but slightly less tendency to cake. |
| Sugar, brown | | 1 yr. | Max. 70% Min. 60% | | Brown sugar should be refrigerated to give it the ratio of humidity it needs to keep soft. |
| Syrups, corn, honey, molasses, sugar | 1 yr. | | | Mold. | Susceptible to mold after container is opened. Refrigerate opened containers. |
| **MISCELLANEOUS** | | | | | |
| Beans, dried (also all lentils) | 1–2 yr. | 2–3 yr. | Max. 60%; Min. 30% | Mold, musty appearance. | More than 60% humidity will cause mold; less than 30% will dry out the product. |
| Candied Peel-Citron | 18 mo. | 3 yr. | | | |
| Cookies, Crackers | 1–6 mo. | 4–12 mo. | Max. 60% | Staling, infestation, rancidity, softening. | Softening can be remedied by placing crackers in the oven to restore crispness. |
| Cracker Meal | 1 yr. | 3 yr. | Max. 60% | Same as above. | Same as above. |
| Dried fruits | 6–8 mo. | | About 75% | Sogginess or hardness, crystallization, infestation. | Higher than 75% humidity will result in sogginess; less than that will dry the fruit out to the point of hardness. |
| Gelatin | 2–3 yr. | 3–4 yr. | Max. 70% | Caking. | |

**DRY STORES CHART (cont.)**

| Products | Cool Storeroom | Refrig. | Humidity | Signs of Deterioration | Notes |
|---|---|---|---|---|---|
| **MISCELLANEOUS (cont.)** | | | | | |
| Dried Prunes | | 15 mo. (see notes) | About 30% | Infestation, sweating, fermenting, molding, excessive drying out and sugaring. | Best temperature is between 40°–50°F. (4°–10°C). Store on skids away from walls and away from strong-odored products. |
| Jams, Jellies | 1 yr. | 2–3 yr. | Max. 60% | Color change, crystallization, caramelization. | Red colored jams and jellies lose color if stored at excessively high temperatures. All these products will caramelize at high temperatures. |
| Nuts | 1 yr. | | | Mold, infestation, rancidity. | If vacuum packed, they will keep better. |
| Pickles, Relishes | 1 yr. | 3 yr. | Max. 60% | Pickles soften, develop hollow centers, cloudy brine. | Important to keep away from strong light, particularly dill pickles. |
| Potato Chips | 1 mo. | | Max. 50% | Staleness, rancidity. | May be recrisped by heating in oven. |
| Coconut, sweetened | 4–6 mo. | | | Browning, mold, off flavor, sogginess. | If only soggy, may be reclaimed by heating in oven. |
| Dates, pasteurized | 8–12 mo. | 8–12 mo. | Max. 65% | | |
| Dates, raw | 1–2 mo. | 8–12 mo. | Max. 65% | | |
| Eggs, powdered | 4 mo. | 1 yr. | | Caking, off odors, mold. | If moldy, discard. |
| Vegetables, dehydrated | 7–12 mo. | 4 yr. | Max. 60% | | |

## STORAGE CAPACITY DATA

| Commodity | Storage Type | Size of Container Ft. or Inches | cm | Weight per Container | Floor (Shelf) sq. ft. | Area cm² |
|---|---|---|---|---|---|---|
| Meat (Carcass) | Track, Hooks | 1 ft. of track for 1/4 | 30.5 of track for 1/4 | 150 lb.  68 kg— 1/4 carcass | 2 | 1858 |
| Meat (Cuts) | Tubs | 2 ft. diam. × 10½-in. | 60.9 diam. × 26.7 | 40 lb.  18.1 kg | 3.5 | 3251 |
| Meat (Cuts) | Trays | 18 × 26 × 3-in. | 45.7 × 66 × 7.6 | 40 lb.  18.1 kg | 3.3 | 3065 |
| Meat (Cuts, Beef) | Fibre Box | 28 × 18 × 6-in. | 71.1 × 45.7 × 15 | 140 lb.  63.5 kg | 3.5 | 3251 |
| Meat (Cuts, Pork) | Wood Box | 28 × 10 × 10-in. | 71.1 × 25.4 × 25.4 | 55 lb.  24.9 kg | 2.0 | 1858 |
| Milk | Can | 13½ in. diam. × 25-in. | 34.3 diam. × 63.5 | 10 gal.  37.6 l | 1.2 | 1115 |
|  | Case | 13 × 19 × 7-in. | 33 × 48.3 × 17.8 | 1/2 pt. (24)0.2 l | 1.7 | 1579 |
|  | Case | 14⅛ × 17½ × 7-in. | 35.9 × 44.5 × 17.8 | 1/2 pt. (35)0.2 l | 1.7 | 1579 |
| Canned Milk | Case | 19 × 13 × 7½-in. | 48.3 × 33 × 17.8 | (6) No. 10 cans 38 lb.  17.2 kg | 1.7 | 1579 |
| Cheese, American | Dairy | 13½ diam. × 7½-in. | 34.3 diam. × 17.8 | 20–30 lb.  9–13.6 kg | 1.3 | 1208 |
| Ice Cream | Cans | 9 in. diam. × 18¼-in. | 22.9 diam. × 46.4 | 5 gal.  18.8 l |  |  |
|  | Cartons | 9 × 10-in. | 22.9 × 25.4 | 2½ gal.  9.4 l |  |  |
| Butter (Margarine) | Boxes | 17¼ × 14 × 10-in. | 43.8 × 35.6 × 25.4 | 60 lb.  27.2 kg | 1.6 | 1486 |
| Bacon | Slab | 10 × 24 × 2-in. | 25.4 × 60 × 5 | 15 lb.  6.8 kg | 1.6 | 1486 |
| Salt Pork | Slab | 12 × 30 × 2-in. | 30.5 × 76.2 × 5 | 15 lb.  6.8 kg | 1.6 | 1486 |
| Shortening | Can | 16 in. diam. × 17-in. | 40.6 diam. × 43.2 | 50 lb.  22.7 kg | 1.8 | 1672 |
| Cooking Oil | Can | 9½ × 9½ × 13-in. | 24.1 × 24.1 × 33 | 5 gal.  18.8 l | 0.7 | 650 |
| Grain | Sack | 18 × 33 × 11-in. | 45.7 × 83.8 × 27.9 | 98 lb.  44.5 kg | 4.0 | 3716 |
| Sugar | Sack | 18 × 33 × 11-in. | 45.7 × 83.8 × 27.9 | 100 lb.  45.3 kg | 4.0 | 3716 |
| Potatoes | Sack | 18 × 33 × 11-in. | 45.7 × 83.8 × 27.9 | 100 lb.  45.3 kg | 4.0 | 3716 |
| Onions | Sack | 18 × 33 × 11-in. | 45.7 × 38.8 × 27.9 | 100 lb.  45.3 kg | 4.0 | 3716 |
| Flour | Sack | 18 × 33 × 11-in. | 45.7 × 83.8 × 27.9 | 100 lb.  45.3 kg | 4.0 | 3716 |
| Eggs | Wood Cases | 26 × 12 × 13-in. | 66 × 30.5 × 33 | 45 lb.  20.4 kg | 2.2 | 2044 |
| Eggs (Frozen) | Cans | 10 × 10 × 12½-in. | 25.4 × 25.4 × 31.7 | 30 lb.  13.6 kg | 1.0 | 929 |
| Fruit | Lug | 14 × 17 × 6-in. | 35.6 × 43.2 × 15.2 | 30 lb.  13.6 kg | 1.7 | 1579 |
| Citrus | Crate | 12 × 12 × 24-in. | 30.5 × 30.5 × 60 | 75–80 lb. 34–36.3 kg | 2.0 | 1858 |
|  | Carton | 11½ × 17 × 11-in. | 29.2 × 43.2 × 27.9 | 75–80 lb. 34–36.3 kg | 1.4 | 1301 |
| Apples | Box | 10½ × 18 × 11½-in. | 26.7 × 45.7 × 29.2 | 44 lb.  20 kg | 1.3 | 1208 |
|  | Carton | 12½ × 19 × 11-in. | 31.7 × 48.3 × 27.9 |  |  |  |
| Apricots | Box | 12½ × 16⅛ × 5/8-in. | 31.7 × 41 × 15.9 | 44 lb.  20 kg | 1.6 | 1486 |
|  | Crate | 16 × 16 × 5-in. | 40.6 × 40.6 × 12.7 | 25 lb.  11.3 kg | 1.4 | 1301 |
| Berries | Crate | 11 × 11 × 22-in. | 27.9 × 27.9 × 55.9 | 24 lb.  10.9 kg | 1.8 | 1672 |
| Cherries | Lug | 13½ × 16 × 6-in. | 34.3 × 40.6 × 15.2 | 36 lb.  16.3 kg | 1.7 | 1579 |
| Grapefruit | Box | 11½ × 11½ × 24-in. | 29.2 × 29.2 × 60 | 25 lb.  11.3 kg | 1.5 | 1394 |
| Grapes | Box | 6 × 16 × 13½-in. | 15.2 × 40.6 × 34.3 | 68 lb.  30.8 kg | 1 | 992 |
| Lemons | Box | 10 × 25 × 13-in. | 25.4 × 63.5 × 33 | 30 lb.  13.6 kg | 1.4 | 1301 |
| Limes | Box | 10 × 19 × 10-in. | 25.4 × 48.3 × 25.4 | 75 lb.  34 kg | 2.2 | 2044 |
| Melons | Carton | 16 × 23½ × 8½-in. | 40.6 × 59.7 × 21.6 | 35 lb.  15.9 kg | 1.3 | 1208 |
|  | Crates (Flat) | 13½ × 16 × 5-in. | 34.3 × 40.6 × 12.7 | variable | 2.6 | 2415 |
|  | Crates | 12 × 22 × 12-in. | 30.5 × 55.9 × 30.5 | variable | 1.4 | 1301 |
| Peaches | Box | 13¼ × 16 × 5-in. | 33.7 × 40.6 × 12.7 | variable | 1.8 | 1672 |
| Pears | Box | 13½ × 21 × 8½-in. | 34.3 × 53.4 × 21.6 | variable | 1.4 | 1301 |
| Pineapple | Crate | 12 × 33 × 11-in. | 30.5 × 83.8 × 27.9 | 45 lb.  20.4 kg | 1.7 | 1579 |
| Beets | Crate | 18 × 22 × 13-in. | 45.7 × 55.9 × 33 | 70 lb.  31.8 kg | 2.7 | 2508 |
| Brussel Sprouts | Box | 11 × 21 × 10-in. | 27.9 × 53.4 × 25.4 | 70 lb.  31.8 kg | 2.8 | 2601 |

**STORAGE CAPACITY DATA (cont.)**

| *Commodity* | *Storage Type* | *Size of Container* *Ft. or Inches* | *cm* | *Weight per Container* | | *Floor (Shelf) sq. ft.* | *Area cm²* |
|---|---|---|---|---|---|---|---|
| Cabbage | Crate | 18 × 22 × 13-in. | 45.7 × 55.9 × 33 | 25 lb. | 11.3 kg | 1.7 | 1579 |
| | Bag | 16 × 32 × 11-in. | 40.6 × 81.3 × 27.9 | 80 lb. | 36.3 kg | 2.8 | 2601 |
| Carrots | Crate | 18 × 22 × 13-in. | 45.7 × 55.9 × 33 | 100 lb. | 45.3 kg | 3.5 | 3251 |
| Cauliflower | Crate | 18 × 22 × 9-in. | 45.7 × 55.9 × 22.9 | 75 lb. | 34 kg | 2.8 | 2601 |
| Celery | Crate | 24 × 21 × 11-in. | 60 × 53.3 × 27.9 | 40 lb. | 18.1 kg | 2.8 | 2601 |
| | Crate | 22 × 16 × 21-in. | 55.9 × 40.6 × 53.4 | variable | | 3.5 | 3251 |
| | | | | variable | | 2.5 | 2323 |
| Lettuce | Crate | 19 × 20 × 14-in. | 48.3 × 50 × 35.6 | variable | | 2.6 | 2415 |
| | Carton | 14 × 22 × 10-in. | 35.6 × 55.9 × 25.4 | variable | | 2.1 | 1950 |
| | Crate | 13 × 21 × 10-in. | 33 × 53.3 × 25.4 | variable | | 1.9 | 1765 |
| | Paper Box | 13½ × 21 × 10-in. | 34.3 × 53.3 × 25.4 | variable | | 2.0 | 1858 |
| Sweet Potatoes | Crate | 14 × 15 × 12-in. | 35.6 × 38.1 × 30.5 | 50 lb. | 22.7 kg | 1.5 | 1394 |
| Rhubarb | Box | 11½ × 18 × 6-in. | 29.2 × 45.7 × 15.2 | 15–20 lb. | 6.8–9 kg | 1.5 | 1394 |
| Tomatoes | Box | 13½ × 16 × 17-in. | 34.3 × 40.6 × 17.8 | 30 lb. | 13.6 kg | 1.4 | 1301 |
| FROZEN FOODS | | | | | | | |
| Turkey | Box Hens | 17 × 25 × 8-in. | 43.2 × 63.5 × 20.3 | variable | | 3.0 | 2787 |
| | Box Toms | 16 × 22 × 11-in. | 40.6 × 55.9 × 27.9 | variable | | 2.5 | 2323 |
| Chickens | Box (Ice) | 12½ × 18 × 8½-in. | 31.8 × 45.7 × 21.6 | 16–32 lb. | 40.6–81.3 kg | 6.1 | 1486 |
| Vegetables | Paper Container | 5¼ × 4 × 1¾-in. | 13.3 × 10 × 4.4 | 10 oz. | 284 gm | * | |
| | Paper Container | 5¼ × 4 × 1¾-in. | 13.3 × 10 × 4.4 | 12 oz. | 340 gm | * | |
| | Paper Container | 5½ × 4 × 1¾-in. | 13.3 × 10 × 4.4 | 16 oz. | 453 gm | * | |
| | Paper Container | 10 × 5 × 2½-in. | 25.4 × 12.7 × 6.4 | 2½ lb. | 1.1 kg | * | |
| | Paper Container | 10½ × 8 × 3-in. | 26.7 × 20.3 × 7.6 | 5 lb. | 2.3 kg | .5 | 465 |

*Area does not apply to very small containers.

| | | | | | | | |
|---|---|---|---|---|---|---|---|
| Fish | Paper Container | 9½ × 7 × 2½-in. | 24.1 × 17.8 × 6.4 | 5 lb. | 2.3 kg | .5 | 465 |
| Fruit | Paper Container | 12 × 8¼ × 3-in. | 30.5 × 21 × 7.6 | 5 lb. | 2.3 kg | .7 | 650 |
| Meat | Paper Container | 12¼ × 10 × 2½-in. | 31.1 × 25.4 × 6.4 | 10 | | .8 | 743 |
| | Paper Container | 13¼ × 9½ × 2½-in. | 33.7 × 24.1 × 6.4 | 10 | | 1.0 | 929 |
| | Paper Container | 14 × 10¼ × 2¼-in. | 35.6 × 26 × 57.2 | 10 | | 1.0 | 929 |

CANNED FRUIT, VEGETABLES

| | | | |
|---|---|---|---|
| Standard No. 2½ | Can | 4 × 4¾-in. | 10 × 12 |
| Coffee 1 lb. (453 gm) | Can | 5⅙ × 3⅝-in. | 13.1 × 9.2 |
| Standard No. 5 | Can | 5⅛ × 5⅞-in. | 13 × 14.9 |
| Standard No. 10 | Can | 6 3/16 × 8¼-in. | 8.1 × 21 |
| Standard Gallon | Can | 6 3/16 × 8¾-in. | 8.1 × 22.2 |
| Dry Milk | Can | 6⅝ × 7½-in. | 16.8 × 44.5 |

**STORAGE CAPACITY DATA (cont.)**

| Commodity | Storage Type | Size of Container Ft. or Inches | cm | Weight per Container | Floor (Shelf) Area sq. ft. | cm² |
|---|---|---|---|---|---|---|
| STANDARD BOXES (CANNED FRUIT-VEGETABLES AND MISCELLANEOUS) | | | | | | |
| 6-oz. (170 gm) | | | | | | |
| Cans | 8 Doz. | 22½ × 11¼ × 7¼-in. | 57.2 × 28.6 × 18.4 | | 1.7 | 1579 |
| 8-oz. (226 gm) | | | | | | |
| Cans | 6 Doz. | 16½ × 11 × 10-in. | 41.9 × 27.9 × 25.4 | | 1.2 | 1115 |
| No. 2 Tall | 2 Doz. | 14 × 10½ × 9⅜-in. | 35.6 × 26.7 × 8.6 | | 1.0 | 929 |
| No. 2½ | 2 Doz. | 16½ × 12½ × 9¾-in. | 41.9 × 31.8 × 24.8 | | 1.4 | 1301 |
| No. 5 | 12/Case | 15½ × 10¼ × 11¼-in. | 39.4 × 26 × 28.6 | | 1.2 | 1115 |
| No. 10 | 6/Case | 19 × 12⅝ × 7-in. | 48.3 × 32.1 × 17.8 | | 1.5 | 1394 |
| Sherry Wine | 12/Case | 10½ × 13 × 13-in. | 26.7 × 33 × 33 | | 1.0 | 929 |
| Champagne | 12/Case | 17 × 21½ × 11¾-in. | 43.2 × 54.6 × 29.8 | | 2.5 | 2323 |
| | | 16 × 21 × 7-in. | 40.6 × 53.3 × 17.8 | | 2.3 | 2137 |

*Source: A Short Course in Kitchen Design, Joseph Laschober.*

canned foods. In pastas they may create checking (cracks) that break down the product during cooking.

*Humidity* is another vital factor in storage. When too high, it hastens the growth of bacteria and molds, and attracts infestation. With all naturally dry and dehydrated products, excess humidity will create caking, which may render the product totally unusable. In some cases, however, humidity must be kept moderately high or the product will dry out.

*Light* is still another factor. Many highly colored (especially red) products will fade quickly if exposed to direct sunlight. This problem occurs most with items packed in transparent material. However, strong sunlight can cause trouble in goods packed in opaque containers also. Solar radiation may raise the temperature inside cans to a level considerably above that of the storeroom and possibly to a point that hastens deterioration.

*Cleanliness* helps discourage infestation and eliminates the chance of bagged items absorbing dust. Ventilation is important because it keeps temperature down and reduces humidity.

Therefore, a storeroom for semi-perishables should be cool, dry, away from direct sunlight, clean, and well-ventilated.

The cooler and drier conditions are, the better for most semi-perishables. An average temperature of 60° to 70°F. (16° to 21°C) is adequate, but lowering it to 50°F. (10°C) will extend the storage life of many products and reduce the rate of quality loss.

On the other hand, the higher the temperature, the faster the loss. Foods generally keep three times as long at 70°F. (21°C) as at 100°F. (38°C) An average relative humidity of between 50 and 60 percent is satisfactory for most foods. However, such important commodities as cereals really should be kept at humidity below 40 percent. If it is possible to use separate areas for the "special case" products, humidity can be regulated somewhat by chemical devices.

Use a dating system to make sure that older stock is always used first. Supervisory personnel who know what to look for in spoilage should make periodic, careful inspections.

Products with strong odors should be held separately so that there is no chance of odor transfer. Most items should be placed on shelves. Use platforms or pallets for floor storage. Be careful not to stack items so high that lower layers are damaged.

***Storing Foods Packed in Glass:*** Products packed in glass with metal or cork stoppers should be inverted to prevent tops from drying out and leaking. Keep goods away from walls, particularly outside ones, to guard against damage from condensation and to insure good ventilation. Barrels or drums are good for storing opened, partially-used items. These barrels or drums can be put on wheels to make them mobile.

A good exhaust fan is an excellent idea in any storeroom. In general, it should be adequate to give the room four complete air changes an hour. Naturally, the storeroom should not have any exposed steam or hot water pipes or machinery that are likely to give off heat.

Install accurate thermometers in prominent places within the room to keep personnel aware of the temperature.

The prevailing climate naturally has an effect on the storeroom setup. In northern regions a fan will probably be sufficient in the summer to keep the temperature under control. Establishments in the North, however, may face the danger of sudden freezing during the winter.

Southern installations may have to shift certain critical products to refrigerated storage during the hot summer months. Refrigeration, of course, is optimum for most semi-perishables, but most foodservice operations have a hard enough time finding the necessary refrigerated space for fresh products.

***Keeping Sun Out:*** If the storeroom has windows, they should be frosted to eliminate direct sunlight. However, the artificial lighting inside should be bright and generous to help personnel keep the room clean and do a thorough job of inspecting the goods.

Glazed tile is the recommended finish for the walls of the storeroom; however, painted masonry or plaster is also satisfactory. Materials such as wood or wallboard are not recommended because they are not vermin proof.

Walls and floors should be tightly constructed and vapor sealed underground. Metal shelving is preferred with a maximum height of 7 ft. 6 in., (228.6 cm) supports every 48 in. (121.9 cm) at least, and average depth of 18 to 21 in. (45.7 to 53.3 cm). Space between shelves varies, of course, with the size of containers they are designed to hold.

Aisles between the shelves should be at least 30-in. (76.2 cm) wide or, if dollies and hand trucks are being used, 42 in. (106.7 cm)

The U.S. Department of Agriculture estimates that a foodservice establishment serving 100 to 200 meals daily should have 120 to 210 sq. ft. (11.1 to 19.5 m²) of dry storage space. One serving 200 to 350 meals should have 210 to 240 sq. ft. (19.5 to 22.3 m²). From 350 to 500 meals served requires 240 to 384 sq. ft. (22.3 to 35.7 m²), and 500 to 750 meals, 384 to 675 sq. ft. (35.7 to 62.7 m²).

## STORING CANNED FOODS

By volume, canned foods represent the largest category among semi-perishables used in foodservice today and therefore merit special attention. They are also probably the least understood from a storage standpoint. The tendency seems to be to consider them almost nonperishables.

According to the National Canners Association, most canned foods may be stored satisfactorily for a year under good conditions such as those outlined above. If refrigerated, canned foods may be safely kept much longer.

However, management of nutrition-conscious operations should plan purchasing so that no canned goods are kept anywhere near a year. Even though canning does preserve food significantly, it does not stop deterioration entirely when the products are kept at room temperature.

Canned goods on the shelf six months after purchase will still be satisfactory, but they will not be quite as high quality as the day they arrived. It is plain that this loss of quality is not good business. Storage expense has been incurred, while the original purchase value has decreased.

Research has not reached the point yet at which a recommendation of not more than three or six or nine months' supply can be made. Instead, it can only be recommended that buying be on as short term a basis as is practical for a particular situation.

### Heat, Dampness Enemies of Canned Goods

The storeroom for canned goods, therefore, should be cool, well-ventilated, and dry. But it is not unusual to find such foods stored in a warm room adjacent to the engineroom or with hot steam pipes lining its ceiling. Such high temperatures impair the color and flavor, if not the wholesomeness, of the product.

Storing canned foods at too low temperatures is just as injurious as storing them at those too high. A damp area may cause the outside of cans to sweat and rust, but does not damage the product unless the rusting is severe enough to penetrate the can.

It is just as safe to keep canned food in the can it comes in—if the can is cool and covered—as it is to empty the food into another container. The important thing to remember in storing any unused portion of canned food is to put it in the refrigerator as you would any other cooked food.

## CAN OPENERS

If opening canned foods is part of the storage procedure, be sure to select a can opener that can handle the required number of cans. If there are to be long production runs in the opening of cans that are all the same size, can openers are available that match requirements. One manual model that can open 12 to 100 cans consecutively takes only one downward pull of the handle to remove entire can lid. Unit is 20-in. (50 cm) high, weighs 50 lb. (22.6 kg), takes cans 10-in. (25.4 cm) tall, 8-in. (20.3 cm) in diameter.

For more than 100 cans, an air-operated opener that requires two-hand operation for greater safety is available; it is 20-in. (50 cm) high, weighs 55 lb. (24.9 kg), will open cans 10½-in. (26.7 cm) tall, 6½-in. (16.5 cm) in diameter. Models are also available to handle cans that are 22-in. (55.9 cm) high.

Heavy-duty, electric can openers that come in either counter or portable models will open up to 700 cans per hour of all sizes and types. The portable model is lightweight but sturdily built. Heavy-duty, manual table models come in two sizes and are designed for speedy, safe operation.

The removable can opener at The Foxfire Restaurant, Anaheim, CA, is simply but effectively mounted. Mounting plate is attached underneath table. Sides of square hole in table top were turned down to form a guide for the body extension of the can opener; can opener then was inserted through opening to eliminate usual problem of cleaning around the edges of mounting plate normally attached to table top.

## STORING PERISHABLE FOODS

The amount of refrigerated storage required by the individual operation, like the dry storage, depends on many factors—type of operation, seating capacity, menu, volume of business, clientele, forms in which perishables are received, and frequency of deliveries.

Under normal conditions, separate refrigerated storage is provided for meat and poultry, fresh fruit and vegetables, and dairy products. In operations where fish and shellfish are featured extensively, a refrigerated fish box is an essential. Where frozen foods are stored for any length of time, a refrigerated storage area capable of maintaining temperatures of 0°F. to −20°F. (−18° to −29°C) is a necessity.

Modern equipment, and changes in the processing of some foods, together with the trend toward convenience or preprocessed foods, are reducing the refrigerated storage space required. Portable metal slide stands, fitted with wire racks, or carts fitted with shelves are storage space savers in walk-in boxes, as they make the best possible use of vertical space.

Operators, too, are finding that less refrigerated storage is required when fabricated and ready-portion meats are purchased and where bulky vegetables are washed and trimmed on receipt or before being placed under refrigeration.

Much of the conventional fixed shelving in walk-in boxes is being supplanted in modern installations by adjustable shelving or portable stands. Portable metal slide stands fitted with wire racks or trays, or carts fitted with shelves, reduce waste motions, as they eliminate much of the rehandling of the foods stored on them.

Fitted with rubber-tired, ball-bearing swivel wheels or ball-bearing, rubber-tired, swivel, pintel casters, this equipment is easily maneuvered and slides in and out of walk-in boxes easily, as the floor is flush with the outside area. Some wheels are also equipped with revolving rubber bumpers, which protect wall areas from being defaced.

Fixed shelving should be of heavy-duty construction and noncorrosive. Such shelving is usually made of stainless steel or galvanized iron. From a sanitary standpoint, it is necessary to reduce to a minimum any crevices and corners that cannot be cleaned easily and quickly.

Mesh or slatted shelving and wire racks permit free circulation of air around the food—an essential for the proper preservation of fresh food.

Reach-in refrigerators are, by and large, located in the preparation and service areas. Drawer-type refrigerators for foods, such as steaks or chops are placed in the chef's work area.

Refrigerators should be fitted with thermometers or be thermostatically controlled. The temperature should be checked frequently. For walk-in boxes, a daily temperature chart with hourly readings should be kept, if at all possible. Any deviation from the normal will then give warning of trouble so that proper action can be taken immediately.

## Fresh Foods Need Air Moisture

Fresh meats, fruit, and vegetables, and dairy products each have definite refrigerated storage requirements regarding temperature and humidity. In commercial storage, where long holding periods are a factor, such requirements are met by having separate cold rooms with different temperature and humidity conditions. These rooms are insulated and mechanically refrigerated. Temperature and humidity are held as constant as possible.

For fresh fruits and vegetables, the air in these storage rooms is maintained with about the same moisture content as the products being stored. As different fruits and vegetables require different temperatures and humidity conditions, more than one produce room is necessary for commercial storage.

In quantity food establishments, where fresh commodities are held for a limited time only, a compromise must be reached, as it is necessary to store several items under the same temperature and humidity conditions. For this reason, many operators consider 38°F. (3°C) the highest refrigerated temperature at which fresh or chilled meats can be stored if they are to be kept at peak of perfection.

Similarly, 45°F. (7°C) is considered by many authorities the highest temperature that can satisfactorily be used to keep fresh fruit and vegetables at their best even though some commodities, such as green peppers, cucumbers, okra, grapefruit, melons, limes, or lemons, might be better stored at temperatures from 45°F. (7°C) to 50°F. (10°C)

To get the best results from refrigerated storage of fresh foods, the following precautions should be taken:

1. Fresh fruits and vegetables must go from loading dock to adequate, accurately controlled, cold storage areas and walk-ins as quickly as possible.
2. Arrange the food to allow free circulation of air around it; cold air is necessary to prevent the food from spoiling.
3. Hang raw meats away from the wall.
4. Keep the newer purchase of the same item in the back and the older purchase in the front so the older one will be used first.
5. Be sure cooked and prepared food items are covered with plastic film wrap or protective paper to prevent loss of moisture as well as to keep drippings from lodging on the food.
6. Discard foods promptly that have passed their usefulness. This practice adds space, prevents overcrowding, increases the circulation of air, and keeps the storage area in proper condition.
7. Keep the refrigerated area spotlessly clean. Wash frequently.
8. Defrost before ¼-in. (6 mm) frost gathers, as frost slows the cooling process. (That is, if the defrosting does not take place automatically.)
9. Open doors only when necessary, as the outside air raises the refrigerated temperature.
10. Check temperatures periodically even though automatic controls are present. Temperatures should be taken at the floor and ceiling levels as well as at the center of the area.

(For more information on refrigeration, see Chapter 11, Refrigeration.)

## STORAGE PRACTICES

Various food items require specific storage practices to preserve maximum flavor values. Recommended practices for several food items with special storage requirements are outlined here:

## Fresh Meats Need Separate Storage Area

Since meat is a perishable food, it requires very careful handling. It must be kept refrigerated from the time it is received until it is prepared for cooking. Refrigeration and sanitation are necessary to keep meat fresh and wholesome.

Fresh and chilled meats should be held in clean refrigerators that maintain temperatures at 33° to 36°F. (0.5° to 2°C) or at most 38°F. (3°C). This temperature range must be carefully regulated so that the minimum does not fall below 33°F. (0.5°C), as a lower temperature darkens the surface of the meat by the slow freezing action.

Fresh or chilled meats should be stored away from other foods. Foreign flavors in meat, especially beef, may be traced to vegetables or aromatic fruits stored in the same refrigerator.

Ground meat, unless frozen, should not be held more than 24 hours. This product spoils rapidly since the entire surface of the meat is exposed. Furthermore, there is a chance that during the grinding process some bacteria on the surface of the meat became mixed with the entire lot. Some of these organisms may continue to grow in the ground meat at temperatures a little above freezing and contaminate it when held longer than 24 hours.

## Keeping Canned Hams

Today's light-cured hams and "tenderized" hams must be stored under refrigeration. They are stored wrapped or covered to prevent the odor from permeating throughout the refrigerator. Fully-cured hams may be stored in a cool room.

Large canned hams must be kept under refrigeration. Some imported small hams, 1 to 3 lb. (453 gm to 1.4 kg), designated sterile products, do not require refrigeration.

Variations from the storage conditions above result in less desirable flavor, loss of product and time, when the meat has to be trimmed due to spoilage, and in some instances complete loss due to deterioration.

Poultry, like other meats, must be stored at temperatures ranging from 33°F to 38°F. (0.5° to 3°C).

## Retaining Moisture in Fruits, Vegetables

Since many fruits and vegetables thrive on coolness and moisture when growing, these products need the same conditions in dry or refrigerated storage. As a rule, most require low temperature and high humidity to preserve their fresh texture, tenderness, flavor, attractive appearance, and nutritive content. They soon lose these desirable qualities when subjected to dry heat or dry cold.

In quantity food operations where these products are held in storage for short periods only, the ideal temperature would be 35°F. to 45°F. (2° to 7°C), but the attainable range is usually 40°F. to 45°F. (4° to 7°C), with satisfactory results.

Humidity of 85 to 95 percent conserves the moisture content of fresh fruits and vegetables in refrigerated storage, and thus prevents the wilting, shriveling, or toughening of the commodity, which will result if moisture leaves the surface of fresh fruits or vegetables.

Since quantity food operators usually buy fresh fruits and vegetables daily, bi-weekly, or tri-weekly, controlling the humidity does not present much of a problem. For products held longer than three or four days, ice or a damp cloth placed over the produce will supply the necessary moisture. Some vegetables packed in bushel containers, such as green beans, tend to pack and heat if held on the premises for any length of time without ice.

**Film Bags.** Some fruits and vegetables are now packaged in film bags or film-covered containers. These can be placed under refrigeration as packaged. Many vegetables are washed and trimmed when received, and put in film bags for storage. These film bags have multiple uses, and come in various sizes, large ones being 29½ × 13 in. (74.9 × 33 cm).

When an impermeable film is used for storing fresh fruits and vegetables at 40°F. to 45°F. (4°C to 7°C) it should be perforated. Ventilation is essential, as these products continue to respire after they are harvested, using up oxygen and giving off carbon dioxide. If there is an accumulation of carbon dioxide and a decrease in oxygen within the unperforated film bag, the commodity develops off flavors and off odors.

The storage life of some fruits—pears, cherries, and apples—is being considerably lengthened by the use of sealed, polyethylene lug liners. In these sealed liners under low temperature storage, the fruit respires at a slower rate than in the standard pack. Decay is reduced, and color brightness and fresh appearance are preserved for longer periods of time than under usual commercial storage and transit conditions.

When the polyethylene-sealed liner lug is removed from low temperature storage and the fruit is held at a higher temperature, the liner must be split open to prevent the build up of undesirable levels of carbon dioxide and the reduction of oxygen in the pack.

**Keeping Corn.**    Corn should be kept cold and moist, as its sugar content changes rapidly to starch when held at a high dry temperature. Tests show that corn can lose as much as 40 percent of its sugar content in 24 hours when not kept cold. This naturally has an adverse effect on the flavor and eating quality of the corn. If the corn arrives at the quantity-food operation fresh, tender, and sweet, it can be kept in good condition if kept cold and moist from the time it is received until it is prepared for cooking. Icing corn retards the loss of sugar. Some tests show that ears of corn with the husks left on retain their flavor better than corn husked at the shipping point.

**Rules for Lettuce Storage.**    Storage practices for lettuce vary, depending on the package. If the lettuce is crated and iced, it should be kept well iced, or covered with a wet cloth in the refrigerator. If it is dry packed in a carton, it still requires a cold temperature and moist air. If the lettuce is placed on a tray or in a dry box in the refrigerator, it should have a wet cloth placed over it.

**Storing Mushrooms.**    Mushrooms do not store well even under the best conditions and should be used as soon as possible. Take every precaution to conserve their moisture. Therefore, they should not be placed uncovered in the refrigerator.

**Preserving Potatoes.**    Prepeeled potatoes have a limited storage life. They can be safely stored not more than seven days, and must be kept refrigerated at all times, preferably at a temperature range of from 32°F. to 40°F.(0°C to 4°C).

On the other hand, some fruits and vegetables do not react favorably to average refrigerated temperatures. Research has shown that potatoes stored at temperatures between 35°F. (2°C) and 45°F. (7°C) undergo chemical changes—some of the starch is converted into sugar. When potatoes with a high sugar content are cooked they develop brown or black spots due to the caramelization of the sugar. This problem is especially noticeable when the potatoes are French fried.

New potatoes should be kept cool. Early and immediate crop potatoes are best stored at 50°F. (10°C) They should be handled with care, as they are easily skinned. Mature potatoes (known as old potatoes) can be stored for a short period at room temperature of 55°F. (13°C); higher temperatures usually produce sprouting.

Sweet potatoes should not be chilled, as they then develop dark streaks, a bitter flavor, and eventually rot. For the few days that they are kept in the quantity food establishment, room temperature is satisfactory. If they are kept at temperatures of 75°F. (24°C) they will sprout.

**Storing Onions.**    If onions are to be stored for any length of time, they should be refrigerated. They should not be stored with other items, such as apples, which might absorb the onion flavor and acquire an unpleasant taste. As onions usually come in mesh bags, they should not come in contact with a wet floor, or commodities from which they will absorb moisture. When onions are to be kept on hand for only a short period, they may be kept in a dry, reasonably cool, well-ventilated place.

**Ripening Tomatoes, Avocados.**    Ripe tomatoes will hold in good condition when refrigerated at 40°F. to 50°F. (4°C to 10°C) But unripe tomatoes are best kept at temperatures ranging from 55°F. to 70°F. (13°C to 21°C) If held for more than eight days below 55°F. (13°C), and then transferred to a warmer place, they will not ripen properly. If rapid ripening is desired, they should be kept at a temperature of 60°F. to 70°F. (16°C to 21°C). At temperatures higher than 70°F. (21°C) ripening is accelerated, but so is decay.

Avocados or alligator pears should not be refrigerated unless they are ripe. To hasten the ripening of firm avocados, keep the fruit two or three days in a warm, humid place. To retard softening, keep the fruit in a cool, dry place at a temperature not below 42°F. (6°C) Firm avocados will soften in a few days when exposed to average summer temperature.

Bananas should not be refrigerated, but kept at room temperature. Those that have become too cold will not ripen properly, will not develop the bright yellow color of prime fruit, and will usually be of poor flavor. Color is the guide to proper time for use. Those that are yellow and tipped with green are partially ripe. Those that are yellow and flecked with brown are fully ripe and should be used immediately or they will be past their prime.

Many salad fruits and vegetables are prepared in advance and stored under refrigeration in gallon glass jars or in film bags to prevent evaporation and to keep the commodity fresh and in good condition for the short time before use.

## MAINTAINING FISH, SHELLFISH AT PEAK QUALITY

Fish is a highly-perishable commodity; the only way the quality of fresh or frozen fish can be maintained is to keep it under refrigeration at all times. Otherwise, bacteria and other microorganisms penetrate the flesh and cause undesirable changes in texture and flavor.

Examine shipments of fresh fish on receipt for signs of spoilage and body changes. The fish should be packed in ice for delivery and should be iced when received. Finely crushed ice is preferable to large pieces that might bruise the flesh of the fish. The ice not only holds the temperature but also keeps the surface of the fish moist and in good condition. Avoid rough handling of the fish, as bruises and punctures of the flesh induce and hasten the breakdown of the tissues.

If frozen fish is placed directly in the refrigerated area without suitable protective covering, undesirable changes take place during the storage period. The gradual loss of moisture causes the fish to become shrunken and dried and to change its texture, appearance, weight, and flavor, and

eventually will cause the fish to suffer freezer burns.

Live crabs, lobsters, clams, and oysters should be kept in a moist, cold atmosphere at approximately 45°F. (7°C). The live crabs and lobsters should be unpacked from the original containers, sorted and spread out so they will be kept moist and cold. They are frequently sprinkled with cracked ice. Oysters and clams are sometimes left in the baskets and kept cold by sprinkling cracked ice over them from time to time.

Scallops, shrimps, crabmeat, lobster meat, shucked clams, and oysters should be kept at a temperature close to 33°F. (0.5°C), but not as low as 32°F. (0°C) or they will freeze.

Frozen shellfish require the same care as frozen fish to preserve full flavor.

## STORING EGGS, EGG PRODUCTS

Fresh eggs may be stored commercially for several months at temperatures as low as 32°F. (0°C). In food establishments, they should be stored within a temperature of 38°F. to 45°F. (3°C to 7°C). They deteriorate when subjected to higher temperatures. Only those required for immediate use should be removed from refrigeration.

Frozen whole eggs, egg yolks, and egg whites that are to be used within a few days are generally stored within a temperature range of 38°F. to 45°F. (3°C to 7°C).

## PRESERVING FROZEN FOODS

Proper freezing alone will not guarantee products of top quality since the packaging and storing conditions are as important as the freezing.

If the frozen product is to be kept for any length of time in refrigerated storage, one of the first requirements is that it be packaged and/or wrapped in material that is moisture vapor proof—tin, glass, latex, coated cellophane, or coated parchment—to prevent the product from losing moisture vapor during the storage period.

When not properly packaged, meat, poultry, fish and shellfish develop freezer burns in storage that detract not only from the appearance of the product, but from its eating qualities as well. Freezer burns generally cause the fat immediately beneath the surface to become more or less rancid, the tissues to get dry and tough, and the red pigment to take on a brown color.

## Temperature Requirements

Once properly packaged, the storage conditions to consider are temperature, humidity, and storing methods. Remember that many properly packaged products will deteriorate under adverse conditions.

Tressler & Evers in "The Freezing Preservation of Foods" state: Today no one questions the fact that frozen foods should be stored at 0°F. (−18°C) or below. Many recognized authorities recommend temperatures as low as −20°F. (−29°C) for the long time storage of certain products. It is the universal opinion that most frozen products may be held in a satisfactory manner at a storage temperature of 0°F. (−18°C). A few products, such as corn-on-the cob, mushrooms, snap

## STORAGE REQUIREMENTS

### Frozen Storage Limitations of Food Products for Commercial Application*

| Food Products | Months |
|---|---|
| FRUIT | 8–12 |
| VEGETABLES | 8–12 |
| Potatoes—French fried, blanched | 2–4 |
| MEATS | |
| Beef—cubed, cutlets, roasts, steaks | 8–10 |
| Lamb and veal—chops, cutlets | 10–12 |
| Pork—chops, roasts | 6 |
| Sausage, smoked pork, ground meat, variety meats | 1–4 |
| Cooked meat, bacon | 1–3 |
| Cooked combination entrees | 2–6 |
| POULTRY | |
| Chickens | 6–12 |
| Turkeys | 3–6 |
| Giblets | 3 |
| Cooked poultry | 1 |
| Cooked poultry entrees | 3–6 |
| FISH | |
| Lean type—cod, haddock | 6 |
| Fatty type—salmon, swordfish, tuna, oysters, clams | 3 |
| Shrimp | 4–6 |
| Lobster, crab | 2–3 |
| SOUPS | 3–5 |
| BAKERY PRODUCTS | |
| Cake batters | 3–4 |
| Cakes, prebaked | 4–9 |
| Cookies | 4–6 |
| Custard and chiffon pies | 1 |
| Fruit pies, baked or unbaked | 3–4 |
| Pie shells, baked or unbaked | 1½–2 |
| Yeast bread and rolls, baked | 3–9 |
| Yeast dough | 1–1½ |

*Note:* All products should be tightly sealed in air/vaporproof containers. They should be frozen properly and held at a temperature of 0°F. (−18°C) or below.

*Foodservice Bulletin #645, Hobart Company.

beans, apples, peaches, poultry, and fatty fish, such as mackerel and salmon, should be stored at $-5°F.$ ($-21°C$)

That frozen foods deteriorate if not held at the proper temperature was forcibly brought out in a comprehensive study undertaken by the U.S. Department of Agriculture (USDA) Western Regional Laboratory on the time-temperature tolerance of frozen foods.

More than 50,000 samples were tested over a period of several years in specially constructed rooms, which permitted accurate control and systematic variation of product temperatures representing the ranges found in commercial and institutional handling. Again, it was demonstrated that zero or lower temperatures prove satisfactory for the majority of frozen foods. But fluctuations of temperature above zero must be avoided. All chemical reactions that result in loss of quality accelerate as temperature rises from $0°F.$ ($-18°C$)—from zero to $5°F.,$ ($-15°C$) $10°F.,$ ($-12°C$) $20°F.,$ ($-7°C$) $25°F.,$ ($-4°C$) etc.

The findings also dispelled the erroneous assumption that a cold and hard package is adequately protected against loss of quality. It was emphasized that many products hard at $20°F.,$ ($-7°C$) and $25°F.,$ ($-4°C$) showed quality that had been impaired.

The study also showed that all temperature damage to the frozen food is retained indefinitely, regardless of handling and care afterward.

Since a constant and uniform temperature is all-important, the freezer storage area should not be used for the freezing operation. All frozen food should have a central internal temperature of $0°F.$ ($-18°C$) In other words, before being placed in freezer storage, frozen products should be as cold or colder than the storage temperature, to prevent fluctuation.

The humidity of the storage area should be carefully controlled. Very high humidity is an advantage in refrigerated storage with temperatures below $32°F.$ ($0°C$). Otherwise, at low temperature air that is low in humidity will attempt to gain moisture from the products being stored. Then the products stored dry out, unless packaged to prevent this from occurring.

These are the conditions required for best possible storage of frozen foods. Time limitations for frozen food storage are shown in the preceding chart. (For more information on storage freezers, see Chapter 12, Storage Freezers.)

## BRAIN TEASERS—STORAGE

1. Goods for storage are usually delivered at the _____ (Fill in.)

2. The person receiving deliveries should check items for quantity, weight, size and/or count. Why? _____

3. The two types of food for which storage should be planned are dry and refrigerated. Space for dry stores should have four qualities. (Name two.) _____

4. Of the following items, cross out those that should not be put in the dry stores area: No. 10 cans, frozen food, dishes, glasses, fresh meat, bags, cartons.

5. What are semi-perishable foods? _____

6. Is the following statement true or false? (Check right answer.) Packaged or canned foods will not spoil. True ____ False ____

7. Using the dry stores chart, list the length of time the following items can be stored: Chocolate milk _____ Canned fruit _____ Salt _____ Margarine _____ Cereals _____ Brown sugar _____

8. Canned goods stored at too high temperatures will not keep well. Is there damage when they are kept at too low temperature? (Check right answer.) Yes ____ No ____

9. Can meat be stored with other foods? (Tell why or why not.)_____

10. How long can fresh ground meat be held safely?_____

*(For correct answers, see page 251.)*

**FIGURE   9.2**
On delivery, produce is stored off the floor in cooler at the Bonaventure Hotel, Los Angeles. Heavy duty solid shelving holds supply of fruits and vegetables required for hotel's menus.

**FIGURE   9.3**
Dry storage area at the Americana Hotel, New York City, has regular wire shelving with shelves off the floor to make cleaning easier.

**FIGURE 9.4**

Adjustable wire shelving permits convenient organization of supplies in the dry storeroom at Sam Houston Jr. High School, Irving, Tex. Note that corner posts have been eliminated to make full use of available space. Floor surface is quarry tile and storeroom is well-lighted and ventilated. Area is directly accessible from production area.

**FIGURE 9.5**
View inside central dry storage room at Food Service Facility, California Highway Patrol Academy, Bryte. Shelving is modular, assembled from components. Items are arranged to speed inventory.

**FIGURE 9.6**
Loading and receiving dock area at the Food Service Facility of the California Highway Patrol Academy, Bryte. Doors are entrances to refrigerated storage rooms. Concealed air curtains are installed above doorways. Storage space was allocated on the basis of multiple deliveries.

**FIGURE   9.7**
There is no possibility of food and chemical confusion at Doctor's Hospital, Tulsa, Okla. All chemicals are kept in their own storage room pictured here. This is done to keep chemicals totally separate from the food storage and preparation areas.

**FIGURE   9.8**
Dry storage space was doubled when facilities at Doctor's Hospital in Tulsa, Okla. were enlarged to take care of 130 new beds. The area is well-lighted, easy to keep clean with its quarry tile floor, coved corners, and shelves well above floor level. The metal shelving combines fixed and mobile units.

**FIGURE 10.1**
Scales are positioned on shelf between the vegetable preparation table and the garde manger station at the Old King Cole Restaurant, New York City.

# Chapter Ten

# Scales

With data processing systems in prospect for more and more foodservice operations, the role of the scale is newly fortified. Not so long ago, the potent argument for installing scales was "loss at the back door," and very impressive the projected figures were. More recently, data on substantial losses traced to overportioning and inaccurate weighing of ingredients during preparation speedily justified the installation of scales in preparation and serving areas.

In his outline based on "The Industry's First Textbook," published in *Foodservice Equipment Specialist*, the late Warner Kerzmann divided scales into three types for three different applications. They were listed as:

1. Receiving scales, generally large, with capacities up to several hundred pounds, are part of the receiving and storage operation, where they are used to check weights of incoming shipments.
2. Preparation scales, usually balance type, are used mostly by bakers, chefs, and cooks.
3. Portion-control scales are used to check weight where meat is cut on premise, in hos-

pitals for diet purposes, and to check or control serving sizes.

## NEW SPOTS FOR SCALES

To be sure that scales stand guard in every area needing controls, check these "scale profiles" of two contemporary operations noted for their canny approach to costs:

A listing of scale locations in the Palmer House, Chicago, covers kitchen, commissary, and butcher shop; types and locations: receiving—1 floor built-in and 1 bench scale; commissary—1 bench scale; butcher shop—2 hanging scales, 5 portion-control scales and 1 bench scale; pastry and ice cream shop—1 bench and 2 table scales; coffee house—1 hanging and 1 portion-control scale; main kitchen—1 hanging and 4 portion-control scales; Petite Cafe Kitchen—1 portion-control scale; food controller—2 portion-control scales.

Robert Buchanan, former director of residence halls foodservice, Northern Illinois University, DeKalb, suggested these locations: (For further information on the use of scales during that period, see Sample Scale Profile, pp. 180–181.)

"I would locate scales in a hidden fashion on the cafeteria hot counter area so that we could accurately weigh casserole-type items placed on the dinner plate.

"I would mount the scale below the steam table with the dial extended through the top of the counter so it is easily viewed by the server but hidden from the customers' view. I would deduct the tare weight of the plates and then place the casserole serving on the plates to weigh the casserole portions."

There is general agreement that use of scales will assure:

- Careful checking of incoming merchandise to eliminate losses
- Basis for accurate inventory
- Foundation for dependable cost-control system
- Accurate weighout of ingredients in food preparation
- Portion control in preparation of prepackaged foods at processing level

## PURCHASING POINTERS FOR SCALES

When purchasing scales, choice should be based on:

- Accuracy
- Speed and ease in using
- Easy reading
- Durability
- Compactness
- Attractive and easy-to-clean design and finish
- Decisions as to whether large number of small scales strategically placed will increase efficiency
- Springs of sturdy construction
- Space required by scale
- Dial position
- Metric equivalents for weights in pounds and ounces
- Metric-only markings
- Protection for pendulum mechanism when scale is not in use
- Need for portability
- Clear definition for figures and graduations.

Some special points to keep in mind when deciding on scales:

- Time required for adjustment of beams and counter-weights—One platform scale automatically extends the resolution and accuracy in its weight of 50-(22.7 kg), 100-(45.4 kg), 200-(90.7 kg) and 500-lb. (226.8 kg) capacity (with metric equivalents) as the load increases, without need for the worker to change load cells. Platform size of scale is 13½-in. (34.3 cm) × 19 in. (48.3 cm). The scale has solid-state components with simple controls and electronic digital read out. It can also be used to count pieces up to 99,999.
- Relation of scales to mixer equipment (i.e., kitchens using 60- or 80-qt. mixers should have a formula scale that will weigh quickly and accurately from 1/2 oz. to 50 lb.)
- Where floors are uneven, adjustments needed for stability: one dial floor scale has wheels that counteract unevenness.

## TYPES OF SCALES

Types of scales found in foodservice operations include:

Floor scales
Suspended platform scales
Overhead track scales
Built-ins
Portion scales
Counter or table scales
Dough or bakers' scales
Balancing scales
Portion and bench scales, standing and heavy duty.

Scales capacity ranges from 50 to 6000 lb. in one line, with other manufacturers listing 5 and 10-lb. portion scales as well as 1/10 (45.3 gm) plus or minus 1/1000 lb. (0.453 gm) scale markings for spices.

Portion scales are available in a choice of markings: 32 oz, with 1/4-oz. markings; 5 lb. with 1-oz. markings; 25 lb., 1-oz. markings; 500 grams, 2-gm markings; 1000 grams, 2-gm markings; combination of 34 oz. and 1000 grams; combination of 5 lb. and 2200 grams; combination of 11 lb. and 5 kg; combination of 25 lb. and 11 kg.

## SCALE SIZES

Space requirements and capacities of several scales (below) will help in estimating areas needed for scales.

## ACCURATE SCALE READING

Scale design is now emphasizing easier operation. Some of the developments that assure quick and accurate scale reading:

- Scale dials that may be installed in any one of eight positions.
- Balance indicator.

- Use of china marking pencil to mark dial for predetermined portion weight. Place plate on platform, rotate dial to zero, then uniform servings can be weighed to exact requirements.
- Kitchen scale on which ingredients can be weighed incrementally; that is, after the first ingredient has been placed in the bowl to be weighed, the scale can be reset to zero and the next ingredient weighed without removing the first. In one model this is done by sliding a knob. The base of this unit has combined metric and pound/ounce weight markings and is scaled to 5 lb. in 1-oz. divisions. When weighing bulky items, the flat top can be removed.
- Adjustable dial, which can be used for excluding weight of container and reading net weight of contents only
- Mechanism that eliminates jiggle and provides instant reading

**PORTION SCALE: Capacity 32 oz. (907 gm) × 1/4 oz. (7 gm); diam. 6½ in. × 9¼ in. (16.5 cm × 23.5 cm) high; platform 5½ sq. in. (35.5 cm)**

**BENCH-TYPE COUNTER SCALE:**

| Capacity | | Platform Dimensions | |
|---|---|---|---|
| *lb. and oz.* | *kg and gm* | *In.* | *cm* |
| 30 × 1 | 13.6 × 28 | 10½ × 13½ | 26.7 × 34.3 |
| 50 × 2 | 22.7 × 57 | 10½ × 13½ | 26.7 × 34.3 |
| 100 × 8 | 45.4 × 227 | 10½ × 13½ | 26.7 × 34.3 |

**Platform Scale—36 in. (91.4 cm) High:**

| Capacity | | Platform Dimensions | |
|---|---|---|---|
| *lb. and oz.* | *kg and gm* | *In.* | *cm* |
| 60 × 2 | 27.2 × 57 | 10½ × 14½ | 26.7 × 36.8 |
| 100 × 1 lb. | 45.4 × 453 | 10½ × 14½ | 26.7 × 36.8 |
| 100 × 2 | 45.4 × 57 | 10½ × 14½ | 26.7 × 36.8 |
| 200 × 4 | 90.7 × 113 | 10½ × 14½ | 26.7 × 36.8 |
| 300 × 1 lb. | 13.6 × 453 | 10½ × 14½ | 26.7 × 36.8 |
| 50 × 1 | 22.7 × 28 | 13 × 19 | 33 × 48.3 |
| 100 × 2 | 45.4 × 57 | 13 × 19 | 33 × 48.3 |
| 200 × 4 | 90.7 × 113 | 13 × 19 | 33 × 48.3 |
| 300 × 1 lb. | 13.6 × 453 | 13 × 19 | 33 × 48.3 |

**Bakers' Dough Scales:**

| Capacity | | Beam | | Size | |
|---|---|---|---|---|---|
| *lb.* | *kg* | *lb. and oz.* | *gm* | *In.* | *cm* |
| 8 lb. | 3.6 kg | 1 lb. × 1/4 oz. | 453 × 7 | 10 × 19 | 25.4 × 48.3 |
| 8 lb. | 3.6 kg | 1 × 1/4 | 453 × 7 | 12 × 22 | 30.5 × 55.9 |
| 16 lb. | 7.3 kg | 2 × 1/4 | 907 × 7 | 12 × 22 | 30.5 × 55.9 |

• Reading chart magnified and optically projected on mirror set behind protective glass shield. Figures and graduations appear bright and bold even in brightly-lighted room.

Less expensive scales for portion control have shock resistant styrene cases that are easy to clean and rustproof.

## WEIGHING PREPORTIONED ITEMS

Selective preset scales make it possible to check a number of preportioned items in succession that are all supposed to weigh the same amount. A pointer can be positioned at desired weight and worker has only to see that it is at desired point, or note—if it is over or under—by how much.

Also useful for portion control where close tolerances are required are scales with easy-to-read 1/8- and 1/4-oz. markings. Called miniatures by one manufacturer, scales can be purchased with a variety of accessories: a potato rack to hold French fries; oversize platforms [4½ × 6 in. (11.4 × 15.2 cm)] for sliced meats and cheeses.

## KEEPING SCALES CLEAN

Accurate scale operation requires a continuing maintenance program. The Scale Manufacturers Association, Inc., makes these recommendations:

Obsolete scales should be discarded; modern, up-to-date scales repaired when necessary and maintained on a regular basis. A scale is really a rather unique business machine. Unlike most other machines, the scale will continue to function even if it is worn out or inaccurate, but it will not be performing correctly.

Keep scales clean and dry. Dust, dirt, food scraps, and other foreign matter can clog up the sensitive inner parts of a scale and build up friction, which causes resistance to movement and impairs accuracy. Good scale maintenance and care keeps scales accurate.

One operator reported he did not find it as easy to keep scales clean as he felt it should be. He wanted a unit in which the mechanism was better sealed to prevent moisture used in the cleaning process from getting in and damaging the scale's mechanism.

His problems have been solved with new models whose clear plastic lenses keep out dirt and moisture and protect dials. They are guaranteed rustproof.

At Northern Illinois University the system that has been developed for maintenance and repair has proved especially successful:

"We have contracts with two scale manufacturers for all of their equipment. These contracts are for service, inspection and repairs, three times each year.

"The first inspection is made in the fall prior to school opening; the second during the Christmas recess, and the third in the spring.

"We use blue trouble report tags, located adjacent to the piece of equipment. Employees and managers note any noise, malfunction, or troubles on these tags. This helps the servicemen, especially if they check the equipment when the employees are not in the kitchen. They will then check all the items that are mentioned on the trouble notice cards attached to the equipment."

## SCALE RECORDERS

Increasingly, the need for permanent records is being recognized; therefore, the printing scale, especially for receiving purposes, becomes more and more of a necessity. To meet this demand there are scale-recording devices, such as the following:

Tape-driven dial with optional printer that records each weighing on tape, ticket, or form

Simple touch of print bar prints exact load weight on tape, ticket, or form in less than a second

One scale recorder indicates information in any one of these ways—single ticket; multi-copy tickets; single tape recordings; double tape recordings (one rolls up inside machine); ticket and tape recording; any size ticket; adaptable with read out for automatic office recording machines; adaptable for automatic labeling system. The recorder operates with a standard typewriter ribbon.

## SYSTEMS THAT INSURE USE OF SCALES

As with all foodservice equipment, the big challenge is to get employees to use scales as the operation's system requires. Here are two approaches that have successfully kept employees scale conscious:

One way to develop systematic, correct use of scales is to require that a supervisor check the employees' regular use of scales. In one operation, the chief storeroom clerk was given responsibility for insuring that all goods received, especially meat, were billed by weight and checked on sealed scales. In other places individual food unit supervisors are responsible for seeing that their employees use portion scales to check the entrees each day. This procedure helps show what the standard portion looks like.

"As in every other foodservice routine, getting proper use of scales, or any other procedure or equipment, is dependent on constant reminder and constant supervision.

"Our routines are set forth for the individual supervisors, as well as the employees in a check list of activities which must be accomplished in each of the operating units. Incorporating such items as checking out the standard portion of the entrees for that particular day on the routine check list helps remind everyone that the use of the portion scale is a requirement."

New employees at Northern Illinois University get in the habit of using scales because they see the older employees using the scales and want to use them also. Usually, new employees are taught the proper use of scales in the second lesson of their employee-training program. NIU recipes are all in weights (except liquids), which is further incentive for using scales.

## CASE STUDIES OF SCALES IN FOODSERVICE

In one nationwide survey among scale users, these unique approaches were discovered:

IN THE RECEIVING AREA—"Floor scales have been installed in receiving areas so that we can load up trucks, mobile refrigerator shelves, or pallets with merchandise and place them on the floor scale. The trucks have the weight painted on them, the total weight will show on the scale and from this total weight the truck weight will be deducted. In that way we know the exact weight of the incoming merchandise."

ONE-MOTION STORAGE—"In our approach to one-motion storage, meat, for example, is unloaded on to portable shelving. The portable shelving is then pushed onto the floor scale, weighed, and moved on to freezer storage.

"If the item is hamburger, the required quantity can be defrosted and moved on the same shelving to the grill area. This reduces handling and gives control by weight."

INGREDIENT WEIGHING ROOM—"In our last installation we incorporated within the facility an ingredient weighing room. We believe that it is much easier to train one employee to weigh items accurately than it is to train eight people.

"The system operates like this: The food production manager makes out a requisition slip the day before production and the ingredients are moved, late in the afternoon, to the weighing room. The ingredients are then weighed in batch amounts for cooking.

"Each item of the recipe is weighed and placed on a cart designated for the proper area. If 120 gal. (454.2 l) of chili are to be made, the recipe is extended, weighed, and placed in the proper container or bag on the cart for two 60-gal. (227.1 l) size batches, ready to be delivered to the steam kettle area.

"In our four largest units we have purchased a scale mounted on rubber-tired, adjustable wheel stands, equipped with a quick tare device that allows the deduction of the weight of the pan before weighing the food item. The scale is in graduations of 1/10 of 1 lb.

"Our thought here is that recipes may be set up in the future in tenths of a pound as it is easier for extension. In addition, 1/10 of a pound increments are necessary and considered desirable for electronic data processing, a future project. The scale also has a magnifying system that is easily read by employees to get exact weights."

FOR SPECIAL WEIGHING—"We use a scale designed to weigh 1/10, plus or minus 1/100 lb., to weigh accurately small amounts of spices and salts.

"Portion scales in kitchen can be preset for desired ounces for use in periodic checking of food items that have been received as preportioned items."

**SAMPLE SCALE PROFILE**
(Based on reported use of scales at Residence Hall Food Service, Northern Illinois University, DeKalb, IL)

| Residence Hall | Type | Location | Use |
|---|---|---|---|
| Gilbert Hall–488 men Opened—1951 | 1 Utility Scale - weight to 24 lb. | Located next to cook's table in kitchen—on stainless steel table next to slicer | Weighing of some small amounts of ingredients. |
| | 1 Portion Scale - 5 lb. + or – 1/4 oz. | | Weighing meat and cheese portions |
| | 1 Platform Scale | Back entrance | Weighing items when receiving, e.g., meat |
| Williston Hall– 234 women Opened—1917 | 1 Fan Scale-40 lb. | Kitchen pantry | Weighing small amounts of ingredients, e.g., spices |
| | 1 Portion Scale - 5 lb. + or – 1/4 oz. | Main kitchen—next to slicer | Used in weighing portions of meat and cheese |
| Adams Hall– 188 women Opened—1946 | 1 Platform Scale | Downstairs—basement area | Weighing items when received, e.g., meat |
| | 1 Portion - 5 lb. + or – 1/4 oz. | Kitchen area | Weighing for correct portions, e.g., meat |
| Neptune Central– 1550 women Opened—1960 | 1 Portion Scale - 10 lb. + or – 1/4 oz. | Kitchen area | Weighing serving portions, e.g., meat, cheese |
| | 1 Scale with indicator and quick tare device 1/10 of lb., 120 lb. capacity | Cook's area | Weighing pans, e.g., meat |
| | 1 Baker's Scale | Storeroom | Weighing small items |
| | 1 Floor Scale | Receiving area | Weighing items when received, e.g., meat |
| | 1 Counter Scale | Salad department | Weighing salad ingredients |
| Snack Bar Opened—1960 | 1 Postage-type Scale | Snack bar | Weighing soft-serve orders, e.g., malts |
| Lincoln Hall– 1,000 co-eds Opened—1962 | 2 Scales—5 lb. + or – 1/4 oz. | Cook's area | Weighing meat for serving, and checking serving on serving line |
| | 1 Scale with indicator, quick tare device 1/10 of lb., 120 lb. capacity | Kitchen—mobile | Weighing ingredients |
| | 1 Floor Scale | Receiving area | Weighing incoming orders |
| | 1 Scale—1/10 + or – 1/100 of lb. | Cook's area | Weighing spices and small amounts of ingredients |

**SAMPLE SCALE PROFILE (cont.)**

| Residence Hall | Type | Location | Use |
|---|---|---|---|
| | 1 300-lb. capacity Scale | Storeroom—downstairs | Weighing meat being taken out of freezer and other ingredients |
| Douglas Hall–1,000 Co-eds Opened—1963 | 1 1000-lb. Floor Scale | Receiving area | Weighing items when received, e.g., meat |
| | 1 Scale with indicator, 1/10 of lb., 120-lb. capacity | Cook's area (mobile) | Weighing ingredients |
| | 2-Portion Mod. Scales —10 lb. + or – 1/4 oz. | Cook's department | Weighing individual portions |
| | 1 Balancing Scale—capacity: 300 lb. | Storeroom | Weighing various items |
| | 1 Scale—10 lb. capacity, + or – 1/4 oz. | Test Kitchen—downstairs | Weighing ingredients for test purposes |
| Grant Towers–designed for 2,000 1st phase: 1965–1,000 2nd phase: 1966–1,000 | 1 Portion Scale—1/10 + or – 1/100 of lb. | Ingredient room | Weighing up spices, small amounts. |
| | 1 Scale: 4-lb capacity | Ingredient room | Weighing ingredients |
| | 2 Scales with indicator and quick tare device 1/10 of lb. | Ingredient room | Weighing up to 200 lb. of ingredients |
| | 2 Portion Scales—5 lb. + or – 1/4 oz. | Kitchen | Used for weighing portions, e.g., meat |
| | 1 Table Scale | Kitchen (mobile) | Used for portion weights |
| | 1 Platform Scale | Receiving area | Weighing items when receiving |

## BRAIN TEASER—SCALES

1. What are receiving scales used for? _____

2. What kind of scale is used to weigh foods for hospital diets? (Circle right answer.) Receiving Scale Preparation Scale  Portion Control Scale

3. List three types of scales found in foodservice operations.
   (1) _____ (2) _____ (3) _____

4. How are scales used to weigh a number of items, one after the other, that should all weigh the same amount?_____

5. If pointer on scale moves upward above preset weight, items will weigh: (too much) (too little). (Circle right answer.)

6. Why are printing scales in greater demand now? _____

7. Using Sample Scale Profile, tell one location where platform scale is used _____
   portion scale _____

   *(For correct answers, see page 251.)*

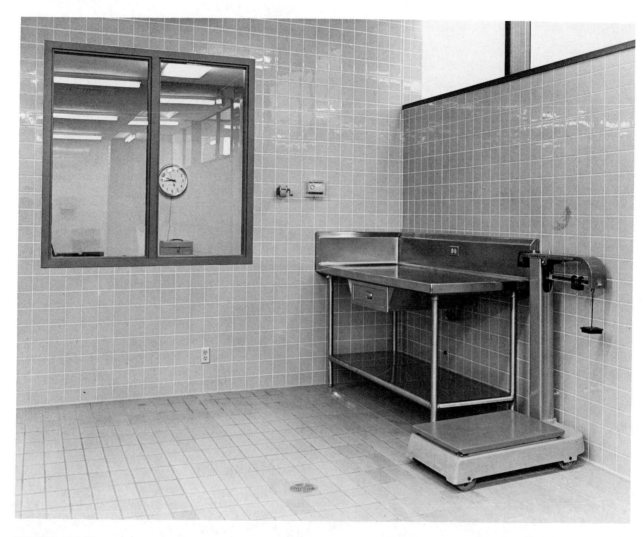

**FIGURE 10.2**
Both weighing in and counting of delivered items were planned for in the receiving area of Sam Houston Junior High School, Irving, Tex. Platform scale on casters can be easily maneuvered for weighing of products. Table provides space for counting and inspecting small items. The manager's office on the other side of the window assures easy supervision of receiving.

**FIGURE 11.1**
Reach-in refrigerator for storage of items needed by waitresses is positioned at end of fully equipped waitress station. Eight of these stations at Indian Lakes Country Club, Bloomingdale, Ill. provide ice, water, beverages, and condiments. They also contain plug-in for portable banquet carts. All food items for banquets are put in hot, cold, or freezer temperature carts.

# Chapter Eleven

# Refrigeration

## CONTROLLING COST OF ENERGY FOR REFRIGERATION

Today's approach to refrigeration centers on energy savings. The two most important factors in controlling refrigeration energy costs are the selection of a unit with the proper amount and type of insulation, and the proper use of the unit.

The better the insulation in refrigerated equipment, the smaller the refrigeration system can be. Relatively speaking, smaller refrigeration systems consume less electricity and, therefore, cost less to operate.

The value of ample insulation was well-demonstrated during the 1977 blackout in New York City. A survey of one manufacturer's customers in the city found that not one lost any product because of the blackout, even though some of these units were without electricity for as long as 44 hours.

When a new piece of refrigerating equipment is required, energy consultant Gerald B. Speen points out that only the extra cost paid for high performance should be considered. This extra or incremental cost, not the total cost of the equipment, is the amount that must be recovered through energy savings. Therefore, the higher-efficiency units usually can be justified. If the savings are great enough, the operator's additional investment will be repaid over and over as the years go by.

Much power is used by refrigeration systems to provide cold and freezing temperatures to preserve and store food. One effective way to reduce energy use substantially and to extend the lifetime of the unit is through the use of packaged refrigeration systems. The condensing units are mounted in a temperature-controlled enclosure that creates a favorable operating environment for the units.

The temperature range commonly supplied by refrigeration units is 38° to 40°F. (3° to 4°C). Both reach-ins and walk-ins usually are designed to *hold* temperatures of prepared food rather than to bring them down. If, for example, warm or hot food is being brought into a walk-in, the refrigerator will need a larger compressor and coils to supply the extra energy required to lower the temperature of this food.

Therefore, proper use of refrigeration equipment requires that food be quickly and safely cooled somewhat before being placed in the refrigerator. Food should NOT be allowed to cool to room temperature, however, as bacteria grow below 145°F. (63°C) making food unsafe to serve.

Proper use, the second important factor in making the best use of refrigeration energy, means planning ahead:

• Schedule time for adequate cool down of items to be refrigerated.
• Work out loading and unloading requirements to minimize opening of refrigerator doors.
• Set up adequate program of preventive maintenance.

The expansion of refrigerated storage requirements in today's foodservice operation is a companion development to the increasing use of menu items prepared off premise during slack periods or well ahead of serving time.

## CHOOSING REFRIGERATION

Refrigerated storage is now available in these types of equipment:

1. Walk-in (can be used as reach-ins, roll-ins, display units)
   Reach-in
   Roll-in (while all walk-ins may accommodate or be modified for carts, some walk-ins are sized especially for them)
   Compartmentalized (all walk-ins can be compartmentalized)
2. Pass-thru
   Counter Refrigeration
   Display Refrigeration
   Mobile or Portable Refrigeration
   Refrigerated Dispensers.

Unless it is a portable model, a refrigerator or storage freezer may be either self-contained or have remote refrigeration units. In self-contained refrigerators or storage freezers, compressor and condensors are mounted as part of the cabinet. In remote units, the refrigeration units are located away from the cabinet or reach-ins.

As the cost of space rises, the search for space "extenders" intensifies. One answer is the potential space saving of walk-in, refrigerated storage space located away from the kitchen, even, in some cases, outside the building but accessible from inside.

But labor costs may dictate another location. To keep refrigerated foods handy to the cook, the salad person, or waiter, refrigeration may be built into work areas or may be part of mobile units that can be positioned in whatever spot is most convenient to work areas.

Wherever the refrigerating mechanism is installed, its ultimate aim continues to be to extend the safe holding periods for fresh and prepared foods.

Here are the desirable holding temperatures for the three primary food categories.

| | |
|---|---|
| Meats and Poultry | 33 to 38°F. (0.6 to 3°C) |
| Dairy Products | 38 to 46°F. (3 to 8°C) |
| Vegetables and Fruits | 44 to 50°F. (7 to 10°C) |

## HOW MUCH SPACE FOR REFRIGERATION?

How much space to set aside for each type of food and where to locate it look like tough questions. The experts have created formulas to figure satisfactory answers. The answers will, of course, differ as widely as the methods used by the experts in arriving at them.

Reach-in refrigeration cabinets are generally sized by cubic capacity. Walk-ins are described in terms of width by length by height. Cubic foot capacity of refrigeration cabinets cannot be translated directly into storage cubes. Allowances must be made for the evaporator coil(s) and fan(s), racks or shelving, and space in which to reach or walk.

To estimate refrigerated food-storage requirements, first determine:

1. What percentage of a typical meal will consist of fresh food?
2. How many days' supplies must be maintained for each food type in refrigerated storage?

The following refrigerated space allocations are recommended for use in preliminary planning:

20 to 25 percent for meat, with portion-ready cuts requiring one-half to one-third less space;

30 to 35 percent for fruits and vegetables;

20 to 25 percent for dairy products (including space set aside in serving areas);

5 to 10 per cent for salads, sandwich material, bakery products, and leftovers.

## CALCULATING REFRIGERATION NEEDS

A "five factor" formula for estimating refrigeration needs is based on:

1. Volume of storage required per typical meal served when use of fresh items is at its peak. The volume per meal is indicated in these figures:

| | |
|---|---|
| Meat and Poultry | .010–.030 cu. ft./meal (0.28–0.85 dm³/meal,) |
| Dairy | .007–.015 cu. ft./meal (0.2–0.42 dm³/meal,) |
| Vegetables and Fruits | .020–.040 cu. ft./meal (0.57–1.13 dm³/meal,) |

The lower figures are more applicable to schools; the average figure to hospitals and employee-feeding installations, and the higher figure to deluxe, waiter-service dining rooms featuring extensive menus using a near maximum of fresh, refrigerated foods.

2. The maximum number of meals to be served between deliveries.

3. Usable refrigerator storage height.

4. Estimate of actual usable space by subtracting unusable space between shelves, aisle space, and space allotted between product and outside walls for air circulation.

5. Estimate of lost space for exterior walls and walls between compartments.

In "A Short Course in Kitchen Design,"* Joseph Laschober, FFCS (Food Facilities Consultants' Society), suggested calculating space needs this way:

*Not in print.

Assuming that the spacing between shelves is 18 in. (45.7 cm) each sq. ft. (929 cm²) of shelving will hold 1½ cu. ft. (42.5 dm³) of food. This means that each sq. ft. of shelf will contain about 65 lb. of food. The total weight of food to be stored divided by 65 will equal the entire amount of shelf space (in sq. ft.) (in cm²) needed for the installation.

## LB (kg) OF FOOD PER FT. OF SHELVING

Charted here is data on the pounds of food that can be stored per lineal foot (30.5 cm) of shelf for different width shelves and also for complete 5-tier shelf units.

Note how important it is to use every available inch of shelf width and length. Every linear inch (2.5 cm) of space wasted means loss of storage for several pounds (kg) of food.

Suggested areas required for refrigerator storage in square feet (dm²) for three types of foodservice have been figured on a meals per day basis:

Employee Feeding Operations—for 400 meals, 75 to 120 sq. ft. (697 to 1115 dm²); 800 meals, 110 to 134 sq. ft. (1022 to 1245 dm²); for 1200 meals, 140–175 sq. ft. (1301 to 1626 dm²); for 1600 meals, 170 to 210 sq. ft. (1579 to 1951 dm²).

School Feeding Operations—for 200 meals, 25 to 35 sq. ft. (232 to 325 dm²); 400 meals, 35 to 50 sq. ft. (325–465 dm²); 500 meals, 40 to 55 sq. ft (372 to 511 dm²); 800 meals, 55 to 70 sq. ft. (511 to 650 dm²); 1000 meals, 70 to 90 sq. ft. (650 to 836 dm²).

Centralized Hospital Dietary Service—based on the number of beds; area required for refrigerated storage for 50 beds, 40 to 50 sq. ft. (372–465 dm²); 100 beds, 80 to 100 sq. ft. (743 to 929 dm²); 160 to 200 beds, 200 sq. ft. (1858 dm²); for 400 beds, 320 to 400 sq. ft. (2973 to 3716 dm²).

### Refrigeration for Plated Portions

Factors that will help determine the amount of refrigerated storage needed for portions to be stored on plates in reach-ins include:

## WIDTH OF SHELVES

| | 12 in. 30.5 cm | 14 in. 35.6 cm | 18 in. 45.7 cm | 21 in. 53.3 cm | 24 in. 61 cm | 27 in. 68.6 cm |
|---|---|---|---|---|---|---|
| *Lb. (kg) Per Lineal Foot of Shelving* — Per each shelf (12-in. (30.5 cm) spacing) | 45 lb. 20.4 kg | 52 lb. 23.6 kg | 67 lb. 30.4 kg | 79 lb. 35.8 kg | 90 lb. 40.8 kg | 102 lb. 46.3 kg |
| Per shelf unit 5 tiers high | 225 lb. 102 kg | 262 lb. 118.8 kg | 335 lb. 152 kg | 395 lb. 179.2 kg | 450 lb. 204 kg | 510 lb. 231.3 kg |

- Plate size used for holding portions
- Capacity for such plates on 18 × 26-in. (46 × 66-cm) pan or tray
- Height needed for plate plus food
- Number of trays that can be fitted into door opening
- Required number of portions to be stored.

(Data to help figure various storage needs is charted on following pages.)

## MOVING FOODS FROM REFRIGERATION

The location of refrigeration should be based on well-planned movement of items to preparation and service areas. Determine the point at which the ratio of employee trips to savings in space cost is in balance. It may be better to roll deliveries a bit further than to have preparation workers making many lengthy trips to get foods from locations nearer to receiving than preparation areas. Consider using less costly labor for transporting refrigerated items.

Mobile carts properly loaded will cut down trips, too. Where component parts of refrigerators are movable, the cost of transporting foods from preparation to service areas may be reduced appreciably. Here are some food transport planning ideas involving goods held in refrigerated storage:

At Hillcrest Jr. High School in Shawnee Mission, Kansas, salad bowls and plates are placed on 18 × 26-in. (46 × 66-cm) colored fibre glass bun pans—12 to 24 on each pan—and then are filled with salad ingredients. Bun pans are then placed in portable carts and wheeled only 35 ft. (1067 cm) from central salad department into a pass-thru refrigerator between two double service cafeteria lines for storage until lunch time.

At Bowling Green, OH, State University refrigeration is located approximately 8 to 10 ft. (243.8 to 305 cm) from the cooking area and about 35 ft. (1067 cm) from the delivery door.

One hospital installation has deliveries made to a preliminary preparation area where one bank of refrigeration is installed. From there food travels to a second refrigerated storage area in an upstairs kitchen where the food is actually cooked and served.

At Cardinal Stritch College, Milwaukee, WI, a refrigerated cook's table is placed in the center of the very efficient hollow square cooking center. Rolling carts pick up raw foods for trips to and through machines and on to refrigerated pass-thrus in the kitchen.

## MENU DETERMINES REFRIGERATION

A large volume of fresh produce and frozen and fresh shellfish used at Castagnola's Lobster House determined the refrigeration selected for the salad pantry. A large dual-temp refrigerator with separate spaces for refrigerated and frozen food provides adequate back-up storage for bulk items. Two pull-out ice bins store fresh shellfish. A pass-thru refrigerator is used for waitress pick up. Large refrigerated bases in the work counter, with pans recessed in the top, serve for a la carte

**SPACE NEEDED FOR FOOD ITEMS STORED ON 18- × 26-IN. (46 × 66 CM) PANS**
**(Capacity per door opening is based on standard, half-height doors)**

| *Item* | *Size of Serving* | *Dish Used* | *Height of Food and Plates* In. | *Height of Food and Plates* cm | *Space Between Pans* In. | *Space Between Pans* cm | *No. of Portions Per Pan* | *No. of Pans For:* 50 Portions | *No. of Pans For:* 100 Portions | *Capacity per Door Opening — Food File* No. of Pans | *Capacity per Door Opening — Food File* No. of Portions | *Capacity per Door Opening — Mobile Food File* No. of Pans | *Capacity per Door Opening — Mobile Food File* No. of Portions |
|---|---|---|---|---|---|---|---|---|---|---|---|---|---|
| Milk | ½ Pint | Carton | 3½ | 8.9 | 4 | 10 | 40 | 1¼ | 2½ | 6 | 240 | 5 | 200 |
| Cole Slaw | No. 12 Dipper | Fruit Nappie | 2½ | 6.3 | 3 | 7.6 | 21 | 2½ | 5 | 8 | 168 | 7 | 147 |
| Chopped Vegetable Salad on Lettuce | No. 8 Dipper | 7⅜ in. Plate | 3 | 7.6 | 3 | 7.6 | 8 | 6¼ | 12½ | 8 | 64 | 7 | 56 |
| Chef's Salad | ¾ cup | Salad Bowl | 2 | 5 | 2 | 5 | 11 | 4½ | 9 | 12 | 132 | 11 | 121 |
| Gelatin Salad on Lettuce | 2½ × 2½ × 1½ in. | 6⅜ in. Plate | 2¼ | 5.7 | 3 | 7.6 | 11 | 4½ | 9 | 8 | 88 | 7 | 77 |
| Cottage Cheese | No. 12 Dipper | Fruit Nappie | 3½ | 8.9 | 4 | 10 | 21 | 2½ | 5 | 6 | 126 | 5 | 105 |
| Cup Custard | — | Cup Custard (Hall) | 2½ | 6.3 | 3 | 7.6 | 40 | 1¼ | 2½ | 6 | 240 | 5 | 200 |
| Pie | 1/6 | 6⅜ in. Plate | 1⅞ | 4.7 | 2 | 5 | 11 | 4½ | 9 | 12 | 132 | 11 | 121 |
| Cake | 3 × 3 × 1½ in. | 6⅜ in. Plate | 2½ | 6.3 | 3 | 7.6 | 11 | 4½ | 9 | 8 | 88 | 7 | 77 |
| Fruit Cup | No. 12 Dipper | Sherbet Glass (stem) | 3⅛ | 3.1 | 4 | 10 | 40 | 1¼ | 2½ | 6 | 240 | 5 | 200 |
| Cream | 1-oz. | Paper Cup | 1⅝ | 4.1 | 2 | 5 | 125 | ½ | 1 | 12 | 1620 | 11 | 1485 |
| Fruit Juice | 4-oz. | 5-oz. Glass | 3⅝ | 9.2 | 4 | 10 | 84 | ¾ | 1¼ | 6 | 504 | 5 | 420 |
| Cantaloupe Boats | 1/6 | 7⅜ in. Plate | 3 | 7.6 | 3 | 7.6 | 8 | 6¼ | 12½ | 8 | 64 | 7 | 56 |

salad preparation. Plate dispensers in refrigerated areas chill salad plates.

In Castagnola's Coffee shop, refrigerated drawers in the cooking assembly keep adequate food supplies close at hand. Adequate back-up refrigeration reduces traffic to the preparation areas.

## WHAT WALK-INS OFFER

A 17 × 31 × 7-ft, 6-in (518 × 945 × 238 cm) high, three-compartment sectional walk-in installed in the vegetable preparation area at the University of California, Berkeley, helps to organize food production.

With continuing energy-saving improvements in design and quality of insulation, walk-ins are assuming greater importance. Walk-ins are feasible, according to one authority, for any operation that serves 300 to 400 meals per day. Another, citing supply, transportation, and price uncertainties, says walk-in coolers and walk-in frozen food holding units are necessities for an operation serving 100 meals a day.

In today's operation, walk-in refrigerated storage:

• Permits use of a greater variety of foods
• Encourages quantity buying at lower discounts
• Eliminates frequent, costly deliveries.
• Offers lower operating costs
• Has lower purchase price
• Provides additional refrigeration capacity for same investment
• Permits quantity buying of raw foods when prices are low
• Provides more space for leftovers, thus cutting down on food loss.

In large foodservice operations, walk-ins are commonly specified for (1) fruits and vegetables, (2) meats, poultry, and fish, and (3) dairy products. There may also be a walk-in near the bake shop, a salad walk-in, and one for garbage. Where walk-in refrigeration follows this plan, each kind of refrigerated food can be kept under the best temperature and humidity conditions.

## Roll-In Units For Walk-Ins

Walk-in coolers can serve many functions. Naturally, they can also be used for roll-in units. They can be equipped with standard insulated reach-in doors and also with hinged or sliding glass doors so the same unit can be used for both storage and display.

Since a single unit requires only one refrigeration system, it is usually more economical to operate than several units with multiple refrigeration systems. Also a single refrigeration system results in lower maintenance costs. When comparing cost per cubic foot of storage area, walk-ins may be less expensive to purchase and operate than standard reach-ins.

Walk-ins, when used as reach-ins, are more efficient to stock than standard reach-ins. In walk-ins, the shelves are loaded from inside the unit from the rear of the shelves. Therefore, stock rotation is automatic, with the oldest product being most accessible from the glass doors. Also, unlike the procedure with some standard reach-ins, the doors do not have to be propped open while shelves are being restocked, and restocking does not interfere with other employees.

Today's walk-ins are usually assembled from metal-clad sections or modular panels that feature thin-wall construction available "off-the-shelf" to form walls, floors, and ceilings. Or they may be built locally. Many use urethane foamed-in-place insulation that has twice the insulating value of conventional materials.

## Outside Location for Walk-Ins

In some cases, walk-ins are installed outside the main building, abutting a wall of the food-preparation area. A door cut into the wall of the kitchen provides access from the inside. Deliveries can be made from outside, if a door to the outside is feasible. Although the walk-in is located entirely outside the building, its access from inside makes it convenient without using any interior space.

Outside space is more economical for both new and existing buildings. With a prefab unit, the cost of the space is predetermined. Acquiring the unit is just like buying a refrigerator from the appliance store—it is ready to plug in and operate immediately.

A leasing plan that permits adding prefab refrigerated space without capital investment can release funds for other needs.

Other advantages of outside walk-ins:

- In a leased facility, the landlord usually will not charge any extra rent for the area occupied by the outside walk-in.
- Compared with enlarging a building to accommodate a walk-in, the outside installation has lower construction costs, lower real estate taxes, and lower insurance premiums. Since the walk-in is a piece of equipment, not real property, insurance premiums on the unit remain the same whether it is located inside or out.
- Even though an outside walk-in is used as a building extension, it is considered tangible property. Therefore, it qualifies for fast depreciation and the investment tax credit just as though it were located inside.

## Enlarging Sectional Walk-Ins

A simple system is now available for enlarging prefabricated walk-ins. Simply remove the end or side of the walk-in, where the size increase is desired, by turning the locking arm back from its locked position. Add new sections. Replace original section. Enlarged walk-in is all ready for use. One caution: It may be necessary to enlarge the refrigeration system when the size of the walk-in is increased.

Prefabricated walk-ins can be enlarged to take care of increased requirements. They can also be relocated easily. The metal skins do not permit penetration of spilled foods or rodents or vermin. These models are available with factory assembled, self-contained refrigeration systems, complete and ready for immediate duty, or refrigeration components (condensing unit, blower coil, etc.) for remote application. Exteriors and interiors may be galvanized steel, textured aluminum, stainless steel, white vinyl, or white paint. Stainless steel, the most durable and most-easily cleaned, is also the most expensive. Less-costly finishes are porcelain, organisol vinyl applied to

steel, or aluminum alloys. Units may be insulated with foamed plastics. Some walk-in manufacturers offer 10-year guarantees.

The installation of prefabricated walk-ins has been planned for speedy completion. One 6 × 8 ft. (182.9 × 243.8 cm) model can be erected by two inexperienced men in three to four hours. The lightweight sections are easy to handle, with locking devices to allow for accurate and easy assembly and to insure tight seams where panels meet. Locking devices are easy to operate and assure tight joining of sections.

## Preventing Heat Transfer

The ability of the insulating material used in refrigeration to prevent heat transfer is of particular importance. One manufacturer recommends that refrigerated facilities be insulated with a material having an "R" value of at least 32. ("R" value measures the ability of insulation to resist the passage of heat from one side of the material to the other.) Manufacturers of refrigeration equipment will supply information about the heat resistance of the insulating material used in their units.

## Walk-In Checklist

Points to be checked when selecting walk-ins are summarized by Kotschevar and Terrell in *Food Service Planning*:

- Walls, ceilings and floors that are vapor-proof, easily cleanable and durable.
- Walk-in floor preferably on level plane with outside floor (insulation installed below floor level); otherwise, outside floor or inside floor laid with gradual incline to offset difference in levels.

Ramps, either inside or outside the walk-in, can also be used at less cost than inclined floor construction. Or the floor panels of the walk-in can be set in a depression so the prefab floor is level with the outside floor.

- Complete seal over insulation materials to keep moisture from penetrating.
- Sturdy, well-insulated doors with heavy-duty, corrosion-resistant, lock hardware. Many doors come with a choice of locking systems: key lock, padlock, or locking bar. Some latch handles provide for both a key lock and a padlock.
- Type of door best suited to use: glass sliding, glass reach-in, solid reach-in, or large door with level threshold for fork-lift trucks. Special swing doors are available to permit the uninterrupted movement of carts in and out of the walk-in. These doors can also be modified for use with hand trucks and lift trucks. On coolers, the doors can be installed in tandem with the standard insulated doors.
- Emergency opening devices on the inside.
- Shelving and other interior equipment adjustable, durable, sturdy, of noncorrosion materials. Cantilevered shelving is available.
- Outside thermometers.
- Sized to handle mobile equipment in use in the operation.
- Adequate storage space—1½ to 2 ft. (45.7 to 61 cm)—on either side of aisle.
- Length of compressor running time.
- Aisles 42-in. (106.7 cm) wide are preferable since they are wide enough to accommodate mobile equipment. If lift trucks are used, there should be work and turning space in storage aisles, and special flooring to withstand the traffic of heavy-wheeled equipment.
- Audio-visual alarm systems to alert personnel to changes in holding temperature, which might affect proper storage of product.

## Controlling Door Openings

Walk-in doors should not be opened unnecessarily. Propping them open while employees are putting food into the unit or removing food from it is not necessary. All walk-ins manufactured by reputable companies have inside safety releases for the doors so that it is impossible for an employee to be locked inside the unit. Even exterior locking bars are equipped with safety releases.

One successful solution to keep employees from leaving cooler doors open during peak periods is being used at the International House of Pancakes, Portland, ME. The operation has installed a transparent door that is made of 4-in. (10 cm) wide vinyl strips. Each of these strips has rounded edges; the strips are precision-designed to overlap. Gravity automatically pulls the strips together as soon as worker clears the cooler door. The transparent door also makes it easy to check cooler.

At Town and Country Manor, a retirement and medical center in Santa Ana, CA, walk-in doors have self-closing hinges that shut doors open less than 90 degrees—an important energy saver.

## Estimating Walk-in Needs

One approach to estimating the required walk-in refrigeration space recognizes that needs differ widely. A luxury restaurant in a central location in a major city that served a great variety of foods and required meat-aging facilities would need much more walk-in space than a busy highway diner with a relatively limited menu.

Or an industrial plant cafeteria serving a limited menu would not need as much capacity as a large hotel.

A simple "rule of thumb" is offered however: 1 cu. ft. (28.3 dm$^3$) of usable refrigerated walk-in space for each three meals served per day. Applying this yardstick, a restaurant serving 500 people three meals a day should have at least 500 cu. ft. (14159 dm$^3$) of walk-in storage space.

Another method for estimating walk-in needs is based on 25 lb. (11.3 kg) of food requiring 1 sq. ft. (928 cm$^2$) of walk-in space or 45 lb. (20.4 kg) requiring 1 cu. ft. (28.3 dm$^3$).

One addition to the streamlined kitchen at Beth Israel Medical Center, New York City, was a large walk-in refrigerator that holds 40 tray carts, each with a 20-tray capacity. This refrigerator allows the tray-assembly crew to complete its work at 2:30 P.M. and the entire dinner meal to be refrigerated until tray service begins at 5:30 P.M.

## Humidity Control

Carefully plan the temperature and humidity conditions in walk-ins, whether permanent or prefabricated. The relative humidity inside the walk-in depends primarily on the temperature difference between the evaporator coil and the air inside the unit and requires precise calculation of refrigeration load and proper specification of refrigeration system components. Manufacturers can make the necessary calculations to assure correct humidity control.

When deciding location of the walk-in, make sure that constant supervision can be maintained easily.

If outside walk-ins have an outside door in addition to the door that opens into the kitchen, deliveries do not disrupt the regular duties of kitchen personnel. In many areas, however, security risks prevent the feasibility of an outside door. Walk-ins located outdoors can be erected on concrete insulated slabs, with weatherproof roofs of prefabricated aluminum, plastic, or standard roofing materials.

## Preventive Maintenance for Walk-Ins

A preventive maintenance program that will minimize walk-in energy costs is outlined here:

1. Use the right operating temperatures. If the thermostat is set unnecessarily low, equipment works harder and electric bills increase.
2. Organize the products stored in the walk-in for fewest door openings. Warm air enters every time the door is opened. (Never prop the door open.)
3. Clear stored products away from the cooling coils.
4. Turn off inside lights when the walk-in is unoccupied. Lights consume electricity and generate heat.
5. Remove and discard any unnecessary packing materials—these slow the cooling of storage materials.
6. Leave space between stored products, allowing air to circulate freely. Slotted shelves promote air movement.
7. Keep compressors clean. They should be vacuumed regularly to prevent clogging, which increases electricity use.
8. Be sure the compressors are placed so that they get enough air. Keep them away from anything that restricts airflow.

9. Pay close attention to upkeep and repair of equipment; worn out or ill-kept walk-ins waste electricity and money.

Proper maintenance of all refrigeration equipment is very important to preserve foods, reduce service costs and cut energy costs. In addition to carrying out proper maintenance procedures, operators should also contract with a dealer or service agency for a start-up and a one-year service policy.

## WHAT REACH-IN REFRIGERATORS OFFER

Reach-in refrigerators can serve a single purpose or many, depending on the demands of the operation. A standard cabinet can provide pan holding slide inserts, food file or sheet pan or tray inserts, baker's food file inserts, wire shelves, pull-out shelves, and mobile food file inserts. All of these can be installed, rearranged, or removed overnight. In one model it is also possible to arrange to thaw frozen food overnight. Some dual models combine a refrigeration unit and a defrosting unit in one cabinet.

Reach-ins can also add a decorative note, since vinyl-clad or sprayed finishes and vinyl bonded to steel are now being used. Bonded vinyl, which can be cleaned with hot soapy water then rinsed with hot clear water, comes in six colors and can be used both inside and outside reach-ins.

Reach-in refrigerators in high-volume operations provide storage in preparation centers; in smaller operations they may provide all refrigerated storage. Reach-in cabinets may be self-contained or remote. If self-contained, the condensing unit is attached either at the bottom or on top of the cabinet. For remote cabinets the compressor unit is located away from the cabinet, usually in another room or, if in the same room, at some distance from the cabinet.

Selection factors to be given prime consideration:

- Proper sizing—estimate requirements carefully; be sure the cubic feet ($dm^3$) capacity will meet needs
- Use of sliding doors or windows to save space
- Even flow of refrigerated air at all levels

- Adequate insulation that is moisture resistant and nonsettling
- Sturdily constructed doors, solid or glass, full or half height, swinging or sliding, left or right hinged
- Welded outside and inside seams, or seamless construction
- Adequate locking devices
- Strong shelves
- Legs that are solid and adjustable
- Condenser located for easy cleaning.

One manufacturer of reach-ins has engineered an energy-saving condensate-evaporation system that requires no electric heaters.

## Setting Reach-in Requirements

Needs for reach-in storage will depend on the amount of food to be stored at one time and the length of time it must be stored. Generally 25 to 30 lb. (11.3 to 13.6 kg) of food can be stored per cu. ft. (28.3 dm$^3$).

If a reach-in refrigerator is opened frequently, consider the possibility of half-height doors instead of full-height doors. Every time a full-height door is opened, the heated kitchen air rushes in so the refrigeration system will run more. If the refrigerator is located near a cooking station, it is essential to use half-height doors. Also, 1 in. (2.5 cm) of asbestos should be added to the refrigerator end nearest the cooking equipment.

## Cleaning and Maintenance Routines for Reach-ins

To maintain self-contained reach-ins, one manufacturer suggests:

1. Know where fuses are located. If unit fails to operate, fuses are the first thing to check.
2. This refrigerator defrosts automatically; thus no defrosting need be scheduled.
3. Condenser should be cleaned periodically for proper air circulation and more efficient operation.
4. Allow as much air as practical around the unit. (Do not block air circulation by placing cartons or cases in front of condensing-unit grille.)

To keep reach-ins clean, follow these directions:

- Clean the inside of the cabinet once a week. Use a mild soap or detergent, rinse thoroughly, and wipe dry with a clean soft cloth
- Wipe up food or juice spills immediately after they occur
- Clean the door gaskets weekly with a damp cloth.
- Eliminate unpleasant odors by placing an open dish of unused coffee grounds or activated charcoal inside the cabinet.

As one refrigeration expert points out, it is much more practical to make the component part of the refrigerator movable than it is to put the refrigerator itself on wheels. Many food carts are now designed to fit into refrigeration areas. Often these refrigerated spaces are located near serving areas and as soon as preparation is completed carts of foods are rolled into these refrigerated areas.

Many kitchens are using mobile shelving to move both food and utensils between preparation centers and refrigerated areas. Supplies can be wheeled wherever needed and located in the most efficient position. Mobile shelving can be any number of shelves high, up to 56-in. (142.2 cm) long and 27-in. (68.6 cm) wide. Rubber bumpers and back or end ledges offer added protection.

By keeping equal size packages or cans together—easy to do with adjustable shelves—only the exact amount of height need be used, and overall vertical capacity is increased.

For complete flexibility, use carts from which individual shelves can be removed or added at any time. Shelving is a minor part of the entire cost of the refrigerator, yet every inch (2.5 cm) of space gained with shelving increases the capacity and value of the walk-in refrigeration units.

## Holding Cabinets

However, mobile cabinets equipped with their own refrigeration units are of special value in certain situations, especially banquet service, where they act as holding units for salads and desserts. Items can be placed in a mobile holding cabinet several hours before serving and can be wheeled to point-of-service.

Air temperatures in these cabinets are thermostatically controlled; unit is set to cut in at 42°F. (6°C) and out at 38°F. (3°C) to maintain proper temperatures.

A condensation-collection pan designed for easy removal and emptying is imperative. In selecting cabinets to travel, be sure that casters are heavy duty and easily maneuvered.

One model has adjustable angles for pans and can use pans of the following dimensions: 20 × 22-in.(51 × 56 cm) and 10 × 20-in. (25 × 51-cm) full and half-size roasting and baking pans; 18 × 26-in. (46 × 66-cm) bun pans; 14 × 18-in. (36 × 46 cm) service trays; 12 × 20-in. (30 × 51-cm) steam-table pans.

Wire rods hold plates fast and slide on stainless steel tracks; new solid shelving is designed for easy cleaning and peak transfer of cold.

Plate carriers also can be inserted that will hold eight plates 8- to 10½-in. (20.3 to 26.7 cm) in diameter per carrier.

## Saving Energy with Roll-ins

To save energy when using roll-in refrigerators always make sure the entire cart is rolled into or removed from the unit at once, rather than opening and closing the door several times to put in or take out a few food items. If frequent door opening is necessary, a reach-in should be used instead. Utilizing the proper equipment keeps the compressor from running more than is necessary.

Another energy-saving idea is planning the use of refrigeration so that refrigerator doors are opened and closed the least number of times possible. Keeping storage areas orderly will also reduce the need for holding doors open any longer than the minimum.

Forced-air refrigeration gently circulates air evenly, keeping cold temperatures constant throughout these cabinets. Pans and trays cannot block the flow of cold moist air that maintains desired temperatures and keeps food moist.

The cold-wall type of refrigeration system (no blower or evaporator plate) is used for holding and transporting uncovered, preplated foods that would be adversely affected by the forced air circulation of a conventional refrigerator. These mobile refrigerators can also be used to advantage in fast-food operations, to back up serving lines, and for buffets and smorgasbords.

## Load Potential

One model is available with either adjustable universal slides or adjustable angle slides. Each pair of angle slides will hold either one 18- × 26-in. (46 × 66-cm) pan or two 14 × 18-in. (36 × 46 cm) trays; each pair of universal slides holds one 18 × 26-in. (46 × 66-cm) pan, two 14 × 18-in. (36 × 46-cm) trays, or one 12 × 20-in. (30 × 51 cm) pan. A unit 70¾-in. (1797 mm) high × 36-in. (914 mm.) deep × 29¹³⁄₁₆-in. (757 mm) wide, with inside working height of 47¾ in. (1212 mm), has maximum angle slide capacity of 30 pairs or universal angle capacity of 15 pairs. It has a dial thermometer on door, sturdy push handles, wheels that roll easily, and bumper bolted to chassis. Temperature range from 32° to 42°F. (0° to 6°C) can be set with knob on adjustable thermostat.

Larger models of the same type have a maximum pan surface area of 21 in. × 28 in. (533 mm × 710 mm) with loading possibilities for universal slides in any combination of the following sizes:

1—18 in. × 26 in. Pan
(457 mm × 660 mm)
2—14 in. × 18 in. Trays
(355 mm × 457 mm)
2—12 in. × 20 in. Pans
(304 mm × 508 mm)
1—20 in. × 20 in. Glass Rack
(508 mm × 508 mm)
1—21 in. × 25½ in. Maxi-Pan
(533 mm × 647 mm)
1—520 mm × 650 mm
Gastro-Norm Pan
(European)
2—520 mm × 325 mm
Gastro-Norm Pans
(European)

In the same model, each pair of angle slides holds any combination of the following:

1—520 mm × 650 mm
Gastro-Norm Pan
(European)

2—520 mm × 325 mm
Gastro-Norm Pans
1—21 in. × 25½ in.
Maxi-Pan (533 mm × 647 mm)

Exteriors of mobile refrigerated cabinets are styled to be decorative enough for public appearances. Also, interiors have coved corners and removable tray slides to make cleaning easy and to insure maximum sanitation. Control lights on some models simplify checking of contents.

## Doors

Refrigerator doors must open easily. One door developed to substitute easy operation for the "hard pull" and the "big push" has been reduced to 46 lb. (20.9 kg) with a 22-oz. (623.7 gm) finger-tip-touch door opener.

The door also closes easily, as it is equipped with cam action, self-closing hinges. Self-closing doors reduce operating costs since they minimize lost energy. Self-closing hinges have been improved by adding springs that increase the force used to close the doors and improve the seal between the door and door handle.

Among recommended door specifications are strong catches; door gaskets that provide reasonable wear; replaceable locking devices; and adjustable strikes.

## NSF SETS STANDARDS

National Sanitation Foundation standards for refrigerator safeguards include:

1. Cabinets or materials easy to clean and keep clean

**MEASUREMENTS OF REPRESENTATIVE REFRIGERATOR ITEMS**
**(For use in determining interspace, width and linear feet of shelving)**

| Product | Package | Approx. | Capacity | Height In. | cm | Width or Diam. In. | cm | Length In. | cm |
|---|---|---|---|---|---|---|---|---|---|
| Butter | box | 64 lb. | 29 kg | 12 | 30.5 | 12 | 30.5 | 14 | 35.6 |
| Cheese | wheel | 20–23 lb. | 9–10.4 kg | 7½ | 19 | 13½ | 34.3 | | |
| Eggs | case | 45 lb. | 20.4 kg | 13 | 33 | 12 | 30.5 | 26 | 66 |
| Milk | can | 10 gal. | 37.7 l | 25 | 63.5 | 13½ | 34.3 | | |
| | case | 24½ pt. | 11.6 l | 10½ | 26.7 | 13 | 33 | 13 | 33 |
| | case | 24½ pt. | 11.6 l | 7 | 17.8 | 13 | 33 | 19 | 48.3 |
| Margarine | box | 60 lb. | 27.2 kg | 10 | 25.4 | 14 | 35.6 | 17½ | 44.5 |
| Meat, portioned | tray | 40 lb. | 18.1 kg | 3 | 7.6 | 18 | 45.7 | 26 | 66 |
| cuts | box | 40 lb. | 18.1 kg | 6 | 15.2 | 18 | 45.7 | 28 | 71.1 |
| cuts | box | 50 lb. | 22.7 kg | 10 | 25.4 | 10 | 25.4 | 28 | 71.1 |
| Apples | box | 35–40 | 15.9–18.1 | 10½ | 26.7 | 11½ | 29.2 | 18 | 45.7 |
| | carton | 40–45 lb. | 18.1–20.4 kg | 12 | 30.5 | 12½ | 31.8 | 20 | 50.8 |
| Berries | crate | 36 lb. | 16.3 kg | 11 | 27.9 | 11 | 27.9 | 22 | 55.9 |
| Cherries, Grapes | lug | 25–30 lb. | 11.3–13.6 kg | 6 | 15.2 | 13½ | 34.3 | 16 | 40.6 |
| Citrus | crate | 65–80 lb. | 29.5–36.3 kg | 12 | 30.5 | 12 | 30.5 | 26 | 66 |
| | carton | 40–65 lb. | 18.1–29.5 kg | 11 | 27.9 | 11½ | 29.2 | 17 | 43.2 |
| Beets, Cabbage | crate | 50–80 lb. | 22.7–36.3 kg | 13 | 33 | 18 | 45.7 | 22 | 55.9 |
| Cauliflower | crate | 40 lb. | 18.1 kg | 9 | 22.9 | 18 | 45.7 | 22 | 55.9 |
| Celery | crate | 55 lb. | 24.9 kg | 11 | 27.9 | 21 | 53.3 | 24 | 61 |
| Lettuce | crate | 40–50 lb. | 18.1–22.7 kg | 14 | 35.6 | 19 | 48.3 | 20 | 50.8 |
| | carton | 40 lb. | 18.1 kg | 10 | 25.4 | 14 | 35.6 | 22 | 55.9 |
| Tomatoes | box | 30 lb. | 13.6 kg | 7 | 17.8 | 13½ | 34.3 | 16 | 40.6 |

2. No floor drains inside cabinets
3. Interior design with all protrusions, e.g., shelf standards or air ducts, easy to remove for cleaning
4. Interior liner completely sealed to prevent seepage

Regularly-scheduled cleaning is the essential step in preventive maintenance. Three points vital to any cleaning program:

1. Fins on evaporator and condensor kept free of all ice and/or dirt
2. Interiors washed out weekly, with all shelves and trays removed for thorough cleaning
3. Exteriors kept spotless at all times.

## REFRIGERATION CASE STUDY

This analysis of the refrigeration in a shopping center restaurant emphasizes the varied applications of refrigeration possible in a food production system:

- Decorative emphasis required color matching refrigerator exteriors to the beige ceramic tile specified for the kitchen. This color coordination was carried through to all the kitchen equipment.

    To keep the colorful finish in good repair, the manufacturer furnished a number of pressure cans of touch-up, air-dry enamel.

    New USDA-approved paints are available to change walk-in colors to match kitchen decor. With one paint system, metal may be prepared and two coats of paint applied in one day. The relatively inexpensive paint is easy to apply.
- Roll-in units are used for all bulk storage. They were designed to take care of the specific needs of the operation. Some slides were removed from the bottom sections of the roll-ins to make room for necessary storage of bulk milk and other sizable items.
- These roll-in units do not have floors since the operator determined that cleaning the floors of the refrigerated space was easier, therefore less costly, than cleaning cart floors.

- Vinyl labels designate the type of food in each refrigerator.
- All stationary refrigerators are set on legs high enough to permit easy sweeping and mopping.
- A pass-thru with glass doors on both sides takes desserts prepared in the kitchen on one side to hold for service pickup by waitresses from the other side.
- The unique method of checking refrigerator temperatures in this kitchen has proved a real cost saver. The night watchman checks the temperature from a dial thermometer installed by the manufacturer. On a special card he records the date and time of each temperature check.

    The dial thermometers have a danger zone and the watchmen are told the number of degrees variation that can be tolerated. Beyond that point, an engineer must be notified immediately. With this system, the percentage of breakdowns and food loss has been less than at two other installations where this organization has automatic alarm systems.
- All refrigeration units, including roll-ins, have magnetic gaskets around doors, and door handles with built-in tumbler locks; all doors are locked at night.
- No interior lights are permitted in refrigerators.
- Swinging doors are used for walk-ins. Where it is desirable to check the contents from the outside, these doors are plexiglas. A training program for those who clean these doors has eliminated potential problems
- Servicing refrigeration equipment in this installation is easier because a number of load centers of electric sub panels are located around the kitchens. Therefore, it is never more than a dozen steps to the sub panel to turn the electricity on or off.
- Drains from the refrigerator coils and from the water-cooled condensing unit on top of the refrigerators empty into special drains designed to prevent any condensate from the coil or water from the compressor from spilling onto the floor. These special drains can also be used as floor drains. To eliminate need for drains, many reach-ins now evaporate their own condensate with compressor heat, usually electric.

- Cast (or extruded) aluminum bumpers have been installed on the refrigerators located on the aisles so carts being moved back and forth do not bump into the refrigerators and dent or scratch them.

These bumpers were fastened to the steel frames inside the refrigerators. To simplify placement of the bumpers, the manufacturer informed the operator where the frames were located. (Do not use steel bolts for this purpose, as the steel will conduct heat in from outside the walk-in to the inside and place an additional load on the refrigeration system. Use plastic bolts instead.)

This carefully planned cart-refrigerator set up puts refrigerated food needed for preparation—whether for salads, desserts, sandwiches or entrees—within arm's reach of preparation personnel.

## REFRIGERATION CASE STUDY

Another case study in refrigeration adapted to an operation's needs is provided by the Foxfire Restaurant, Anaheim, CA. Designed to generate an annual revenue of $1,000,000 with a minimum of highly trained personnel, the restaurant exceeded that goal in its first year.

An intimate dining atmosphere was assured by creating five separate rooms, plus a cocktail lounge, bar, and dancing area.

Back-up refrigeration for the operation includes walk-in refrigeration with reach-in freezers convenient to both receiving and preparation areas. The equipment has self-closing hardware and thermopane glass panels to reveal interior contents without opening the door. Exteriors have dial thermometers plus alarm systems to assure proper temperature control. Approaches are slightly ramped to provide easy access for mobile racks. In the walk-in, cantilevered shelves provide continuous surface and maximum storage capacity. The shelves are positioned 2 in. (5 cm) from walls to permit air circulation. Lightweight shelving in the walk-in refrigerators at the Foxfire Restaurant was chosen for easy handling.

A general storage refrigerator is adjacent to the receiving area. It has walls and ceilings

shielded with aluminum for easy maintenance and sanitation. Floors are quarry tile and coved to raised lower shelf. Lights are vaporproof for efficiency and safety. Double duty for one Foxfire reach-in refrigerator was assured by locating it between cook's preparation station and semi-exhibition cooking station where it can double as a back-up unit.

Perfectly aligned, solid wood doors that are self-closing and have magnetic seals are a decorative element in the Foxfire's waitress pickup station. They serve the practical purpose, with their refrigerated bases, of providing storage for garnishes (note picture in Chapter 7, Infrared Food-Warming Equipment, showing flush-mounted hardware on the doors, an excellent safety feature).

Refrigeration is also available at either end of the semi-exhibition entree-cooking line (See picture, Chapter 6, Broilers). To speed production and provide backup for the broilers, there is a single section, reach-in refrigerator at the left end of the line. At the opposite end, next to the steam cookers, is a dual-temp reach-in, which provides product backup within easy reach for that end of the line.

The employee entrance at Foxfire Restaurant is flanked by service buildings that hold compressors for all the major refrigeration systems. One location houses compressors for walk-in refrigeration and bar refrigeration requirements; the other, compressors for refrigeration in the semi-exhibition cooking station and salad bar. The main electrical switch gear is also installed in the area. The remote location provides outside access for servicing, good air circulation for compressors, and eliminates ambient heat that would have to be offset if compressors were inside the restaurant.

## SPECIALIZED REFRIGERATION

The development of specialized equipment has made it possible to insert refrigeration at many different preparation points and service areas.

In the salad and pantry pickup section of The Apple Tree Inn, North Kansas City, MO (see picture, Chapter 7, Infrared Food-Warming Equipment), waiters can work at their own speed due to a special refrigerated set up. Two pass-thru refrigerators are kept stocked with predished desserts, salads, and salad accompaniments.

Like all kitchen areas in New York City's Old King Cole Restaurant, the broiler area is designed to be self-sufficient. It has enough refrigeration to hold all items of meat and fish at an arm's length away from the broiler. Items are prepared in the butcher shop, placed on standard sheet pans used throughout the operation, and brought to the short-order refrigerator at the broiler. The sheet pans slide into the refrigerator to eliminate transfer and handling. All foods can be finished off with only one direct turn by the broiler man; he turns only to place the finished food on a shelf ready for waiter pickup.

Salad table under-counter units offer refrigerated space for three ⅓-pans or six ⅙-pans behind a 17½ × 24½-in. (44.5 × 62.2 cm) door opening; two ⅓- and 8⅙-pans behind a 17½- × 16½-in. (44.5 × 41.9 cm) door opening. Door storage in some models also provides space for dressings. In these tables a special air circulation system holds natural moisture in vegetables and meats.

Quick, cold sandwich preparation in a minimum of space is also possible with refrigerated sandwich units. These vary in size. Offered in one line are sandwich units in 2-, 4-, 5- and 6-ft. (61-, 121.9-, 152.4-, and 182.9-cm) lengths, 36 in. (91.4 cm) in height with a variety of pan arrangements to hold fillings at safe and appetizing temperatures.

## Refrigerated Drawers

Called "one of the most interesting applications of refrigeration," refrigerated drawers are turning up almost everywhere in preparation and service areas. The most common location, and one considered most efficient for a refrigerated drawer, is below another piece of equipment for which it provides a source of back-up supply.

Citing as an example of this application, refrigerated drawers located directly below fryers and griddles in a short-order unit, a manufacturer admits, "There are those who would disagree

with my point of view, feeling that too much usable space is lost through drawer construction." (Having heating and refrigerating equipment close together is also questioned by some designers.)

"Certainly a small amount of space is lost, but, in my opinion, the efficiency which is gained by locating refrigeration—of a design that does not require bending or stooping—directly beneath a piece of equipment far outweighs the small amount of refrigerated storage space which is lost because of the type of construction which must be employed.

"As can readily be seen, a conventional refrigerator must always be located away from an operating unit like the grill. As a result a great deal of efficiency is lost as the attendant walks back and forth between the refrigerator and his station.

"This loss can be partially overcome with the use of a refrigerated base. However, use of a drawer is even more efficient as bending or stooping is not required to gain access to the refrigeration and its contents are immediately visible to the employee."

Fish-storage refrigerators combine 4 or 8 self-closing drawers that hold molded, high-impact plastic pans (approved for food storage). They are 16-in. (40.6 cm) wide × 18⅞-in. (47.9 cm) long × 6½-in. (16.5 cm) high. Drawers have easy-grip handles.

Refrigerated drawers on the front cooking line at the Red Onion Restaurant, Huntington Beach, CA, are located under griddles used to prepare that mainstay of Mexican menus, the tortilla. Refrigerated drawers are designed to hold standard-size pans. The drawers selected can refrigerate enough supplies for the station to cover peak periods.

## Dessert Display Cases

Properly refrigerated dessert display cases are called a merchandising must, counted on to build volume in many operations. One display refrigeration unit has been designed as a vertical refrigerated showroom for desserts and pastries. It requires only 8 sq. ft. (7432 cm²) of floor space, and has three full-length glass doors with shielded fluorescent lights to spotlight the specialties presented in it.

In another refrigerated display unit that offers 8.5 cu. ft. (2506 dm³) of inside storage space, two full rows of pies or salads can be highlighted. These cases are designed to hold food that is already at 40°F. (4°C); they should not be used to attempt to bring warmer food down to this temperature.

## Beverage Dispensers

Refrigerated fruit juice dispensers designed to hold 2½ and 5 gal. (9.4 and 18.9 l) are equipped with small self-contained refrigerating units.

Milk dispensers and milk coolers both offer refrigerated capacity for this basic beverage.

## Water Coolers

With the wide variety of water coolers currently available, cooled water sources can be spotted throughout an establishment. Location and equipment possibilities are varied enough to meet the specific requirements of cafeterias, restaurants, or schools (child size). Coolers are available for wall and counter installation as well. Waitress units are often equipped with small refrigerated dispensing units for cream, butter, cocktails, salads, fountain supplies, and similar items.

## BRAIN TEASER—REFRIGERATION

1. What are the two basic types of refrigeration? _____ and _____

2. Refrigeration is designed to hold temperature of food rather than to bring the temperature down. For this reason, hot food should be (rushed into refrigerator) (cooled slightly before being put into refrigerator). (Circle right answer.)

3. When locating refrigeration, is it better to have deliveries rolled further or to have preparation employees make more trips to refrigerated units? (Fill in right answer.) _____

4. How is much food being moved into refrigerated units today? _____

5. Using chart entitled Space Needed for Food Items Stored on 18 x 26-in. Pans, how many pans will it take to hold 100 portions of cottage cheese served with a No. 12 dipper? ____

6. List one way in which walk-ins are important to today's foodservice operation. _____

7. Walk-ins can be installed in (Circle right answer.) (semi-exhibition cooking area) (outside of building)

8. Doors to walk-ins should be propped open while moving food in and out. True ____ False ____ (Check right answer.)

9. Where is reach-in most likely to be located in high-volume operations? _____

10. Half-height doors should be considered for reach-ins if doors are opened once a day ____ doors are opened frequently ____ (Check right answer.)

*(For correct answers, see page 251.)*

**FIGURE   11.2**
Speeding the cook's work at The Apple Tree Inn, Kansas City North, Mo. is the pass-thru refrigerator above located at the end of the hot food pick-up counter. It holds various toppings for baked potatoes and other refrigerated items needed to finish or accompany hot entrees. Waiters also have access to this refrigerator for ingredients they need to add to complete plating.

**FIGURE   11.3**
Chilling refrigerator designed for roll-in units has self-contained refrigeration system that chills large volume of hot precooked food with high velocity convected air. It can reduce food temperatures from above 140°F. to 45°F. (60° to 7°C) in as little as two hours.

**FIGURE   11.4**
An unusual solution to providing an area for additional school lunch storage space was the erection of this dry storage area adjacent to the kitchen with panels of the type usually used in constructing walk-in coolers and freezers. It is 12- by 12-ft. and holds supplies for both the breakfast and lunch program at Haleyville School, Commercial Township, N. J. Since panels are insulated, heating installation was not needed.

**FIGURE   11.5**
Orderly storage assured proper air circulation for refrigerated products. Self-closing doors that automatically shut from a 45 degree angle help to cut down open door time.

**FIGURE   11.6**
Walk-in at Hyatt Regency kitchen is sized for food production required in the dining rooms of the 400-room hotel. Located adjacent to the Commonwealth Convention Center in Louisville, Ky., hotel will help handle foodservice for guests attending conventions and other special events scheduled there.

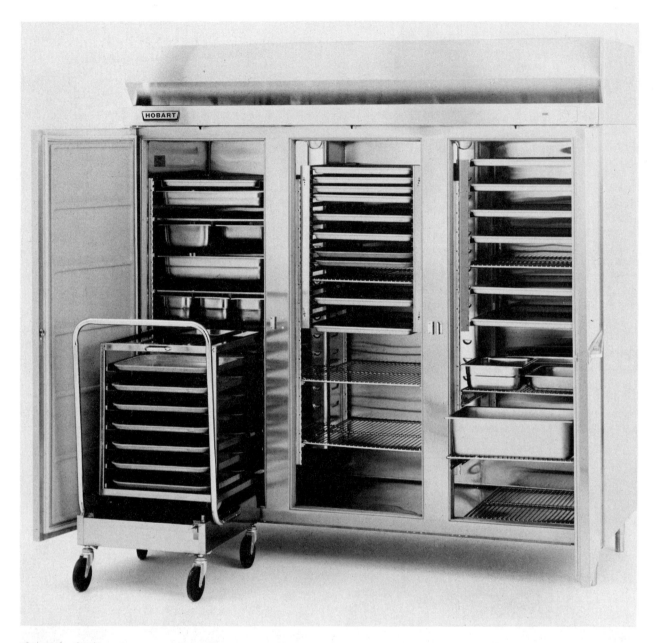

**FIGURE 11.7**
Advance planning assures best possible use of varied types of interior equipment available for refrigerator storage. Pans can be put in on tray slides (replacement for shelving) as at upper left section in photo; on trays in roll-in section, lower left; baking pan tray slides, top center; wire shelves located for deeper containers, bottom center; 10 adjustable levels that will each hold one 18- by 26-in (46- by 66-cm) pan or two 14- by 18-in. (36- by 46-cm) pans, upper right; pull-out shelves, lower right.

**FIGURE 11.8**
A cook/package/chill production system in use at Memorial Hospital System, Southwest Unit, in Houston puts major emphasis on controls possible in an ingredient room. This is where all pre-preparation and portioning for production is done. Portioned ingredients in containers are immediately moved into an ingredient refrigerator which serves as a buffer zone between pre-prep and production. This cold storage room holds packaged food after production is completed.

**FIGURES   11.9a and 11.9b**
Between the cold food plating table and the patient tray belt at Doylestown (Pa.) Hospital are two pass-thru refrigerators. Salads, desserts, and sandwiches are prepared and plated onto 18- by 26-in. (46- by 66-cm) bun pans, then
loaded into refrigerators as above. Special hold-open door stops permit the sliding refrigerator doors to self-close, except when they are opened to the maximum limit. In that position, the stops hold and doors stay open to permit loading of filled bun pans. Picture on next page shows trays of cold food being removed from tray belt side of pass-thru
when trays are being loaded.

**FIGURE 11.10**
This roll-in refrigerator at Indian Lakes Country Club, Bloomingdale, Ill. holds plated products in vertical racks. Adjacent soft ice cream machine is used for preparation of parfaits also held in roll-in racks in refrigerator.

**FIGURE   11.11**
Walk-in dairy cooler at Doctor's Hospital, Tulsa, Okla. has all stainless steel shelving with raised ''bubbles'' in shelving to permit air circulation. Roll-in racks containing finished foods are also held in this walk-in.

**FIGURE  11.12**

Cold food preparation area at Doctor's Hospital, Tulsa, Okla. has large walk-in cooler at the rear. Good flow from coolers to preparation area to coolers to service areas has helped step up production for 130 new beds. Walk-in refrigerator and freezer space was doubled.

**FIGURE   11.13**
Roll-in, quick chill refrigerator at right in this picture of The Apple Tree Inn's meat preparation area is also located next to room containing special hickory smoke oven. Products from either area can be easily transferred into the refrigerator.

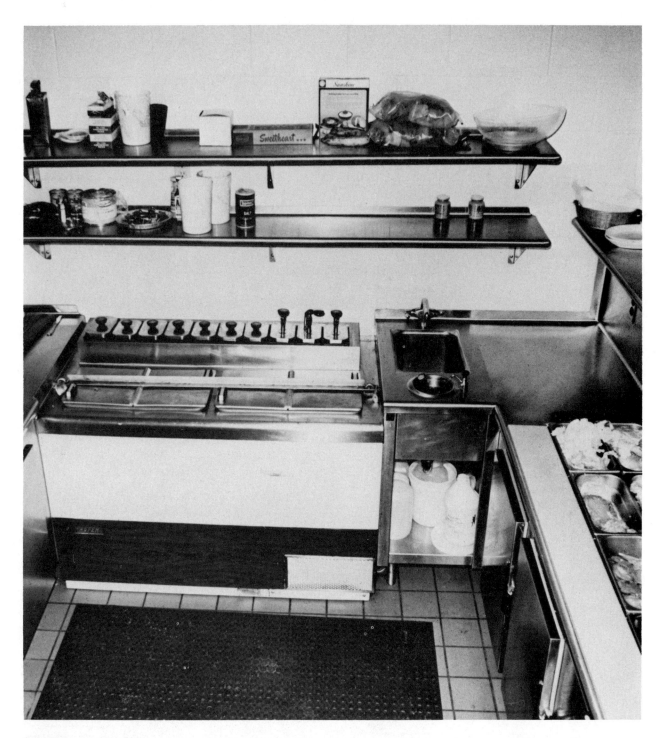

**FIGURE   11.14**
This ice cream, chilled dessert, and salad service station at the Sheraton St. Louis Hotel makes maximum use of refrigerated back-up. Foodservice for this luxury hotel located in a convention center has to be supplied for six separate
areas serving 8500 meals per week. Under-counter refrigeration on either side of U-shaped station keeps refrigerated
supplies close to preparation point. Locked ice cream case prevents pilferage when station is not in use. Sanitary service for ice cream set-up is assured with dipper well equipped with running water located at right of ice cream case.
Salad ingredients set out for preparation are held at safe temperatures in cold pans on refrigerated bases.

**FIGURE   11.15**

This picture illustrates a most unique adaptation of an existing piece of equipment to serve a special purpose at Bob Burns Restaurant, Woodland Hills, Calif. The two units, one at left and one in the center, that are mounted on the elevated shelf and flush to the wall are basic refrigerated milk dispensers. They have been modified with interior liners that hold cut lettuce. The liners are equipped with chutes and chutes incorporate a metering baffle controlled by a pressure plate inside the door. To use the dispenser, the waitress opens the small door in the unit and places a stainless steel bowl against the pressure plate which in turn opens the baffle releasing the salad base. When the bowl is filled, she releases the pressure plate by removing the bowl which permits the spring-loaded baffle to close. The larger circular raised flanges in the counter are where these salad mixing bowls are positioned. When a bowl is removed for service it is immediately replaced with another permitting the refrigerated base to chill the salad mixing bowl. The smaller circular wells house the vessels containing the dressings. The refrigerated base is used for back-up supplies and one section in each of the two stations is equipped with a special rack to accommodate plates for chilling. The designer of this system achieved both an efficient, self-contained work station and ease of maintenance.

**FIGURE   11.16**
Cold table at right in picture of cook's finishing station at the Foxfire Restaurant, Anaheim, Calif. has refrigerated bases. Self-closing refrigerator doors close easily as they are equipped with stainless steel roller guides. Stainless steel adapters in the drawers provide maximum capacity for the No. 200 modular pan and its increments which are used throughout the production and serving areas to increase efficiency and save labor.

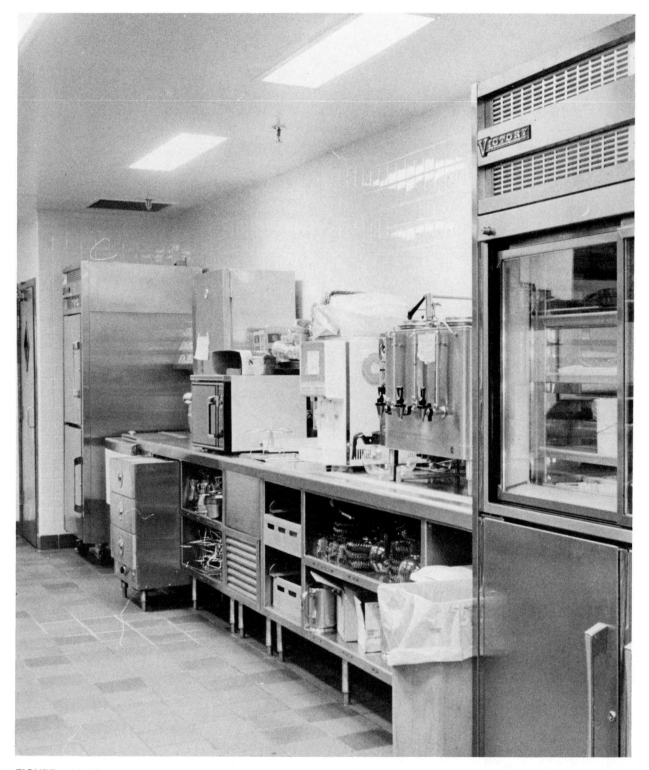

**FIGURE    11.17**
From salads in the pass-thru refrigerator at right through beverage equipment to freezer storage on tray slides for desserts at far left, waitresses have little difficulty completing orders at this pick-up station. It is located at Columbian House Restaurant, Bolingbrook, Ill.

**FIGURE  12.1**
Food storage needs anticipated for the future have led to the design of storage freezers that can also be used as refrigerator units by simply moving a switch. The selector switch changes operation from refrigerating to holding freezer as needs require.

# Chapter Twelve

# Storage Freezers

Frozen foods are a major component of today's menus. As the use of frozen foods continues to increase, storage space for frozen foods expands accordingly. At the same time, new aids to the use of frozen foods are being devised that save energy and speed reconstitution.

## STORE FROZEN FOODS IN SEPARATE UNITS

It is now generally accepted that frozen-food holding cabinets or storage freezers cannot be used successfully for the freezing of food. Where on-premise freezing is needed, separate freezing equipment is required to provide the necessary subzero temperatures. Much new equipment is available for operations that do their own freezing.*

Since the majority of foodservice operations buy foods already frozen, most of the information

*For detailed information on blast freezing of quantity foods, see Eulalia Harder, *Blast Freezing System for Quantity Foods*, Vols. 1 and 2. Boston: CBI Publishing Co., 1980.

in this chapter will cover reach-in and walk-in storage freezers. Equipment that thaws frozen food rapidly is a problem solver for many operations, and is also described in this chapter.

Frozen-food holding cabinets or reach-ins are being located at more preparation points in kitchens. Some kitchens have found that the steps saved cut labor costs enough to offset costs of operating such units even alongside the range.

Prefabricated or sectional walk-ins for frozen food storage can also be located outside preparation areas to take advantage of less costly space, and, if security permits, with an outside door for off-hours delivery.

## RISING CURVE OF FREEZER SPACE NEEDS

The increased use of frozen food reflects its many advantages for foodservice operations: improved scheduling of production, portion control, labor savings, consistent quality, and ability to expand limited menus while keeping costs in line. Operators must have enough frozen food storage space to buy advantageously and to provide needed variety.

Aware of the profit possible through use of convenience foods, many operators are pre-preparing foods in their own kitchens on slow days for use on busier days, a practice that can level the work load and help "hold the line" on labor costs.

It is now agreed that the faster food freezes, the better it turns out, since sharp freezing keeps ice crystals small and undetectable. Actually, food freezing should be a 3-step process: (1) refrigeration to cool; (2) sharp freezing; (3) holding at low temperature. Foods should be frozen in blast freezers or tunnel freezers, not in frozen-food holding areas or storage freezers. Frozen food needs to be *stored* at 0°F. (−18°C); food must be *frozen* at temperatures ranging from −25°F. (−32°C) to −100°F. (−73°C).

When foods are frozen in areas that also contain stored frozen foods, the foods being held may deteriorate. Therefore, freezing capacity, located separately and distinguished from the storage freezers, must be provided to freeze food items in quantities necessary to meet menu requirements.

To clarify the need for separate equipment, new emphasis is being put on correct terminology. Equipment designed to store frozen food is usually called a storage freezer, whether it is a reach-in unit, space in a walk-in, or an entire walk-in designed to be a storage freezer. Such equipment is kept at 0°F. to −10°F. (−18° to −23°C). A 0° to −10°F. (−18° to −23°C) temperature capability is urged by some designers who feel it offers greater safety for stored frozen foods.

Equipment that freezes food is referred to as a processing freezer, a blast freezer, or a tunnel freezer.

New types and varieties of frozen food are continually being introduced by processors. Tailored to a wide range of operating requirements, frozen foods are being welcomed as problem solvers. They are successfully replacing a sizable portion of on-premise food production.

## NEW LOCATIONS FOR STORAGE FREEZERS

More frozen food cabinets are appearing and are showing up in unexpected places. The cook, the baker, the salad maker, and counter workers for some time have been using frozen raw ingredients to prepare some dishes. Current use of these ingredients as well as frozen entrees is being stepped up to the point where efficiency requires the placement of equipment for frozen food storage in all of these work areas.

Frozen food storage units come in counter types that provide storage capacity plus a usable work area, especially desirable where space is at a premium. They can be mounted to desirable working heights and may be provided with tray inserts, pan inserts or, when specially ordered, with drawers. Their cooling systems may be self-contained or remote.

Mobile frozen-food storage cabinets or storage freezers can be placed in any location. Models are available with decorative trim that helps them fit easily into open-to-view preparation and serving areas. Heavy-duty casters and easy-to-manage push handles make moving these units easy. The interior design and exterior surface assure easy cleaning.

All frozen food, whether prepared on premise or off, should be put immediately into reach-in, under-counter, counter, or walk-in storage freezers.

## ESTIMATING STORAGE FREEZER REQUIREMENTS

Operators need to know today's menu needs and tomorrow's probable changes to figure out their frozen food storage requirements. In addition, the following facts should be known when deciding how much frozen food storage space will be necessary:

- Quantities of off-premise prepared foods or ingredients specified during peak periods
- Frequency of frozen food deliveries
- Possibility of buying larger frozen quantities to reduce per lb. or per serving costs
- Maximum length of time on-premise prepared frozen items are held
- Amount of on-premise frozen foods to be stored
- Unusual consumption peaks
- Short term space needed for predished foods
- Time and equipment factors, if any, involved in proper defrosting.

(See charts below and on page 206 for food-holding capacity data.)

Since frozen foods come in packages and pans of uniform, known sizes, it is easy to calculate storage space requirements by combining cabinet (reach-in) or walk-in freezer specifications with food container sizes and quantities. Here are cubic storage capacities of some popular walk-in models: 4 × 6-ft. (121.9 × 182.9 cm)—117 cu. ft. (3313 dm$^3$); 6 × 8-ft. (182.9 × 238.8 cm)—184 cu. ft. (5210 dm$^3$); 8 × 10-ft. (238.8 × 304.8 cm)—435 cu. ft. (12318 dm$^3$); 10 × 18-ft. (304.8 × 548.6 cm)—1022 cu. ft. (28940 dm$^3$). Obviously the term *walk-in* would be meaningless if all

## STORAGE SPACE REQUIREMENTS FOR FROZEN FOOD ITEMS IN BOXES AND CARTONS

*Boxes and/or Cartons*

| Item | Capacity | Dimension In Inches | Dimension In Centimeters | Cu. Ft. | Number Boxes and/or Cartons Stored Per Door Opening Level | Number Boxes and/or Cartons Stored Per Door Opening Half-Height |
|------|----------|---------------------|--------------------------|---------|-------|-------------|
| Vegetable | 2½ lb. (1.1 kg) | 9⅝ × 5⅜ × 2½ | 24.4 × 5.4 × 6.4 | 13 | 25 | 125 |
| Vegetable | 12 oz. (340 gm) | 5⅜ × 4 × 1½ | 5.4 × 10 × 3.8 | 192 | 113 | 565 |
| Potatoes, French fry cut | 30 lb. (13.6 kg) | 18 × 11½ × 10⅛ | 45.7 × 29.2 × 25.7 | | 2 | 4 |
| Breaded fish stick | 6 lb. (2.7 kg) | 10⅛ × 8 × 2¾ | 25.7 × 20.3 × 7 | 7 | 22 | 66 |
| Lobster tail | 5 lb. (2.3 kg) | 14⅞ × 7¼ × 3⅜ | 37.8 × 18.4 × 8.6 | 4 | 11 | 36 |
| Rainbow trout | 5 lb. (2.3 kg) | 12⅞ × 8¼ × 2¾ | 32.7 × 21 × 7 | 6 | 17 | 51 |
| Shrimp | 5 lb. (2.3 kg) | 11⅝ × 6¼ × 2¾ | 22 × 16 × 7 | 8 | 17 | 74 |
| Shrimp | 2 lb. (907 gm) | 7⅝ × 5⅜ × 2⅛ | 19.4 × 13.7 × 5.4 | 19 | 56 | 180 |
| Poultry Chicken Parts | 10 lb. (4.5 kg) | 18¼ × 10¾ × 2¾ | 46.4 × 27.3 × 7 | 3 | 10 | 26 |
| Turkey roll | 11 lb. (5 kg) | 17⅛ × 5 × 5 | 43.5 × 12.7 × 12.7 | 4 | 6 | 30 |
| Meat, ground beef | 50 lb. (22.7 kg) | 20¾ × 15¾ × 5¼ | 52.7 × 40 × 13.3 | 1 | 1 | 8 |
| Dairy products Butter | 32 lb. (14.5 kg) | 11 × 11 × 11 | 27.9 × 27.9 × 27.9 | 1 | 4 | 8 |
| Cheese | 30 lb. (13.6 kg) | 12 × 12 × 8½ | 30.5 × 30.5 × 21.6 | 1 | 3 | 9 |
| Pie | 1 lb. 8 oz. (679 gm) | 8¼ × 8¼ × 1⅝ | 21 × 21 × 4.1 | 16 | 7 | 112 |
| Ice cream Rectangular | 1 pt. (0.5 l) | 3⅜ × 4 × 2½ | 8.6 × 10 × 6.4 | 55 | 63 | 441 |
| Rectangular | ½ gal. (2 l) | 6⅞ × 4¾ × 3½ | 17.5 × 12 × 8.9 | 15 | 26 | 130 |
| Round | 2½ gal. (9.5 l) | 9½D × 10H | 24.1D × 25.4H | 1 | 7 | 14 |
| Fruit | 30 lb. (13.6 kg) | 10D; 13H | 25.4D; 33H | 1 | 6 | 12 |
| | 10 lb. (4.5 kg) | 7¼D; 8¾H | 18.4D; 22.2H | 3 | 11 | 33 |
| | 8½ lb. (3.9 kg) | 6¼D; 8¾H | 15.9D; 22.2H | 5 | 14 | 52 |
| | No. 10 can | 6⅛D; 7H | 15.6D; 17.8H | 10 | 16 | 48 |
| | 6½ lb. (2.9 kg) | 6⅛D; 7H | 15.6D; 17.8H | 6 | 16 | 48 |
| | 4½ lb. (2 kg) | 6⅛D; 4⅝H | 15.6D; 11.7H | 10 | 16 | 80 |
| | No. 5 can | 4¼D; 7H | 10.8D; 17.8H | 13 | 28 | 84 |
| Fruit juice Orange juice | 2½ lb. (1.1 kg) | 4⅛D; 5½H | 10.5D; 14H | 19 | 28 | 112 |
| Concentrated orange | 12 oz. (340 gm) | 2¾D; 4⅞H | 7D; 4.9H | 49 | 86 | 430 |
| Concentrated orange | 32 oz. (907 gm) | 4D; 5⅝H | 10D; 14.3H | 19 | 36 | 156 |
| Concentrated lemon | 18 oz. (510 gm) | 3½D; 4⅝H | 8.9D; 11.7H | 34 | 50 | 250 |
| Horseradish | No. 303 can | 3⅛D; 4¾H | 7.9D; 12H | 37 | 56 | 280 |

**STORAGE SPACE REQUIREMENTS FOR FROZEN FOOD ITEMS ON 18 × 26-IN. (46 × 66 cm) BUN PANS**

| Item | Size of Serving | Dish Used | Height of Food and Plates | Space Between Pans | No. of Portions Per Pan | No. of Pans for: 50 Portions | 100 Portions | Capacity per Door Opening Food File No. of Pans | No. of Portions | Mobile Food File No. of Pans | No. of Portions |
|---|---|---|---|---|---|---|---|---|---|---|---|
| Milk | ½ pint (0.2 l) | Carton | 3½" (8.9 cm) | 4" (10 cm) | 40 | 1¼ | 2½ | 6 | 240 | 5 | 200 |
| Cole Slaw | #12 Dipper | Fruit Nappie | 2½" (6.4 cm) | 3" (7.6 cm) | 21 | 2½ | 5 | 8 | 168 | 7 | 147 |
| Chopped Vegetable Salad on Lettuce | #8 Dipper | 7⅜" (18.7 cm) Plate | 3" (7.6 cm) | 3" (7.6 cm) | 8 | 6¼ | 12½ | 8 | 64 | 7 | 56 |
| Chef's Salad | 3/4 cup (170 gm) | Salad Bowl | 2" (5 cm) | 2" (5 cm) | 11 | 4¼ | 9 | 12 | 132 | 11 | 121 |
| Gelatin Salad on Lettuce | 2½ in. × 2½ in. × 1½ in. (6.4 by 6.4 by 3.8 cm) | 6⅜" (16.2 cm) Plate | 2¼" (5.7 cm) | 3" (7.6 cm) | 11 | 4½ | 9 | 8 | 88 | 7 | 77 |
| Cottage Cheese | #12 Dipper | Fruit Nappie | 3½" (8.9 cm) | 4" (10 cm) | 21 | 2½ | 5 | 6 | 126 | 5 | 105 |
| Cup Custard | — | Cup Custard (Hall) | 2½" (6.4 cm) | 3" (7.6 cm) | 40 | 1¼ | 2½ | 6 | 240 | 5 | 200 |
| Pie | 1/6 | 6⅜" (16.2 cm) Plate | 1⅞" (4.8 cm) | 2" (5 cm) | 11 | 4½ | 9 | 12 | 132 | 11 | 121 |
| Cake | 3 in. × 3 in. × 1½ in. (7.6 by 7.6 by 3.8 cm) | 6⅜" (16.2 cm) Plate | 2½" (6.4 cm) | 3" (7.6 cm) | 11 | 4½ | 9 | 8 | 88 | 7 | 77 |
| Fruit Cup | #12 Dipper | Sherbet Glass (stem) | 3⅛" (7.9 cm) | 4" (10 cm) | 40 | 1¼ | 2½ | 6 | 240 | 5 | 200 |
| Cream | 1 oz. (28 gm) | Paper Cup | 1⅝" (4.1 cm) | 2" (5 cm) | 135 | ½ | 1 | 12 | 1620 | 11 | 1485 |
| Fruit Juice | 4 oz. (114 gm) | 5-oz. (192 gm) Glass | 3⅝" (9.2 cm) | 4" (10 cm) | 84 | ¾ | 1¼ | 6 | 504 | 5 | 420 |
| Cantaloupe Boats | 1/6 | 7⅜" (18.7 cm) Plate | 3" (7.6 cm) | 3" (7.6 cm) | 8 | 6¼ | 12½ | 8 | 64 | 7 | 56 |

the cubic feet (dm$^2$) in a walk-in were considered usable for storage. Assuming that all storage is to be on shelves, one manufacturer estimates the usable shelf space in a 4 × 6-ft. (121.9 × 182.9-cm) walk-in as about 70 sq. ft. (650 dm$^2$). The estimate for 6- × 8-ft. (182.9 × 238.8 cm) walk-in is about 90 sq. ft. (836 dm$^2$) of shelf space. Cantilevered shelving systems can increase the storage capacity of walk-ins by eliminating the front post and also providing more flexibility in loading and unloading the shelves.

## STORAGE PROCEDURES FOR FROZEN FOOD

Because frozen foods are very sensitive to temperature change, these storage procedures are recommended:

- Frozen food items must be stored in a 0°F. (−18°C) area as soon as received and not

allowed to stand at room temperature for any length of time. As the temperature of frozen food products rises above 0°F. (−18°C), the rate of deterioration increases rapidly, even if the product stays "solid." Original quality of frozen foods never returns once they begin to deteriorate from partial thawing.

- Foods to be stored in frozen food storage cabinets must be properly packaged in moisture-vapor-proof material or containers to prevent dehydration, oxidation, discoloration, odor absorption, and loss of volatile flavors.

- Whenever possible, store food items in their original shipping cartons. If there are breaks in the cartons, or cartons take too much space, rewrap the items in vapor-proof, moisture-proof paper.

- Keep freezer doors closed as much as possible because kitchen heat that is let into the freezer when doors are open must then be cooled, thus adding to energy costs. Train employees to open doors in frozen food storage areas or storage freezers only when necessary. To minimize door openings, plan to remove as many items as possible at one time. Sometimes putting some frozen items in the refrigerator for brief periods will reduce the need to open storage freezer doors.

- Tightly sealed or wrapped food helps to prevent dehydration and oxidation, and also to prevent excess frost formation on the sides of a freezer and on evaporator coils.
- Placing food products loosely on shelves to obtain good air circulation within a cabinet or walk-in storage freezer is vital for temperature control.

## VARIETY OF FROZEN FOOD STORAGE EQUIPMENT

Fortunately, current design in frozen food storage equipment is varied enough to meet the demands of any location. Self-contained, reach-in cabinets, push-in units installed over insulated flooring, under-counter or under-cooking equipment units, frozen food cabinet pass-thrus, even portable frozen food transportation units, as well as walk-in space of any dimensions, are now available.

Transportation frozen food cabinets are designed to transport frozen food from freezer storage areas to remote dining rooms or to other institutions. These cabinets may be loaded the day or night before, held at freezing temperatures, then be transported by truck. Upon arrival at their destination, the cabinets become storage freezers when the condensing unit is plugged in.

### Mobile Storage Freezers

The cold-wall type of storage freezer (no blower or evaporator plate) is used for holding and transporting uncovered, preplated foods that would be adversely affected by the forced air circulation of a conventional freezer.

These mobile freezers are also useful in fast-food operations, to back up serving lines, or for buffets and smorgasbords. Mobile storage freezer cabinet exteriors are styled to be sufficiently decorative for public appearances. At the same time, interiors have coved corners and removable tray slides to make cleaning easy and to insure maximum sanitation. Control lights on some models simplify checking of contents.

## WHAT TO LOOK FOR IN REACH-IN STORAGE FREEZERS

When considering reach-in equipment for frozen food storage, check these points:

- Construction—properly sealed; easily cleaned
- Exterior—rust resistant; in keeping with decor if location makes this an important factor
- Adequate insulation
- Doors—well-constructed; easily opened; hinges easy to operate
- Lights—adequate; automatic light switch on door, if desired
- Shelves—easy to clean and adjust; maximum load provisions
- Condensing Unit—sufficient horsepower; type; location; necessary ventilation
- Temperature Control—visible thermometer or temperature record; automatic alarm system
- Defrosting System
- Amount of floor space required.

If a reach-in storage freezer is opened frequently, the possibility of half-height doors instead of full doors should be considered. Every time a full-height door is opened, the heated kitchen air rushes in, causing the refrigeration system to run more. If the storage freezer is located near a cooking station, half-height doors, and 1-in. (25 cm) asbestos should be added to the end nearest cooking equipment.

Although usually equipped with wire shelves, reach-ins for frozen food storage can be adapted to a wide variety of institutional requirements through optional accessories such as tray and pan slides and roll-out shelves.

Reach-ins may use either forced air or freezer plates to maintain temperatures; those with plates cannot be automatically defrosted. Systems for automatic defrost or handling of condensation have been kept simple. Manufacturers have prepared step-by-step directions for maintenance.

## Installing Storage Reach-Ins

Installation tips for frozen food storage reach-ins:

1. Make certain reach-in freezers have been properly installed; i.e., the cabinet should be level front to back and right to left, and connected to the required electrical power supply. Be sure units rest solidly and evenly on all four corners.
2. When first turning on a freezer, make sure its automatic defrost timer is set so it will not go into the defrost cycle during the peak service period.
3. In most cases, frozen food cabinets should be located away from any equipment that generates heat; if self-contained, they should be installed to permit necessary air circulation.

Never keep pans or any other supplies on top of a storage freezer with a top-mounted compressor.

## Cleaning Routines for Reach-Ins

Cleaning procedures for reach-in storage freezers are easy:

- Clean the inside of the unit once a week. Use a mild soap or detergent, rinse thoroughly, and wipe dry with a clean soft cloth. Wipe up food or juice spills immediately after they occur.
- Clean the door gaskets weekly with a damp cloth.
- Eliminate unpleasant odors by placing an open dish of unused coffee grounds or activated charcoal inside the cabinet.

## VARIATIONS IN WALK-IN STORAGE FREEZERS

Walk-ins are available with areas that can be used to hold frozen food, or an entire walk-in can be designed solely for frozen food. They come in a wide range of standard, ready-to-install models. Freezer space in a combination refrigerator/ freezer walk-in can be designed with reach-in doors and areas for roll-in units. Sufficient walk-in space for bulk storage permits the operator to buy ahead.

Combination refrigerator/storage freezer walk-in units provide 35°F. (2°C) temperatures in the refrigerator section and 0° to –10°F. (–18° to –23°C) temperatures for the storage freezer section. Prefabricated or sectional walk-ins are also widely used as storage freezers, located either adjacent to preparation areas or outside the building but with access from the kitchen.

Knowing what kind and thickness of insulation does the best job in storage freezers is necessary to get the most for the buyer's dollar and to keep energy costs as low as possible (see insulation data in Chapter 11, Refrigeration).

Walk-ins come in a variety of exterior treatments and a range of prices. Stainless steel is considered the most durable and most easily cleaned, but is the most expensive. Less-costly finishes include porcelain, organisol vinyl applied to steel or aluminum alloys.

## Writing Specifications for Walk-In Freezer Storage

When preparing specifications for walk-in, freezer storage areas, include these factors:

- Needed cubic content for storage or processing
- Exterior—material offering long life, easy cleaning at desired cost
- Interior—tight, easy to clean
- Insulation—adequate for temperatures required
- Assembly—easy, tight, minimum cost
- Refrigeration System—adequate; if not self-contained, geared to conditions in location where it will be installed; capacity sufficient to maintain required temperature level
- Defrost System—type of control; automatic
- Door construction
- Floor Level—designed to permit easy movement of foods in and out
- Transportation Cost
- Alarm System
- Accessories—e.g., shelving, floor racks, display doors

In addition to these factors one expert emphasizes that "the glue that pulls them together into a sound product is the reputation of the manufacturer. One failure, involving a load of food, can pay for a lot of invoice difference between competing makes of equipment."

## Locating Outdoor Walk-In Storage Freezers

Prefabricated or sectional walk-in equipment for frozen food storage, designed for installation outside, with entrance from the kitchen, increasingly is being specified. Installing units outside can release expensive inside space for more profitable use and permit buying in larger quantities for maximum discounts. If there is an entrance from the outside and security permits, deliveries can be made at any time without disturbing kitchen personnel. Often purchasing larger quantities and offering flexible delivery schedules will gain extra discounts from suppliers.

Assess these factors to determine the most efficient location for prefab walk-in units: traffic, access, loading or unloading requirements. Units are delivered completely equipped and ready for immediate operation. Equipment may also be leased and is designed to be easily expanded in size as frozen food holding needs change.

## Walk-In Maintenance

These preventive maintenance steps for walk-ins with storage freezer areas are recommended by one manufacturer:

1. Use proper operating temperatures.
2. Organize stored products for fewest door openings.
3. Keep cooling coils clear of stored product.
4. Eliminate unnecessary packaging material.
5. Turn off inside lights when walk-in is unoccupied.
6. Leave air space between stored products.
7. Use proper defrost cycles.
8. Keep compressors clean.
9. Make certain compressors get adequate air.

## Walk-In Installation

Factors to consider when installing walk-in storage freezers:

- Supply proper electrical service of sufficient amperage and voltage at compressor location.
- If installed in an existing building with wood floors, check and reinforce floors if necessary to accommodate weight of walk-in unit with its estimated product load.

## Location and Size of Walk-In Doors

Carefully consider door design and location; both affect employee productivity and energy costs. Before deciding about doors, gather information about the institution's own food handling methods, as these practices affect width and height selection and dictate most satisfactory door dimensions.

In locating walk-in doors, one manufacturer recommends placing doors where they will provide most convenient access into the area and permit greatest use of interior walls.

Other door factors to consider: whether right-hand or left-hand swing works best; automatic closing devices; foot-operated opening devices; glass panels for easy checking of contents; provisions to handle sweating; best materials—metal, plastic or glass.

In many installations, today's labor costs and the problems of meeting peak production requirements for many expensive menu items offset the costs of dealing with the ambient heat of the range if frozen food storage is located nearby. Properly insulated walk-ins can be used in high-temperature areas with little effect on the operating cost of the unit, according to one manufacturer.

## STORAGE FREEZER CAPACITY FOR 8600 MPW

Frozen-food handling facilities at the University of California's giant Student Center graphically illustrate the increase in locations and types of equipment needed when an operation plans to use frozen food.

In this three-level operation, which serves 55,000 meals a week, there is a walk-in for receiving frozen foods on the first floor; a walk-in used mainly for leftovers on the second floor; reach-in frozen food cabinets under serving counters in the cafeteria, and upright frozen food cabinets on the third floor.

One large employee foodservice, serving more than 8,500 cafeteria meals and 100 executive meals per week—plus two coffee breaks daily—has frozen food facilities that include two walk-ins—598½ cu. ft. (16948 dm³); one reach-in (in experimental area)—42½ cu. ft. (1203 dm³); one reach-in (baker's area)—21¼ cu. ft. (602 dm³); one pass-thru frozen food cabinet—13⁵⁄₁₂ cu. ft. (380 dm³); ice cream cabinets—18 cu. ft. (510 dm³) and one serving-counter frozen-food cabinet—24½ cu. ft. (694 dm³).

## SPECIAL ADAPTATIONS FOR FROZEN FOOD STORAGE

Adaptation of an ice cream freezer adds self-service opportunities for waiters at The Apple Tree Inn, North Kansas City, MO. Located at the end of the salad and pantry pickup line, the freezer holds a special frozen salad that waiters quickly can add to their trays.

In the lower left corner next to the French fryers is a freezer storage base that holds frozen raw shrimp and French fries ready for the fryer (see picture Chapter 5, Fryers). The top of the freezer base is used to process shrimp before they go into the fryers.

An ice cream case mounted on casters for easy daily loading from walk-in freezer is pictured in Chapter 11, Refrigeration. It separates the dessert station from the salad station at Bob Burns Restaurant, Woodland Hills, CA. Ice cream case holds enough to supply both lunch and dinner needs. Reach-in refrigerator in left of picture holds chilled desserts.

## SPECIALIZED THAWING AND STORAGE REFRIGERATORS

Earlier in this chapter it was pointed out that foods should be frozen quickly, in specialized

freezing equipment if done on-premise, and then stored in reach-in or walk-in freezers. Delivered frozen food also requires immediate storage at 0°F. (−18°C).

Are the speed and methods of thawing also important? The answer is "yes." Some foods may be thawed rapidly in a microwave oven, a steam cooker, or in other ways. Other foods may or should be defrosted more slowly. But to leave the product standing at room temperature invites spoilage. A slower but safer way that saves energy is to permit the product to defrost in a refrigerator. However, there are at least three disadvantages to that method. (1) Other foods in the refrigerator will be frozen or unduly cooled. (2) A considerable amount of refrigerator space is tied up in an inefficient process. (3) An uneconomically large food inventory must be carried because an extra two or three days are needed for work-in-progress, i.e., thawing frozen food.

To overcome some of the disadvantages of refrigerator defrosting of frozen foods, manufacturers offer reach-in and roll-in refrigerators designed to thaw foods automatically and then to hold them at proper temperature until needed. The principle is to apply enough warmth to the food in the refrigerator to meet the thawing schedule and to offset the cold given off by the frozen food to prevent the temperature in the box from dropping so much as to affect other foods there.

One means of achieving this result is by reversing the refrigeration cycle: When heat is needed in the box, the refrigerator takes it from the air in the room—the reverse cycle; when cold is needed to maintain storage temperature, heat is removed from inside the box and exhausted to the room—the conventional cycle.

There are also self-contained refrigerator systems capable of thawing frozen foods quickly in a controlled air temperature range of 40° to 43°F. (4° to 6°C). A timing control starts the thaw cycle. During thawing, alternating cycles of heating and refrigeration maintain uniform and safe air temperatures. At the end of predetermined thawing time, the cabinet automatically returns to conventional storage temperature of 38°F. (3°C).

Items to be thawed can be rolled into unit. A 2-section model can thaw up to 400 lb. (181.4 kg) of frozen foods. The unit is equipped with visual alarm indicator light that lets workers know if temperatures exceed safe limits, power indicator light that goes on if power goes off, indicator that shows temperature inside unit, and a thawing timer.

Aside from preserving the safety and quality of thawed food, the thawing cabinet helps the operation achieve a systematic and rational production cycle. The frozen food can be put in the thawing refrigerator in the evening and be ready for cooking any time the next day. As the thawed food dwindles or is removed, the cabinet is available as an ordinary refrigerator. By evening, again, there is space for the next supply of frozen food to be thawed.

## FREEZER STORAGE FOR THE FUTURE

With frozen convenience food items available and the expansion of frozen preservation, foodservice operations are demanding an increasing amount of low-temperature refrigerated equipment. Today, storage is required for 40°F. (4°C) refrigerated products. Tomorrow, the need may well be for low-temperature storage. A convertible unit operated with a selector switch has been designed to meet this need to vary refrigerated storage capability.

As the manufacturer points out:

Technically, the equipment is made feasible through the use of wide range refrigeration equipment which can handle the 40°F. (4°C) requirement without overloading the motor and still have adequate motor cooling capacity at the low temperature range to avoid burn out. It is designed to hold within the range of a nominal 40°F. (4°C) cabinet to a nominal 0 degree F. (−18°C) cabinet. The extremes of 50°F. (10°C) and −10°F. (−23°C) are not recommended.

As a frozen food unit, the cooling coils, condensing unit size, controls and defrost system are sized to handle these load requirements. When the selector switch is changed to the normal temperature position, none of these elements is changed. The defrost system is still physically there, but electrically it is isolated from the operational circuit. The condensing unit and cooling coils are larger than normally used, which means only that they are required to operate a smaller percentage of the time than in a standard cabinet.

The design intent for this equipment is to supply equipment as used in standard applications for either frozen food storage or normal temperature refrigeration. It is not intended for use as a processing freezer, for rapid safe thawing of frozen foods, or as special temperature laboratory equipment.

## BRAIN TEASER—STORAGE FREEZERS

1. Food can be frozen in storage freezers. (Check right answer.) True ____ False ____

2. Using the chart Storage Space Requirements for Frozen Food Items in Boxes and Cartons, how many 2-lb. boxes of shrimp can be stored per cu. ft. if unit has level, or full, door opening? _____

3. Counter model storage freezers provide (extra work space) (no work space). (Cross out wrong answer.)

4. To figure out how many cartons a walk-in storage freezer could hold, should space be allowed for foods to be brought into the unit? (Check right answer.) Yes ____ No ____

5. Frozen food quality improves if it is allowed to stand a long time before it is put into freezer storage. (Check right answer.) True ____ False ____

6. If frozen food shipping containers are broken, they (should go into storage right away) (items should be tightly rewrapped and put into storage right away). (Cross out wrong answer.)

7. A pan of rolls should be put next to a top-mounted compressor on a storage freezer until time for service. (Check right answer.) Yes ____ No. ____

8. How often should door gaskets on reach-in storage freezers be cleaned? _____

9. Why is it a good idea to locate a walk-in freezer outside the building? (products are farther away) (frozen products can be purchased in larger quantities) (Circle right answer.)

10. What new piece of equipment makes it easier for an operation to use frozen food items on its menu? _____

*(For correct answers, see page 251.)*

**FIGURE   12.2**
Door of walk-in cooler that leads to frozen food storage area at Sam Houston Junior High School, Irving, Tex. is made of transparent acrylic. Shelving for both refrigerator and frozen food storage area is of all stainless steel construction to eliminate rust. Dial thermometers on exterior wall provide easy visual checks at all times on temperatures inside both freezer and refrigerated storage areas.

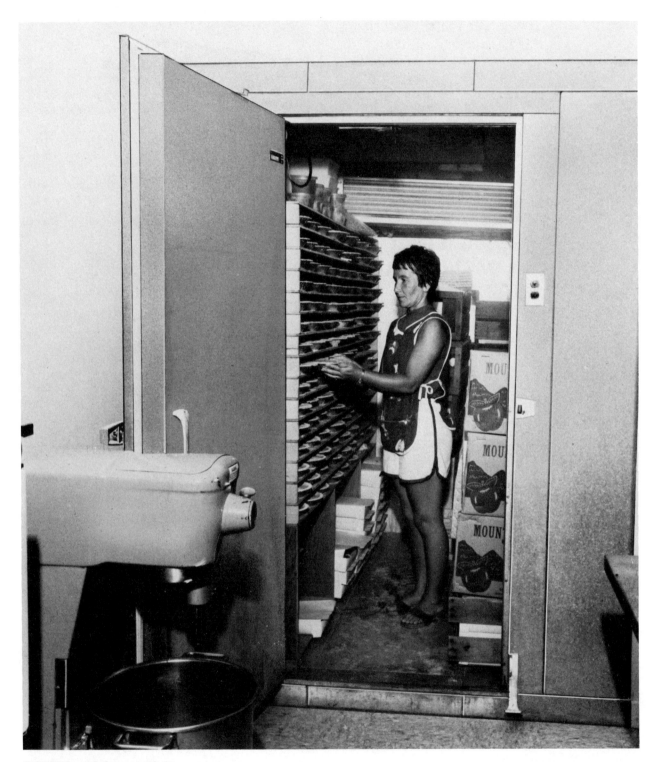

**FIGURES   12.3a and 12.3b**
This 6- by 10- by 7 ft. 6 in.  (182.9- by 304.8- by 228.6 cm) walk-in storage freezer holds unbaked apple pies at −10°F. (−23°C) at Allenholm Farm, South Hero, Vt. It is one of 2 units needed for the operation which sells 60,000 bu. of apples per year either as fresh fruit or processed into pies and applesauce. About 13,000 pies are baked and sold each year. Before pie apples are sliced for baking, they are held in walk-in cooler pictured above.

**FIGURE   12.4**
Combination storage freezer and refrigerator has 40°F. (4°C) section and 0°F. (−18°C) section behind half height doors.

**FIGURE   12.5**
Frozen food holding cabinet with two sections side by side provides extra work space as well as convenient frozen food storage. Either a stainless steel or hard maple cutting board top can be provided.

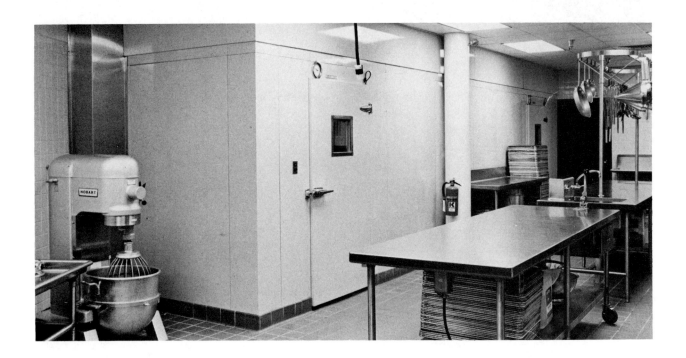

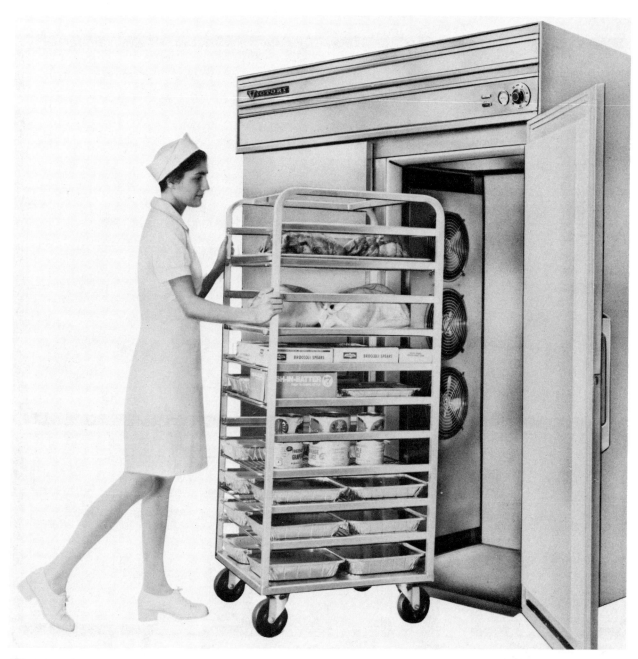

**FIGURE   12.7**
Up to 400 pounds (181.4 kg) of frozen food can be thawed evenly and quickly in this 2-sectional thawing refrigerator. Unit keeps foods between 40° (4°C) and 43°F. (6°C) while thawing. When food had thawed the preset length of time unit automatically becomes a conventional storage refrigerator with 38°F. (3°C) temperature.


**FIGURE   12.6**
(See facing page.) This is the main walk-in refrigerator and freezer storage area at Indian Lake Country Club, Bloomingdale, Ill. Units are prefabricated, or sectional, with flush floors. Area is well lighted and windows in unit doors cut down on door openings since visual checks of interiors are possible.

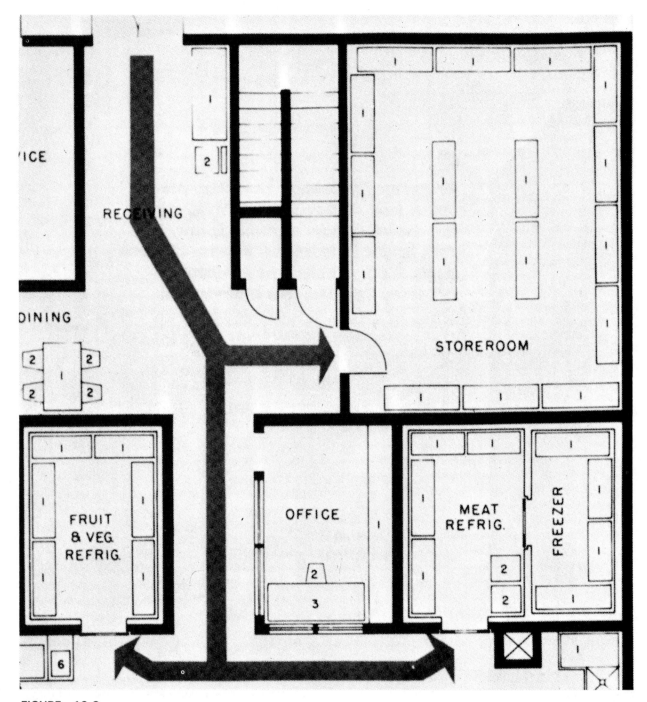

**FIGURE  12.8**
Direct route for food supplies from receiving to storage—dry, refrigerated, and frozen food, is traced on flow chart for
Birnam Wood Golf Club kitchen, Santa Barbara, Calif.

**FIGURE   12.9**
The rear one-third of this walk-in cooler is a frozen food storage area. Area is entered from cooler section and both cooler and frozen food sections have reach-in doors on each side. Full length cooler door is at right in this installation at the Commonwealth Convention Center, Louisville, Ky. Foodservice facilities in the Center are flexible enough to serve from 75 to 5000 people at once.

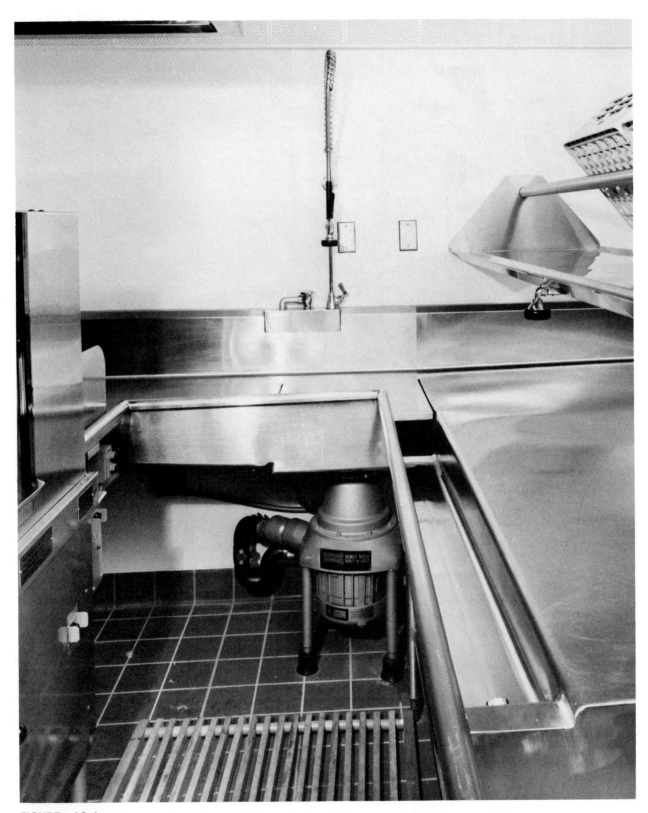

**FIGURE   13.1**
Not all waste handling is done in one spot in foodservice operations. Waste handling in the warewashing section at
Bob Burns Restaurant, Woodland Hills, Ca. successfully combines these elements: a scrapping trough is pitched to
the disposer; a flatware trap, or guard, is provided to protect the disposer; the trough is equipped with a manually
operated water flushing inlet.

# Chapter Thirteen

# Waste-Handling Equipment

Thirty to 40 percent of the supplies received in a foodservice operation are eventually disposed of as waste, according to one estimate. Reducing this quantity as much as possible cuts the costs of waste handling.

Waste removal or handling can be done in many ways:

1. A food waste disposer using a continuous flow of fresh water grinds and flushes waste directly into the sewage system. This practice is not always permissible, as many sewage systems cannot manage the extra load of waste from disposers. Septic tanks often prohibit the use of disposers also. In some areas it is necessary to refrigerate garbage to meet sanitation requirements.
2. Compactors, either bag compactors or stationary units, can be used. With a bag compactor a ram compresses the waste into a bag or carton; the unit is usually mobile; and waste volume can be reduced as much as 4 to 1. Bags are removed from machine for final storage and/or pickup.

Some units discharge compacted waste into a cardboard container, which can be removed from the compactor and sealed to contain odors, then stored until a trip to the dump is scheduled.

## OUTSIDE LOCATIONS

Stationary compactors, usually located outside the building, are a fixed device with a large, detachable container that holds the compacted waste. Eight cubic yard containers may be emptied on site into a mobile compactor.

3. Incinerators can burn most waste, except glass and metal. Newer restrictive codes require that scrubbers be installed and waste be fed into the incinerator carefully to prevent pollutants from coming out of the stack.
4. Shredders will handle cans, bottles, crates, and bulky waste.
5. Waste-pulping systems are designed to comply with waste-disposing regulations, especially where local codes or ordinances pro-

hibit feeding solid waste into sewage systems. Semidry pulp is suitable for land fill.

Locate pulpers where waste occurs in an operation. Waste is pulped in water to form a slurry, which is sent through piping to a water-press at a final pickup point. Waste emerges, much reduced, as semidry pulp, and goes into a container to be taken away. The water used to transport the waste is recycled to handle more waste.

6. Can crushers, aluminum foil container washers, bottle crushers, and balers are also available to solve specific disposal problems.

Choice of equipment depends primarily on the relative costs of garbage removal.

## TRASH, CAN STORAGE REQUIREMENTS

In many operations, waste handling is done in a separate location. One designer recommends that the trash and can storage room should be located adjacent to the receiving area with its doors opening only onto the dock. Isolating the trash room from the kitchen and food storage area is desirable for reasons of sanitation. Also, having the doors opening only to the dock allows the trash man to pick up after closing hours.

One of the operations carried on in the trash and can storage room is can washing. This activity affects the construction of the trash room. The floor must be concrete and the surface should be finished concrete or tile.

If food refuse must be trucked away, a garbage storage room will be needed. Refrigeration must be provided for this room to maintain the temperature at approximately 50°F. (10°C). A good size for this room is 6 by 8 ft. (182.9 by 243.8 cm). In many instances, the can storage and garbage storage functions can be combined in one room if it is constructed without windows and kept in the 50°–55°F. (10°–13°C) temperature range.

Conveniently located just off the loading dock at Sam Houston Junior High School, Irving, TX, the can-washing room makes handling of garbage cans easy, yet it is separate from receiving so

that incoming goods will not be contaminated. The area has can-washing equipment and a drying rack.

Space and equipment were also provided to clean all vegetables prior to storage at Sam Houston Junior High School. Resultant waste is quickly moved to nearby loading dock.

The canwasher and space to store other miscellaneous cleaning equipment are in a room near the outside dock at Middle Tennessee Mental Health Institute, Nashville. Can washing is minimized since a portable compactor decreases the amount of trash going out of the kitchen.

## WASTE HANDLING AT POINT OF ORIGIN

Handling waste at point of origin has paid off for the Old King Cole Restaurant in New York City. Each area has its own garbage cans, which are lined with plastic bags. These are picked up periodically and taken on a cart by elevator to the basement. Here they are compacted and refrigerated until taken away. The trash elevators are separate from the food or room service elevators, and trash leaves the premises without re-entering any food areas. The cans are also washed in the trashroom, which is at a different level than the kitchen.

## COMPACTOR TYPES

Vertical compactors have been designed to fit into a variety of kitchen designs. The exteriors can be covered with wallpaper, formica, or other kinds of paneling.

One compactor handles waste in a 4-sided, steel container on casters that holds a carton or plastic bag. Carton or bag on casters is rolled in through an access door. A safety interlock will not permit machine to operate unless access door is closed and locked securely. Waste is fed into the box through a trash door, and compacting starts when a button is pushed. When the cardboard box is full of compacted waste, a signal indicates that the box can be sealed and slid off the container onto a dolly or hand truck. One model has a 20-to-1 compacting ratio.

## Mobile Compactors

Mobile compactors for all-purpose use take less than 5 sq. ft. (46.5 dm²) of floor space. They plug into any 115 volt outlet. After compaction, waste can be packed into bag, box, or reusable container.

## WASTE SYSTEMS

At Augustine's Restaurant, Belleview, IL, a well-planned waste system has saved $300 a month for 1,200 meals a day. A waste equipment system installed in minimum space near the dishmachine reduces food scraps, paper, and corrugated box wastes by about 90 per cent. A through-the-wall unit discharges pulped wastes into a separate collection room. The unit recirculates water used in the pulper back to the scraping table to flush waste material quickly down the 28-ft. (71.1 cm) trough to the pulper.

**Pulper Unit Beneath Scrapping Table.**  With one pulper unit that is installed beneath the dish scrapping table, workers need only remove silver, and push plate waste onto tray mat. Mat and food waste and any other disposable items are fed directly into pulper. This same model can also be used as a free-standing unit.

This model speeds self-bussing if all items on a tray are disposable (frequently the case in school foodservice units) and this unit is installed at a pass-thru window. Waste items are sent to the pulper by a flush-down system.

In a satellite system, waste from a typical 435-student school consisted of aluminum foil trays (5 × 6½-in. (12.7 × 16.5 cm) with a foil overwrap, 5-in. (12.7 cm) paperboard trays with plastic shrink film overwrap, milk cartons, straws, napkins, plastic flatware, condiment containers, and food waste. The waste equipment pulped all the waste satisfactorily with minimal residue remaining in the pulper trash box.

Pulper units have pushbutton start-stop controls, can handle up to 1500 lb. (680.4 kg) per hour, and have reduced the volume of waste as much as 85 per cent.

Food and paper scraps from floor carts and food wastes from the food preparation area are fed into a pulper and then into a remote water press at Bellin Memorial Hospital.

## DISPOSER OPERATION

Care and common sense must be used in the operation of any waste-handling equipment. For example, understanding how a disposer works can save time or a service call. A disposer is designed to handle not more than a specific number of pounds of product per hour. To help prevent clogging of a disposer, turn on the disposer and cool water first, then feed the product at an even rate. Turn off the disposer and let cool water run for a minute to help clear the line. Some disposers have automatic controls that take care of these steps. Cool water is needed to keep the disposer cool while it is operating, as well as to help move waste products through.

Maximum efficiency can be obtained in a pulper by feeding waste at a steady, uniform rate. Overfeeding only slows down the pulping action. Dimension of the waste is also important, since the largest waste volume should not exceed more than half the tank diameter. Automatic water level control in the pulper tank ensures optimum efficiency. Water level is adjustable to compensate for the types of materials being fed to the unit. Water saturable materials require a higher water level than plastics or aluminum foil waste.

Good food preparation systems start with receiving and storage areas and procedures that are well-devised. They wind up with well-planned systems of waste disposal.

## BRAIN TEASERS—WASTE-HANDLING EQUIPMENT

1. Why cannot food waste disposers be used in all locations? _____

2. Compactors use a ram to compress waste to be packed in bag or carton. Waste can be sealed to (contain odors) (wait for scheduled trip to dump) (for long term storage on premises) (Circle wrong answer.)

3. Why should trash and can storage area be located away from the kitchen and food storage areas? _____

4. Incinerators can burn glass and metal. (Check right answer.) True ____ False ____

5. If local laws prohibit feeding solid waste into sewage system, which of the following waste disposal systems can be used? (shredder) (waste pulping system) (can crusher) (Circle right answer.)

6. Why should cool water be turned on before and after disposer is used? _____

*(For correct answers, see page 251.)*

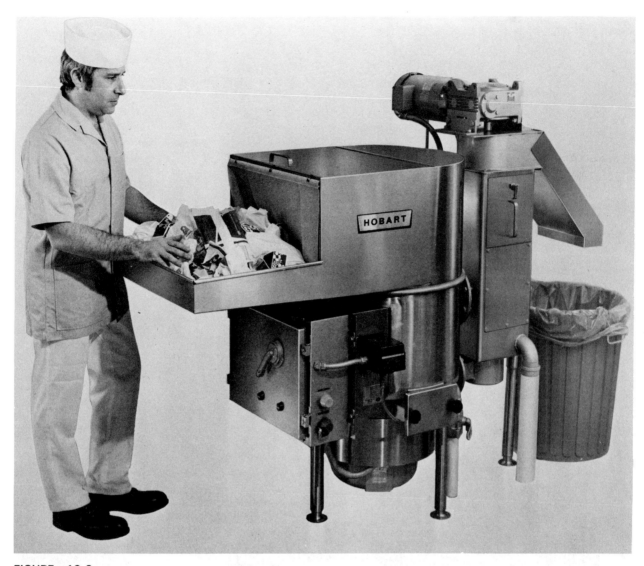

**FIGURE   13.2**
This waste handling unit turns paper, plastic, leftovers, scraps, and cooked bones into neat, semi-dry pulp. The pulping process washes waste, reducing odors. Units are available to handle wastes in amounts up to 1500 lb. (680.4 kg) per hour; can be located in kitchens to keep waste handling costs to the minimum. Nearly 95 percent of the water used in unit is recovered and returned to pulper. This continually flushes unit and only a daily washdown is needed to keep unit clean.

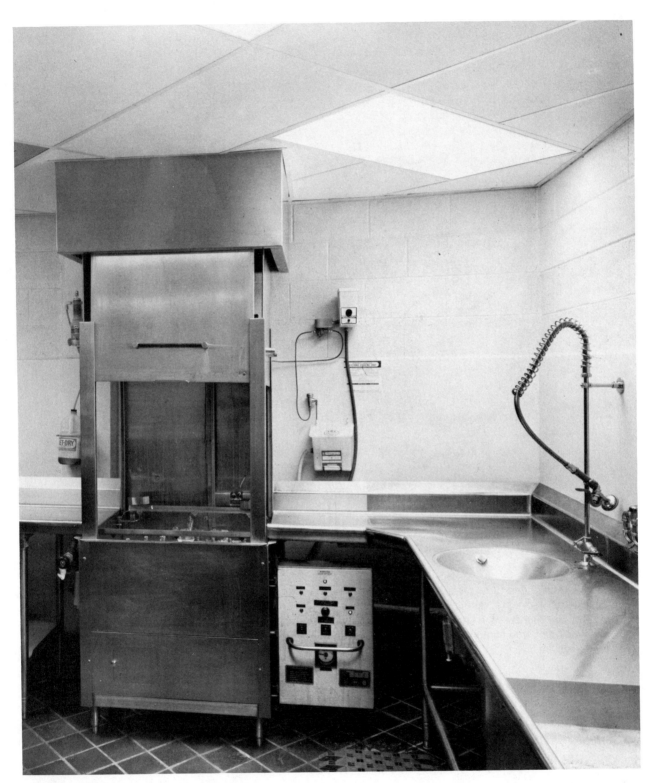

**FIGURE    13.3**
Waste disposal for pot washing at Doctor's Hospital was planned for maximum efficiency. At bottom right is a corner of the huge soak sink, first stop for soiled pots. Next pots are rinsed over disposer, then go around the corner into pot washing machine.

**FIGURE   13.4**
In the vegetable preparation area at Sam Houston Junior High School in Irving, Tex. note that controls for disposer and drain are recessed to prevent accidents. Refuse cans are on casters, an aid to speedy waste removal.

# *Chapter Fourteen*

# How to Clean Equipment:
## Programmed Lessons

The following series of programmed lessons for cleaning various kinds of foodservice equipment were designed for two purposes: (1) to provide basic knowledge for foodservice trainees or students on cleaning equipment, and (2) to guide supervisors in preparing similar materials specific to their own operations for use in employee training. Many foodservice operators, managers, supervisors and dietitians have reported that these programmed training materials have been most useful to workers learning to take care of the equipment it covers.

## HOW TO CLEAN RANGE TOPS

The top of the range is a very important spot in the kitchen because it is the place where many main dishes are cooked. For most customers, the main dishes make the meal.

These stews, sauces, gravies, and soups develop delicious flavors as they cook slowly on the range. It is the slow, steady heat that brings out such flavors. Yet the range can do speedy cooking too.

Whether the cooking is fast or slow, the range top will give off steady heat only so long as it is kept clean. Because so much cooking and dishing up is done on the range top, food often spills over. It should be wiped up immediately. Food that is not cleaned off right away will bake on, and the range top will be much harder to clean later.

Ranges can be heated by gas or by electricity. Your supervisor will tell you which kind you will be working on. You will need to study only the steps for cleaning the kind of range you will be responsible for.

It is not hard to keep the range tops clean. To help you learn how to do it, the steps have been worked out on the next page by the programmed learning method for both electric and gas ranges.

To learn the cleaning routine you need to know, take one piece of paper and cover everything under the heading GAS RANGE TOPS or the heading ELECTRIC RANGE TOPS except the statement numbered 1.

Now read the information in number 1. After you have read all the material you will come to the last sentence. It has a blank for you to fill in. Write the fact that you think belongs in the sentence in the blank.

Now uncover statement 2 and see if the answer in *italics* above it is the same as what you wrote in space 1. If it is not the same, read the information in number 1 over again to be sure you have the first step right.

Now go on to statement 2 and handle it the same way you worked on number 1. Do the same thing for statement 3.

Keep these pages handy so that you can go over them whenever you have any questions about cleaning the electric or gas range top.

## Gas Range Tops

1. At the end of the day's cooking, while the gas range top is still warm, wipe it off all over with a piece of material. Burlap is good for this job. This wiping will remove spilled food before it can burn and become much harder to get off.
(Fill in the following sentence.)
While it is still warm, the gas range top should be wiped with a piece of material to get off all _____.

### Spilled food
2. Take all movable parts out of the range top. These parts may be lids, rings, or top plates. Clean all grease and dirt from them, and also clean the openings they fit into. You can be sure you have done a good job if these movable parts are level when you put them back on the range top.
(Fill in the following sentence.)
All movable parts should be _____ the range top and cleaned. The openings they fit into should also be cleaned.

### Taken out or removed from
3. Clean out any grease or spilled food that you see in cracks or openings. Do not let water spill onto range top at any time. Water can

damage many parts of the range and repairs cost money.

## Electric Range Tops

1. The hotplate and griddle surfaces of the electric range should be scraped with a wire brush or flexible spatula after each use to get all spilled food off the surface.
(Fill in the following sentence.)
Clean the top of the electric range by scraping with a _____ _____ or _____.

### Wire brush or flexible spatula
2. Wipe out the grease trough on the griddle top range thoroughly at least once a day. Wipe out this trough whenever it is so full that grease cannot run through.
(Fill in the following sentence.)
Clean the grease trough on the griddle top range at least _____ _____ _____.

### Once a day
3. Each day remove the grease receptacle and empty it. Then wash it in the pot sink and put it back in the range.

## HOW TO CLEAN STEAM KETTLES

The steam kettle is the work horse of the kitchen. Soup, cereals, vegetables, macaroni, puddings are all cooked in the steam kettle.

In fact, most of the food that is needed in a successful foodservice operation can be prepared in the steam kettle.

The steam kettle works best when it is cared for properly. To make it easy for you to learn how to keep steam kettles clean, the steps have been worked out by the programmed learning method.

To learn how steam kettles should be cleaned, take one piece of paper and cover everything on this page except the statement numbered 1.

Now read the information in number 1. After you have read all the material, you will come to the last sentence. It has a blank space for you to fill in with the proper word.

Now uncover statement 2 and see if the fact in *italics* at the top is the same as what you wrote in space 1. If it is not the same, read the information again to be sure you have the first step right.

You are ready to go on to space 2. Handle it the same way you worked on space 1. Do the same thing for each of the other spaces, uncovering them one at a time.

## Cleaning Steam Kettles

Keep this page handy so you can go over it whenever you have any questions about cleaning steam kettles.

1. It is best to clean the steam kettle right after the food is taken out. First you have to pour some water in the steam kettle. Stir the water around to rinse the kettle. Let it drain out.
(Fill in the following sentence.)
When you start cleaning the steam kettle, right after it is emptied, the first thing to do is pour _____ into it and rinse it out.

### Water

2. If you cannot clean the steam kettle right after the food is taken out, fill it with water above the cooking line. Turn on the steam and heat the water.
When it is time to clean the kettle, take a brush or sponge and scrub the inside of the kettle until all water and food pieces drain out.
(Fill in the following sentence.)
To get all the pieces of food out of the steam kettle, fill with _____ and scrub inside with _____.

### Water and brush or sponge

3. After food pieces are rinsed out of steam kettle, close the drain. Put detergent in a bucket of hot water and pour it in steam kettle. Scrub inside of steam kettle thoroughly. Be sure to scrub both sides of the lids and hinges.
(Fill in the following sentence.)
Use hot soapy water to scrub inside of steam kettle and both sides of _____ and _____.

### Lids and hinges

4. Use some of the same soapy water to scrub the outside of the kettle. This is the time to scrub the legs, the framework around the kettle, and the pipes that connect to the kettle.
(Fill in the following sentence.)
To keep outside of the steam kettle clean, use warm water and _____ it all over.

### Scrub

5. Pick up a bottle brush. Open the drain and while the soapy water runs out, push the brush in and out of the drain pipe and valve. If drain is the kind that comes out, take it out and wash it. Then rinse drain and put it back.
(Fill in the following sentence.)
Some drains can be cleared by pushing a bottle brush through them. You can take other drains out to _____ and _____.

### Clean and rinse

6. Now close drain. Fill kettle about one-third full of water and heat it. Use this hot water to rinse inside and outside of kettle. Open drain and let rinse water out. Leave drain open until you are ready to use kettle for cooking.
Your steam kettle is now ready to turn out more batches of fine food.

## HOW TO CLEAN STEAM COOKERS

Good food is what brings customers to your establishment. Good food starts with clean equipment. Keeping equipment clean is easiest when you know what steps to take.

A new method called programmed learning is being used in this series to show food service workers how to clean various pieces of equipment. To learn how steam cookers should be cleaned, take a piece of paper and cover everything on the next page that follows statement 1.

To find out how to clean steam cookers, read the facts in 1 below. After you have read everything, fill in the fact needed to complete the last sentence.

Next, uncover statement 2 and see if the fact above the 2 is the same as what you wrote in space 1. If it is not the same, read the information in 1 over again to be sure you have the first step right.

Now go to number 2. Handle it the same way you worked 1. Do the same for each of the four remaining statements, uncovering them one at a time.

Keep this page handy so you can go over it whenever you have any questions about cleaning the steam cookers in your unit.

## Cleaning Steam Cookers

1. Be sure steam cooker is cool before you start to clean it. Remove shelves and shelf supports from cooker and take them to the sink. Wash them thoroughly with warm water and mild detergent. You may need to soak some of the pieces to soften hardened food that will not wipe off. Rinse cleaned shelves and supports and let them dry.
(Fill in the following sentence.)
The first thing to be done in cleaning a steam cooker is to take out _____ and _____.

### Shelves and shelf supports

2. Clean inside of cooker compartment thoroughly with warm water and mild detergent. Be sure to get any spilled food out of the compartment, as foods left in the compartment are unsanitary and may discolor the metal. Rinse inside of compartment thoroughly.
(Fill in the following sentence.)
You must wash out the inside of the compartment in the steam cooker carefully to get out any _____.

### Spilled food or caked-on food

3. Wash the compartment doors inside and out with warm water and mild detergent. Also wash molding around the door. Cleaning the compartment doors is especially important if greasy foods are cooked often. Rinse inside and outside of doors.
(Fill in the following sentence.)
To keep grease from forming on inside of steam cooker door, wash with _____ and _____.

### Warm water and mild detergent

4. Now that the steam cooker has been thoroughly cleaned inside, you can replace shelf supports and shelves. Put them back so shelves stay firmly in place.
(Fill in the following sentence.)
You can count on getting good food from your steam cooker when it has been _____.

### Carefully or thoroughly cleaned

5. Wash the inside of the steam cooker with warm water and noncaustic cleaning compound. Do not use steel wool or any metallic, abrasive cleaner that will mar the finish. Rinse dry and polish all outside surfaces with a soft cloth.
(Fill in the following sentence.)
To keep from marring the outside of the steam cooker, wash with warm water and _____.

### Noncaustic cleaning compound

6. Until steam cooker is to be used again, leave door slightly open so compartment can dry. The steam cooker is now ready to turn out more of the good food that means satisfied customers and a successful foodservice operation.

## HOW TO CLEAN DECK AND CONVECTION OVENS

Deck ovens and convection ovens take care of the preparation of many important menu items. They bake, roast, oven-broil, oven-fry, cook casseroles, and reconstitute frozen foods. Many kitchens have both deck and convection ovens so it will help you to know about both kinds.

Deck ovens are also called peel ovens or stack ovens; they have been used in foodservice kitchens for many years. They can be made up of one, two, or more oven compartments placed one on top of the other in one piece of equipment. There may be several of these stacks of ovens in one area of the kitchen or they may be located in separate preparation areas.

The oven compartments can be 7 in., 8 in., 12 in., or 16 in. in height. The smaller compartments or decks are for baking pies, cakes, and other small items. The larger compartments can hold large turkeys or roasts.

Deck ovens can bake or roast many items at one time. The heat for baking the foods comes from the bottom of the deck. It is called the hearth and foods to be baked in deck ovens are placed on the hearth.

Convection ovens are a much newer piece of equipment. They were designed to speed up some of the baking and roasting. The baking and roasting heat in convection ovens is pushed all through the unit. The heated air rushes all around the foods placed in the convection oven so foods can be cooked on two or more racks in the oven rather than only on the hearth.

The rush of hot air all around the food items makes convection ovens especially useful for reconstituting the frozen food items used in so many foodservice operations today.

Keeping these ovens clean means keeping them ready to turn out the good roasts or bakery items that make people want to keep eating in the same restaurant, drive-in, dining room, or school foodservice.

Deck and convection ovens can have several different kinds of finishes and there are directions here for cleaning various finishes. Your supervisor will tell you what finishes are used in the ovens in your kitchen, and you can learn how to clean those particular finishes.

There are also range and pizza ovens in many kitchens and the information on cleaning deck and convection ovens will help you in cleaning them.

Keeping the ovens clean is an important job. You can learn how to do it by studying the steps on these pages. They have been worked out for you by the programmed learning method.

Before you go further, take one piece of paper and cover everything on the rest of the next column except the statement numbered 1.

Now read the information in number 1. After you have read all the material in 1, you will come to the last sentence. It has a blank for you to fill in. Write the words in the blank space that you think belong in the sentence.

Now uncover statement 2 and see if the words above the 2 are the same as the words you wrote in space 1. If they are not the same, read the information over again to be sure you have the first step right.

You are ready to go on to number 2. Handle it the same way you worked on 1. Do the same thing for each of the other statements, uncovering them one at a time.

Keep these pages handy so you can go over them whenever you have any questions about cleaning deck or convection ovens. Remember that deck ovens are also called peel or stack ovens.

Before you begin to clean any oven be sure the oven is turned off. If it is a gas oven, turn the burners off; if it is an electric oven with an on-off switch, turn switch off. Let oven cool. Now you are ready to take the first step in cleaning the oven.

## Cleaning Deck, Stack or Peel Ovens

1. Scrape all sugar, oil or carbon deposits from valve and door handles and edges of doors with a scraper. Do a thorough job of getting all of it off.
(Fill in the following sentence.)
Use a _____ to clean off sugar, oil, or carbon that has built up on valve and door handles or door edges.

**Scraper**
2. Brush out combustion chamber daily with a small broom or brush; clean up spilled foods that fall beneath oven doors.
(Fill in the following sentence.)
When foods fall under doors, clean up with a _____.

**Broom or brush**
3. When black finish on outside of oven is cool, dip a cloth in light oil and wipe all over the outside of the oven. Next take a dry cloth and wipe the outside of the oven dry.
(Fill in the following sentence.)
After you wipe outside of oven with oil, go over it again with a _____ _____.

**Dry cloth**
4. If food has baked on or grease has splattered on stainless steel facing or interior of ovens,

use stainless steel cleaner after oven has cooled to take off baked-on food or grease. When you rub cleaner over oven, be sure to rub it in the same direction as the grain of the metal.
(Fill in the following sentence.)
To get baked-on spills off stainless steel, use _____ _____ _____.

### Stainless steel cleaner

5. When stains are so hard that they will not come off with regular stainless steel cleaners, work on them with a piece of steel wool. Rub lightly with the steel wool. If you rub too hard, you will scratch the oven.
(Fill in the following sentence.)
If you have to use steel wool to get some stains off stainless steel parts of the oven, be sure to rub it _____ over the surface.

### Lightly

6. If shelves need cleaning, use a long handled scraper. You can take the shelves out and scrub them at the pot sink if the scraper does not do the job.
(Fill in the following sentence.)
To get shelves clean, _____ or _____ them.

### Scrape or scrub

7. On aluminum or painted interiors do not use wire brush, steel wool, domestic cleaners or solutions containing ammonia, lye, or soda ash. Ask your supervisor to give you the right cleaner.

## Convection Ovens

Be very careful if you use scouring powder on the outside of the oven. It is very hard to get scouring powder off the oven. If it is not completely removed, it can damage the oven. Scouring powder can scratch and fog glass and can also damage or take off special coatings that are put on some ovens.

1. Go over stainless steel fronts on oven with a damp cloth. If spots will not come off with a damp cloth, use cloth wrung out in water

that has had detergent added. This will get stubborn spots off.
(Fill in the following sentence.)
When spots are hard to get off, use _____ in the water you dip your cleaning rag in.

### Detergent

2. Clean parts of the oven that have a special silver finish with a cloth that has been dipped in a detergent solution.
(Fill in the following sentence.)
Special silver finishes on ovens can be wiped off with a _____ dipped in a detergent solution.

### Cloth

3. Clean porcelain oven linings and door linings with an oven cleaner compound or with a cloth that has been moistened with water and detergent. Windows in the oven can also be cleaned with a cloth that has been dipped in water and detergent.
(Fill in the following sentence.)
Either water and detergent or _____ _____ _____ will clean porcelain oven and door linings.

### Oven cleaner compound

4. Take chrome finish racks and rack supports out of the oven and clean them in the pot sink. At the same time be sure to take out pan from the bottom of the oven, which is put there to catch spills. Scrape out spilled foods and clean pan at pot sink. Dry racks, rack supports, and spill pan and put back in the oven. Now it is ready to be used again.

## HOW TO CLEAN REVOLVING OVENS

The food that is baked in revolving tray or rotating ovens goes round and round as it cooks and comes out crisp and full flavored at the end of its ride. The trays of food roasting and baking while they slowly move through the oven have given this piece of foodservice equipment its name.

Revolving ovens come in two sizes. In the larger ovens, the trays are attached by hangers to the mechanism that revolves them in a circle from the front to the back of the oven. When the trays are in motion they look like the carts on a ferris wheel.

The smaller revolving oven is a compact version of the larger oven. It is designed to fit in the line with other standard kitchen equipment and has trays that revolve from side to side. Because the trays move from side to side the compact oven does not have to be as deep.

Revolving ovens are used to roast turkeys, hams, beef roasts, chickens, bread, pies, Danish pastry, pizza, and casseroles. Cleaning problems are most often caused by the grease that splatters from roasting meat or the fruit that boils over when pies are baking.

When pans of food to be cooked in revolving ovens are not carefully placed on the trays, the pans may spill and that spillage also adds to the cleaning problems. The more quickly spilled foods are wiped up the easier it is to keep the revolving oven clean.

These spillover problems are most easily solved when ovens are cleaned often and carefully. If grease and other spilled foods are left to pile up on the bottom of the oven, they can catch fire. Revolving ovens are easy to keep clean because you can get right inside the oven to remove dirt.

The steps needed to clean revolving ovens of all sizes have been worked out for you by the programmed learning method. You can learn how to clean a revolving oven by studying the steps on this page.

Before you go further, take one piece of paper and cover everything below except the statement numbered 1.

Now read the information in number 1. After you have read all the material in 1, you will come to the last sentence. It has a blank for you to fill in. Write the words in the blank space that you think belong in the sentence.

Now uncover statement 2 and see if the words above the 2 are the same as the words you wrote in space 1. If they are not the same, read the information over again to be sure you have the first step right.

You are ready to go to number 2. Handle it the same way you worked on 1. Do the same thing for each of the other statements, uncovering them one at a time.

Keep this page handy so you can go over it whenever you have any questions about cleaning the revolving oven.

## Cleaning Revolving Ovens

1. Be sure oven is cool before you start to clean it. The oven temperature should be the same as room temperature. Use a mild detergent with a damp cloth to clean the outside of the oven. Do not use harsh cleaners, as they will damage the surface.
(Fill in the following sentence.)
Outside walls of the oven can be wiped clean with a _____ _____ and a _____.

**Mild detergent and damp cloth**
2. Scrape all food particles off tray coverings inside the oven. Take trays out of oven and wash them in the sink. If the frames that hold the trays need cleaning, take them to the sink and scrub them.
(Fill in the following sentence.)
Scrape food off trays, then take trays to _____ and _____.

**Sink and wash them**
3. Clean spilled food from floor of oven with either a vacuum cleaner or a counter brush and dust pan.
(Fill in the following sentence.)
All food spilled on the floor of the oven should be cleaned up with a _____ _____ or _____.

**Vacuum cleaner or counter brush**
4. Before you go inside the oven to clean, be sure the main electrical power switch is cut off or that the main gas supply valve is turned off. When cleaning large ovens, never ride on trays unless another person is standing by and USE ONLY HAND CRANK to move trays if worker is cleaning them.

## HOW TO CLEAN MICROWAVE OVENS

The microwave or electronic oven helps keep customers happy because it gets food orders out in a hurry. Food is cooked fast in microwave ovens because the heat comes from electronic tubes. These tubes send heat deep inside the food at the same time they heat the outside of the food. With these ovens, food can be cooked much faster than ever before.

A food service operation that has a microwave or electronic oven can use it to cook frozen foods rapidly. The oven can also reheat prepared foods in a matter of seconds even though they have been chilled in the refrigerator until time to go into the oven.

The microwave oven makes it possible to please patrons with a greater selection of menu offerings since food can be prepared ahead of time and cooked fast when it is needed.

Like all foodservice equipment, the microwave oven works best when it is kept clean. You can learn how to clean electronic or microwave ovens by studying the steps on this page. They have been worked out for you by the programmed learning method.

Before you go further, take one piece of paper and cover everything on the rest of this page except the statement numbered 1.

Now read the information in number 1. After you have read all the material you will come to the last sentence. It has a blank for you to fill in. Write the words in the blank space that you think belong in the sentence.

Now uncover statement 2 and see if the words above the 2 are the same as the words you wrote in space 1. If they are not the same, read the information over again to be sure you have the first step right.

You are ready to go on to number 2. Handle it the same way you worked on 1. Do the same thing for each of the other statements, uncovering them one at a time.

Keep this page handy so you can go over it whenever you have any questions about cleaning microwave or electronic ovens.

Before you begin to clean the microwave or electronic oven, be sure the oven is turned off. If there is an on-off switch on the oven, turn it OFF. Now you are ready for the first step in cleaning the oven.

## Cleaning Microwave Ovens

1. When grease collects or food burns on the inside of an electronic or microwave oven, it cuts the cooking power of the oven. Slower cooking will slow service to the customers so be sure to wipe up all food that spills right away, before it can burn on. Use a damp cloth that has been soaked in a mild detergent to wipe up spills.
(Fill in the following sentence.)
You need to wipe up spilled food in the microwave or electronic oven or else it will burn on and _____ .

**Cut cooking time or slow food service**
2. You can get hardened food off the inside or the outside of the oven by soaking the spots with a damp cloth. Never scrape at burned-on food or use any scouring pads, powder, or other abrasives.
(Fill in the following sentence.)
Get hardened food spots off the outside of the oven by soaking the spots with a _____ .

**Damp cloth**
3. Wash the outside of the oven every day with a soft cloth that has been dipped in warm water mixed with a mild detergent. After you have washed the outside of the oven thoroughly, rinse it with clear water. Dry with a soft cloth or paper towel.
(Fill in the following sentence.)
Use a soft cloth, warm water, and _____ _____ to wash the outside of the oven.

**Mild detergent**
4. Wash the inside of the microwave or electronic oven every day, too. Wring a soft cloth out in warm water and mild detergent and wipe all over the inside of the oven with it.
(Fill in the following sentence.)
Wash the inside of the oven with a soft cloth and _____ _____ .

**Warm water**
5. Rinse the inside of the oven with clear water. Dry carefully with a soft cloth. Your microwave or electronic oven is now ready to turn out food in a hurry for your customers.

## HOW TO CLEAN BROILERS

Steak is the celebration food of a majority of today's diners. Since steak is a high-cost entree, it must always be well-prepared. The clue to the well-cooked steak is the broiler.

There are two kinds of broilers; (1) the horizontal overhead broiler, which may be electric, conventional gas, or infrared, and (2) char or underfired broilers.

Both kinds of broilers are designed to give off high heat so that meat can cook in its own juices. In this kind of cooking, no fat needs to be used.

Horizontal broilers can handle casseroles or fish, as well as steaks and chops. Char broilers, however, are generally limited to steaks and chops. Char broilers inject the popular charcoal-broiled taste as the meat juices and drippings fall on the hot coals, briquettes, or radiant rock, and give a smoky flavor to foods being broiled at high temperatures.

Either kind of broiler needs to be kept clean if it is to handle the maximum number of orders. Study the steps on these pages to learn the proper cleaning routine for broilers.

Before you go further, take one piece of paper and cover everything in the next column except the statement numbered 1.

Now read the information in number 1. After you have read all the material in 1, you will come to the last sentence. It has a blank for you to fill in. Fill in the blank space with the word or words that you think complete the sentence correctly.

Next uncover statement 2 and see if the words above the 2 are the same as the words you wrote in space 1. If they are the same you have the first step right.

You are ready to go on to statement 2. Handle it the same way you worked on number 1. Do the same thing for each of the other statements; uncover them one at a time.

Keep these pages handy so you can go over them whenever you have any questions about cleaning horizontal overhead broilers or char underfired broilers.

## Horizontal Overhead Broiler

This is the way to clean a horizontal overhead broiler:

1. Wipe the outside of the broiler every day with a cloth dampened in water that contains a noncaustic cleaning compound. Rinse, dry and polish the outside of the broiler with a soft cloth.

(Fill in the following sentence.)
After washing the outside of the broiler, use a _____ _____ to dry and polish it.

**Soft cloth**
2. When you clean the inside of the broiler, be sure you use a cloth that is not too wet. Wring it hard, as you should never get water into the broiling compartment. Go over the inside surfaces of the broiler with a damp cloth.
(Fill in the following sentence.)
Never get _____ into the broiling compartment.

**Water**
3. If food has burned on the inside of the broiler, scrape it off with a long-handled scraper or brush. Do not use cleaners that will mar or scratch the lining on the inside of the broiler.
(Fill in the following sentence.)
Use a _____ or _____ to get burned-on food off the inside of the broiler.

**Scraper or brush**
4. Remove the pans that catch grease from the broiler. Empty them and wash them. Be sure to dry these pans thoroughly. Then put them back under the broiler. Now you have the broiler ready to go.

## Char or Underfired Broiler

This is the way to clean a char or underfired broiler. This kind of broiler will have a hood above it to take off smoke. The hood will need a regular cleaning so it does not get too clogged to take out smoke and grease particles. Some hoods have special cleaning systems. You will learn about the cleaning of hoods from your supervisor.

1. Lift off the grids that rest on the top of the char broiler and wipe them clean with a damp cloth. Under the grids are baffles. Take these out next and wipe them clean with a damp cloth.
(Fill in the following sentence.)
Use a _____ _____ to clean the grids and baffles.

**Damp cloth**

2. Now clean heat source for the char underfired broiler with a scraper (or wire brush, if particles of food have burned on). Next, wipe with a rag dampened in detergent water.
(Fill in the following sentence.)
To get burned-on food off the broiler, use _____ or _____.

**Scraper or wire brush**

3. Remove and empty drip trays and wash them with detergent and water. Dry thoroughly and put them back under the broiler.
(Fill in the following sentence.)
After you wash drip trays, be sure you get them _____ before putting them back under the broiler.

**Dry**

4. Where charcoal briquettes are used for broiling, all ashes and burned matches should be cleaned out from the pilot area. Also clean ashes out of the fire box with a vacuum cleaner or brush. Now go over the outside of the broiler with a cloth dampened in water that contains a noncaustic cleaning compound. You have the char broiler ready for high-speed production.

## HOW TO CLEAN COFFEE-MAKING EQUIPMENT

If customers like the coffee, they are inclined to like everything about an eating place. Customers think coffee is good if it is hot, full flavored, and has a fresh-made taste.

Coffee-making equipment that is kept clean and in good working order makes good coffee. There is an easy way for you to learn how to keep coffee-making equipment clean. It is called programmed learning. It helps you learn the facts.

On these pages we are using programmed learning to teach the cleaning methods for four kinds of coffee making equipment. Your first step is to take one piece of paper and cover everything on this page that follows statement number 1.

To learn how to clean each kind of coffee-making equipment, start by reading the facts in the statement numbered 1. After you have read them, write in the fact that you think will complete the last sentence.

Next uncover statement 2 and see if the fact in *italics* above it is the same as what you wrote in space 1. If it is not the same, read the information in number 1 over again to be sure you have the first step right.

Now go on to statement 2. Handle it the same way you worked on 1. Do the same thing for any remaining statements, uncovering them one at a time. Keep these pages handy so you can go over them whenever you have any questions about cleaning coffee equipment.

## Coffee Urns

1. After each batch of coffee, when all the coffee has been poured from the urn, pour hot water through the urn to rinse it. Pour in a little more hot water and brush all around the inside of the urn; be sure you brush top to bottom and all around. Now rinse out the urn with more hot water until water comes out clear.
(Fill in the following sentence.)
The inside of the coffee urn should be _____ and _____ after each batch.

**Brushed and rinsed**

2. At the end of each day, clean the coffee urn again and rinse it several times with hot water. Remove faucet cap on top of gauge glass. Put brush in gauge glass and run it down inside. Use hot water and urn cleaner. Rinse gauge glass with hot water. Put gauge glass back on urn.
(Fill in the following sentence.)
After urn is cleaned out with hot water, the gauge glass liner should be brushed with _____.

**Hot water and urn cleaner**

3. Scrub faucet, rinse with hot water. Wipe outside of urn all over with a damp cloth or sponge. Then wipe dry and polish with a clean dry cloth. Remove cover and clean it.
(Fill in the following sentence.)

Use a damp cloth to wipe the outside of the urn clean.
Polish urn with a _____ _____.

**Dry cloth**

4. Fill clean urn with water and leave water in urn until it is time to make the next batch of coffee. Rinse urn bags in clean, cold water and leave in pan of clean water until time to use the urn again.

These steps will keep urn fresh so that coffee made in it comes out full flavored with the fresh-made taste that customers like best.

## Glass Coffee Makers

1. Rinse out top and bottom bowls of glass coffee makers with clean water after each batch is made. Rinse cloth filter in hot water and store in container of cold water until time to make next batch.
(Fill in the following sentence.)
After each batch of coffee is made, rinse out _____ and _____ bowls of glass coffee makers.

**Top and bottom**

2. At end of shift, scrub out top and bottom bowls of glass coffee makers with cleaning solution. Use stiff brush to clean insides of bowls and filter tube.
Rinse top and bottom bowl and tube thoroughly with hot water. When bowls are sparkling clean, coffee will have fresh flavor.

## Pressure Method Coffee Brewers

1. At the end of shift, run fresh water through the coffee brewer to remove loose soil. Remove cover, brewing chamber and coffee container. Pour water and urn cleaner into coffee reservoir. Scrub coffee reservoir and drain it. Rinse with clear, hot water to get all of the cleaning solution out.
(Fill in the following sentence.)
Remove loose soil in coffee brewer by pouring _____ _____ through it.

**Fresh water**

2. Put cover, brewing chamber and coffee container in pot sink, and clean with urn cleaner. Rinse thoroughly with clear hot water.
(Fill in the following sentence.)
To remove urn cleaning solution, use clear hot water to give covers, brewing chamber and coffee container a _____ _____.

**Thorough rinse**

3. Unscrew faucet bonnet, clean out cap and top cap of sight glass gauge on outside of coffee brewer. Use a straight cleaning brush to clean inside of sight glass gauge. Rinse gauge, bonnet and caps and put back together.
(Fill in the following sentence.)
Clean sight glass gauge with a _____ _____ _____.

**Straight cleaning brush**

4. Clean inside of machine with a damp cloth or mild stainless steel cleaner. Wipe dry and polish with a clean dry cloth.
Keep approximately one inch of water in coffee reservoir until time to make next batch of coffee.
When you are ready to make the next batch, drain out standing water and start with fresh water.

## Automatic Percolators

1. Each time percolator is emptied, wash inside of percolator and coffee container or basket with warm, soapy water. Next rinse with hot water. NEVER PUT PERCOLATOR IN WATER.
(Fill in the following sentence.)
Wash automatic percolator and coffee container with _____ _____ _____
Rinse. Never immerse percolator in water.

**Warm soapy water**

2. Scrub the inside of the tube with a stiff percolator-tube brush. Run clear water through the faucet to clean it out thoroughly after brushing.
(Fill in the following sentence.)

The inside of the tube should be washed with a _____ _____.

### Stiff brush

3. Wipe outside of automatic percolator with a clean damp cloth. Rub outside of percolator dry and polish with dry cloth. Do not use steel wool or any metallic abrasive cleaner on the outside.
(Fill in the following sentence.)
Wipe the outside of the percolator with a _____ _____ cloth, polish with a _____ _____.

### Clean, damp; dry cloth

4. Store clean automatic percolator with cover partly off so air can circulate inside the percolator and keep the inside from picking up odors.
Fresh and clean equipment is what every foodservice operation needs to make full-flavored coffee and keep customers satisfied.

# A Glossary of Foodservice Equipment Terms

In an attempt to assure that foodservice equipment terms have the same meaning in all parts of the country, the Food Facilities Consultants Society* has compiled this glossary. It is a project that has taken considerable time and effort. FFCS members have made this contribution because of their beief in the importance of standardizing terms used in equipment listings on kitchen plans to achieve a national uniformity. Through the generosity of the FFCS Board of Governors, we are being permitted to publish this glossary as a valuable addition to *The Complete Book of Cooking Equipment*. We are grateful to FFCS for sharing this basic material with us. J.W.

## A

**Au Gratin Oven**   Enclosure with hinged door mounted on top of a broiler. Also called finishing oven.

## B

**Bain Marie**   Sink-like depression in a table top with a water bath heated by steam, gas or electricity into

*Now known as the Foodservice Consultant Society International (FCSI).

which containers of food are placed to keep foods heated. Often used by chefs as a double boiler. Also called sandwich unit when used for refrigerated foods in sandwich preparation.

**Bake Oven**   See Oven.

**Baker's Stove**   See Pot Stove.

**Baker's Table**   Table whose top has 4" to 6" high curbing along the rear and sides to minimize spillage of flour onto floor during preparation. Often furnished with mobile or tilt-out ingredient bins under the top.

**Banquet Cart**   Insulated or non-insulated mobile cabinet with a series of interior shelves and/or racks to hold plates and/or platters of food. Usually equipped with an electric heating unit or refrigeration device.

**Bar Workboard**   Equipment below the top of a bar containing sinks, drainboards, cocktail mix stations, ice storage chests, beverage coolers, glass washers, etc. Also called sink workboard.

**Barbecue Grill**   A live charcoal or gas fired, open hearth, horizontal grill having spits set across the top of the unit with rotisserie-type drive mechanism along the front working side.

**Barbecue Machine**   See Rotisserie.

**Beef Cart**  Mobile unit, with or without bottled gas, alcohol or electric heating unit. Used for display and slicing of roast beef in the dining room.

**Beer Cooler**  Cooler in which kegs, cans or bottles of beer are refrigerated. The direct draw cooler is a low counter type with self-contained tapping equipment and dispensing head(s).

**Beer Dispenser or Tapping Cabinet**  Refrigerated or ice-cooled insulated cabinet with beer, soda and/or water dispensing heads, drainer plate and pan recessed flush with the bar top and a drain trough under. Usually built into a liquor bar top, between workboards.

**Beer System**  A method for tapping beer from remotely-located refrigerated kegs and transporting it through pressurized, refrigerated, and insulated lines to dispensing heads located at one or more stations in the bar and/or backbar.

**Beverage Carrier**  See Carrier.

**Bin**  Semi-enclosed, rectangular or round container, open on top, with or without lift-off, sliding, or hinged cover. Floor-type bins are usually mobile, of height to roll under a table top. Bins under a baker's table may be mobile or built-in to tilt out. An ingredient bin may be usd for flour, sugar, salt, beans, dry peas, etc. A vegetable storage bin has a perforated or screened body. An ice storage bin is fully enclosed and insulated with hinged or sliding insulated door(s) at the front; it is normally stationary, and set under an ice-making machine (head). A silverware (flatware) or cutlery bin is small and mounted in a holder set on or under counter top with other bins.

**Blender**  Vertical mixing machine with removable cup or jar, having mixing and stirring blades in the bottom and mounted on a base with a drive motor. Normally set on a table or counter top. Used in preparing special diets in hospitals, mixing cocktails in bars, as well as to whip or puree food generally at home.

**Blower (Evaporator) Coil**  See Unit Cooler.

**Blower-Dryer**  Motor-driven attachment with a blower and electric or steamheated coil, mounted on top of a dishwasher for quick drying of ware at the end of the final rinse cycle.

**Board**  A rectangular or round board, small for easy handling, set on a hard surface or counter top, to prevent dulling the knife blade when cutting food. It can be made of laminated or solid hard rock maple, or composition of rubber or thermal plastic material. Usually furnished with a handle or grip. Sandwich and steam table boards are rectangular and narrow; they are mounted on a sandwich unit or the corresponding section of a counter top. Also called Work Board in preparation areas of a kitchen.

**Boil-In-Bag**  A clear plastic waterproof pouch containing foods which are heated by immersing the package in boiling water.

**Bone Saw**  See Meat and Bone Saw.

**Booster**  See Hot Water Booster.

**Bottle Breaker**  Motor-driven device with revolving, horizontal, open top pan, in which empty glass bottles are safely flogged with steel bars.

**Bottle Chute**  Flexible cylindrical tubing to convey empty bottles from bar to bottle storage bin, or breaking or crushing device. Load end is usually located at the cocktail mix station.

**Bottle Crusher**  Motor driven device with rollers or reciprocating plate(s) to crush bottles, plastic containers and cans. The unit is mounted on a stand with a waste receptacle beneath to receive crushed and broken articles. The loading chute is provided with a spring-loaded or gravity-hinged door.

**Bottle Disposer**  System consisting of bottle chute and storage bin, bottle breaker or bottle crusher.

**Bottle Trough**  Trough suspended along the front of a bar workboard, usually at the cocktail mix station, to hold various bottles of liquor or mixer used often. Also called Speed Rail.

**Bowl**  A round bottom container open at top for mixing food. The salad bowl is a shallow type for mixing and displaying leafy vegetables. A coffee bowl is the lower of a two-piece, siphon-type coffee maker, used as a decanter.

**Braising Pan, Tilting**  See Fry Pan, Tilting.

**Bread Molder**  Machine with a series of rollers and conveyor belts to shape the ball of dough to pan bread, hearth bread or long rolls of varied length.

**Bread Slicer**  1. Motor-driven machine with a multiple set of reciprocating knives in a single frame through which bread is pushed, or vice versa. 2. Motor-driven or hand-operated machine with a single revolving knife to slice single slices while a bread loaf is moved along in a chute by a gear driven plate. Slice thickness may be varied.

**Breading Machine**  Horizontal rotating cylinder, set on a base with a drive motor and filled with breading mix. Food is placed in one end, carried through the cylinder by an internally mounted auger, and discharged at the other end. Food is tumbled in breading mix.

**Breath Guard**   See Display Case Sneeze Guard.

**Briquette**   One of the coal-size pieces of permanent refractory material used in open hearth, gas-fired grills to provide radiant broiling heat.

**Broiler, Backshelf**   Broiler with gas-heated ceramic radiants or electric heating elements, having an adjustable sliding grill. The unit is normally mounted on a panel and brackets above the rear of the range. Also called Salamander Broiler.

**Broiler, Char or Open Hearth**   1. Horizontal type with gas-heated briquettes under a grill at the top. 2. Horizontal type with non-glowing electric strip heaters at the top. May also be equipped with an adjustable electric grill above the top grill to broil both sides at once.

**Broiler, Charcoal**   Horizontal type with removable bottom pan containing glowing charcoals to radiate high heat into the bottom of foods set on a grill above. Mounted on stand or enclosed cabinet or masonry base.

**Broiler, Conveyor**   1. Horizontal-type unit with openings at both ends using a motor-driven, grill-type conveyor to transport food between or under gas-fired ceramics or electric heaters. 2. Horizontal-type unit, open at both ends, using a motor-driven, revolving, heated griddle to transport food under gasfired ceramics or electric heaters.

**Broiler, Pop-Up**   Enclosed horizontal-type unit with a slotted opening in the top and gas-heated radiants on both sides of the cavity. Food is placed in an elevating mechanism and broiled on both sides at the same time. Similar to a pop-up toaster.

**Broiler, Pork and Spare Rib, Chinese**   Counter- or stand-mounted, narrow depth broiler with 2 or 3 decks, each having gas burners and radiants, for cooking pork slices and spare ribs in metal platters.

**Broiler, Upright**   Vertical type with an opening at the front, and gas-heated radiant ceramics or electric heating elements at the top of the cavity. Food is placed on a sliding adjustable grill set under the radiants. May be mounted on counter top, oven or cabinet base, or stand. Often aligns with ranges. May be equipped with removable charcoal pan.

**Broiler-Griddle, Combination**   1. Unit with front opening with griddle plate set into top, equipped with gas-heated radiants under the griddle. Radiants heat food and griddle simultaneously 2. Unit with front-opening door(s) having gas-heated radiants at the top of the cavity and food placed on a sliding or swinging type griddle plate set below.

**Buffet Unit**   One or more mobile or stationary counters having flat surfaces, with cold pans or heated wells at the top, on which chafing dishes, canape trays or other food displays can be placed for self service.

**Bun Divider**   See Roll Divider.

**Butcher Block**   Rectangular or round shape—6″ 10″, 14″ or 16″ thick—consisting of hard rock maple strips, kiln dried, hydraulically pressed together, glued and steel doweled through. Work surface of block is smoothed surface of ends of strips. Block mounted on open type wood or steel legs.

**Butter Chip Dispenser**   Enclosed insulated unit with mechanical refrigeration or ice to hold tiers of butter pats placed on chips, and dispensed one at a time. Normally set on a counter top. Also called Butter Chip Cooler.

## C

**Cafeteria Counter, Serving Counter**   In a cafeteria, top which is usually provided with recessed cold pans, recessed pans for hot foods section, display and protector cases, and drain troughs for beverages; set on legs or masonry base with enclosure panels, semi- or fully-enclosed cabinets with refrigeration or warming units beneath; all as required to accommodate foods to be served. Unit may be equipped with tray slide.

**Can Crusher**   Motor driven machine with rollers or reciprocating plates or arms to crush cans and break bottles. Unit mounts on stand with space under for refuse receptacle to receive crushed articles. Also called can and bottle crusher.

**Can Opener**   1. Hand-operated or motor-driven device fastened to the top of a table, wall, cabinet, etc. to open individual cans. 2. Portable, motor-driven device capable of opening cans while still in case.

**Can Washer**   1. Enclosed cabinet with spray heads for washing the interior and exterior of a can, mounted on open legs. 2. Round platform with a rotating spray head at its center for washing the interior of a can, mounted on a stand with foot-operated water valves. 3. Rinse nozzle built into a floor drain and connected to a hand-operated, quick-opening mixing valve.

**Can Washer and Sterilizer**   Enclosed cabinet with spray heads for washing the interiors and exteriors of cans, mounted on open legs, provided with detergent dispenser and 180°F. (82°C) hot water rinse or steam mixing valve for final rinse. See Pot and Pan Washer.

**Carbonated Beverage System**   See Soda System.

**Carbonator**  Motor-driven water pump, with tank and control valves, to combine cold water and $CO_2$ gas in a storage tank, producing soda water. Used for soda fountains, carbonated beverage dispensers, and dispensing systems.

**Carrier**  A unit for carrying food, beverages, and ware by hand for short distances, furnished with grip(s) or handle(s). Could be an enclosed cabinet, insulated, heated, or refrigerated; or a wire basket or rack.

**Cart**  Mobile unit of varying structure: as an open shelf or shelves; a semi- or fully-enclosed cabinet with single or multiple compartments whch may be insulated. Used for transporting food or ware, and for cleaning and storage.

**Cash Drawer**  Shallow drawer located under a counter top at the cashier end. Often provided with removable, compartmented insert for currency and coins.

**Cashier Counter**  See Check-Out Counter.

**Cashier Stand**  Mobile or stationary stand with solid top set on four legs, or semi-enclosed body open at bottom. May be provided with foot rest, cash drawer, and tray rest on one or both sides.

**Cereal Cooker**  Rectangular unit with heated water bath, having one or more openings in top with lug holders, into which pots with lugs are fitted to prevent the pot from floating. Cooker may be gas, electric or steam heated. Unit may be floor or wall mounted, and equipped with water filler and gauge.

**Check-Out Counter**  Counter located between a cafeteria serving area or kitchen and a dining room, for use by checker and/or cashier. Also called Cashier Counter.

**Chinese Range**  Range with one or more large-diameter gas burners on an inclined top, and a raised edge around each burner opening. Food is cooked in shallow bowls called Woks. Range top is cooled by water flowing from a front manifold to a rear trough, with strainer basket at one end. A swing spout faucet mounted on high splashguard at rear fills the bowl when the spout is turned 90 degrees.

**Chopping or Cutting Block**  See Butcher Block.

**Clam Opener**  Device with hand-operated, hinged knife and fixed, vee-shaped block attached to a table top.

**Cleaning Cart**  Mobile unit with one or more compartments for soiled linen, waste, and water for mops and wringer.

**Coffee Filter**  Perforated metal container, or disposable paper or muslin bag in coffee maker or urn to hold bed of coffee grounds.

**Coffee Grinder**  1. Bench-mounted, hand- or motor-driven machine with bean hopper at the top, grinding mechanism, and discharge chute with holder for container or filter beneath. 2. Coffee grinding attachment for a food machine.

**Coffee Maker**  1. Hand or automatically operated, electric-heated unit in which a measure of hot water at the proper temperature is poured over a measured bed of coffee grounds contained in a filtering unit. The extracted beverage is discharged into a container and/or serving unit. 2. Hand or automatically operated, electric-heated unit in which a measure of hot water at the proper temperature is combined with a measure of instant coffee mix and discharged into a container. 3. Unit consisting of one or more sets of upper and lower bowls set on gas- or electric-heated range. The measure of water boiled in the lower bowl is forced by pressure into the upper bowl containing measured coffee grounds. When the set is removed from the heat source, the cooling lower bowl creates a vacuum, causing the liquid to flow back down through a filter in the bottom of the upper bowl. The upper bowl is then removed to permit use of the lower bowl as a server or decanter.

**Coffee Mill**  See Coffee Grinder.

**Coffee Percolator**  Covered cylindrical container with up to 120 cups capacity, electric or gas heated. Percolating device in center causes heated water to flow over measured bed of coffee grounds contained in a filtering basket at top. Unit is normally hand filled. Heating unit keeps coffee warm for serving. Bottom has draw-off faucet.

**Coffee Range**  Counter unit consisting of one to four low-rated gas or electric burners for making coffee with siphon-type coffee makers.

**Coffee Urn**  Enclosed container of water with jar (liner) set into top. Urn water is heated by gas, electric or steam. A measure of hot water at proper temperature is poured over measured bed of coffee grounds contained in a filtering unit. Beverage collects in jar and is discharged through bottom connection to draw-off faucet. Urn water is not used for coffee making. Equipped with water inlet valve to fill urn body.

**Coffee Urn Battery**  Assembly of units consisting of one or more water boilers and one or more coffee urns heated by gas, electric or steam. Battery is complete with piping, fittings and controls between boiler(s) and urn(s).

**Coffee Urn, Combination**  1. Coffee urn with water inlet valve and additional draw-off faucet for hot water to make tea and instant beverages. 2. Pressure siphon type has sealed water and hot air chambers with piping control between water jacket and jar. 3. Twin type has two coffee jars set into top of single container. Urn body is usually rectangular in shape. 4. Automatic type has electrically operated device to pump and measure hot water at thermostatically controlled temperature.

**Coffee Warmer**   Counter top range with one or more gas, electric or canned heaters to maintain coffee at serving temperature; each with coffee bowl or decanter. Also called Coffee Server.

**Cocktail Mix Station**   Section of bar workboard where drinks are poured or mixed. Usually includes open top ice storage bin and wells for mixer bottles and condiments.

**Cold Beverage Dispenser or Urn**   See Iced Coffee/Tea Urn.

**Cold Pan**   Insulated depressed pan set into a table or counter top; provided with waste outlet; may be refrigerated with crushed ice, refrigeration coil fastened to the underside of the lining, or a cold plate. A perforated false bottom is provided when ice is used.

**Combination Steam Cooker and Kettle**   See Cooker and Kettle, Combination.

**Compressor, Refrigeration**   See Condensing Unit, Refrigeration.

**Condensate Evaporator**   Finned coil through which compressed refrigerant flows, absorbing the heat inside refrigerator or freezer.

**Condensing Unit, Refrigeration**   Assembly consisting of mechanical compressor driven by electric-powered motor with either air or water cooling device. 1. Open-type unit has major components separate but mounted on same base. 2. Hermetic-type unit has major components enclosed in same sealer housing, with no external shaft, and motor operating in refrigerant atmosphere. 3. Semi-hermetic-type unit with hermetically sealed compressor whose housing is sealed and has means of access for servicing internal parts in field.

**Condiment Cabinet**   Semi- or fully enclosed cabinet, mobile or stationary, having several removable or intermediate shelves to store cook's or baker's condiments and spices in the cooking and preparation areas.

**Condiment Shelf or Rack**   Shelf or rack mounted above or under a table top to hold several condiment items for use by the cook or baker.

**Condiment Stand**   Standard-height, mobile or stationary stand having a solid top with receptacle for holding condiment containers, and tray rest on one or both sides. May be open type with legs, enclosed type with cabinet base and shelves, or may have insulated cold pan and refrigerated base.

**Confectioner's Stove**   See Pot Stove.

**Container, Food and Beverage**   See Bin, Carrier.

**Convection Oven**   Gas or electric heated. Heat is circulated through the oven interior with fan or blower system. Interior may be equipped with racks and/or shelves. Ovens may be stacked or set on stand. Oven bottom may be constructed as part of the platform of a mobile basket rack cart.

**Convenience Food**   Any food item that has been processed by any method from the raw state, packaged for resale and/or further processing or use at later date.

**Cook's Table**   Table located in the cooking area of kitchen for cook's use.

**Cooker and Kettle, Combination**   One or more steam-jacketed kettles with one or more steam cookers mounted in top of single cabinet base or tops of adjoining cabinet bases. May be for direct steam operation, or provided with steam coil, gas- or electric-heated steam generator in the base under the steam cooker(s).

**Cooker/Mixer**   Direct steam, gas, or electric steam-jacketed kettle, with hinged or removable agitator mounted to supporting frame or brackets.

**Cookie Dropper**   Motor- or hand-driven machine used to portion and shape drops of cookie dough using dies. Unbaked cookies are dropped onto baking sheet pans or conveyor belt. Also called Cookie Machine.

**Corn Popper**   Enclosed unit with transparent front and ends, transparent doors on the working side, electrically-heated popcorn popper suspended from the top, and warming heaters for storage of finished popcorn. May be mounted on counter or enclosed base.

**Cotton Candy Machine**   Machine with round tub and spinning unit, and electric heating unit for converting sugar into cotton candy. May be set on counter top or stand.

**Creamer**   1. Insulated container for cream, having ice or mechanical refrigeration, and provided with adjustable draw-off faucet for each cream measure. Often anchored to counter or wall. Also called Cream Dispenser. 2. Soda fountain unit with self-contained ice cream cabinet.

**Creamer Rack**   Rectangular basket of wire or plastic construction with compartments to fit glass creamers. Used to wash, fill, and store creamers.

**Crusher**   See Bottle Crusher, Can Crusher, Compactor, and Ice Crusher.

**Cryogenic Freezer**   See Freezer (3).

**Cubing Machine**   See Dicing Machine.

**Cutlery Box** Unit consisting of one or more compartments for storage and dispensing of flatware (knives, forks, spoons). Often set on a counter or table top, and sometimes built into the front of a cabinet under the top, or as a drawer.

**Cutting Board** See Board.

# D

**Deep Fat Fryer** See Fryer.

**Defrost System** Refrigeration system for a freezer consisting of a blower evaporator coil, heating unit and controls. Electric type employs heating elements; hot gas type uses heat exchanger to remove frost from the coil and allow condensate to flow to the drain pan under the coil.

**Dessert Cart** Cart with several shelves for display and serving of desserts. May be equipped with mechanical or ice-refrigerated cold pan or plate, and with transparent domed cover.

**Detergent Dispenser** Device mounted on a dishwasher or sink for storage and dispensing of liquid detergent, or mixture of powdered detergent and water, into the wash tank of the unit through the pump manifold or incoming water line. Some units are equipped with control device, electrically operated, to detect detergent strength in tank.

**Dicing Machine** Bench-mounted, hand- or motor-driven, two-operation machine that first forces food through a grid network of knives in a square pattern and then slices the food the same length as the side of the square. May be attached to food-mixing or cutting machine. Also called Dicing Attachment or Cubing Machine.

**Dish Box** See Carrier.

**Dish Cart** Cart for storage and dispensing of clean or soiled dishes. Usually of height to roll under counter or table top.

**Dish Table** Work surface with raised sides and end(s) having its surface pitched to a built-in waste outlet, adjoining a sink or warehousing machine. There may be a soiled table used for receiving, sorting and racking ware, located at load end of the sink or washing machine; and a clean table at unload end for draining of rinse water, drying, and stacking ware.

**Dispenser** Unit for storage and dispensing of beverages, condiments, food, and ware. May be insulated and refrigerated or heated. May be provided with self-leveling device. May be counter- or floor-mounted, stationary or mobile type.

**Display Case** A semi- or fully-enclosed case of one or more shelves, mounted on counter top or wall, for display of desserts. Semi-enclosed type have transparent end panels and sneeze guards along customers' side to protect uncovered foods. Refrigerated type have insulated transparent panels and doors. Heated type are usually provided with sliding doors and electric heating unit, with or without humidifier.

**Dolly** Solid platform or open framework mounted on a set of casters, for storage and transportation of heavy items. May be equipped with handle or push bar.

**Dough Divider** Motor-driven, floor-type machine to divide dough (usually for bread) into equally-scaled pieces. Pieces are removed from work surface by conveyor to next operation. Normally used for bread dough. Also called Bread Divider.

**Dough Mixer** 1. Motor-driven machine with vertical spindle to which various whips and beaters are attached. Bowl is raised to the agitator. Mixers of 5- to 20-quart capacity are bench mounted. Mixers of 20- to 140-quart capacity are floor type. 2. Motor-driven, floor-type horizontal machine with tilting-type bowl and horizontal agitator(s) for a large dough batch. Also called Kneading Machine or Mixer.

**Dough Molder** See Bread Molder.

**Dough Proofer** See Proofer, Proofing Box or Cabinet.

**Dough Retarder** May be upright reach-in, low counter bench-type, or walk-in refrigerator with series of racks or tray slides and/or shelves, in which dough is kept cool, to retard rising.

**Dough Rounder** Motor-driven, floor-mounted machine into which a piece of dough is dropped and rounded to ball shape, by means of a rotating cone and fixed spiral raceway running from top to bottom. See Roll divider and Rounder.

**Dough Sheeter** Motor- or hand-driven machine with a series of adjustable rollers to roll dough to sheets of even thickness. Also called Pie Crust Roller.

**Dough Trough** Large tub with tapered sides, usually mounted on casters, for storing and transporting large batches of dough. Some troughs have gates at the ends for pouring dough when the trough is lifted above a divider and tilted.

**Doughnut Fryer** See Fryer.

**Doughnut Machine** Unit consisting of hand- or motor-driven batter dropper and shallow fryer. Doughnuts are conveyed through heated cooking fat or oil bath, turned over, and discharged out of bath into drain pan.

**Drainer**  See Drain Trough, Kettle Drainer.

**Drink Mixer**  Vertical, counter-type unit with one or more spindles with motor at top. Switch is activated by drink cup when placed in correct position. Also Malted Mixer.

**Drop-In Unit**  Any warming, cooling, cooking, or storage unit that is dropped into an opening in a counter or table top and is fitted with accompanying mounting brackets and sized flange.

**Dunnage Rack**  Mobile or stationary, solid or louvered platform used to stack cased or bagged goods in a store room or walk-in refrigerator or freezer.

**E**

**Egg Boiler**  Electric, steam or gas-heated unit with removable timed elevating device(s) to raise basket(s) or bucket(s) out of boiling water bath. Containers are lowered by hand. Ferris wheel type unit will automatically lower and raise baskets through water bath. Also called Egg Timer.

**Egg Timer**  See Egg Boiler.

**Electronic Oven**  See Microwave Oven.

**Equipment Stand**  See Short Order Stand.

**Evaporator**  See Condensate Evaporator, Unit Cooler.

**Extractor**  1. See Juice Extractor. 2. See Grease Filter. 3. See Water Extractor.

**Extruder**  See French Fry Cutter.

**F**

**Fat Filter**  1. Gravity type has disposable paper or muslin bag strainer set in holder on top of fat container. Unit is placed under drain valve of fat fryer. 2. Siphon type uses disposable paper or muslin bag strainer over fat container, attached to rigid siphon tube mounted on fat fryer, with other end of tube in fat tank. 3. Motor-driven, pump-type, portable or mobile, uses disposable paper strainer. Has flexible hose from fat tank to strainer. Strainer set on fat container.

**Filter**  1. See Coffee Filter. 2. See Fat Filter. 3. See Grease Filter.

**Finishing Oven**  See Au Gratin Oven.

**Fire Extinguisher**  Hand-operated, sealed with chemical inside, most commonly wall mounted and provided with control and directional hose, or horn.

**Fish Box**  1. Ice-refrigerated, insulated cabinet with counter-balanced hinged or sliding door(s) at the top, and drawer(s) at the bottom front. 2. Ice or mechanically refrigerated cabinet with tier(s) of self-closing drawers with insulated fronts. Also called Fish File.

**Fish File**  See Fish Box.

**Fish and Chip Fryer**  See Fryer.

**Flatware**  Term for knife, spoon and fork used by the diner.

**Floor Scale**  1. Unit fixed in a pit, its platform flush with finished floor. May have dial or beam mounted on top of the housing at the rear of platform framing, plus tare beam. Used for weighing heavy objects on mobile carriers. 2. Mobile type—See Platform Scale.

**Food Carrier**  See Carrier.

**Food Cutter**  1. Motor-driven, bench- or floor-mounted machine with a rotating shallow bowl to carry food through a set of rotating horizontal knives whose axis is perpendicular to the radii of the bowl. Knives are set under hinged-up cover. 2. Motor-driven, floor-mounted high-speed machine with vertical tilting bowl having a vertical shaft with rotating knife. Also called vertical cutter/mixer or sold under various brand names.

**Food Freshener**  Electrically operated unit to introduce live steam to the exterior or interior of food, heating it to serving temperature without loss of moisture. Cabinet type has a hinged cover or drawer for warming the exterior of foods. Hollow pin-type heats food interior through injection.

**Food Merchandiser**  Refrigerated, heated or non-insulated case or cabinet with transparent doors, and possibly transparent ends. Used for display and sometimes self-service of foods.

**Food Shaper**  1. Motor-driven unit with loading hopper, bench or floor mounted. Shapes food into rectangular or round patties of varying thickness. May be equipped with paper interleaving, removing, and conveying devices. 2. Attachment to meat chopper to shape ground food into rectangles of varied thickness. Also called Food Former.

**Food Warmer**  1. Insulated mobile or stationary cabinet with shelves, racks or tray slides, having insulated doors or drawers. May be electric, steam or gas heated, and provided with humidity control. 2. Infrared lamp or electric radiant heating element with or without a glass enclosure, mounted above the serving unit in a hot food section.

**French Fry Bagger**  Motor-driven machine to convey, measure, and insert French fried potatoes into paper bag blown open to receive product.

**French Fry Cutter** Hand-operated or motor-driven machine, or attachment to food machine, that pushes potato through grid of knives set in square pattern in frame.

**French Fryer** See Fryer.

**Fry Pan, Tilting** Rectangular pan with gas or electric-heated flat bottom, pouring lip and hinged cover. Floor mounted on a tubular stand or wall mounted on brackets with in-wall steel carriers. A small electric pan may be table mounted on legs. Also called Braising Pan, Tilting Griddle or Tilting Skillet.

**Fryer** 1. Floor- or bench-mounted unit heated by gas or electricity with tank of oil or fat into which foods are immersed. Common type has deep tank. Special types have shallow tanks for fish, chicken, doughnuts, etc. and a basket conveyor type has a shallow tank for draining with baskets, arms, mesh type belt, or rotating auger to move foods through the bath. Pressure type has a lift or hinged cover to seal the top of the fryer tank.

**Fudge Warmer** Counter-mounted, electrically heated, insulated pot with hinged or lift-off cover and ladle.

# G

**Glass Washer** 1. Multi-tank horizontal machine with hand-activated rinse nozzle in one tank, revolving brushes in a second tank, and final rinse nozzles in a third. 2. Single or double tank doortype or rack-conveyor-type dishwasher.

**Grater** 1. Bench-mounted, hand- or motor-driven machine in which food is forced against the face of a revolving grater plate by a pusher or hopper plate. 2. Part of vegetable slicing attachment to food machine.

**Grease Filter or Extractor** 1. Removable rectangular or round frame having several layers of wire mesh or baffles and mounted in the exhaust equipment above or behind cooking units. 2. A series of baffles mounted in exhaust equipment, from whose surfaces grease deposits are flushed with wash water into a waste outlet. 3. Manifold mounted water nozzles in exhaust equipment producing a fine spray mist which collects grease from laden air and drains through a waste outlet.

**Griddle** Extra thick steel plate with a ground and polished top surface, heated by gas or electricity. Surface edges are raised, or provided with gutters and drain hole leading to catch trough or pan. May be set on counter top with legs, stand, or oven base.

**Griddle Stand** See Short Order Stand.

**Grinder** 1. See Meat Chopper. 2. See Coffee Grinder.

# H

**Hamper** See Linen Hamper.

**Heat Exchanger, Steam** Boiler with coils to generate clean steam with possibly contaminated house steam. Used for steam cooking units.

**High speed Cooker** See Steam Cooker.

**Hors d'Oeuvre Cart** Cart with platforms on ferris wheel having several food containers on each platform. Used for display and service.

**Hot Chocolate Dispenser or Maker** 1. Counter-mounted, electrically heated glass bowl with agitator, or insulated tank with agitator for dispensing premixed hot chocolate. 2. Counter-mounted, electrically heated unit that combines measure of heated water with measure of chocolate mix, and dispenses mixture at touch of button.

**Hot Dog and Hamburger Broiler** Semi- or fully-enclosed cabinet with glass doors and panels for display. An electric heater under the top radiates onto hot dogs in baskets or on pins on wheel, or onto hamburgers laid on platforms mounted on motor-driven ferris wheel. Food rotates while cooking.

**Hot Dog Steamer** Counter-mounted cabinet with transparent display panels and hinged covers or doors. The unit is electrically heated with a water bath and immersion device to generate steam for heating hot dogs, and dry heat for warming rolls.

**Hot Food Cabinet** See Food Warmer, Carrier.

**Hot Food Table or Section** See Steam Table.

**Hot Plate** Counter-top and floor-mounted unit with one or more open gas or tubular electric burners arranged left to right and/or front to rear. French hot plates are round or square solid steel plates, gas or electrically heated.

**Hot Water Booster** Electric, steam-, or gas-heated insulated tank or coil used to raise the incoming hot water from house temperature to sanitizing temperature, as required by code. Booster may be mounted inside housing or at end of warewashing machine, under warewashing table, or may be remotely located.

**Housekeeping Cart** Cart with one or more semi- or fully-enclosed compartments for clean linen, a compartmented tray at the top for supplies, a cloth hamper for soiled linen, and a waste receptacle.

**Humidifier** Electric, steam or gas-heated unit used to evaporate and distribute water inside proofing equipment and hot food warmers. May be fixed or removable attachment.

# I

**Ice Breaker**   See Ice Crusher.

**Ice Chest**   See Ice Storage Bin.

**Ice Cream Cabinet**   1. Mechanically refrigerated low-type chest with removable, hinged, flip-flop covers, used for storage and dispensing of ice cream. 2. Mechanically refrigerated upright cabinet with hinged door(s), for storage of ice cream.

**Ice Cream Display Cabinet**   Ice cream cabinet with sliding or hinged transparent doors or covers. Mostly used in self-service stores.

**Ice Cream Freezer**   Floor- or counter-mounted machine with mechanically refrigerated cylinder, having a dasher to mix and refrigerate an air-and-ice cream mix to flowing ice cream. The product is then placed inside a hardening cabinet.

**Ice Cream Hardening Cabinet**   Low cabinet with a lid(s) or upright cabinet with hinged door(s), insulated and refrigerated at a very low temperature to set ice cream hard.

**Ice Crusher**   1. Motor-driven or hand operated floor- or counter-mounted machine with spiked rollers, to crush large pieces of ice or ice cubes. 2. Attachment mounted between an ice cube making machine and an ice storage bin, having a damper for directing cubed ice to motor-driven rollers with spikes to crush ice as required.

**Ice Cuber**   See Ice Maker.

**Ice Dispenser**   A floor-, counter-, or wall-mounted stationary ice storage bin with motor driven agitator and conveyor mechanism, or gravity feed, that dispenses a measure of ice (cubed or crushed) through a discharge chute into a container at working level.

**Ice Maker**   Floor-, counter- or wall-mounted unit containing refrigeration machinery for making cubed, flaked and crushed ice. Maker may have integral ice storage bin. Larger capacity machines generally have a separate bin in which ice is received via a connecting chute. Capacity is rated in pounds of ice per 24-hour day.

**Ice Maker and Dispenser**   Floor-, counter-, or wall-mounted ice maker with storage bin and dispensing mechanism. See Ice Maker, Ice Dispenser.

**Ice Pan Display**   See Cold Pan.

**Ice Plant**   1. An assembly consisting of a large capacity ice maker that empties into a walk-in freezer or ice storage bin(s) on the floor below via directional chute(s). 2. A large capacity, floor-mounted ice maker, having a small capacity bin connected to vertical and horizontal conveyors with insulated sleeves for transporting ice to large capacity bin(s).

**Ice Shaver**   Hand-operated or motor-driven, floor- or bench-mounted machine whose rotating plate or wheel has a sharp knife which produces ice like snow when forced against the face of a cake of ice. Also called Snow Cone Machine.

**Ice Storage Bin**   Insulated mobile or stationary cabinet of one or more compartments with hinged or sliding door(s) or cover(s). It is commonly mounted under an ice-making machine, with opening(s) in the top to receive product(s) and is fitted with a waste outlet in the bottom. Ice is normally scooped out of bin. Unit may be built into counter.

**Ice Vendor**   Floor-mounted, mechanically refrigerated freezer with a coin operated mechanism to release a measure of loose or bag of ice cubes at working level.

**Iced Coffee/Tea Urn**   Urn with stainless steel or transparent glass jar and drawoff faucet. Stainless steel type may be insulated. Glass jar may be equipped with ice compartment suspended from cover. Also called Iced Tea/Coffee Dispenser.

**Infrared Heater or Warmer**   Unit consisting of one or more lamps or electric strip heaters, with or without protective covering or reflector, mounted in a bracket or housing. Usually set over hot food serving and display areas, or inside enclosed displays. Unit produces infrared heat to keep food warm.

**Infrared Oven**   Oven having heat generated and radiated from electric infrared heating elements encased in a glass tube, or from an exposed quartz infrared plate.

**Injector, Rinse**   See Rinse Injector.

**Injector, Steam**   See Steam Injector.

**Insert**   Rectangular pan or round pot set into the top of a steam or hot food table.

# J

**Juice Extractor**   1. Counter-mounted motor-driven ribbed cone having base with drain hole for juice. Half of fruit is pressed by hand, down onto cone. 2. Bench- or floor-mounted motor-driven machine that slices fruit in half, and squeezes halves between nesting cones. 3. Hand-operated bench-type machine that squeezes fruit halves between inverted cones. Also called Juicer.

## K

**Kettle Drainer**  Mobile sink with screen or strainer basket, waste outlet with adjustable tailpiece, and push handle.

**Kettle, Electric Heated**  1. Stationary or tilting two-thirds steam-jacketed, or stationary full steam-jacketed kettle with electric immersion heater in water between shells. Kettle is floor-mounted inside housing or attached to housing with tilting mechanism. Tilting device may be hand or power operated. Stationary unit may be hand or power operated. Stationary unit is provided with water filler, hinged cover and draw-off valve. Tilting-type has pouring lip and may have draw-off valve, hinged cover and water filler. 2. Stationary or tilting two-thirds steam-jacketed kettle set into top of cabinet base with remote electric heated steam generator adjoining kettle. Kettle provided with hinged cover, water filler and draw-off valve.

**Kettle, Flat Bottom**  Rectangular pan with flat bottom having inner and outer shells. Live steam is introduced between shells, heating inner shell for cooking. Kettle is tilting type, floor-mounted on tubular stand, or wall mounted with brackets and in-wall steel chair carriers. Kettle front has pouring lip. Top has hinged cover.

**Kettle, Gas Heated**  1. Stationary full or two-thirds steam-jacketed kettle with a gas burner under the bottom of its outer shell to heat water between shells. The kettle is floor-mounted inside housing, and provided with a water filler and hinged cover. 2. Stationary or tilting two-thirds steam jacketed kettle set into the top of a cabinet base with remote gas heated steam generator adjoining the kettle. The kettle provided with hinged cover, water filler and draw-off valve. 3. Stationary floor-type direct-fired kettle with a single shell, mounted inside insulated housing, with a gas burner under bottom of shell, draw-off valve and hinged cover.

**Kettle, Steam-Jacketed**  Kettle having live steam introduced between the inner and outer shell to heat the inner shell for cooking. Deep type kettle generally is two-thirds jacketed. Shallow-type kettle generally is fully jacketed. May be mounted to the floor with tubular legs or pedestal base, or mounted to the wall with brackets and in-wall steel chair carriers. Tilting- or trunnion-type may be floor- or wall-mounted, having a worm gear device for hand operation. The stationary kettle has a draw-off valve. The tilting kettle has a pouring lip and may have a draw-off valve. The kettle may be equipped with lift-off or hinged cover, filling faucet, water cooling system, thermostat, etc.

**Kettle, Table Top**  Two-thirds steam-jacketed kettle, tilting type, with operating lever up to 20 qt. capacity, or tilting worm gear device for 40 qt. capacity; all direct steam, electric heated. All kettles have a pouring lip. Tilting type have 20 and 40 qt. capacity with a lever handle. Oyster stewing kettle is shallow tilting type kettle.

**Kettle, Tilting or Trunnion**  See Kettle, Steam-Jacketed; Kettle, Flat Bottom.

**Kneading Machine or Mixer.**  See Dough Mixer.

**Knife Rack**  Slotted wood or stainless steel bar set away and attached to edge of table top or butcher block. This forms a slot into which cutlery blades are inserted and held up by handles of same while the handles protrude at the top.

**Knife Sharpener**  1. Bench-mounted, motor-driven machine with rotating stones forming a vee to grind edges on both sides of a blade. 2. Attachment to slicing machine. 3. Grinding wheel attachment to food machine having an attachment hub.

## L

**Linen Cart**  Cart with several compartments for storage of clean linen. May be semi- or fully-enclosed.

**Linen Hamper**  1. Stationary or mobile metal cabinet with hinged metal cover. 2. Stationary or mobile framework with round cloth bag or cloth sides, ends and bottom.

**Lobster Tank**  Transparent tank open at the top, and with a water wheel at one end. Tank bottom is lined with special salt. Mounted on a stationary or mobile enclosed base with a filtering and mechanical refrigeration system for tank water. Also called Trout Tank, with salt omitted.

## M

**Machine Stand**  Mobile or stationary stand with solid or open frame top, mounted on open legs or cabinet base, with adjustable dimensions to suit a specific machine or device.

**Malted Mix Dispenser**  Counter- or wall-mounted unit with a transparent, covered hopper, having a lever for dispensing a measure of malted mix powder.

**Meat and Bone Saw**  Floor-mounted, motor-driven band saw with upper and lower pulleys, stationary cutting table with gauge plate and movable carriage.

**Meat Chopper**  Table- or floor-mounted, hand or motor-driven horizontal machine. Food placed in top mounted hopper is fed by a stomper into cylinder with tight fitting auger to drive food against rotating knife and perforated plate. Also called Meat Grinder.

**Meat Grinder**   See Meat Chopper.

**Meat Hook Rack**   One or more wood or metal bars mounted on a wall or floor stand, with fixed or removable sharp pointed metal hooks. Also called Meat Rail.

**Meat Roaster, Steam-Jacketed**   Shallow steam-jacketed kettle with cover and draw-off valve.

**Meat Tenderizer**   Counter-mounted machine having two sets of round knives with spaced cutting edges, set apart on slow speed rollers. Meats are inserted into a slot in the top, pass through the rollers and are discharged at the bottom front through which the meats to be tenderized pass.

**Menu Board**   Sign with fixed or changeable letters, or removable lines listing the food items and prices.

**Meter, Water**   See Water Meter.

**Mexican Food Machine**   Device used to hold a vee-shaped tortilla when filling it to make a taco.

**Microwave Oven**   Stand- or counter-mounted oven in which foods are heated and/or cooked when they absorb microwave energy (short electromagnetic waves) generated by magnetron(s).

**Milk Cooler**   1. Low, insulated chest with mechanical or ice refrigeration, for storing and dispensing half-pint to two-quart containers of milk. 2. Counter or stand mounted refrigerator with one or more 2- to 10-gallon containers equipped with sanitary tube connections which extend through flow control handles for dispensing loose or bulk milk.

**Milkshake Machine**   See Drink Mixer, Shake Mixer.

**Mix Cabinet**   Low counter-type or upright reach-in refrigerator in which the mix for frozen shakes or ice cream is stored.

**Mixer, Dough**   See Dough Mixer.

**Mixer, Drink**   See Drink Mixer.

**Mixer, Food**   Motor-driven machine with vertical spindle having several speeds on which various whips and beaters are mounted. Bowl is raised up to agitator. Mixers of 5 to 20 quart capacity are bench-type. Mixers of 20 to 140 quart capacity are floor type.

**Mixer Stand**   Low height stationary or mobile stand with four legs and a solid top to support a mixer up to 20 quart size. May be provided with undershelf and vertical rack for mixer parts.

**Mixer, Vertical Cutter**   See Vertical Cutter/Mixer.

**Mixing Tank**   Vertical type has center, bottom or side-mounted agitator assembly. Horizontal type has end agitator assembly. All are floor-mounted and provided with removable or hinged cover and draw-off valve. Tank may be provided with recirculating pump and filtering system.

**Molder, Food**   See Food Shaper.

**Modular Stand**   Low height, open, stationary stand with four or more legs, having an open framework top, to support heavy-duty modular cooking equipment.

## N

**Napkin Dispenser**   Counter top unit for storage and dispensing of folded paper napkins. Napkins forced to head plate by spring.

## O

**Oven**   Fully enclosed insulated chamber with gas, electric or oil-fired heat, provided with thermostatic control. Deck type units have chambers or sections stacked one above the other. Bake type decks are approximately 7" high inside. Roast type decks are 12" to 14" high inside.

**Order Wheel**   Metal or wood spoked wheel with clips or hooks on its perimeter, located between cooks' and servers' areas, on which order slips are placed to maintain rotation and visibility.

**Oyster Opener**   See Clam Opener.

## P

**Pan and Utensil Rack**   1. One or more bars and braces suspended from a ceiling, or mounted on posts or a wall, housing fixed or removable hooks for hanging pots, pans and utensils. 2. Upright mobile or stationary unit, open or semi-enclosed, with tiers of angle- or channel-shaped slides to support pans. 3. Heavy-duty rectangular wire basket to hold pans and utensils upright in a pot washer.

**Pan Washer**   See Pot and Utensil Washer.

**Pass-Thru Window or Opening**   Trimmed opening between kitchen and serving areas having a shelf for a sill. May be equipped with hinged or sliding door or shutter.

**Peanut Roaster**   Electrically heated enclosed display case with hinged cover at the top.

**Peeler**   Floor- or bench-mounted machine having a vertical, stationary, abrasive-lined cylinder open at the top, a motor driven agitator bottom plate, and an over-the-rim water supply. Product discharged through door in cylinder side. Waste water is discharged at bottom and may be equipped with a peel trap basket that can be hung on a pipe over sink, or set inside a cabinet base under the peeler. May also be equipped with garbage disposal unit.

**Peeler Stand**   1. Special height mobile stand, open-type, with four legs. 2. Special height enclosed cabinet with adjustable legs, a door designed to house a trap basket, and a waste outlet.

**Pellet Heater**   Counter-mounted, electric heated, insulated cabinet having one or more vertical cylinders in which metallic discs, inserted at the top, are heated. Discs are dispensed at the bottom through drawer type device.

**Pie and Pastry Case**   See Display Case.

**Pizza Oven**   Baking-type oven of one or more decks, gas-, electric- or oil-fired, having temperature range from 350 to 700°F. Deck(s) are of heat retaining masonry material.

**Pizza Sheeter**   See Dough Sheeter.

**Platform Scale**   Mobile unit with a dial or beam, for weights up to 1500 pounds. May be floor- or stand-mounted.

**Platform Skid**   See Dunnage Rack.

**Popcorn Machine**   See Corn Popper.

**Pot and Utensil Washer, or Potwashing Machine**   Machine of one or more tanks with hood or wash chamber above, inside which large ware is washed, using very big, high pressure pumps. Water is pumped from tanks and sprayed over ware placed in racks or set on a conveyor or platform. One or more final fresh water rinses sanitizes ware. Machine has a 34'' to 36'' working height. 1. Door-type, single tank machine has power wash and final rinse only. 2. Door-type, two-tank machine has power wash and power rinse tanks, and final rinse. 3. Belt conveyor machine is straight-through type machine having one to three tanks plus final rinse. Ware is set directly on a belt. 4. Revolving tray table type has two to three tanks plus final rinse. Ware is set directly on turntable platform.

**Pot Filler**   Faucet or valve with a hose mounted at a range, pot stove or kettle to fill a vessel direct.

**Pot Stove**   Low, floor-mounted single burner stove with high Btu or kw rating for use with large stock pots.

**Prefabricated Cooler**   Walk-in type refrigerator or freezer having insulated walls, ceiling and floor fabricated in a shop and assembled on the job site. The insulated floor and base of the walls may be constructed as part of the building.

**Preparation Table or Counter**   Unit located in the preparation area of a kitchen, for cutting, slicing, peeling and other preparation of foods.

**Prerinse or Prewash Sink**   Sink constructed as an integral part of a soiled dish table, located near a dishwashing machine, and furnished with removable perforated scrap basket(s) and spray hose.

**Pressure Cooker**   See Steam Cooker.

**Pressure Fryer**   See Fryer.

**Pre-Wash**   Separate machine or built-in section of a warewashing machine with tank and pump or fresh water supply. Pump recirculates water over ware; fresh water type sprays over ware; before pumped wash section of machine.

**Proof Box or Cabinet**   Fully-enclosed cabinet with gas, steam or electric heater and humidifier. Sometimes unit may be insulated type with thermostatic and humidity controls. Box may be mobile. Traveling type proofer has a conveying mechanism inside the overhead cabinet, as in large commercial bread bakery.

**Protector Case**   A single shelf mounted on posts with transparent shield at the front, or front and ends. Mounted over a counter top at hot food or sandwich sections to protect uncovered food.

**Pulper**   Floor-mounted garbage and waste disposal machine with a vertical cylinder, grinder plate and knives, and sump compartment for non-grindable matter. Waste material is ground in a deep water bath to form a slurry which is piped to a water extractor. Water from the extractor is recirculated to the pulper.

# Q

**Quartz Oven**   Oven which employs an electrically heated quartz plate or infrared quartz element inside a glass tube to generate heat. Also called Infrared Oven.

# R

**Rack: Cup, Dish, Glass, Plate or Tray**   1. Rectangular or round-shaped basket of wire or plastic construction, with or without compartments or intermediate lateral supports, used for washing and/or storage of small ware. Racks are self-stacking type for cups and glassware. 2. See Tray Rack for upright unit.

**Rack Pan**   See Pan and Utensil Rack.

**Rack Washer**   Machine of one or two tanks with hood or wash chamber over, with one or two doors, using large size high pressure pumps, and final sanitizing rinse. Steam or electric heated water is pumped from tanks and sprayed over racks wheeled onto tracks inside washer. Machine is made to recess in floor to have tracks set flush with finished floor.

**Range**    Unit with heated top surface or burners which heat utensils in which foods are cooked, or cook foods direct. Some ranges are equipped with an insulated oven base. Hot or even heat tops, and fry or griddle tops, are gas- or oil-fired, or electrically heated. Open or hot plate tops have electric or gas burners. Fry or griddle tops are gas- or oil-fired, or electrically heated.

**Reel Oven**    See Revolving Tray Oven.

**Refrigerated Table**    Table top mounted on counter-type refrigerated base.

**Refrigerator Shelves**    Shelves of wire, solid, embossed or slotted material with reinforced hemmed edges, mounted on tubular posts with adjustable sanitary brackets. May be in stationary or mobile sections.

**Revolving Tray Oven**    Gas, electric or oil-heated oven with a motor-driven ferris wheel device inside having four or more balanced trays. Bake or roast pans are loaded and unloaded from a single opening with a hinged down door. Steam may be added for humidity requirements of products.

**Rinse Injector**    Device mounted to top or side of washing machine for storage and automatic dispensing of liquid water softener into the final rinse manifold.

**Roast Oven**    See Oven; Convection Oven; Revolving Tray Oven.

**Roaster, Meat, Steam-Jacketed**    See Meat Roaster, Steam-Jacketed.

**Roll Divider**    Hand- or motor-operated machine that divides a ball of dough into equal pieces. Hand-operated unit is stand- or table-mounted. Motor-driven unit is floor mounted with a cabinet base and may be combined with a rounding device. Also called Bun Divider.

**Roll Warmer**    1. Enclosed cabinet with a telescoping cover, heated by pellet or glowing charcoal under a false bottom. 2. Enclosed insulated cabinet with electric heating elements, and humidity controls. The unit is provided with one or more drawers in a tier at the front; it sets on a counter top, legs or a stand, or is built into a counter. Also called Bun Warmer.

**Rotisserie**    1. Upright enclosed cabinet with a vertical grill having gas-fired ceramics or electric heating elements. A side-mounted motor drives revolving spits set in a tier in front of the heaters. The unit has hinged or sliding glass doors. 2. Upright enclosed cabinet containing a motor driven ferris wheel provided with food cradles or baskets passing under gas-fired ceramics or electric heating elements. 3. Enclosed, square, upright cabinet with meat suspended from top in center revolving motor driven cradle, heated by four infrared lamps radiating from the corners. 4. Also see Hot Dog and Hamburger Broiler.

## S

**Salad Case**    Unit consisting of a refrigerated counter with refrigerated food pans set into the top, and a refrigerated or nonrefrigerated display case mounted on the counter top.

**Salamander**    A backshelf or cabinet mounted over the rear of a range or steam table, and absorbing the heat therefrom to keep foods on it warm.

**Salamander Broiler**    See Broiler, Backshelf.

**Saw, Meat and Bone**    See Meat and Bone Saw.

**Scale**    See Floor Scale; Platform Scale.

**Self-Leveling Dispenser**    See Dispenser.

**Service Stand**    A stationary cabinet with a solid top at a working height used in a restaurant; may have shelves, bins, drawers, and refrigerated section for storage of linen, flatware, glassware, china, condiments, water and ice.

**Settee Bench**    Bench with upholstered seat and upholstered back.

**Shake Maker**    Floor- or counter-mounted machine with one or two mechanically refrigerated cylinders, having dashers to mix and refrigerate an air-and-milk mixture to a flowing frozen dessert beverage. Unit may be equipped with syrup tanks and pumps, and mixing spindle to blend various flavors in shakes.

**Shrimp Peeler and Deveiner**    Bench-mounted, motor-driven machine that removes vein and shell from shrimp and prawn.

**Silver Burnisher, Holloware and Flatware**    Machine with a tumbling barrel or vibrating open top tub filled with steel balls and compound, in which silver plated utensils are placed. Tumbling or vibrating action causes steel balls to roll down plating onto base metal. Units may be bench- or floor-mounted, or made mobile to roll under a table top.

**Silver Washer and Drier**    Floor-mounted machine with a fixed or removable tumbling drum set inside a wash chamber with a hinged cover for washing, sterilizing and electrically drying flatware. The removable drum has a perforated bottom and top cover. The fixed drum has a hinged cover and perforated ends. Machine has wash, rinse and final sterilization rinse cycles. Electrically heated air is blown through wash chamber and drum to dry flatware.

**Sink**  1. Preparation, Cook's or Utility: one or two-compartment type with drain-board on one or both sides, each compartment averaging 24" square. 2. Pot and Pan or Scullery: two, three or four-compartment type with drainboard on one or both sides, and possibly between compartments. Each compartment should be minimum 27" left to right, and average 24" front to rear.

**Slaw Cutter**  Floor- or bench-mounted machine with revolving slicer plate and hopper. Cored and quartered cabbage heads inserted in hopper are forced against slicer plate and product discharges through chute below.

**Slicer**  Bench- or stand-mounted machine with a stationary motor driven round knife and slice thickness gauge plate, and reciprocating feed trough or carriage. Flat trough may have hand and/or spring pressure type feed plate. Gravity trough may have hand or automatic feed plate. Trough may be hand-operated or motor driven. Slicer can be equipped with automatic stacking and conveying device.

**Slicer, Bread**  See Bread Slicer.

**Slicer, Vegetable**  See Vegetable Slicer.

**Slush Maker**  Floor/counter mounted machine with one or two mechanically refrigerated cylinders having dashers to mix and refrigerate a water mixture to a flowing frozen dessert beverage.

**Smokehouse, Chinese**  Floor-mounted, enclosed, insulated roasting cabinet with gas burners and baffle plates, hinged door(s), duct connection and flue at top, and removable grease pan inside the bottom. Meat, fish and poultry are mounted on skewers inside. Interior walls and door have deflector plates to direct drippings into the grease pan.

**Sneeze Guard**  See Display Case.

**Snow Cone Machine**  See Ice Shaver.

**Soda Dispenser**  1. Part of soda making and refrigeration system: dispensing head attachment for mounting on a soda fountain, bar, counter or at a waiter station, complete with drainer. 2. Enclosed cabinet, ice or mechanically refrigerated, to dispense premixed soda or combine soda water and syrup stored in a cabinet or remote tanks. 3. Floor- or counter-mounted cabinet with a self-contained soda and refrigeration system having remote or self-contained syrup tanks.

**Soda Maker**  Unit consisting of mechanical refrigeration system, carbonator and soda storage tank.

**Soda System**  Assembly consisting of soda maker, syrup tanks, syrup, soda and refrigeration tubing, and soda dispensing head(s) and/or cabinet(s). Also known as Carbonated Beverage System.

**Soft Ice Cream Maker**  Floor- or counter-mounted machine with one or two mechanically refrigerated cylinders having dashers to mix and refrigerate air and ice cream mix to a flowing frozen dessert. Unit is equipped with hand or foot operated dispensing head or control.

**Soiled Dish Pass Window**  Trimmed opening in a partition between dishwashing and serving areas, having the soiled dish table as a sill. The opening may be equipped with hinged or sliding door or shutter.

**Soup Station**  Section of cook's table or cafeteria counter with a hot food receptacle, rectangular or round, set into the top.

**Speed Rail**  See Bottle Trough.

**Spice Bench**  Table with stationary cabinet above rear or below top, or mobile cabinet(s) under the top. Cabinet(s) have two or more spice drawers or bins.

**Squeezer, Juice**  See Juice Extractor.

**Steam Cooker**  Enclosed cabinet with one or more sealed compartments having individual controls into which (chemically clean) steam is introduced for cooking or heating. Cooker may be direct connected or equipped with gas-fired, electric or steam coil generator in the base. 1. A cooker with compartments in tiers cooks with low pressure steam. Each compartment has a hinged door with a floating inner panel and a sealing gasket made tight with a wheel screw. Unit is floor-mounted, or if direct connected, may be wall-mounted. 2. Cooker with high pressure has self-sealing door(s) with a gasket made tight by interior steam pressure. May be floor-, counter- or wall-mounted. Also called High Speed Cooker.

**Steam Jacketed Kettle**  See Kettle, Steam-Jacketed.

**Steamer, Dry**  See Food Freshener.

**Steamer, Hot Dog**  See Hot Dog Steamer, Steam Cooker.

**Step-In Cooler/Freezer**  See Walk-In Refrigerator/Freezer.

**Stock Pot Stove**  See Pot Stove.

**Storage Rack**  Unit consisting of one or more shelves mounted on angle, channel or tubular posts, for storage of goods or ware.

**Stove**  Floor- or counter-mounted unit with one or more open gas or electric burners. Also called Hot Plate.

**Swill Trough** 1. Depression in dish table approximately 6″ to 9″ wide, and 2″ to 6″ deep, equipped with waste outlet, strainer basket, and perforated cover. 2. Extra sink compartment of shallow depth located between compartments of pot washing sink, equipped with strainer basket.

# T

**Table** Top with solid flat surface, mounted on floor with legs, on wall with brackets and legs, or on semi- or fully-enclosed cabinet. May be stationary or mobile. May have shelves under, shelves over, and tool drawer(s).

**Tea maker or Dispenser** 1. See Coffee Urn. Same as coffee urn with tea laid in strainer. 2. Counter-mounted unit to combine instant tea mix with heated water for hot tea or cold water for ice tea.

**Tenderizer** See Meat Tenderizer.

**Timer, Egg** See Egg Timer.

**Toaster** 1. Counter-mounted pop-up type having two or four slice capacity. Electric only. 2. Counter-mounted conveyor type with a motor driven conveyor carrying the product between electric or gas-fired radiants. 3. Sandwich type: See Grill.

**Tray Make-Up or Assembly Conveyor** Motor-driven or gravity-type horizontal conveyor to transport trays between various food loading stations.

**Tray Rack** Upright mobile or stationary unit, open or semi-enclosed, having angle, channel or tubular posts and one or more tiers of angle or channel-shaped slides to support trays or pans. Rack may be built-in to cabinets or suspended from under table tops.

**Tray Slide or Rail** Horizontal surface to accommodate the width of a tray, extended out from, and running the length of, cafeteria counter top. May be constructed of solid material with or without raised edges and vee beads; or of several tubular or solid rails or bars. Mounted on and fastened to brackets secured to counter top and/or counter body. Also called Tray Rest.

**Tray Stand** Low height mobile or stationary four-legged stand with solid top. Top may have raised back and sides to prevent tray stacks from falling over.

**Trough, Swill** See Swill Trough.

**Trout Tank** See Lobster Tank.

**Truck** See Cart.

# U

**Undercounter Sink Workboard** See Bar Workboard.

**Unit Cooler** Semi-enclosed cabinet open at front and rear or top and bottom, depending on air flow, with a motor-driven fan blowing air through a mechanically refrigerated finned coil. Device is normally suspended inside a refrigerator or freezer. Also called blower (evaporator) coil.

**Urn, Coffee/Tea** See Coffee Urn.

**Urn Stand** Stationary stand with a solid top having raised edges all around, recessed drain trough(s) with waste outlet and a drainer plate flush with the top. Raised, die-stamped openings are used to connect lines to an urn. Top set on open base with shelf, semi-enclosed cabinet with bottom (and intermediate) shelf, or enclosed cabinet with bottom (and intermediate) shelf and door(s). May also be equipped with fold-down step.

# V

**Vegetable Peeler** See Peeler.

**Vegetable Slicer or Cutter** 1. Hand- or motor-driven counter-mounted machine having rotating removable plates with varied knives. Product is forced against plates and knives for slicing, dicing, grating, shredding, etc. 2. Similar attachment to a food machine with rotating removable plates and knife arrangements.

**Vegetable Steamer** See Steam Cooker.

**Vertical Cutter/Mixer** Floor-type machine with a vertical tilting mixing bowl having a 25 to 80 quart capacity. The bowl is equipped with a two speed motor and a high speed agitator shaft at bowl bottom with cutting/mixing knife. A hand or motor-driven stirring and mixing shaft is fixed to the bowl's cover. A strainer basket may be included.

**Waffle Baker, Grill or Iron** See Grill.

**Water Boiler** 1. One or more urns of coffee urn battery, heated by gas, steam or electricity, to bring water to boil for making beverages. Usually connected to other urns with water piping and controls. Can be used separately. 2. Gas-, electric-, steam- or oil-fired unit to heat water for use in kitchen.

**Water Extractor** Floor-mounted machine located at the terminal of a waste pulping system. The device augers pulp in a slurry out of the tank to a pressure head at the top, extracting water which is then recirculated into the system. The pulp is discharged into a chute to a waste receptacle.

**Water Heater**    Counter-mounted instant electric heating device with faucet for making tea and hot chocolate drinks.

**Water Station**    Section of a counter or stand with a glass and/or pitcher filling faucet and drain trough.

**Window, Soiled Dish Pass**    See Soiled Dish Pass Window.

**Wine Rack**    Fixed or portable folding type unit with alternating stacked compartments open at front and rear to support wine bottles in a horizontal position for storage and display.

**Wok**    See Chinese Range.

**Wood Top**    Table top constructed of kiln-dried, hard rock laminated maple strips, hydraulically pressed together, glued and steel doweled through.

# Answers to Brain Teasers

## RANGES
1. Soups, Sauces, Newburg
2. Solid hot top, Open top burners, solid griddle
3. Large quantities
4. Quickly
5. Down or Off
6. Slop water over range tops
7. Scraping, NEVER use water to remove burned-on particles
8. Wipe surface clean of all grease and food particles
9. Before
10. Stock kettle work
    Pan broiling
    Sauteing
    Stewing
    Pan boiling

## STEAM KETTLES
1. Steam
2. Tilting kettles placed on tables, Steam kettles standing on floor, Kettles mounted from wall
3. 200 gal. (754.9 l)
4. Vegetables, Macaroni, Soups, Beef Stew
5. All answers correct
6. Off
7. Soaking

8. Out; Fine metal sponge or brush
9. Should be cleaned
10. Draining rinse water out

## STEAM COOKERS
1. At one time
2. Potatoes, Poultry, Puddings, Fish
3. Small batches of food just before service
4. All answers correct
5. Both answers correct
6. 18 pans; 30 to 35 lb. (13.6 to 15.9 kg)
7. Wiped up immediately
8. Tall or flat; solid or perforated
9. Locked in place
10. Automatically defrosted

## TILTING BRAISING/FRY PANS
1. Uses energy-efficient steam
2. Shut off when desired temperature is reached; maintain oil at proper temperature; permits cooked items to be held at serving temperatures for some time (any answer is correct)
3. Yes
4. Dips out; tips over and pours out
5. Pouring lips; self-locking tilt mechanism

## OVENS—DECK, REVOLVING
1. Bake, Roast, Oven-broil, Oven-fry, Cook casseroles, Reconstitute frozen food (any 3 answers)
2. Lower
3. Large roasts or poultry
4. First
5. Each other; Sides of oven
6. For 3 ways to save energy, see p. 51
7. Merry-go-round
8. See page 61 for list of items and check your answers
9. Heat
10. (a) Worker can get inside oven to clean after it has cooled down. (b) Trays are removable and can be scrubbed in sink. (c) Tray frames also come out and can be taken to sink

## OVENS—CONVECTION
1. Rapid reconstitution of frozen food items; rapid reheating of preprepared foods; roasting; baking
2. Constantly moving heated air strips away from cold air in oven chamber, speeds up heat absorption process.
3. b
4. True
5. Check chart p. 66 for answer
6. Need to be carefully arranged
7. True
8. Will be open the shortest possible time
9. Commercial oven light bulbs should always be used as home or domestic oven light bulbs may shatter and spoil a whole oven load of food.
10. For causes of uneven baking and roasting, see pp. 57–58

## OVENS—MICROWAVE
1. (a) reheating single serving of precooked food; (b) heating food for service at beginning or end of meal period; (c) speedy defrosting; (d) eliminating preparation and service bottlenecks
2. Radar and television
3. Speeds up
4. Time
5. 10 times as long, as the microwave oven would give out the same amount of heat-producing energy for both loads. This heat can zero in on 1 lb. of food or be divided over 10 lb. Microwave cooking is guided by time, not temperature.
6. See list of food items on pp. 72–73
7. Special doorlocks that shut off microwave generator automatically whenever door is opened
   Electronic "chokes" that reduce microwave leaks
8. One compartment microwave oven; microwave oven with higher power and a larger cavity, which can heat more items at the same time

9. Easy
10. Plastic, glass, paper. China can also be used if it does not have metal (gold or silver) trim or content.

## GRIDDLES
1. Below
2. Above and below
3. Where people can watch them
4. a. c. d. e. f. g.
5. Should be carefully followed
6. Daily
7. So foods will not stick during cooking
8. When they are new and after they are cleaned
9. Any four of the following foods can be cooked on the griddle:

| | |
|---|---|
| hamburgers | steak |
| bacon and eggs | frankfurters |
| sandwiches | pancakes |
| fried potatoes | fruit |
| | onion slices |

10. The sharp edge of a scraper will mar the griddle surface permanently if it strikes the griddle

## FRYERS
1. 
| | |
|---|---|
| Fried chicken | Croquettes |
| Fried shrimp | Doughnuts |
| French fries | Fried fish |
2. Unload or dump
3. Conventional restaurant types
   Pressure fryers
   Semi-automatic, high-production fryers
4. Cleaning or special cleaning
5. Keep it clean or clean regularly or clean whenever fryer needs it
6. Temperature of fat is too high
7. Turned down
8. The amount of fat absorbed by the food fried in it. (Turnover, that is fat absorbed by foods fried in it, can be 10 to 40% of the fat used in frying)
9. Drain wet foods before putting them in fryer
10. Cannot. Salt shortens life of frying fat

## BROILERS
1. Most expensive
2. Horizontal or overhead broilers
   Infrared
   Char or underfired broilers
   Specialty broilers
3. Steaks and chops
4. Above top of heavy-duty range or above a spreader plate as part of back shelf assembly
5. High production capacity
   Fast heatup

6. Tongs
7. By feel or way in which meat springs back; knowing how to judge doneness takes experience
8. No
9. Meat can be dipped in oil, brushed with butter, butter and oil or liquid browning to assure browning.
10. Never get water inside of broiler.

## ⚔ INFRARED FOOD-WARMING EQUIPMENT
1. Heats only object it is directed at
2. Lamps, portable units, overhead models, metal tubes under hoods, table models
3. 140°F. (60°C)
4. Lower temperature of food being held so drafts should be prevented wherever possible.
5. Pizza
6. Any pressure in handling tubes that might break them
7. By putting plug in proper electrical outlet
8. No
9. Plates warm up very slightly; are never too hot to hold comfortably

## SPECIALTY EQUIPMENT
1. Meat with bone in
2. Bowl and cutting or chopping parts are easy to remove
3. Speed makes cutting very fast so shorter time is safer; machine can be restarted if more cutting is necessary
4. Bagels, English muffins
5. All through the day
6. Yes
7. Small
8. No
9. Swing-away water filler
10. Chafing dish, hibachi, fondue pot
11. Can sear food without overcooking
12. Because pizzas bake in a very few minutes so door is constantly being opened to load or unload pizzas, which lowers oven temperature
13. Yes
14. So many Mexican dishes are topped with melted cheese
15. Daily
16. Increases

## ෆ STORAGE
1. Loading dock
2. To make sure goods are those ordered.
3. Well-ventilated, well-lighted, dry, clean
4. Frozen food, fresh meat
5. Packaged food products
6. False

7. 6–12 months; 1 year; indefinitely; 1 month or 3 months; 6 months; 1 year
8. Yes
9. No, as it may pick up off-flavors
10. Not more than 24 hours

## SCALES
1. Checking weight on incoming shipments
2. Portion control
3. Floor scales, suspended platform scales, overhead track scales, built-ins, portion scales, counter or table scales, dough or baker's scales, balancing scales
4. Use preset scales with pointer set at right amount
5. Too much
6. Greater need for permanent records
7. Check Sample Scale Profile for right answer

## REFRIGERATION
1. Reach-in and walk-in
2. Cooled slightly before being put in refrigerator
3. Have deliveries rolled further
4. Mobile carts
5. Five
6. Can carry greater variety of food; can do quantity buying; cut down on deliveries
7. Outside of building
8. False
9. Preparation centers
10. Doors are opened frequently

## STORAGE FREEZERS
1. False
2. 19; 56
3. Extra work space
4. Yes
5. False
6. Rewrapped tightly and put into storage immediately
7. No
8. Once a week
9. Frozen products can be purchased in larger quantity
10. Thawing and storage refrigerator

## WASTE-HANDLING EQUIPMENT
1. Sewage and septic systems cannot handle extra load of waste
2. Contain odors and held till dump trip is scheduled
3. Prevent contamination; assure sanitation
4. False
5. Waste pulping system
6. To keep disposer cool and to feed waste products through

# Index